THE RIGHT WAY
TO LOSE
A WAR

Also by Dominic Tierney

*Failing to Win: Perceptions of Victory and
Defeat in International Politics*

*FDR and the Spanish Civil War:
Neutrality and Commitment in the Struggle That Divided America*

*How We Fight: Crusades, Quagmires, and the
American Way of War*

To my parents

Contents

Contents

Part III
The Right Way to Win a War

Preface

I'm only alive because a war dragged on too long.

My great-grandmother Charlotte Ann was born in Lancashire, England, in 1887. She worked as a weaver in the cotton mills, where she met a man named John Ethelbert Margerison. They married in 1911 and had two children, Sally and Mary.

In 1914, World War I broke out and John joined the Royal Field Artillery. In his poem "MCMXIV," Philip Larkin wrote about the husbands heading off to the front with an innocence long since vanished: "the men / Leaving the gardens tidy, / The thousands of marriages, / Lasting a little while longer."

The fighting on the western front quickly descended into stalemate. Trenches stretched for hundreds of miles across France and Belgium like distended varicose veins. Despite the military deadlock, both sides refused to make peace. Inspired by dreams of expansion and hatred of the enemy, the belligerents dismissed any idea of negotiating.

And so the war went on. With new technologies like machine guns and high-explosive shells, the combatants learned how to kill but not how to win. As poet Carol Ann Duffy has written, "The frozen, foreign fields were acres of pain."

In February 1916, the Germans struck at the French fortress of Verdun but were halted by desperate resistance. *They shall not pass.* The ten-month storm of steel produced a collective tally of nearly one million dead and injured. In July 1916, the British attacked

John and Charlotte Ann Margerison (Author's collection)

the German lines at the Somme River in northern France with a ferocious bombardment that was heard in London, 160 miles away. But the fearsome cavalcade failed to break the German defenses, and the British army suffered sixty thousand casualties on the first day of the battle. Still there were no peace negotiations.

And so the war went on. In 1917, the British assault on Pass-chendaele in Flanders bogged down in a wretched hell of mud and death. Hundreds of thousands of casualties were incurred for the capture of just five miles. British reinforcements "shambled up past the guns with dragging steps and the expressions of men who knew they were going to certain death," one veteran wrote. "In sullen silence they filed past one by one to the sacrifice."[1]

Unlike many of his Lancashire pals, John Margerison was still alive. If the belligerents had brokered a truce in 1914, 1915, 1916, or 1917, he would have returned home to Charlotte Ann. But any hope for an armistice was ground into dust as the combatants strove for a decisive victory to justify their terrible loss.

And so the war went on. In 1917, the United States entered the campaign on the side of Britain and France. The following year, in March 1918, Germany gambled everything on a massive spring offensive to win the war before American troops arrived in strength.

On April 12, 1918, John wrote to Charlotte Ann, scribbling in pencil on three pieces of paper. It was almost ten o'clock at night: "I feel that I must write a few lines to you before I lie down to sleep." It might be "a few days before I have the chance again." The German attack was brutal. "Things are very rough our way, as you will be aware, can't say whether we are winning or not, just now. Certainly the Boche is sparing nothing to crush us." But John was comforted by thoughts of home. "I am still living in hope for the time to come when we shall be united again and war shall be no more."

Four days later, John was killed in action. He was thirty-three. According to a British officer, "a team of horses which he was driving was hit by an enemy shell and death was instantaneous."

The Margerisons were just one of ten million European families ripped apart by the storm of war. But death sometimes brings life in its wake. Charlotte Ann eventually remarried. Her new husband was a much older man, a widower named William Tracy. She brought her two children, Sally and Mary, into the marriage. He came with six kids. And they had two more children together — one of whom was my grandfather, John Tracy. Without the shell blast that killed John Margerison in 1918, my grandfather would almost certainly never have been born.

World War I continued long past the point when the combatants

John Margerison's last letter, April 12, 1918 (Author's collection)

should have rationally ended the fighting. The countries that lost the war were left crippled and embittered. Even the winners were physically and psychologically traumatized. The protracted conflict sowed fetid seeds of revolution and revenge that yielded a second global cataclysm just two decades later.

Today, as we see in Afghanistan, we're little closer to solving the puzzle of ending a stalemated or failing war. To learn how to forge a path out of conflict, we must sometimes analyze war with a dispassionate eye. But we should always remember that beneath the abstract language of strategy lie families like the Margerisons.

In his last letter in 1918, John sent a special message to his five-year-old daughter: "Tell our Sally father sends his love to her and that I am expecting to hear of her being good at school." In 2015, Sally turned 102 years old. She's one of the last remaining strands connecting our generation to the Great War.

PART I

THE WRONG WAY TO LOSE A WAR

CHAPTER I

The Dark Age

At 9:44 p.m. on July 27, 1953, Private First Class Harold B. Smith had just sixteen more minutes of the Korean War to survive before the cease-fire came into effect at 10:00 p.m. You can imagine this twenty-one-year old marine from Illinois, out on combat patrol that evening, looking at his watch. Smith didn't have to be in Korea. He had already served his time in the Philippines. But he volunteered for the fight. He also didn't have to be on patrol that evening. But he offered to take the place of another guy who went out two nights before.

Suddenly, Smith tripped a land mine and was fatally wounded. "I was looking directly at him when I heard the pop and saw the flash," recalled a fellow marine. "The explosion was followed by a terrible scream that was heard probably a mile away."[1] Another soldier said, "I was preparing to fire a white star cluster to signal the armistice when his body was brought in."[2]

Twenty-two years later, on April 29, 1975, Lance Corporal Darwin Judge and Corporal Charles McMahon were marine guards near an air base outside Saigon in South Vietnam. Judge was an Iowa boy and a gifted woodworker. He once built a grandfather clock that still kept time decades later. His buddy,

McMahon, from Woburn, Massachusetts, was a natural leader. "He loved the Marines as much as anybody I ever saw in the Marines," said one friend.[3]

The two men had only been in South Vietnam for a few days. They were part of a small U.S. security force that remained after the main American withdrawal in 1973. McMahon and Judge arrived just in time for the military endgame, as North Vietnamese troops bore down on Saigon. McMahon mailed his mother a postcard: "After this duty, they may send us home for a while.... I'll try to write when I have time and don't worry Ma!!!!"[4]

At 4:00 a.m. on April 29, a Communist rocket struck Judge and McMahon's position and the two men died instantly. In the chaos of the final American exit from South Vietnam, with helicopters desperately rescuing people from rooftops, McMahon and Judge's bodies were accidentally left behind. It took months to negotiate their return.

On the early evening of November 14, 2011, Army Specialist David Hickman was traveling in an armored truck through Baghdad. Hickman, from North Carolina, had been in ninth grade when the Iraq War started in 2003. He was a natural athlete with a black belt in Tae Kwon Do. "He always seemed like Superman," said one of his friends.[5]

A massive explosion ripped into Hickman's truck. It was a roadside bomb—the signature weapon of the Iraqi insurgents. Hickman was grievously wounded. The next day, just before midnight, the army visited Hickman's parents in North Carolina to tell them their son was dead.

Smith, Judge, McMahon, and Hickman were the final American combat fatalities in Korea, Vietnam, and Iraq, respectively. An unknown soldier will have the same fate in Afghanistan. These men are the nation's last full measure of devotion. The final casualty in war is uniquely poignant. It highlights the individual human price of conflict. It represents the aggravated cruelty of near survival. It has all the random arbitrariness of a lottery. The Soviet-made 122 mm rocket that killed Judge and McMahon in 1975 was famously inaccurate. It could have landed anywhere in the vicinity. But it fell just a few feet from the marines. Sergeant Kevin Maloney found their bodies and wondered, "Why them and not me?"[6]

The closing casualty has particular resonance in a war without victory. Who could expect anyone to be the final soldier, as the saying went in Korea, to *die for a tie*? Or even worse, as former navy lieutenant John Kerry remarked during congressional testimony on Vietnam in 1971, "How do you ask a man to be the last man to die for a mistake?"[7] One of David Hickman's buddies said about Iraq, "I'm just sad, and pray that my best friend didn't lay down his life for nothing."[8]

Most of all, the final casualty underscores the value of ending a failing conflict. If we could have resolved the wars in Korea, Vietnam, and Iraq earlier—even just a few minutes earlier— Smith, Judge, McMahon, and Hickman's lives would have been the first to be spared.

And now we can imagine Smith, Judge, McMahon, and Hickman standing in three great lines of the American dead from these wars. Arranged single file in the order they fell in battle, the columns stretch back like solemn processions. As we conclude the violence a day earlier, a month earlier, or a year earlier, more and more of these men and women are spared.

How can we end a deteriorating war? Is it possible to withdraw from a stalemated or losing campaign without abandoning our interests or betraying our values? When military victory is no longer possible, can we escape with a draw or a minor failure rather than endure a complete debacle? In other words, is there a *right* way to lose a war?

Today, these are critical questions because we live in an age of unwinnable wars, where decisive triumph has proved to be a pipe dream. Since 1945, the United States has suffered a string of military stalemates and defeats in Korea, Vietnam, Iraq, and Afghanistan.

Time and again, in the face of a worsening campaign, Washington struggled to cut the nation's losses and find an honorable peace. Following battlefield failure, the United States groped for the exit like a man cast in darkness. We're good at getting in but bad at getting out. Or, as Barack Obama put it in 2014, "I think Americans have learned that it's harder to end wars than it is to begin them."[9]

In Korea, we spent two years negotiating a truce, even as brutal attritional fighting continued. In Vietnam, peace talks lasted for five years, with little to show for it. It took twenty-one days to capture Baghdad in 2003 and 3,174 days to leave Baghdad. We seized Kabul in November 2001—and we're still there. The price for these failed exit strategies was paid in American lives, domestic discord, crippled presidencies, and devastation for the local people.

In an era when American wars usually end in regret, we need to think seriously about military failure: why it happens and what we can do about it. *The Right Way to Lose a War* is a user's guide for ending a failing conflict. The book offers a road map for withdrawing from a difficult campaign without seeing everything collapse. And it explains how we can turn around America's military fortunes and start winning again.

But before we consider how to get out of a military quagmire, we need to understand why we get lured into the morass in the first place.

The Golden Age

On June 5, 1944, the eve of D-day, U.S. general George S. Patton strode onto a makeshift stage in southern England to address thousands of American soldiers. "Americans play to win all of the time," said Patton. "I wouldn't give a hoot in hell for a man who lost and laughed. That's why Americans have never lost nor will ever lose a war, for the very idea of losing is hateful to an American."[10]

It was the golden age of American warfare. Patton could look back on a century of U.S. victories in major wars. Victory means that Washington achieved its core aims with a favorable ratio of costs and benefits.[11] Major war means an operation where the United States deployed over fifty thousand troops and there were at least one thousand battle deaths on all sides.[12]

The golden age began in 1846, when the United States locked horns with Mexico. For eighteen months, the United States won battle after battle. In the 1848 Treaty of Guadalupe Hidalgo, Washington paid $15 million to Mexico, and assumed several million dollars' worth of Mexican debts, in return for seizing about half of Mexico's territory and creating the modern American Southwest. Northern Whigs recoiled at the acquisitive U.S. objectives. But the Mexican-American War was popular with most Americans, especially Democrats in the South and West, who believed in the nation's Manifest Destiny to expand from sea to shining sea.

Two decades later, the Civil War was widely seen in the North as a heroic struggle for Union and emancipation, which saved, in Lincoln's words, "the last best hope of earth."[13] The nation emerged through a hellfire of fratricidal slaughter to preserve the United States, in the words of a sergeant from Indiana, as "the beacon light of liberty & freedom to the human race."[14]

The Spanish-American War of 1898 heralded the emergence of the United States as a new great power. The campaign was a wildly popular adventure where Washington brushed aside Spanish forces, freed Cuba from Madrid's grasp, and annexed Puerto Rico, Guam, and the Philippines. Theodore Roosevelt became a national celebrity after he charged up San Juan Heights accompanied by the Rough Riders and an embedded journalist. "Up, up they went in the face of death, men dropping from the ranks at every step.... Roosevelt sat erect on his horse, holding his sword and shouting for his men to follow him."[15]

Not every U.S. war in this era was a clear-cut triumph. Following the Spanish-American War, for example, the United States suppressed a nationalist insurgency in the Philippines at a high cost of over four thousand American dead, and over two hundred thousand Filipino civilian fatalities—mostly from famine and disease related to the war. It was a harbinger of the darker era of warfare to come.[16]

But the United States soon returned to the path of victory. The country was a late entrant into World War I, joining the fray in 1917, three years after the opening salvos. U.S. intervention proved decisive in breaking the stalemate and defeating Germany. When the armistice was finally reached in 1918, the United States was clothed in immense physical power and moral prestige.

In 1944, as Patton addressed the troops, the glorious era was about to reach its pinnacle. "By God," he said, looking ahead to D-day, "I actually pity those poor sons of bitches we are going up against."[17] World War II passed into history as the good war: a struggle of moral clarity and total commitment against the architects of the Holocaust. The campaign was a testament to the valor-studded splendor of American warfare.

The century from 1846 to 1945 was defined mainly by conventional interstate wars, where the United States fought enemy countries on a clear battlefield. Our army met their army, we won decisively, and then we imposed our terms. World War II epitomized America's talent for overwhelming opposing states with mass production, logistics, and technology. At its peak capacity, American industry churned out a new aircraft every five minutes and forty-five seconds. The atom bomb was the ultimate expres-

U.S. troops raising the flag on Iwo Jima in the Pacific came to symbolize victory in World War II. (Office of War Information, National Archives, ARC identifier: 515086)

sion of American technological prowess. "To say that everything burned is not enough," recalled one witness at Nagasaki. "It seemed as if the earth itself emitted fire and smoke, flames that writhed up and erupted from underground."[18]

The price of military triumph was often immense. In the Civil War alone, there were around 750,000 American fatalities—more than the deaths in every other U.S. war combined.[19] The journalist Ambrose Bierce wrote about one soldier who fell at Shiloh in 1862. He had been "a fine giant in his time." But now he "lay face upward, taking in his breath in convulsive, rattling snorts, and blowing it out in sputters of froth which crawled creamily down his cheeks, piling itself alongside his neck and ears."[20]

Despite the sacrifice, from the 1840s onward, Americans consistently strode into what Winston Churchill called the "broad sunlit uplands" of victory.[21] The costs of conflict were staggering, but so were the benefits. The Civil War saved the Union and emancipated the slaves. World War II ensured the survival of liberal democracy in Western Europe. If we classify the Philippine campaign as a draw, or an ambiguous outcome, the overall tally comes to five victories, one draw, and no defeats. For Americans, golden-age conflicts became the model of what war ought to look like.

The Dark Age

And then, all of a sudden, we stopped winning major wars. The end of World War II was a turning point in America's experience of conflict. The golden age faded into the past, and a new dark age of American warfare emerged. Since 1945, Americans have experienced little except military frustration, stalemate, and loss.

The martial dusk fell in June 1950, when Communist North Korea invaded non-Communist South Korea. Fearing that the Soviet Union and China were set on world domination, Washington led an international coalition to aid Seoul. The campaign began brightly, as U.S. forces defended South Korea from invasion, and then took the offensive to roll back communism in the North. American soldiers captured Pyongyang and took photos of each other sitting behind Kim Il Sung's massive desk.[22]

In November 1950, however, China unexpectedly intervened with hundreds of thousands of troops, landing a hammer blow on American forces. In one of the biggest battlefield defeats in American history, U.S. troops retreated south through an icy wasteland. The fighting in Korea descended into a grim stalemate until a truce was finally reached in 1953, at a cost of nearly 37,000

American lives. For a nation used to golden victories, Korea was a confusing and wearying experience—in the words of cartoonist Bill Mauldin, "a slow, grinding, lonely, bitched-up war."[23]

Worse was to follow. In 1965, South Vietnam was crumbling in the face of a Communist insurgency. President Lyndon Johnson sent half a million American soldiers into what he called "that bitch of a war."[24] Trying to resuscitate South Vietnam, the United States found itself chained to a corpse. For the first time in American history, the nation faced outright military defeat—and, most shockingly, against North Vietnam, a "raggedy-ass little fourth-rate country," as LBJ put it.[25]

Despite the deaths of 58,000 Americans, South Vietnam still fell to communism. The war sapped U.S. resources, divided American society, deepened popular distrust of government, eroded the nation's self-identity as a vessel of goodness in the world, damaged America's global image, and helped to destroy the careers of two presidents—Johnson and Richard Nixon. The American army that went to Vietnam was more impressively equipped than at the start of any previous war. The American army that left Vietnam was unraveling, as discipline deteriorated and drug use became rampant. Henry Kissinger, the secretary of state from 1973 to 1977, said, "We should never have been there at all."[26]

The 1991 Gulf War was a successful military operation, where the United States liberated Kuwait from Saddam Hussein's grip at low military cost. A quarter of a million American soldiers launched a surprise left hook assault across the Iraqi desert, and within 100 hours the ground campaign was over. The U.S. Army's official history of the war described "the transformation of the American Army from disillusionment and anguish in Vietnam to confidence and certain victory in Desert Storm."[27]

The Gulf War was tarnished, however—not by what we did, but by what we *didn't* do. The White House portrayed the war as a morality tale, and cast Saddam Hussein as the second incarnation of Hitler. This story is meant to end with the overthrow of the ruthless tyrant. But President George H. W. Bush brought the curtain down before the final act by refusing to march on Baghdad. It was a wise decision. Bush's own son might attest to the dangers of seeing the performance through to regime change and beyond.

For many Americans, however, the outcome of the Gulf War felt hollow and unsatisfying. Polls showed that the American public didn't think the campaign was a victory—because Saddam remained in power.[28] It was a war from the dark age rather than the golden age. As Bush wrote in his diary, "It hasn't been a clean end—there is no battleship *Missouri* surrender. This is what's missing to make this akin to WWII, to separate Kuwait from Korea and Vietnam."[29]

A decade later, the United States regressed back to disillusionment and anguish. Harold Macmillan, the British prime minister from 1957 to 1963, reportedly said, "Rule number one in politics: never invade Afghanistan."[30] In October 2001, the United States swaggered into this harsh and beautiful land. Within two months, the Taliban were routed from Kabul and fled south toward the Pakistan border.

But the war was not over. The Taliban recovered and escalated their attacks, setting the stage for today's stalemated conflict. The United States and its allies have largely rid Afghanistan of Al Qaeda and established a range of health and education services. The Afghan election of 2014 went surprisingly smoothly. The ink-stained finger was a symbol of defiance from those who voted.

But after a dozen years of fighting against a resilient insurgency, with over two thousand Americans killed and twenty thousand wounded, and the expenditure of over $600 billion, the campaign is too costly to be considered a success. Today, no one is talking about victory. Instead, many Afghans are warily positioning themselves for the post-American era and the possibility of deepening civil war. In 2014, as the bulk of U.S. forces prepared to leave the country, the UN reported that Afghan civilian deaths and injuries had jumped 24 percent from the previous year.[31] Meanwhile, one poll found that only 17 percent of Americans supported the campaign in Afghanistan—making it the least popular war in U.S. history.[32]

An even bleaker tale played out in Iraq. On March 20, 2003, America's "shock and awe" bombardment lit up the sky in Baghdad, as President George W. Bush declared, "We will accept no outcome but victory."[33] After Saddam Hussein was toppled, however, the mission degenerated into America's fourth troubled war since 1945. Regime change triggered the collapse of civil government and widespread unrest, involving Saddam loyalists, sectarian groups, and foreign jihadists.

Each morning, dawn's early light revealed car-bomb smoke drifting across Baghdad and a harvest of hooded bodies—a grim installment toward the overall tally of one hundred thousand civilian deaths. In his novel, *The Yellow Birds,* Iraq War veteran Kevin Powers described the pointless grind in Iraq: "We'd go back into a city that had fought this battle yearly; a slow, bloody parade in fall to mark the change of season."[34] In 2007, the surge of American troops helped pull Iraq back from the brink of catastrophe. But the balance sheet from the war remained steeply negative. Al Qaeda claimed a new battlefield, Iran was strengthened by the removal of its nemesis, Saddam Hussein, anti-Americanism surged, 4,500 U.S. troops were killed, 30,000 Americans were injured, and more than one trillion dollars was expended.

Zbigniew Brzezinski, the national security advisor to President Jimmy Carter, told me, "The Iraq War was unnecessary, self-damaging, demoralizing, delegitimizing and governed primarily by simplistic military assumptions that didn't take into account the regional mosaic in which Iraq operates and the internal mosaic inside Iraq."[35]

The U.S. record in major wars since 1945 is one success (the Gulf War), two stalemates or draws (Korea and Afghanistan), and two losses (Vietnam and Iraq). In terms of victory, we've gone from five-for-six in the golden age to one-for-five in the dark age. Even the win in the Gulf has an asterisk because many Americans feel ambivalent about the result.[36]

The dark age is a time of protracted fighting, featuring the three longest wars in American history (Afghanistan, Iraq, and Vietnam). It's a time when the ultimate price of conflict is usually far higher than Americans would have accepted at the start. It's a time when wars are synonymous with individual presidents rather than with the country as a whole—Truman's war, LBJ's war, Nixon's war, Bush's war, Obama's war—as we blame the White House for a divisive adventure. It's a time when military heroes are thin on the ground. It's a time when movies and novels about war describe political conspiracy and futile struggle. It's a time when the signature illness for veterans is post-traumatic stress disorder. It's a time when the most resonant images of conflict are children napalmed, helicopters rescuing Americans and Vietnamese from rooftops, and intertwined naked bodies at Abu Ghraib. It's a time when Walter Cronkite's famous summary of Vietnam in 1968, "we are mired in stalemate," provides an apt motif.[37]

The dark age is a far cry from the "Veni, vidi, vici" of the golden age. Like Joe DiMaggio, victory in war seems like the relic of a bygone era. Why do we keep struggling on the battlefield? There are always unique reasons why wars deteriorate. Human error or simple bad luck may derail a campaign. But such an abrupt reversal in the nation's military fortunes calls for a deeper explanation. Americans didn't suddenly become less competent or brave after 1945. So what did change?

To find out the answer, let's turn the clock back two thousand years.

Into the Wild

In AD 9, three Roman legions—cogs in the greatest war machine the world had ever known—marched into the Teutoburg Forest in Germania. The woods swallowed them up.

The Roman governor of Germania was Publius Quinctilius Varus, a prominent senator with little repute on the battlefield. When Varus was informed that a small number of Germanic tribesmen had rebelled, he decided to quash the rising with shock and awe: three legions plus auxiliaries, amounting to over twenty thousand men.

The supposed rebellion, however, was a trap laid by a Germanic nobleman named Arminius. Like a sleeper agent, the twenty-five-year-old Arminius pretended to be a trusted ally. He grew up in Rome, fought for the imperial cause, and became a Roman citizen. Now he plotted an insider attack.

A conventional contest on open ground between Roman legions and Germanic tribes would be a killing field. The legionnaires were highly skilled with the *gladius* sword and the *pilum* javelin. They wore body armor and wielded large rectangular shields. They fought in a formidable triple-line formation that smashed through most opponents. By contrast, the Germanic tribesmen entered battle with minimal protection, carried spears and small swords, and were untrained in large-unit warfare.

But Arminius had no intention of fighting on open ground. He knew his enemy. He had lived with Romans and fought with Romans. He understood their tactics and how to beat them. Arminius gathered an alliance of Germanic tribes and lured the Roman force into an ambush in unfamiliar terrain.

Providence smiled on Varus one last time as whispers reached him of Arminius's treachery. But Varus refused to believe that

Rome's loyal servant would turn traitor, so he set out confidently into the Teutoburg Forest. Expecting no opposition, Varus's troops were stretched thin along a winding path. Eventually, the army reached a choke point: a narrows between marshland and hills. It was here that Arminius struck, attacking the Romans from the flank. According to Roman historian Cassius Dio, "They came upon Varus in the midst of forests by this time almost impenetrable."[38]

The battlefield environment gave the Germanic tribesmen a decisive edge. Arminius's men knew the paths. Lightly equipped, they could move swiftly and strike in hit-and-run style. In the narrow boggy ground, the Romans couldn't maneuver effectively. Violent rain soaked many of the large wooden Roman shields and made them too heavy to use. Still, Arminius resisted a single decisive battle. Instead, he spent four days wearing down the Roman troops with attritional raids and a hail of spears.

In the shadows of the dark forest, almost the entire Roman force was killed or captured. Witnessing the army's doom, Varus took his own life. When Emperor Augustus heard news of the catastrophe, he proclaimed, "Varus, give me back my legions!"[39] The tide of empire receded in the north. Rome never again tried seriously to conquer Germania.

Varus's calamitous defeat in the Teutoburg Forest was the result of Roman power and the changed battlefield environment. Rome's military strength, unparalleled road system, and talent for organization and logistics propelled its armies into distant Germania. But the unfavorable terrain and weather at Teutoburg diminished Rome's edge, and even turned its strength into a liability. Power sent Roman soldiers into the forest; the harsh setting ensured they never left.

It was a similar story for the United States after 1945. American power projected U.S. forces into far-flung conflicts. But the new era of civil wars and unconventional fighting tempered the benefits of material strength, and even rendered it counterproductive.

Otto Albert Koch depicts the battle of the Teutoburg Forest in this 1909 painting enti-tled Varusschlacht. (Lippisches Landesmuseum Detmold; www.lwl.org)

Power cast American troops into distant wars; the changed battle-field environment meant the outcome was regret.

After World War II, the United States bestrode the world like a colossus, with an economy three times larger than that of its closest rival, the USSR, and a monopoly on atomic weapons. Washington constructed an entire new architecture of national security, including the Department of Defense, the CIA, and a global system of alliances. The military–industrial complex was permanently carved into the American landscape like Mount Rushmore. From the polio vaccine to rock and roll, from Hollywood to Harvard, America's worldwide influence was unmatched. In 1941, Henry Luce, the publisher of *Time* and *Life,* celebrated what he called the "American century."[40]

These globe-girdling capabilities transformed how Americans viewed foreign threats and created a constant temptation to use force. Faraway countries of which Americans knew nothing, such as Korea and Vietnam, were suddenly seen as vital bastions of U.S. security, requiring direct military intervention.

Power tends to broaden a nation's horizons. Robert Kagan wrote, "A man armed only with a knife may decide that a bear prowling the forest is a tolerable danger. . . . The same man armed with a rifle, however, will likely make a different calculation."[41] Similarly, a weak country may conclude it can live with an aggressive rival. A strong state, however, may find the same danger to be unacceptable. Blessed with the inheritance of World War II, the United States marched confidently into the forest to confront the Soviet bear.

After all, who else would take responsibility? Franklin Roosevelt had once imagined that "Four Policemen" would oversee the postwar order: the United States, Britain, China, and the Soviet Union. But Britain was bankrupt. China was devastated by civil war from 1946 to 1949, and then governed by Mao's leftist revolutionaries. And the Soviet Union was enemy number one. Only the United States could contain the Communist threat, ensure open international trade, and protect global security.[42]

U.S. power also unleashed an underlying and deeply embedded missionary streak in American culture. We often see our values of liberty and democracy as universal. We assume that if you scratch a foreigner, you'll find an American trying to get out. A newly resplendent United States could shape the world in its own image and bring freedom to the South Koreans and South Vietnamese alike. In 1961, John F. Kennedy promised to "pay any price" in order "to assure the survival and the success of liberty."[43]

Following the end of the cold war, American power reached new heights. With the Soviet Union dead and buried, the United States began spending almost as much on defense as every other country in the world combined. The torrent of U.S. interventionism poured into new channels: humanitarian missions like Somalia and an expansive war on terror. Washington engaged in more major wars in the fifteen years after the cold war (the Gulf War, Afghanistan, and Iraq) than in the previous forty-five years (Korea and Vietnam).

It's no coincidence that Washington's most intemperate military adventure—the invasion of Iraq in 2003—occurred during the time of America's greatest and most unfettered power. Iraq was a luxury war: an optional extravagance that only a hegemon might consider. The United States had so many resources it could choose to fight a vague and distant threat on the far side of the world. "We're history's actors," said a senior advisor to George W. Bush, "and you, all of you, will be left to just study what we do."[44]

Of course, there's more to the tale of American interventionism than simply material capabilities. Domestic politics, economic pressures, presidential personalities, and other forces all played a role. But power is the vital catalyst that spurred Americans to seize the sword: *Could* intervene so easily became *should* intervene.

If material strength encouraged the use of force, what kind of conflict was the United States getting itself into? After 1945, Americans discovered the same lesson as the Romans two millennia before: The battlefield environment can suddenly change and throw even the most capable military off balance.

First, the good news: Since World War II, countries have almost stopped fighting each other. The traditional model of conventional interstate conflict—where governments declare war on each other, departments of war oversee the campaign, armies conquer and annex territory, and empires rise and fall—has been dismantled piece by piece. Governments have ceased declaring war. Departments of war have been renamed departments of defense. And territorial expansion by force is no longer acceptable. When Iraq invaded Kuwait in 1990, it was the first time that one UN member state annexed another, and the aggressor was forcibly removed by a broad international coalition.

Of course, countries have not suddenly become paragons of virtue. International politics is a contact sport, full of furious rivalry and intense competition. Interstate wars do still happen, like the conflict between Iran and Iraq in the 1980s—a particularly brutal struggle where the combatants rained missiles on each other's cities and Iraq ran cables through marshland to electrocute Iranian troops en masse.

But interstate wars have become very rare. World War II was the thunderous crescendo that presaged what historian John Lewis Gaddis called "the long peace."[45] Great powers haven't fought each other for over sixty years. There were no interstate wars at all from 2004 to 2007—a peaceful run that ended with a tiny border skirmish between Eritrea and Djibouti.

Many respectable countries have basically given up the war game, including America's old adversaries like Mexico, Spain, Germany, Italy, and Japan. In much of the world, war has lost its luster of glory and honor. Which leader of a great power today would declare, as Theodore Roosevelt once did, that "no triumph of peace is quite so great as the supreme triumphs of war"?[46] The good news of interstate peace is preached most loudly in Europe. In the early twentieth century, European countries "were made by and for war," but by the end of the century, they "were made by and for peace."[47] One can now picnic safely on the Franco-German border.

There are many reasons why Pax, the Roman goddess of

peace, has ascended over Mars, the god of war. Memories of the world wars diminished the appeal of using force. Nuclear deterrence stabilized relations between the major powers. The spread of democracy cultivated a zone of peace among elected regimes. The creation of institutions like the United Nations spurred the peaceful settlement of disputes. Globalization and international trade deepened the linkages between countries and made interstate conflict seem costly or irrational.

But now for the bad news: Conflict still exists in the form of civil wars, or organized violence within the boundaries of a state. Of course, the guerrilla who seeks to overthrow a constituted government by force and subversion is nothing new. The term dates back to the Spanish insurgents who battled against Napoleon. And weaker sides have used stealth, hit-and-run raids, and evasion since the earliest days of warfare.[48]

The insurgent, however, now dominates the military stage. The percentage of conflicts that were civil wars (rather than interstate wars) rose from 66 percent in 1896–1944, to 79 percent in 1945–1989, to 87 percent in 1990–2007.[49] Warfare today occurs "amongst the people," in the cities, in the villages, and in the streets.[50]

Insurgents didn't get the memo that war is over. Following World War II, the collapse of the European empires and the creation of brand-new countries governed by strongmen and kleptocrats provoked a wave of civil wars. The end of the cold war and the disintegration of the Soviet Union spurred another spike in internal conflict. After the mid-1990s, the incidence of civil war began to fall back — but then increased again in the wake of the Arab Spring in 2011, with violence in Libya, Syria, and elsewhere. In 2014, Ukraine descended into civil war, as Russia fostered a separatist movement in eastern Ukraine and seized the Crimean Peninsula. Some insurgents fought for independence or unification. Others were inspired by religion or ideology. And still others were motivated by personal enrichment—vulture warriors picking at the carcass of a dying nation.

International terrorists also ignored the end of war. Al Qaeda seeks to carry out spectacular attacks that inspire support, provoke enemies to overreach, and shake the foundations of the international system. On 9/11, the United States was struck, not by an army, but by nineteen men. This tiny band bypassed the nation's defenses like a virus and used America's strength against itself—employing aircraft as guided missiles.

In recent years, the lines between terrorism and insurgency have blurred. Al Qaeda has evolved from a focused terrorist group into a broad network of militias that wage guerrilla war and seek to govern territory in countries like Iraq, Syria, Yemen, Somalia, and Mali.

Conflicts today are mainly relegated to a few dozen failed or failing states that are breeding grounds for warlords, insurgents, and criminals. For the United States, foreign civil wars are a major security danger, causing humanitarian crises, refugee flows, and terrorism. The 2002 National Security Strategy concluded, "America is now threatened less by conquering states than we are by failing ones."[51]

With its unmatched power following World War II, the United States marched into the forest to confront the danger. But Washington chose an unfortunate moment to discover its inner interventionist. As the battlefield environment shifted from interstate war to civil conflict, military campaigns became ugly at best and unwinnable at worst.

Guerrillas are not invincible. In history, most insurgencies failed. During the nineteenth century, for instance, governments routinely brushed rebels aside. But in the twentieth century, the outcome of guerrilla wars began to change. After 1945, regimes defeated large-scale insurgencies only around one-third of the time. The British tried and failed to stabilize Palestine. The French lost in Indochina and Algeria. The Russians were beaten in Afghanistan. Israel struggled in Lebanon. The Dutch were bested in Indonesia. And the United States suffered a grim sequence of interventions in Vietnam, Afghanistan, and Iraq.[52]

In the new battlefield environment, American power often proved ineffective or even counterproductive. From 1846 to 1945, the United States had a minuscule peacetime army but won almost every major campaign. After World War II, Washington constructed the most expensive military machine that ever existed and endured seven decades of martial frustration.

As the United States became more powerful, it increasingly intervened in far-flung lands against culturally alien enemies it didn't understand. Early American foes—Mexico, the Confederacy, Spain—were fairly familiar. But over time, our opponents—North Korean, Chinese, and Vietnamese Communists, Afghan insurgents and Iraqi guerrillas—grew steadily more exotic.

Fighting alien adversaries on the far side of the globe hands the opponent home-field advantage. We're strangers in a strange land. We don't comprehend the local geography, religions, traditions, ethnic politics, or languages. In 1950, most GIs had never been out of the United States. Now they were thrown into the mud, poverty, and ancient culture of Korea. The GIs sometimes saw the enemy as an indistinguishable mass of "gooks" and "chinks." Decades later, in 2006, there were one thousand American officials in the Baghdad embassy, but just thirty-three spoke Arabic and only six were fluent.[53]

For the local people, we may seem like aliens. We descend from nowhere and start reordering their society. Our destructive machines of war resemble the Martian tripods in H. G. Wells's *War of the Worlds.* Shouting in a strange tongue, gesticulating widely, and armed to the teeth, American soldiers can be a terrifying spectacle. U.S. intervention may provoke an antibody response, as local traditionalists rally against the threatening intruder, creating what David Kilcullen called "accidental guerrillas."[54]

America's material strength has another curse. For a global hegemon like the United States, each war is just one of many competing security commitments around the world. For the enemy, however, the conflict is a life-and-death struggle that occupies its entire attention. It's limited war for us, and total war for them. We have more power; they have more willpower.

During the 1974 Rumble in the Jungle boxing match, Muhammad Ali famously used a "rope-a-dope" strategy against the hard-hitting George Foreman. Ali absorbed blow after blow until Foreman punched himself out. In the same manner, the Vietnamese insurgents endured Washington's punishment until Americans were unwilling to fight any longer. In 1965, Maxwell Taylor, the U.S. ambassador to South Vietnam, said the Vietcong "have the recuperative power of the phoenix [and] an amazing ability to maintain morale."[55]

The insurgent David enjoys a further advantage over the American Goliath: The locals are not going anywhere. Everyone knows that Washington will leave in the end, so its long-term value as an ally is questionable. But after the American circus packs up and heads out of town, the insurgents will still be there, with long memories about their friends and enemies. In Afghanistan, according to diplomat Richard Holbrooke, "The biggest problem we face is that the Pakistanis know that sooner or later we're leaving. Because that's what we do. And that drives everything."[56]

Washington was unable to wield its power effectively in the new battlefield environment. The U.S. military was stuck in the golden age, clinging to an old playbook based on conventional interstate war. Mass production, high technology, and big unit warfare had delivered victory time and again against enemy countries. Washington tried the same tactics against insurgents with free-fire zones and enemy kill counts. William Westmore-land, the U.S. commander in Vietnam, said the solution to the insurgency lay with one word: "firepower."[57]

But these tactics proved disastrous in the era of civil wars. Counterinsurgency is very different from interstate war and requires a unique skill set. Defeating guerrillas means winning hearts and minds. Counterinsurgents should move among the people as the fish swim in the sea—securing the population, developing networks of human intelligence, and boosting the legitimacy of the regime. Indiscriminate firepower can cause collateral damage and recruit more enemies. One study found that areas of South Vietnam bombed by the United States tended to shift over to insurgent control.[58] The U.S. military believed that with enough high explosives it couldn't lose the Vietnam War, but as defense analyst Andrew Krepinevich pointed out, more likely it couldn't win.[59]

The United States also failed to learn from its experience fighting insurgents. According to historian Russell Weigley, the U.S. military has repeatedly battled guerrillas, but each time it "had to relearn appropriate tactics at exorbitant costs" and viewed the experience "as an aberration that need not be repeated."[60] In the wake of Vietnam, the U.S. Army decided it would never fight guerrillas again and threw away the manual—literally destroying its notes on counterinsurgency. Instead, the top brass planned incessantly for an interstate war against the Soviet Union in Europe.[61]

After the cold war ended, the U.S. military continued to neglect counterinsurgency and nation-building. Stabilization missions were dismissed as "military operations other than war," or MOOTWA. The chairman of the Joint Chiefs of Staff reportedly said: "Real men don't do MOOTWA."[62]

The United States perfected its mastery of conventional interstate war—even as this kind of conflict became increasingly obsolete. A new generation of communication systems, smart bombs, and stealth weapons produced a "revolution in military affairs" that could "find, fix, and destroy" opponents at long range and high speed. The George W. Bush administration pursued a vision of military "transformation," where agile high-technology warfare guaranteed swift victory. Washington spent vast sums on big-ticket hardware designed for interstate campaigns — the F-22 Raptor, the F-35 Joint Strike Fighter, and the Virginia-class fast attack submarine. Against a decaying tin-pot dictatorship like Saddam's regime, it was all too easy.

These new capabilities, however, were ineffective against a complex insurgency. The U.S. military could hit almost anything with pinpoint accuracy — but what if we couldn't see the enemy? American troops also lacked some of the more mundane equipment needed in dark-age wars. At a town-hall-style meeting in 2004, one soldier told Secretary of Defense Donald Rumsfeld that the troops deploying to Iraq didn't have armored Humvees. "We're digging pieces of rusted scrap metal and compromised ballistic glass that's already been shot up...picking the best out of this scrap to put on our vehicles to take into combat." Rumsfeld replied, "You go to war with the army you have...not the army you might want or wish to have at a later time."[63]

But the army you have is the result of the choices you make. In 2007, Robert Gates, the secretary of defense, said that after Vietnam, "the Army relegated unconventional war to the margins of training, doctrine, and budget priorities." As a result, "it left the services unprepared to deal with the operations that followed: Somalia, Haiti, the Balkans, and more recently Afghanistan and Iraq — the consequences and costs of which we are still struggling with today."[64]

Whereas the United States failed to adjust to the new era of war, guerrillas raised their game. These are not your great-grandparents' insurgents. Modern rebels searched for America's weak spots. And unlike the U.S. Army, the guerrilla is a quick study.

Mao Zedong and others developed a blueprint of revolutionary war that inspired insurgents around the world. Guerrillas should engage in protracted war: playing defense, hiding within the population, consolidating their strength, before finally taking the offense. Patience was a virtue. The Chinese Communists fought for twenty-seven years. The Vietnamese Communists fought for thirty years. In the words of French military theorist Roger Trinquier, the insurgent would be "invisible, fluid, uncatchable."[65] More recently, radical Islamists have adopted guerrilla warfare as part of a revolutionary strategy to defeat what they call the "near enemy" of apostate regimes in the Middle East and the "far enemy" of the United States and the West.

In a counterrevolution in military affairs, insurgents devised innovative tactics to overcome American power. When U.S. aircraft carpet bombed Vietcong positions, the guerrillas took the war underground, building an extensive network of tunnels outside Saigon (now expanded in size so that larger Western tourists can squeeze through).

Today, the Taliban survive on estimated revenues of just $250 million per year. Harvard University's annual operating budget of $4 billion could bankroll sixteen Taliban-style insurgencies.[66] But the Taliban — whose name means "students" — did their homework. They learned about American tactics. Copies of the U.S. military's counterinsurgency training manual were found in a Taliban camp. The Afghan guerrillas built networks with Iraqi rebel groups and honed their use of improvised explosive devices, which caused almost two-thirds of coalition casualties.[67]

After 1945, insurgents played an ace card: national self-determination. The idea that every nation should decide its own fate free of external compulsion has become widely accepted — and is even inscribed into the UN Charter. During the cold war, Communist insurgents in Vietnam and elsewhere fused together nationalism with Marxism in a "national liberation movement."[68] More recently, the Taliban combined nationalistic appeals against the foreign occupier with demands for stricter forms of Islam. As the French discovered in Algeria and the United States found in Vietnam, trying to hold back the tide of nationalism can be a futile endeavor.

Rebel movements also proved skillful at securing backing from outside countries. Foreign aid is vital to the success of an insurgency. With external support, insurgents are twice as likely to win as the regime. If insurgents lose this outside assistance, the regime is four times as likely to win.[69]

Guerrillas benefited from a snowball effect, as each rebel victory created new potential allies. After the Communists won the Chinese civil war in 1949, Beijing became the arsenal of insurgency in the developing world. Ho Chi Minh spent years living in China and was profoundly influenced by Mao's revolution. Ho said the relationship between the Chinese and the Vietnamese was like "ten thousand loves." China's aid to the Vietnamese Communists was critical in the defeat of France and the United States—although the ten thousand loves would ultimately wither and fade.[70]

In summary, after 1945, civil war emerged as the dominant kind of conflict and guerrillas became more formidable opponents. Inspired by nationalism, willing to learn and adapt, and utilizing new sources of international support, the insurgent presented a significant new challenge. But the United States was slow to adjust to the new era and continued to prioritize an outmoded model of conventional interstate war. As a result, weaker opponents repeatedly threw the U.S. military to the mat, judo-style.

The Paradox of War

We live in an age of power, peace, and loss. Since 1945, the United States has emerged as the unsurpassed superpower, relations between countries have been unusually stable, and the American experience of conflict has been a tale of frustration and defeat.

This raises the first paradox: *We lose because the world is peaceful.* The decline of interstate war and the relative harmony among the great powers is cause for celebration. But the interstate wars that disappeared are the kind of wars that we win. And the civil wars that remain are the kind of wars that we lose. As the tide of conflict recedes, we're left with the toughest and most unyielding internal struggles.

It's also hard to win great victories in an era of peace. During the golden age, the United States faced trials of national survival, like the Civil War and World War II. The potential benefits were so momentous that Washington could overthrow the enemy at almost any cost in American blood and treasure and still claim the win. But in wars since 1945, the threats are diminished. Since the prize on offer is less valuable, the acceptable price we will pay in lives and money is also dramatically reduced. To achieve victory, the campaign must be quick and decisive—with little margin for error. Without grave peril, it's tough to enter the pantheon of martial valor.

There's a second paradox: *We lose because we're strong.* U.S. power encouraged Americans to follow the sound of battle into distant lands. But the United States became more interventionist just as the conflict environment shifted in ways that blunted America's military edge. As a result, Washington was no longer able to translate power into victory. If America was weaker, its military record might actually be more favorable. With fewer capabilities, the idea of invading Iraq would have stayed in the realm of dreams.

Indeed, the two paradoxes are connected. American power helped usher in the age of interstate peace, as Washington constructed a fairly democratic and stable "free world" in the Western Hemisphere, Western Europe, and East Asia, fashioned institutions like the United Nations, and oversaw a globalized trading system. But this left intractable civil wars as the prevailing kind of conflict. And American power also tempted Washington to search for monsters to destroy in far-flung locations. In other words, power and peace are the parents of loss.

No one wants to go back to the days of weakness, war, and winning. A favorable record in major conflict is poor compensation for global catastrophe. But as we enjoy the fruits of power and peace, we should steel ourselves for more battlefield setbacks. The dark age of American warfare looks set to endure. In the future, conflict will likely remain dominated by civil wars. American strength will continue to lure presidents into foreign intervention. The U.S. military will resist preparing for counterinsurgency. Guerrillas, by contrast, will learn and adapt—and bloody the United States.

Exit, Pursued by a Bear

During the golden age, the problem was how to mobilize American might to destroy an enemy state, and where to hold the ticker-tape parade. In the dark age, our challenge is different. Most major wars turn into unwinnable conflicts, and we must learn how to extricate the country from a quagmire, escape with a tolerable draw, or even find the right way to lose. In the wake of battlefield failure, how can we leave without seeing everything we fought for crumble into ashes?

What we need is an *exit strategy*. The term first arose in the business world to describe how investors or business owners could sell their stake in an operation. The phrase later gained currency in the political realm after the U.S. intervention in Somalia in the 1990s, and refers to a responsible military withdrawal. An exit strategy is designed to remove U.S. forces, protect our core interests and values, and leave behind some measure of order and stability.[71]

In the wake of military loss, the stakes are incredibly high. Losing the right way—or the wrong way—may mean life or death for thousands of American soldiers. Battlefield failure can easily turn into a catastrophic rout. The Prussian military theorist Carl von Clausewitz described how the "feeling of having been defeated" could spread like a virus through an army, suddenly breaking its will.[72] During the American Civil War, Confederate troops were remarkably committed through four long years of fighting. But in 1865 a cascade of pessimism suddenly afflicted Southern soldiers and officers. They resisted President Jefferson Davis's order to launch a guerrilla campaign, and the Confederate war effort collapsed.[73]

America's reputation and global image could also be at risk in any withdrawal. If we tear up our treaty commitments in a bid to end the fighting, we could undermine the credibility of our promises elsewhere. As a result, allies may desert us and enemies may no longer be deterred.

Furthermore, military debacles can cast a long shadow over the American home front. In a best-case scenario, wearied Americans will tune out the war. In a worst-case scenario, the exit strategy could spark domestic uproar and congressional rebellion. Opponents may accuse the president of treason for ending the campaign, or ruthless aggression for extending the fighting. There could even be blood on the streets, like the killing of four protesters at Kent State University in 1970. The withdrawal plan may have a dramatic impact on a president's career. Just look at the fate of LBJ, who won a landslide triumph in 1964 and then decided not to run for reelection in the wake of Vietnam.

Following battlefield loss, the future of the target country is on the line, whether it's South Korea, South Vietnam, Afghanistan, or Iraq. Our decisions may condemn thousands to death and millions to tyranny. Worsening civil war in Afghanistan, for example, threatens to extend the country's long national trauma, allow Al Qaeda to return in force, or spread violence to neighboring Pakistan—which has the sixth biggest population in the world, deep social divisions, and a nuclear arsenal.

The moral stakes are momentous. Do we have an obligation to fix what we broke and save our allies in Afghanistan and elsewhere? Or, at some point, must we betray our friends? After South Vietnam fell to communism, hundreds of thousands of Vietnamese were imprisoned, killed, or fled the country as "boat people." But to keep fighting in Vietnam would also have been morally questionable, risking more death and destruction in a futile venture. How can a president make this kind of ethical calculus?

Withdrawing from a losing military campaign is the ultimate test of leadership. For two hundred years, no American president has ever managed to end his own major failing war. Truman in Korea, LBJ in Vietnam, and Bush in Afghanistan and Iraq, all ended up handing the problem over to their successors.

Following battlefield failure, leaders can face what chess players call *Zugzwang,* or "move anguish."[74] In chess, you can end up in an unfortunate situation where every possible move worsens your position. You might prefer not to move at all, but you have to do something—and that something hastens your downfall.

Military failure can also trigger a kind of move anguish. There are no easy choices, just bad and worse. Leave too quickly and everything might collapse, potentially forcing our return. Leave too late and we may expend blood and treasure only to alienate the local population and step further into the mire.

A successful exit strategy requires the entire constellation of leadership skills: courage, wisdom, guile, a capacity to see the big picture, a ruthless streak, and an ability to inspire American and allied support. Presidents must appoint the right people to key positions, spot opportunities and constraints in the environment, and make tough decisions. Extricating the United States from a military debacle won't win a president many awards. But it may be the president's greatest service to the country. In this sense, losing the right way *is* a victory.

In Case of Emergency, Break Glass

In 2006, as Iraq disintegrated, Donald Rumsfeld, the secretary of defense, came to face the music before the Senate Armed Services Committee. When Hillary Clinton accused Rumsfeld of pursuing a "failed policy" in Iraq, Rumsfeld replied, "I don't know that there's any guidebook that tells you how to do it. There's no rulebook, there's no history for this."[75]

Rumsfeld was right about one thing: There's no manual for handling battlefield defeat or withdrawing from a deteriorating war. Far more is written about how wars begin than how they end. And there are almost no books on how to deal with military failure. Difficult conflicts like Korea often become forgotten wars. Ending a difficult conflict is the forgotten part of the forgotten war.[76]

The truth is that we dislike envisaging any kind of loss. American culture is a victory culture. Coded into the American DNA are the fear of failure and the celebration of winning. Writing about Americans in the 1830s, Alexis de Tocqueville described "the most imperious of all necessities, that of not sinking in the world."[77] Today, in the United States and Canada, $3 billion a year is spent on trophies and awards.[78] We're comfortable with loss only when it proves a temporary setback on the road to ultimate triumph, whether it's a Christian prevailing over sin, a pioneer mastering the natural world, or a sportsman reaching the pinnacle. As Patton said, "The very idea of losing is hateful to an American."

Our distaste for thinking about failure is especially true with regard to war. Armed conflict is an expression of American identity and a trial of national vitality. General Douglas MacArthur said, "There is no substitute for victory."[79] In 2006, when Iraq and Afghanistan spiraled downward, prominent books were published with titles like *America's Victories: Why the U.S. Wins Wars and Will Win the War on Terror.*[80] The whole notion of exit strategies, or cutting losses and finding a responsible withdrawal, runs counter to the nation's image, forged in the golden age, of war as a quest for decisive triumph.

How long can we deny a simple fact? *We keep losing.* When America's record at major war is one-for-five, the victory culture starts to look like wishful thinking, unhealthy braggadocio, and illusory triumphalism—good for the nation's self-esteem, perhaps, but not good for handling reality. As the dark age of American warfare approaches its eighth decade, it's time to face up to the hard truths of conflict.

This book is a guide to help the United States—or indeed, any country—march backward out of a quagmire and end a failing war. Much of the advice is aimed at U.S. presidents and senior officials. Other suggestions are for ordinary Americans. Handling battlefield loss requires a collective effort.

The challenges of crafting an effective exit strategy stretch far beyond the traditional battlefield. We must travel from the halls of Congress to the living rooms of America and the courts of global opinion. And we must draw on many different disciplines, including history, military strategy, political science, psychology, leadership, negotiation studies, and communications.

We need to hear from those who personally faced a deteriorating war. This book therefore includes material from dozens of interviews with leading generals, diplomats, and policymakers, including Stanley McChrystal, the U.S. commander in Afghanistan from 2009 to 2010; John Allen, the U.S. commander in

Afghanistan from 2011 to 2013; George Casey, the U.S. commander in Iraq from 2004 to 2007; Ronald Neumann, the U.S. ambassador to Afghanistan from 2005 to 2007; Ryan Crocker, the U.S. ambassador to Iraq from 2007 to 2009 and the U.S. ambassador to Afghanistan from 2011 to 2012; Marc Grossman, the Special Representative for Afghanistan and Pakistan from 2011 to 2012; John Abizaid, the commander of United States Central Command from 2003 to 2007; John McLaughlin, the acting director of the CIA in 2004; Zbigniew Brzezinski, the national security advisor to Jimmy Carter from 1977 to 1981; George Shultz, the U.S. secretary of state from 1982 to 1989; and Sir Graeme Lamb, the commander of the British Field Army from 2007 to 2009.

The book focuses on recent American stalemates and defeats in Korea, Vietnam, Afghanistan, and Iraq. But we will also look at other countries' experiences of ending difficult conflicts, including Finland's attempt to extricate itself from an alliance with Nazi Germany in World War II, France's savage war of peace in Algeria, and the Soviet Union's bleeding wound in Afghanistan. And to get a wider perspective, I traveled to Israel and the Palestinian territories to talk to senior officials from both sides about Israel's withdrawal from Gaza in 2005 — and the lessons learned.

The first part of the book, chapters 2–3, explains why the United States handles battlefield failure badly. Here, we'll look more closely at Washington's exit strategies in Korea, Vietnam, Iraq, and Afghanistan, and see how psychological, domestic, and other forces can trigger dangerous missteps.

The middle part, chapters 4–9, outlines a new exit strategy called "surge, talk, and leave," designed to help Washington withdraw without seeing everything collapse. Chapter 10 shows how the United States can start winning again, by laying out six principles for using force in the dark age of American warfare.

Can't we just skip ahead to the last chapter and discover how to avoid defeat? After all, if we stop losing, then we don't need an exit strategy after loss. But this is like training people in fire prevention—and then shutting down the fire department. To be fully prepared, we must try to avert disaster, and also be ready when a crisis occurs.

Today, attention is naturally focused on the war in Afghanistan. But this is not a book about Afghanistan. It's really a book about the *next* war. We can use America's experience in Afghanistan (as well as Korea, Vietnam, Iraq, and other conflicts) to understand the inherent dilemmas in handling loss, and create guidelines for future quagmires.

Some of the advice may sound like common sense. But common sense is often lacking. Other recommendations are counterintuitive— like determining how the war is going by finding out where a local governor sleeps. Along the way, we'll encounter fascinating stories: how the Founding Fathers were better at ending the War of 1812 than fighting it; how French president Charles de Gaulle dealt with an attempted coup and a potential loose nuke to resolve the conflict in Algeria; and how weeks of diplomacy in Vietnam were spent arguing over the shape of the negotiating table.

CHAPTER 2

Fiasco

On January 13, 1842, a British sentry at Jalalabad, in Afghanistan, looked out into the distant hills. Where was the British army of fifteen thousand men, women, and children that set out from Kabul a week before?

The sentry saw only a dark speck. Through field glasses, it turned out to be a man clinging to a stumbling pony. The gate was thrown open and soldiers rushed out to meet the rider. He was William Brydon, a thirty-year-old Scottish doctor from Kabul. Brydon's body was cut and bruised. His feet were swollen by frostbite. His pony was on the brink of death. The soldiers asked: What happened to the army? Brydon answered, "I am the army."[1]

The First Anglo-Afghan War began three years earlier, in 1839, when Britain invaded Afghanistan. It was the height of Pax Britannica, or the era of British global power. In Central Asia, Britain and Russia competed for supremacy in a high-stakes contest known as the Great Game. London was gripped by paranoia that Afghanistan would fall into the Russian orbit, threatening India, and decided to preempt the danger by forcible regime change.

Elizabeth Butler's 1879 painting The Remnants of an Army *depicts William Brydon's arrival at Jalalabad.*

British troops quickly captured Kabul, toppled Dost Mohammad Khan, the Afghan king, and installed the former ruler, Shah Shuja, in his place. The war was over, it seemed, and British officers took to hunting and playing cricket. The new arrivals imported the necessities of imperial rule, including a grand piano, ceremonial kilts, a parakeet, numerous maidservants, and a wine cellar carried by three hundred camels.

For the British, Shah Shuja was a pliable fellow. For the Afghans, he was an illegitimate puppet. In 1840, an armed rebellion began in Pashtun areas of Afghanistan and quickly swept toward Kabul. Mountstuart Elphinstone, who served in the British East India Company, said it was a hopeless task to maintain Shuja "in a poor, cold, strong and remote country, among a turbulent people like the Afghans."[2] As the mission degenerated into a military fiasco, the only question was: How costly would the British loss be?

Everything hinged on the exit strategy. "You have brought an army into the country," said one Afghan chieftain. "But how do you propose to take it out again?"[3] The British decided to retreat from Kabul to the closest garrison, Jalalabad, ninety miles away. And so, at first light on January 6, 1842, in the midst of the Afghan winter, 4,500 soldiers and over 10,000 camp followers set out for the mountain passes. "Dreary indeed," recalled Lieutenant Vincent Eyre, "was the scene over which, with drooping spirits and dismal forebodings, we had to bend our unwilling steps."[4]

The shambling mass waded through feet of snow with little food or shelter. The soldiers' mustaches and beards were coated in icicles. Their eyes were afflicted by snow blindness. Their frostbitten feet looked like charred logs of wood. Some were captured or hacked to pieces by Afghan tribesmen. Many died of starvation or exposure. Others gibbered in madness or took their own lives. "The snow was absolutely dyed with streaks and patches of blood for whole miles," wrote Eyre, "and at every step we encountered the mangled bodies of British and Hindustani soldiers and helpless camp-followers, lying side by side...the red stream of life still trickling from many a gaping wound inflicted by the merciless Afghan knife."[5]

For the rest of his life, Captain Colin Mackenzie remembered the image of a naked Indian child sitting alone and abandoned on the snow plain. "It was a beautiful little girl about two years old, just strong enough to sit upright with its little legs doubled under it, its great black eyes dilated to twice their usual size, fixed on the armed men, the passing cavalry and all the strange sights that met its gaze."[6] Mackenzie wanted to save the child, but there were too many others alone on the path. He had no choice but to leave her there to die.

The black column of soldiers and refugees thinned like a starving snake. By January 12, a rump force of barely two thousand found their way blocked by swarming tribesmen. A few dozen broke through the enemy lines on horseback. All of them were cut down—except one. Chewing on licorice roots to stave off thirst, Brydon reached Jalalabad to tell the tale.

Soldiers in the fort played bugles to guide any last stragglers to safety. "The terrible wailing sound of those bugles I will never forget," wrote Captain Thomas Seaton. "It was a dirge for our slaughtered soldiers and, heard all through the night, it had an inexpressibly mournful and depressing effect."[7]

After the British withdrew, Dost Mohammad Khan regained his throne. "Not one benefit, political or military, has been acquired with this war," wrote Reverend G. R. Gleig, the British army chaplain in Jalalabad. "Our eventual evacuation of the country resembled the retreat of an army defeated."[8]

The British intervention in Afghanistan is an example of a *fiasco,* or an unwinnable war. This book is a guide to handling fiascos; so let's take a closer look at the concept.

Fiascos happen in wars of limited interests, or military campaigns that don't directly imperil a country's physical security. Wars of national survival, like the world wars, are life-and-death struggles where leaders may need to do whatever it takes to achieve a decisive result. "You ask, what is our aim?" said Winston Churchill in World War II. "I can answer in one word. It is victory, victory at all costs, victory in spite of all terror, victory, however long and hard the road may be; for without victory, there is no survival."[9]

By contrast, wars of limited interests involve lower stakes. The fighting is in a more distant location. The military deployment is smaller. The homeland is not at risk. Therefore, countries can't justify an endless commitment. In the 1840s, for example, Britain had only limited interests in Afghanistan and couldn't keep fighting indefinitely.

Fiascos are triggered by a major military failure. The battlefield situation has deteriorated alarmingly. The wheels are coming off. By the start of 1842, the British faced a dramatically worsening situation as the insurgency reached Kabul.

If a country's interests in the conflict are sufficiently restricted, and the battlefield failure is sufficiently extreme, the result may be an unwinnable war. A decisive victory can no longer be achieved at a reasonable cost. Overthrowing the adversary will forfeit too much blood and treasure, reap too small a dividend, take too long, erode public support, or damage wider objectives. In 1842, the British had no plausible path to a meaningful victory in Afghanistan.

It's sometimes tough to identify exactly when a war turns into a fiasco. In other words, there's no simple metric for determining if a conflict is unwinnable. In the end, claiming that decisive victory is off the table is a judgment call. We must identify what victory represents and estimate the costs, benefits, and risks of seeking this outcome—all based on the unique nature of the campaign.

This assessment may be subjective but it's not arbitrary. As the military situation steadily worsens, the reality of a fiasco becomes increasingly clear. In other words, when the war effort first starts to deteriorate, the situation is often ambiguous and debatable. Then, if the decline continues further, the implausibility of achieving victory comes into sharp focus. At the extreme, following a severe battlefield reversal, the grim truth of an unwinnable war is self-evident. Later, we'll look in more detail at the challenges of assessing progress in wartime—especially in counterinsurgency campaigns—as well as some solutions.

In the wake of a fiasco, leaders must find an exit strategy to cut the nation's losses and protect its interests and values. They need a substitute for victory, such as a tough draw or a tolerable failure.

The idea of cutting losses, or fighting for less than victory, isn't easy for Americans to accept. We like decisive results. American sports matches, for example, almost always end in a clear win or a loss, whereas European sports like soccer and cricket often result in a tie. "If you tried to end a game in a tie in the United States," said NBC's fictional coach Ted Lasso, "heck, that might be listed in Revelations as the cause for the apocalypse."

During the 2014 soccer World Cup, the United States played Germany in the final group game. Because of other results, the United States could progress if it won, drew, or even if it lost—as long as it was by a narrow margin. The idea of losing in the right way seemed risible to many Americans, and reinforced the idea that soccer is an alien sport. "This is the United States of America," said one commentator. "We do not play for ties, or celebrate advancing solely because another team lost."[10]

In a similar vein, we tend to see the outcome of war in binary terms as a victory or a defeat. Any negative U.S. military result is placed in the defeat bracket and feels almost equally intolerable. Who wants to scrape a draw or lose by less? *This is the United States of America.*

The outcome of war, however, is not binary. Instead, there are many gradations of success and failure. An unwinnable war means that decisive victory has been removed from the list of possible outcomes. But this still leaves a wide range of potential results, including a marginal success, a tough draw, a partial failure, or an outright catastrophe. The difference between a draw and a disaster may equal thousands of lives. Therefore, in an unwinnable war, there's still a great deal to play for.

In January 1842, for example, there were many possible resolutions to the First Anglo-Afghan War. None of them involved a British victory. Some roads led to a modest failure. Other paths ended in military catastrophe. Britain chose poorly and lost an entire army.

The British retreat from Kabul is the wrong way to lose a war. But is there a *right* way to lose a war? Is it possible to end a deteriorating conflict without leaving a sole survivor clinging to an injured pony and a dying child along the path?

The success of an exit strategy is about much more than just returning the troops. Otherwise the mission can turn into what foreign affairs analyst Gideon Rose called a "moon landing," designed to transport soldiers far away and bring them home safely with little regard for what's left behind.[11]

Ultimately, an exit strategy should be assessed based on a cost-benefit analysis. Did officials use the available resources efficiently to achieve political goals, limit the loss to national interests and values, and maximize potential gains? Did they carefully compare different courses of action—escalation, de-escalation, or negotiation—and choose the best option? Or were other, and likely more effective, paths out of the conflict available but ignored?

Today, the problem of resolving a fiasco has become all too familiar. Since 1945, four out of five major American wars became unwinnable: Korea, Vietnam, Afghanistan, and Iraq. The only exception—where victory remained on the table—was the Gulf War. How well did the United States handle these military crises?

America's record of dealing with fiascos is largely one of failure. In other words, Washington responded to battlefield reversals in ways that made a poor situation even worse. We stumbled over the finish line, not just losing but losing *badly*. Let's take a closer look at U.S. exit strategies in Korea, Vietnam, Afghanistan, and Iraq—as an important step in discovering the right way to end a difficult war.

Old Baldy

On November 24, 1950, Douglas MacArthur, the commander of U.S. forces in Korea, launched "the end of the war offensive."

American and allied troops had pushed North Korea out of the South, crossed the 38th parallel into the North, captured Pyongyang, and were advancing toward the Chinese border. North Korea was about to be liberated. The iron curtain in East Asia was about to be rolled back. MacArthur said he would bring the boys home by Christmas.

But American soldiers were walking into a trap. Beijing had repeatedly signaled it would intervene rather than accept the fall of North Korea. Washington dismissed the threat as a bluff. Reports emerged of thousands of Chinese troops in North Korea. The danger was brushed aside. Chinese forces mauled several South Korean divisions and then vanished like ghosts. The peril was again ignored. American troops rushed north with confidence born from a century of golden victories and a seemingly invincible commander in MacArthur.

On November 27, Sergeant Gene Dixon was serving with the U.S. Marines near the Chosin Reservoir in North Korea when "all hell broke loose."[12] In a coordinated assault, three hundred thousand Chinese troops struck U.S. and allied forces. "It seemed as if the Chinese were coming at us from all directions," said Dixon, "blowing bugles and yelling throughout the night." Wearing only quilted cotton jackets in a Siberian winter, the Chinese soldiers attacked at close range with machine guns and hand grenades. One Communist general told his men: "Kill these Marines as you would kill snakes in your homes."[13]

"I couldn't believe my eyes when I saw them in the moonlight," recalled Marine Corporal Arthur Koch. "It was like the snow come to life, and they were shouting and shaking their fists — just raising hell. . . . The Chinese didn't come at us by fire-and-maneuver, the way Marines do; they came in a rush like a pack of mad dogs."[14]

Chosin was a death trap. American soldiers were outnumbered eight to one. The marines slogan "every man a rifleman"

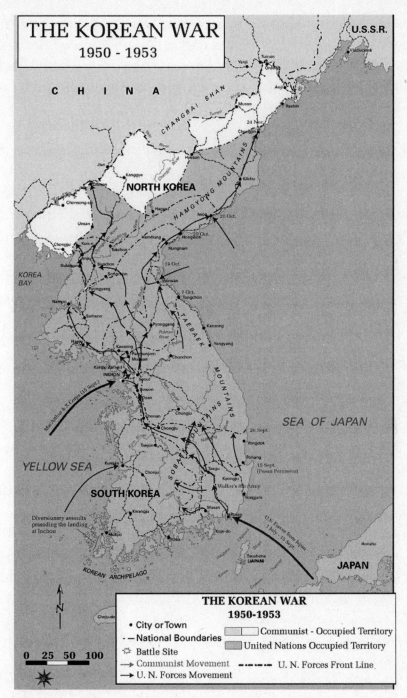

The Korean War (U.S. Military Academy, West Point, Wikimedia Commons)

paid dividends as cooks and truck drivers were thrown into desperate hand-to-hand fighting. In the longest retreat in American military history, U.S. and allied forces withdrew below the 38th parallel. Pyongyang and Seoul fell once more into Communist hands.

Most of all, there was the cold, which reached thirty-five below zero. Frostbitten American troops dragged the icy corpses of their comrades. Mortar bombs left a fiery trail through the frozen air. Soldiers waded through streams and found their clothes turned to ice when they reemerged. "I can recall chipping away at a can of frozen franks and beans, one bean at a time," said Dixon.[15]

On December 10, 1950, Dixon celebrated his twenty-first birthday by walking out of the Chosin Reservoir alive. After suffering over four thousand battle casualties, with thousands more men incapacitated by frostbite and other injuries, the marines were withdrawn from North Korea by sea. The evacuation was over by Christmas.

For American soldiers, China's entry into the Korean War was an odyssey of endurance. For U.S. president Harry Truman, it threatened decisive defeat or an escalation to World War III. The campaign was now unwinnable. With hundreds of thousands of Chinese troops fighting on the enemy side, the cost of conquering North Korea had grown exponentially. Yes, the United States could have mobilized its full might, laid waste to mainland China with atomic weapons, and, most likely, subjugated North Korea. But if the price were a hundred thousand American lives and the erosion of Washington's broader security position, the outcome wouldn't have been a victory. As MacArthur put it, "We face an entirely new war."[16]

How effectively did Truman handle the fiasco in Korea? To Washington's credit, the United States averted a military rout. The president ordered a state of national emergency and expanded American rearmament—more than doubling the size of the U.S.

military within the first year of fighting, from 1.5 million to 3.2 million. In early 1951, the United States regained its military footing in Korea. General Matthew Ridgway whipped demoralized American soldiers into fighting shape by instilling "that sense of belonging to a tightly organized and well-led organization, the feeling that can give momentum to a whole force and make it truly unconquerable."[17] American airpower and artillery ground down the enemy in attacks code-named Thunderbolt, Killer, and Ripper. In March 1951, U.S. and allied forces recaptured Seoul and the front lines returned roughly to the 38th parallel, where the war had begun.

At the same time, Truman avoided dangerous escalation. General Douglas MacArthur wanted to widen the conflict by taking the war to China and even using the atomic bomb. MacArthur, the hero of World War II, was undoubtedly a military genius. But he was also a reckless crusader. Attacking China could have sparked a global conflagration. Truman resisted broadening the war and, in April 1951, fired MacArthur for public insubordination.

In July 1951, the two sides began truce negotiations. The Joint Chiefs thought that the talks would take three weeks. Pessimists said that they might last six weeks. U.S. negotiators were told to pack dress uniforms for the imminent armistice ceremony. If an acceptable deal had been quickly hammered out, Truman could have earned a profile in courage for resolving a dangerous crisis.[18]

But the Korean War didn't end. It took two years of negotiations, over five hundred meetings, and eighteen million recorded words before a deal was eventually reached, in July 1953. As they parleyed, the belligerents continued bloody attritional fighting over hills like Old Baldy, a barren moonlike crest that changed hands eleven times during the campaign.

Neither side was willing to show any hint of weakness. All the major players saw Korea as a stage on which to demonstrate their military prowess and resolve to a global audience. Stalin bankrolled the North Korean war effort and pressed China and North Korea to take a tough stand. The United States also played hardball diplomacy—especially on the issue of prisoners of war. China and North Korea demanded the traditional "all for all" swap of POWs at the end of hostilities. But without thinking through the consequences, Truman insisted that captured Communist prisoners be allowed to defect. Washington's inflexible position on repatriation proved disastrous. This single issue kept the war going for an extra fifteen months.[19]

The final truce terms were similar to those proposed at the start of the talks: a cease-fire along the line of military control. But now nearly twenty thousand more U.S. soldiers were dead. Americans saw the Korean War as a dour stalemate. The failed exit strategy meant that Truman left office in 1952 as one of the most unpopular presidents in U.S. history.[20]

Return to Your Dust

In Jewish folklore, the golem was an artificial being, crafted out of clay and animated by ritual incantations, which performed tasks for its creators. But the golem is ultimately a story of hubris. The creature proved hard to control and ended up destroying its designer.

South Vietnam was America's golem: a synthetic creation, cast from the earth of U.S. material wealth, kneaded into being by American advisors, and inspirited by hymns of freedom. The two decades of South Vietnam's life represent a tale of illusions that ultimately shattered the country and profoundly damaged its maker.

The 1954 Geneva Accords ended French rule in Vietnam and

divided the country into a Communist North and a non-Communist South. It was supposed to be a temporary arrangement pending national elections and unification. But the United States feared the path of unification would lead to a Communist Vietnam and an expansion of Soviet and Chinese influence. Washington rejected the Geneva Accords and sought to fashion South Vietnam into the sentinel of Southeast Asia.

By 1960, a sustained insurgency known as the Vietcong emerged in South Vietnam. (It was also called the National Liberation Front and, after 1969, the Provisional Revolutionary Government.) Backed by North Vietnamese troops and supplies, the Vietcong fought to unite the country under Communist rule.

In 1964, despite years of American aid and the presence of thousands of U.S. advisors, South Vietnam was close to collapse. President Lyndon Johnson faced a stark choice of getting in or getting out. Believing that the fall of South Vietnam would trigger a domino effect of Communist gains in the region, imperil America's reputation, provoke a conservative backlash at home that could destroy the Great Society, and prove a personal humiliation, LBJ chose to get in.[21]

After an alleged North Vietnamese attack on a U.S. naval vessel in the Gulf of Tonkin, Congress authorized the use of force. Johnson compared the Gulf of Tonkin Resolution to grandma's nightshirt because it "covered everything."[22] In March 1965, LBJ began the Rolling Thunder bombing campaign against North Vietnam and dispatched U.S. Marines to protect airfields in South Vietnam. It was the first installment in a steady expansion of American ground forces, which reached 184,000 by the end of 1965, and more than doubled again the following year. Americans were now committed to fight for a country almost wholly lacking in strategic resources or political freedom.[23]

Vietnam may have been an unwinnable war as soon as U.S.

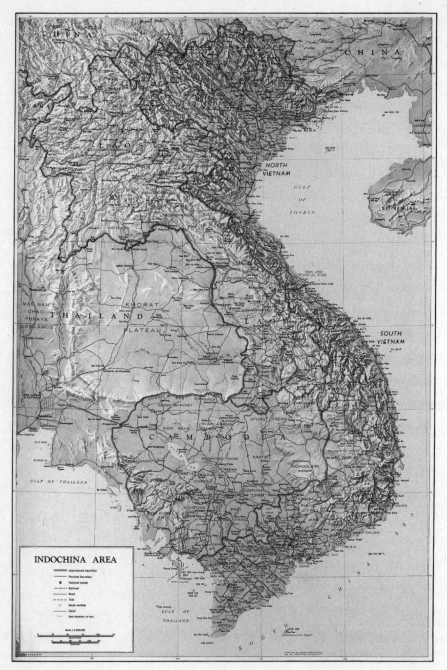

Indochina in 1970 (*Indochina Atlas*, published in October 1970 by the Directorate of
Intelligence, Office of Basic and Geographic Intelligence, Central Intelligence Agency)

A U.S. Marine guards a captured Vietcong prisoner in 1965. (Department of Defense, U.S. Marine Corps, National Archives, ARC identifier: 532434)

forces set foot in the country. In other words, a decisive victory—defined as the suppression of the insurgency and the creation of an independent and secure non-Communist South Vietnam—may have been too costly to achieve from the start. Still, there was some uncertainty about the Communist response to the arrival of American forces.

By 1966, however, Vietnam was clearly a fiasco. With massive bombing and hundreds of thousands of ground troops, the United States could prop up its ailing creation, but the war could not be won at a reasonable cost. Washington was unable to defeat the Vietcong or force North Vietnamese troops to leave the South. The United States strove for a "crossover point" where Communist losses couldn't be replaced—but this moment always lay beyond the horizon. Washington estimated there were 134,000 Communist troops in South Vietnam by the end of 1965 and 280,000 by 1967.

The fundamentals of the campaign favored North Vietnam. The enemy decided when and where to fight, initiating almost nine out of ten engagements. The insurgents were incredibly committed and willing to take punishment on a scale rarely seen in modern warfare. The same couldn't be said for America's ally, South Vietnam, which was riven by coups and lacked legitimacy or a popular base of support.[24] Hanoi could also count on backing from two great powers, the USSR and China. In 1966, China dispatched fifty thousand military personnel to North Vietnam, including engineers and antiaircraft units. In late 1966, Robert McNamara, the secretary of defense, told the president, "The prognosis is bad that the war can be brought to a satisfactory conclusion within the next two years."[25]

With victory an unrealistic goal, the task was now to fashion a viable exit strategy. Withdrawing from Vietnam was one of the most difficult foreign policy challenges in American history. LBJ had planted the U.S. flag, and seemingly put America's reputation on the line—hugely complicating any exit. And Hanoi was intransigent, seeing the war through a prism of Communist ideology and supreme self-confidence.[26]

Johnson responded to the fiasco with a tortuous policy that only prolonged America's agony. "Nobody wanted that war less than Lyndon Johnson," said the president's youngest daughter. "No matter how hard he tried, he didn't seem to be able to get out of that quagmire."[27] For two years, there was no exit strategy as the United States became trapped in endless conflict. LBJ clung to the illusion that gradual escalation would somehow force the enemy to quit, pledging "victory over aggression."[28] Meanwhile, Washington refused to negotiate with North Vietnam unless it first surrendered—or, in other words, accepted an independent and non-Communist South Vietnam.

Finally, after the Communist Tet Offensive of January 1968, LBJ shifted to a new strategy of de-escalation, the cessation of most bombing raids against North Vietnam, and negotiations. In May 1968, the two sides began peace talks in Paris. But the discussions went nowhere as Washington continued to insist that North Vietnam accept an outcome short of unification. Johnson also announced his decision not to run for reelection, handing the riddle of Vietnam to his successor, Richard Nixon.[29]

How did Nixon fare? In his defense, Nixon inherited an almost impossible situation: an unwinnable conflict, 550,000 American troops on the ground, 200 U.S. fatalities every week, declining public support, an increasingly critical Congress, and the stark possibility of being the first president to lose a war—with potentially negative consequences for America's reputation in the cold war and Nixon's own credibility as president.

"We've got to get the hell out of there," said Nixon in March 1971. "No question," replied National Security Advisor Henry Kissinger.[30] The president's policy of "Vietnamization" shifted the burden of fighting to South Vietnam and steadily reduced American troop levels to fewer than seventy thousand in the spring of 1972. The U.S. military adopted more effective counterinsurgency tactics known as "clear and hold," which pacified many rural areas of South Vietnam—although the gains often proved transitory.[31]

Nixon pursued both official and secret negotiations with Hanoi. Finally, in January 1973, the president announced an agreement to end U.S. involvement in the war and received plaudits from across the American political spectrum. North Vietnam had long demanded a new coalition government in South Vietnam, with Vietcong participation. But the final deal allowed the U.S.-backed Nguyen Van Thieu regime to stay in power. Nixon claimed it was "peace with honor."[32] Having achieved détente with the Soviet Union and China, Nixon was "three for three," according to Kissinger.[33]

Ultimately, however, Nixon's exit strategy from Vietnam was a failure. For five months after his inauguration in January 1969, Nixon tried to impose his will on North Vietnam with a mixture of bluffing and firepower. The routine was good cop, *mad cop*. Kissinger was the calm voice of reason, whereas Nixon cultivated the image of an obsessive madman who might irrationally escalate the war—and perhaps go nuclear. Nixon's tactic reminded one White House official of the crazed German scientist in *Dr. Strangelove*. But Hanoi saw through the bluff, forcing a switch to the new policy of Vietnamization.[34]

Although Nixon withdrew U.S. troops from Vietnam, he also widened the war by invading Laos and Cambodia, mining the North Vietnamese port of Haiphong, and expanding the bombing of North Vietnam. Peace talks ultimately dragged on for almost five years—even longer than in Korea. For months, the administration insisted that North Vietnam and the United States simultaneously withdraw their troops from the South, which was an absurd demand when Washington was already unilaterally removing its forces. In the end, another twenty thousand Americans were killed during the Nixon presidency, along with one hundred thousand South Vietnamese soldiers and five hundred thousand North Vietnamese and Vietcong troops.

What did this excruciating process achieve? Yes, Nixon managed to keep Thieu in power. But Washington also agreed that North Vietnam's troops could remain in South Vietnam after U.S. forces left. It was an inevitable concession—and one that rang the death knell for the Saigon regime.

The White House knew the paper peace meant nothing and Hanoi's military victory was just a matter of time. Kissinger sought a "decent interval" between leaving and losing, so that the fall of Saigon would come after the 1972 election. In August 1972, Kissinger told Nixon, "If a year or two years from now North Vietnam gobbles up South Vietnam, we can have a viable foreign policy if it looks as if it's the result of South Vietnamese incompetence.... So we've got to find some formula that holds the thing together a year or two, after which—after a year, Mr. President, Vietnam will be a backwater."[35] Nixon also concluded, "South Vietnam probably is never gonna survive anyway."[36] The deluge was tolerable—but only if it came *après moi*.

President Thieu said the peace terms were "an agonizing solution" that might force him to "commit suicide."[37] Kissinger told the president, "Thieu is right...our terms will eventually destroy him."[38] John Ehrlichman, the president's assistant for domestic affairs, recalled bumping into Kissinger the day after Nixon's "peace with honor" speech. Struck by the president's optimistic words, Ehrlichman offered his congratulations. But Kissinger "told me the truth and it shook me badly." If the South Vietnamese were lucky, Kissinger said, "they can hold out for a year and a half."[39]

In the end, Saigon resisted a little longer: just over two years. During the spring of 1975, North Vietnam crushed southern resistance in a two-month conventional invasion. Congress and the American people had reached their limit. There would be no last-ditch defense of South Vietnam.

In 1975, President Ford looked over a draft speech to Congress on Vietnam. "And after years of effort, we negotiated a settlement which made it possible for us to remove our forces *with honor* and bring home our prisoners." The president crossed out the phrase "with honor."[40]

The broad contours of the 1973 deal had been on the table

since 1968. North Vietnam had previously offered to delay unification if the United States withdrew. Indeed, large chunks of the 1973 text were taken verbatim from the Vietcong's ten-point peace plan of 1969. And tragically, we can go back even further. The settlement that Washington achieved in 1973 was arguably worse than the terms North Vietnam offered in 1965.[41]

What should the United States have done when the war became a fiasco? Given Hanoi's tough stance, there were no easy choices. A sudden abandonment of Vietnam would have been divisive at home and might have triggered dangerous international consequences. Kissinger wrote, "We could not simply walk away from an enterprise involving two administrations, five allied countries, and thirty-one thousand dead as if we were switching a television channel."[42]

But there were other options available between changing the television channel and five more years of futile war. As the military reality came into focus, Washington should have pressed more aggressively for a face-saving exit by calling for a new international conference to settle the fate of South Vietnam. Washington could have accepted a power-sharing deal in Saigon and the neutralization of South Vietnam as part of a process of gradual reunification—even if this path was likely to end in Communist rule. Most importantly, Washington should have focused on its wider goal: preventing a reunified Vietnam from expanding Chinese influence in the region. This remained a plausible aim even if Hanoi won the war because of historical rivalries between Vietnam and China. After all, from Washington's perspective, the war was never really about Vietnam itself: It was about America's broader global position.

In congressional testimony in 1966, former diplomat George Kennan called for "a resolute and courageous liquidation of unsound positions" in Vietnam. No victory was possible, said Kennan, and Washington should push for a compromise peace that was "less than ideal."[43] In September 1967, CIA director Richard Helms presented a secret memo suggesting that the United States could leave Vietnam without a serious loss to its global status. In the same year, the economist and former diplomat John Kenneth Galbraith called for a narrowing of goals in Vietnam and a new Geneva conference.[44]

This was the road not taken. Instead, the United States became committed to the preservation of an artificial country, until its final ignominious collapse. In the Talmud, Rabbi Zeira said to the golem, "You were created by the magicians; return to your dust."

Small Footprint

After 9/11, the United States attacked the Taliban regime in Afghanistan with one of the smallest invading armies in modern history. A few hundred Special Operations Forces and CIA operatives, backed by U.S. airpower and local allies on the ground, overthrew the Taliban and eradicated Al Qaeda's principal safe haven in less than three months.

With the enemy fleeing south toward Pakistan, Washington had a golden opportunity to create a stable regime in Kabul. At this stage, perhaps 80 percent of the Afghan people were favorably disposed toward the international force. But the United States acted as if the mission was over. Washington didn't want to get involved in anything that looked like nation-building. And attention soon switched to Iraq. In 2002, there were only ten thousand U.S. soldiers in Afghanistan, along with five thousand international troops—in a country of around twenty-five million.

Graeme Lamb told me that Afghanistan "required a large commitment of resources, money, and time. On all three counts we shortchanged Afghanistan from the outset."[45] Insufficient troops limited the ability of Hamid Karzai's new Afghan regime to offer a basic level of services or provide for law and order, allowing the Taliban to steadily recover.

By 2006, Afghanistan was a fiasco. There was no plausible way to suppress the guerrillas at a low enough cost to count as decisive victory. The Taliban were resurgent, controlling large swathes of the south and busily setting up a shadow government. Corrupt rule sapped popular support for the regime in Kabul. Helmand Province became the ground zero of global opium production. In the first three years of the war, there were fewer than 10 suicide bombings in Afghanistan. In 2006 alone, there were 139. From 2005 to 2006, the overall number of insurgent armed attacks tripled, from 1,500 to 4,500.[46]

The U.S. goal was now to fashion a workable exit plan to consolidate the gains of the mission and prepare for eventual

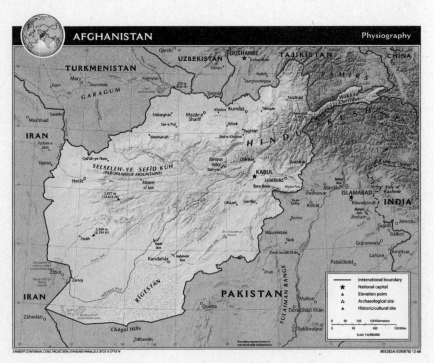

Afghanistan (Central Intelligence Agency)

withdrawal. Washington's response to the fiasco, however, was to whistle past the graveyard. As the Taliban recovered, the United States looked the other way. Iraq was deteriorating at an even quicker pace, and Afghanistan took a backseat. In late 2005, the United States actually planned to withdraw 3,000 of its 20,000 troops in Afghanistan — although, fortunately, the idea was shelved. As late as 2007, there were just 23,500 U.S. troops in the country, along with 25,000 NATO soldiers. Washington was also slow in training Afghan forces. And the Bush administration categorically rejected any negotiations with the Taliban leadership.

Finally, in 2009, the crisis was impossible to ignore. Following a careful review, Obama almost tripled U.S. troop levels, from 38,000 at the start of 2009 to 100,000 in 2010. But there was a crucial caveat. U.S. troops would start withdrawing in mid-2011, barely eighteen months in the future.[47]

Obama's new strategy blunted the Taliban's momentum and averted an immediate crisis — creating a military stalemate on the ground. But the dramatic expansion in American forces combined with a rapid drawdown undermined the potential for sustained gains. The White House also wasted two more years refusing to talk to the Taliban.

Ronald Neumann, the U.S. ambassador to Afghanistan from 2005 to 2007, told me there was "great confusion" among the Afghans about our intentions and plans.[48] On the one hand, Washington signaled a long-term commitment to Afghanistan. In 2012, the NATO Summit in Chicago agreed to withdraw most international forces by the end of 2014 and then create a new NATO successor mission focused on advising and training Afghan troops. At the Tokyo Conference in 2012, the United States brokered $16 billion in international development aid for Afghanistan.

On the other hand, as the Obama administration grew disillusioned with the entire morass, the focus shifted unmistakably to handing over power and getting out. There was talk of a "zero option" with no successor force at all, although Obama eventually announced that around ten thousand U.S. troops would stay after 2014 (this deployment would be cut in half by the end of 2015 and removed almost entirely by the end of 2016). In his 2013 State of the Union address, Obama declared: "By the end of next year, our war in Afghanistan will be over." Note the use of *our* rather than *the*.[49]

The administration's narrative of extrication from Middle Eastern wars threatened to turn into a full-blown retreat from the region—"abandoning Afghanistan to an uncertain future" as former State Department official Vali Nasr put it.[50] The exit strategy was in danger of becoming more about exit than strategy.

Leave-to-Win

After the Gulf War ended in 1991, the United States sought to contain Saddam Hussein through international sanctions and periodic air strikes. In the wake of 9/11, however, the Bush administration dramatically shifted course. The White House became fixated on a potential alliance between tyrants and terrorists. Iraq's suspected weapons of mass destruction (WMD) program could become the arsenal of Al Qaeda. With unsurpassed American power and few domestic constraints, the White House decided to solve the Saddam question once and for all. A surgical regime-change operation would remove the dictator, create a pluralist democracy in Iraq, and remake the Middle East.[51]

The invasion of Iraq in 2003 was a textbook case of combined arms maneuver warfare, as the United States toppled the government in Baghdad at limited cost. But that's where the positive tale abruptly ended. As George Shultz, the former secretary of state, told me, Washington "didn't seem to have thought through what to do with that success."[52] There were too few American troops to stabilize the country, and little or no preparation for the potential collapse of Iraqi institutions and widespread looting. One of the leading experts on democracy promotion, Larry Diamond, described the administration's policy as "gross negligence."[53]

Bush chose as his top administrator in Iraq L. Paul Bremer, a retired Foreign Service officer. The president had never met him.

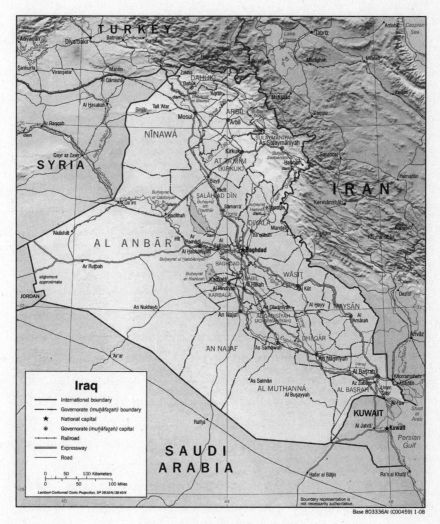

Iraq (Central Intelligence Agency)

Bremer admitted he wasn't an expert on Iraq or the wider issues of postwar reconstruction. And he didn't speak Arabic. Nevertheless, he took the reins for a country of twenty-five million people. He then made two self-destructive decisions: a purge of Baath Party members from public sector work and the disbandment of the Iraqi army. With a few strokes of the pen, the United States created a multitude of unemployed, disgruntled, and armed men.[54]

Iraq descended into civil war, with rival militias battling each other, as well as American and regime forces. Al Qaeda in Iraq carried out spectacular atrocities, including blowing up the United Nations headquarters in Iraq. Ordinary Iraqis were killed at checkpoints. They were killed on buses. And they were killed waiting in line for a police job.

By 2004, the campaign was unwinnable. There was no plausible way to stabilize Iraq at a low enough cost to count as victory. The rebellion had metastasized with multiple Sunni and Shiite insurgent groups. In April 2004, the Abu Ghraib scandal revealed widespread American mistreatment of prisoners and further eroded the legitimacy of the war effort. U.S. fatalities almost doubled, from 486 in 2003 to 849 in 2004. By the end of 2004, hundreds of Iraqi civilians were dying every week. General William Odom concluded, "Bush hasn't found the WMD, Al Qaeda, it's worse, he's lost on that front...he's going to achieve a democracy there? That goal is lost, too....Right now, the course we're on, we're achieving Bin Laden's ends."[55]

Given the blood and treasure already expended in Iraq, and the receding possibility of a secure and democratic country, the United States was now looking at a grim set of outcomes, ranging from a tough draw to an out-and-out catastrophe. How did the White House respond?

The U.S. exit strategy was known as "leave-to-win," which meant withdrawing as quickly as possible. Washington was determined to avoid getting bogged down in a prolonged stabilization

In 2007, a U.S. armored personnel carrier was hit by an improvised explosive device. (U.S. Army, C-52 of 3/2 Stryker Brigade Combat Team)

mission in Iraq. Bush claimed that "sending more Americans would undermine our strategy of encouraging Iraqis to take the lead in this fight. And sending more Americans would suggest that we intend to stay forever, when we are, in fact, working for the day when Iraq can defend itself and we can leave."[56]

The administration sought to hand over sovereignty to Iraqi exiles and handpicked supporters, hastily train Iraqi security forces, let Baghdad take the lead in providing security, and reduce U.S. troop levels from 130,000 to 100,000 by the end of 2006. To minimize the U.S. presence, American soldiers were hunkered down in forward operating bases, or "little Americas," far removed from the Iraqi people, where the troops enjoyed Starbucks coffee and flat screen televisions, and were known as *fobbits.*[57]

As a result of leave-to-win, the United States neither left nor won. Baghdad couldn't take the lead in stabilizing the country, because it was an active participant in the civil war. Iraqi security forces often doubled as death squads. With too few troops to permanently clear areas of insurgents, and with American soldiers isolated from the Iraqi people, the United States was left playing a deadly game of "whack-a-mole." From 2005 to 2006, Iraqi civilian deaths jumped from 20,000 to 35,000. Iraq suffered the greatest number of suicide terror attacks in history.[58]

Meanwhile, the United States resisted negotiating with the insurgents. Paul Wolfowitz, the deputy secretary of defense, read a memo suggesting that the United States reach out to Sunni rebels—and returned it with three words scribbled in the margin: "They are Nazis!"[59]

At the time, John Abizaid was head of U.S. Central Command, with responsibility for the Middle East, North Africa, and Central Asia, including Afghanistan and Iraq. I asked Abizaid whether we waited too long to talk to Sunni insurgents. "Absolutely, we should have reached out immediately." The problem: "What was obvious from my point of view was not obvious to people back in Washington."[60]

Desperate to leave Iraq but facing a worsening crisis, Washington found solace in denial. In 2003, Bremer was briefed about useful lessons from Vietnam and responded furiously. "I don't want to hear the word *Vietnam* in my office. This meeting is over."[61] Meanwhile, Rumsfeld told the press corps, "I don't do quagmires."[62] He described widespread looting as the "untidiness of freedom" and dismissed the Iraqi rebels as "dead-enders."[63] Rumsfeld said: "We don't have an exit strategy, we have a victory strategy."[64] He was right about the first part.

In the ancient Greek legend, Oedipus was told he would kill his father and marry his mother. Tragically, the plan he devised to avert these events only served to make the prophecy come true. In the same vein, the Bush administration's strategy to avoid a nation-building quagmire—leave-to-win—produced exactly the feared outcome. It took over eight years to end the war. During this time, 4,500 Americans were killed, 32,000 were wounded, and hundreds of billions of dollars were spent.[65]

Fight or Flight

It's easy, with all the benefit of hindsight, to cast judgment on American leaders who operated in the midst of crisis and uncertainty. Few scenarios are as challenging as a military fiasco. But even at the time, many prominent voices saw the futility of these exit strategies and pressed for a change of course.

During the 1960s, George Ball, the undersecretary of state for economic and agricultural affairs, was a tragic Cassandra figure, who accurately prophesied what would happen with endless escalation in Vietnam but kept losing the argument. "Once on the tiger's back," he said, "we cannot be sure of picking the place to dismount."[66] Vice President Hubert Humphrey also told LBJ that the odds of success in Vietnam were slim and that the United States should cut its losses. Rather than listen, Johnson sidelined Humphrey from key decision making.[67]

Time and again, Washington struggled to extract the country from a failing war. In the wake of a fiasco, we tried to leave either too slowly (Korea and Vietnam) or too quickly (Iraq and Afghanistan). We failed to adjust our war aims effectively. We negotiated badly, or we refused to negotiate at all. Flawed exit strategies weakened four presidents—Truman, LBJ, Nixon, and Bush—and caused enormous damage to American society.

The question is: Why do we keep losing the wrong way?

CHAPTER 3

The Landscape of Loss

In the early hours of June 22, 1941, a maelstrom crashed into the Soviet Union, in the form of three million Germans, half a million Allied troops, and thousands of aircraft and tanks. After hearing news of the Nazi invasion, Stalin was shocked and depressed. The Soviet dictator had refused to believe intelligence reports of an imminent attack. Now he again denied reality by clinging to the hope of a diplomatic solution. Unfortunately, Hitler was intent on transforming the Soviet Union into a vast German colony: "What India was for England the territories of Russia will be for us."[1]

After Minsk fell at the end of June and the full extent of the catastrophe was laid bare, Stalin suffered a psychological breakdown. "Everything's lost," he told his colleagues. "I give up. Lenin founded our state and we've fucked it up."[2] The next day, Stalin didn't appear at the Kremlin. Exhausted and unable to sleep, he wandered aimlessly around his dacha. For two days, the government was paralyzed and the Germans marched on. Finally, the Politburo top brass visited Stalin and found a haggard figure. "Great Lenin's no more," said Stalin. "If only he could see us now." The dictator feared the officials were about to arrest him: "Why've you come?"[3]

Stalin had never been more vulnerable. The Politburo had this one chance to remove him. But there was no coup at the court of the crimson king. All of Stalin's rivals were long dead. The Soviet premier survived and ultimately recovered his nerve.

Four years later, the military tide had turned and now Soviet armies bore down on Berlin. Hitler and his fanatical inner circle clung to illusions that victory was still possible. Physically deteriorating, with a trembling hand and signs of senility, Hitler believed the grand coalition arrayed against him would disintegrate, and new German miracle weapons like the Me 262 jet fighter would safeguard the thousand-year Reich.

In April 1945, Joseph Goebbels, the German minister of propaganda, read aloud to Hitler from one of the Führer's favorite books, a history of Frederick the Great. Goebbels described Prussia's nadir in the Seven Years' War, when all hope seemed lost and Frederick thought about taking poison. Then, in 1761, the Empress Elizabeth of Russia died, and the enemy alliance unexpectedly collapsed. Listening to the tale, Hitler's eyes brimmed with tears. A few days later, Franklin Roosevelt passed away. Hitler was sure that history would repeat itself and that deliverance was imminent.[4]

It was all wishful thinking. The Allies were determined to see things through. The miracle weapons were too few in number to make any difference. Berlin's delusions only prolonged the devastation for this continent of suffering.

Stalin's and Hitler's experiences give some idea why it's so difficult for leaders to handle military failure. The aftermath of battlefield disaster is a complex, challenging, and uncertain environment to navigate. Loss can be psychologically shattering. It may trigger anxiety, depression, and feelings of helplessness — or, alternatively, a faith in fantastical salvation. The facts are so painful they simply cannot be faced. At the chemical level, stress heightens production of the hormone cortisol, which can reduce memory function, cause rigid thinking, and diminish problem-solving skills.[5]

As the scholar Fred Iklé put it: "Strong men may lapse into strange indecisiveness, precisely at a time when their nation most urgently requires firm decisions."[6]

And mental strain is just one reason why it's difficult to plot a sure course through the landscape of loss. In the wake of battlefield reversals, the glue binding the war effort together may come unstuck. Public support could collapse. Alliances may splinter and fail.

One solution is to prepare ahead of time for exit strategies following military failure—*before* disaster strikes. The aftermath of defeat is no place for desperate improvisation. But Washington rarely plans effectively for such contingencies. When a fiasco occurs, presidents break the "In Case of Emergency" glass and find nothing there.

War Games

Chess masters carefully study endgames. Understanding endgame strategy can help you force a checkmate when you're ahead, or snatch a draw or a win from the jaws of defeat. The final stage of a chess match has its own logic. The weakest piece—a pawn—becomes suddenly vital. As the ground is cleared of pieces, pawns can march across the board and metamorphose into powerful queens. Stalemate is also a possibility. And the king may come out of hiding and take the offense like a dashing Alexander the Great.

José Raúl Capablanca was a genius at chess endgames. Growing up in Havana, Cuba, in the 1890s, he learned the game at age four by watching his father play and then beating him. By 1921 he was world champion. Capablanca's endgames were a thing of beauty. His mind worked backward from victory. He would conceive a winning position, and then secure a small edge early on—say, three pawns to two on one side of the board—which ultimately

Four-year-old Capablanca playing chess against his father in 1892 (Wikimedia Commons)

proved decisive in the finale. "In order to improve your game, you must study the endgame before everything else," said Capablanca. "For whereas the endings can be studied and mastered by themselves, the middle game and the opening must be studied in relation to the endgame."[7]

Of course, endgames in chess and war are very different. In chess, there's no uncertainty about each side's material strength and strategic positions: The pieces are there for everyone to see. But in wartime there's often doubt about the enemy's capabilities and location.

In chess, the endgame is the simplest phase of the match because there are fewer pieces on the board. But in war the endgame may be the most complex phase as new countries enter the fray.

And in chess, it's usually clear you've entered the endgame phase. But in war, you might not even know whether you're in the endgame. The conflict could suddenly and unexpectedly reach its denouement. You go to bed in the middle game and wake up in the endgame.

As a result, it's much harder to plan for the endgame of military conflict. We can't predict exactly what the position will look like at the finish line and script the entire mission.

But in war the need to prepare for endgames remains just as compelling. Without attention to the finale, leaders are leaping in the dark. Therefore, Capablanca's advice holds true: The opening and the middle stages of war should be studied in relation to the endgame. Before any military operation begins, leaders should analyze likely scenarios for concluding the campaign and achieving their goals. As well as planning ahead from the start to the endgame, leaders can work backward from the "checkmate" move—is it even possible to get there?

It's a staggering fact that countries often go to war paying little heed to the endgame. Military plans routinely focus on the first act of the saga and ignore the denouement. Iklé wrote, "Most of the exertion is devoted to the means—perfecting the military instruments and deciding on their use in battles and campaigns— and far too little is left for relating these means to their ends."[8]

In 1941, Japan weighed the merits of launching a surprise attack against the most powerful country in the world, the United States. It was a war of choice, and Japan had plenty of time to carefully think through the decision. Given the gigantic stakes, one might expect Tokyo to have planned extensively for the military endgame. Japanese leaders did debate the best date to strike Pearl Harbor. And they also thought through the likely short-term effects. But they barely considered how the conflict might ultimately finish. Just a few weeks before Pearl Harbor, Japanese officials offered an incredibly vague assessment. "We cannot exclude the possibility that the war may end because of a great change in American public opinion....At any rate we should be able to establish an invincible position....Meanwhile, we may hope that we will be able to influence the trend of affairs and bring the war to an end."[9]

Hideki Tojo, the Japanese prime minister, echoed this sentiment with a reference to the Kiyomizu Temple, a Buddhist shrine in Kyoto that juts out over a steep cliff edge. "There are times when we must have the courage to do extraordinary things—like jumping, with eyes closed, off the veranda of the Kiyomizu Temple."[10] Tokyo made a leap of faith, and every major Japanese city was reduced to ashes.

In recent years, the United States has also failed to think through the endgame of war. "Operational planning guidance," wrote one analyst, "does not integrate exit strategy considerations in the forefront of the planning and execution cycles."[11] Washington tends to focus on the initial combat phase—"taking the hill"—rather than the postwar efforts to stabilize a country and consolidate political gains.[12]

After the United States bombed Iraq in 1998 in a mission called Desert Fox, the prospect of a final showdown with Saddam loomed closer. But General Anthony Zinni, then the head of U.S. Central Command, knew the American military had an issue. "It struck me then that we had a plan to defeat Saddam's army, but we didn't have a plan to rebuild Iraq." In 1999, Zinni organized a war game called Desert Crossing to examine what a post-Saddam Iraq might look like. The game revealed that regime change could trigger a host of problems, including "rival forces bidding for power," fragmentation "along religious and/or ethnic lines," and an upsurge in "Iran's anti-Americanism."[13]

Given these challenges, Zinni pushed Washington to prepare

for the stabilization of Iraq. "We need a plan in addition to the war plan for the reconstruction." The answer, he said: "Not interested. Would not look at it."[14]

A few years later, when Bush set America's target sights on Baghdad, Zinni, who was by now retired, called Central Command. "You need to dust off Desert Crossing." They replied, "What's that? Never heard of it." In just a few years, the corporate memory "was gone."[15]

Washington was playing a new game, and the focus was no longer on the end state. During 2002, the U.S. military carried out a series of simulations as part of its planning for the Iraq War. The U.S. Army's game was called Vigilant Warrior, and the air force's game was named Global Engagement. The scenario was a regime change mission against a fictional country called Nair (which sounds a lot like Iran but actually combined features of Iran and Iraq). These were tabletop games: Risk with added bells and whistles. Comfortingly, both games ended in a decisive U.S. victory.

But one of the participants, Huba Wass de Czege, a retired brigadier general, saw a serious problem. The games were based on a flawed conception of victory. They ended after the United States won the opening rounds on the battlefield rather than when Washington achieved its overarching political goals. The games "tend to devote more attention to successful campaign-beginnings than to successful conclusions." They finish when American control of strategic locations looks like "a matter of time," or, in other words, when "victory seems inevitable to us (not necessarily to the enemy)." The result is a "blind spot at the back-end of campaigns."[16] It's like ending a chess match halfway through. The war games needed more turns to show the challenges that come *after* regime change.

Problems in theory soon became problems in practice. The Iraq invasion plan prioritized the regime-change stage and downplayed the subsequent effort to stabilize the country. A member of the military staff that planned the ground invasion concluded, "Both the planners and the commander had been schooled to see fighting as the realm of war and thus attached lesser importance to postwar issues.... Only a fool would propose hurting the war fighting effort to address postwar conditions that might or might not occur."[17] Tommy Franks, the head of U.S. Central Command from 2000 to 2003, told the deputy secretary of defense where his priorities lay: "You pay attention to the day *after,* I'll pay attention to the day *of.*"[18] As Thomas Pickering, former undersecretary of state for political affairs, told me, the White House believed that "military victory would produce its own rewards magically out of the clouds."[19]

And the United States is particularly unlikely to prepare for endgames *after military failure.* Chess masters spend long hours studying endgames in losing positions. If the middle game goes badly and they enter the finale with less material, can they salvage a draw through superior play?

Frank Marshall was the American chess champion from 1909 to 1936. He personally received the title of grandmaster from no less than Tsar Nicholas II. Marshall was most famous, however, for his prodigious skill at chess "swindles," or extricating himself from difficult positions using tactical skill, time pressure, and psychological warfare. He even wrote a book called *Marshall's Chess "Swindles,"* which described "my victories over certain disappointed gentlemen."[20] As one biographer put it, "His prowess at rescuing the irretrievable took on magical proportions."[21]

But Washington is not interested in planning military "swindles," or studying the endgame of war when it's a piece down. Loss is a dirty word. "Nations are as incapable of imagining their own defeat," wrote cultural historian Wolfgang Schivelbusch, "as individuals are of conceiving their own death."[22] James Stavridis, the former Supreme Allied Commander in Europe, told me,

"U.S. military culture is not particularly compatible with failure planning." One reason is "the culture of 'can-do,' 'we will succeed,' or, as Colin Powell put it, 'perpetual optimism is a force multiplier.'"[23]

Overly positive thinking often infects war games. According to a 1971 review of education in the U.S. Army, war games and other exercises were "generally euphoric in nature—the U.S. Army always wins with relative ease."[24] And this, remember, was in the midst of a military debacle in Vietnam.

More recently, Wass de Czege wrote that U.S. war games "greatly underestimate the difficulty of concluding such campaigns promptly." In reality, "coalitions tend to fray as optimistic expectations fade and the achievement of strategic aims is delayed.... The enemy's definition of winning promptly becomes not losing, or delaying defeat until the coalition tires of pursuing its original strategic ends."[25]

In 2002, the U.S. military organized a simulation called Millennium Challenge. It was one of the biggest war games in history: a three-week-long, $250-million exercise, involving over 13,000 personnel. The official purpose was to test America's capacity to defeat a major adversary in the Middle East. But the top brass had another motive: demonstrating the success of U.S. military "transformation," or the new model of agile high-technology warfare.

Paul K. Van Riper, a retired Marine Corps lieutenant general, was tapped to command the enemy forces. The Pentagon said that Van Riper could play freely with "the ability to win." So that's exactly what he did—by using asymmetric tactics to show the limits of transformation. Van Riper bypassed U.S. electronic surveillance by delivering his orders via motorcycle messenger. When an American fleet gathered for the invasion, Van Riper struck first with cruise missiles and a swarm of suicide bombers in speed-

A U.S. F-117A Nighthawk Stealth Fighter flies over Nevada during Millennium Challenge 2002, symbolizing the era of military "transformation." (American Forces Information Service, Department of Defense, National Archives, ARC identifier: 6630164)

boats. The result was worse than Pearl Harbor. Sixteen U.S. warships were destroyed and over twenty thousand American personnel were killed. Fortunately, it was just a game.

Having been out-fought, the Pentagon now had a chance to explore the consequences of military failure by letting the game play out. Instead, the organizers responded by effectively knocking over the pieces. The simulation was suspended, the American fleet rose from its watery grave and came back to life, and new rules were introduced to ensure victory for the good guys. To help American troops land safely, Van Riper was told to turn off his air defenses and reveal the location of some of his units. Rather than keep the pretense going, Van Riper quit in protest. "It was in actuality an exercise that was almost entirely scripted to ensure [an American] 'win.'"[26] The U.S. military got its victory—and a seeming validation of rapid and decisive operations.

The refusal to think seriously about defeat can infect real war as well as simulated war. When conflict approaches, American officials avoid being distracted by painful scenarios of failure. *What if an insurgency takes root?* Instead, planners focus on taking the first steps in the chosen strategy for victory.

Before the invasion of Iraq, the Bush administration ignored Middle East experts who highlighted the potential risks of regime change. The White House preferred to hear from true believers. According to journalist George Packer, any American official who raised possible flaws with the Iraq invasion plan risked "humiliation and professional suicide."[27]

American planners assumed that U.S. forces would topple Saddam's regime and then quickly redeploy. The Special Inspector General for Iraq Reconstruction concluded that there was "no established plans to manage the increasing chaos" in Iraq. As a result, "when Iraq's withering post-invasion reality superseded [official] expectations, there was no well-defined 'Plan B' as a fallback and no existing government structures or resources to support a quick response."[28]

John Abizaid, the head of U.S. Central Command from 2003 to 2007, told me, "In Iraq we saw a lack of clarity on war ending conditions. There was a heroic assumption that it would be quick and easy. The time horizon was not extended far enough to cover the possibility of an insurgency."[29] Richard Myers, chairman of the Joint Chiefs of Staff from 2001 to 2005, said to me, "Al Qaeda went to the sound of the guns in larger numbers than we thought."[30] Shortly after the invasion, Lieutenant General William Wallace remarked, "The enemy we're fighting is a bit different from the one we war-gamed against."[31]

Stavridis suggested one solution to me: "We should do more deliberate planning for potential failure." For example, we could systematically study past debacles—like the British experience in Afghanistan in the 1840s.[32] This advice echoes the review of army education in 1971: "A strong element of every curriculum should be historical studies which frankly analyze unsuccessful American military efforts...[including]...an objective discussion of what we did, what went wrong, and why. This single action would do more to establish credibility for our instruction than any other known to me."[33]

Inadequate preparation for military endgames — especially in losing positions — means that when a fiasco strikes, Washington is forced to improvise. A high-pressure atmosphere of confusion and stress provides the perfect environment for skewed thinking and a failed exit strategy. Powerful hawkish forces may propel officials toward perilous escalation, with more troops, more bombing, and a widened war. Meanwhile, dovish pressures can pull policymakers toward a precipitous exit that risks a complete collapse on the ground. As a pilot of the state, the president must avoid these obstacles and navigate through dangerous terrain.

The Lure of the Hawk

"Don't matter who did what to who at this point," said drug-gang member Slim Charles in the hit television show *The Wire*. "Fact is, we went to war, and now there ain't no going back. I mean, shit, it's what war is, you know? Once you in it, you in it. If it's a lie, then we fight on that lie. But we gotta fight." Facing battlefield loss, presidents may also conclude that "there ain't no going back." The pressure to escalate the war effort can feel irresistible.

Here, a leader's first enemy is himself — or human psychology. Amid the stress of a military crisis, slow and reasoned thinking may give way to quick gut-check decisions. The experience of failure can exacerbate the effect of psychological "biases," or mental tendencies to think in certain ways, often caused by emotions such as fear or an overwhelming mass of complex information. Crucially, psychological biases don't have random effects. Instead, they systematically unleash a leader's inner hawk and encourage military escalation. These pressures can help prolong a war far beyond the point when rationally it should end.[34]

In HBO's television show *Boardwalk Empire,* set during Prohibition-era America, two criminal kingpins, Arnold Rothstein and Nucky Thompson, engage in a high-stakes poker game. Rothstein loses big when he puts Nucky on a straight and he actually has a flush. Rather than accept the pain and walk away, Rothstein goes "on tilt," which in poker parlance means a mental state of aggressive gambling that can trigger even bigger losses. Finally, one of Rothstein's associates asks Nucky to cut off his credit: "He's a great man...but he doesn't like to lose." Nucky replies: "Nobody likes to, but we all have to learn how."

This is an example of what psychologists call loss aversion, which means we hate losing something more than we like winning something, whether it's a poker game, a tennis match, or a war. The act of forfeiting—even a small amount of something—can feel intolerable. Once we start losing, we're tempted to gamble and try to win it all back, even at the risk of even greater calamity.

Consider a scenario where you have a pretty sweet choice. Option A is to definitely win $850. Option B is to wager, with a 90 percent chance of receiving $1,000 and a 10 percent chance of getting nothing. Here, you're in a happy land that psychologists call the "domain of gains." In other words, you can accept a certain win, or gamble and potentially earn even greater profit but possibly receive nothing. What would you do? Most people act conservatively, choose Option A, and take the sure money.

Now consider a second—and much less appealing—scenario. Option A is to definitely lose $900. Option B is to wager, with a

90 percent chance of handing over $1,000 and a 10 percent chance of sacrificing nothing. Here, you're in an unpleasant realm that psychologists call the "domain of losses." You can accept certain deprivation, or gamble, with a small chance of dodging the bullet entirely but a big chance of owing even more money. In this scenario, people's preferences about wagering change dramatically. Rather than accept a definite loss, most people opt to gamble by choosing Option B.

Interestingly, when presented with these scenarios, people don't respond to the probabilities in a rational way. Mathematically speaking, gambling is actually a superior proposition in the first scenario rather than the second scenario. In the first scenario, a 90 percent chance of receiving $1,000 is preferable to taking $850, whereas in the second scenario, betting is no better or worse than accepting a definite loss. Nevertheless, people are more likely to wager in the second scenario.

So what's going on? When people can make a certain profit they become risk-averse: *A bird in the hand is worth two in the bush.* But when people stare down the barrel of a definite loss, they become risk-acceptant. Sacrificing even a modest amount of something feels unbearable, and so they gamble in the hope of getting back to even — even if they may suffer still greater forfeiture.

Loss aversion pays for the casino's glittering lights. When a gambler starts losing a few chips, he doesn't accept his bad luck and walk away. Instead, he doubles his bets in a bid to win it all back.

And this psychological bias also explains why officials find it so hard to cut their losses and withdraw from a deteriorating war. Accepting even a modest military failure feels unbearable. The lure of the wager that further escalation will somehow recoup all the earlier sacrifices can be overwhelming. In one study, political scientist Jeffrey Taliaferro found that loss aversion made great powers persevere in flagging wars far longer than one would expect based on a rational cost-benefit analysis. Time and again, countries poured lives and money into failing endeavors in the vain hope of getting back to even.[35] In 1965, for example, Vice President Hubert Humphrey urged LBJ to reduce America's involvement in Vietnam but recognized that "it is always hard to cut losses."[36]

Another powerful (and related) bias is "sunk costs," or past expenditures that can't be recovered, like money invested in a project. When making a decision, it's usually wise to ignore sunk costs and focus on future gains and losses. But that's not how people actually think and behave. Instead, we often seek to justify what we've already invested through additional effort.

Imagine that you've purchased a nonrefundable movie ticket online. You look out the window and see appalling weather. But having paid for the ticket, you're determined to get your "money's worth." So you drive in perilous conditions to the movie theater. Then the film turns out to be absolutely terrible. But you sit through the whole thing anyway—a pointless waste of your time. The money invested in the ticket has long vanished, but it hangs like a cloud over your decisions.

The power of sunk costs can be seen in many areas of life. People stay in abusive marriages because of the time they've spent in the relationship. Banks hand more cash to a failing business to rationalize the original lending decision—throwing good money after bad.[37]

No sunk cost is as powerful as the blood and treasure expended in war. Consider a scenario: Would you support destroying a terrorist base if the mission was likely to cost ten American lives? You might decide that the operation is not worth it. But what if we've *already* sacrificed one hundred men trying to take the base, and it will cost ten more lives to succeed? Suddenly, the ten fatalities seem tolerable. The earlier deaths encourage us to invest further lives. At Gettysburg, Abraham Lincoln turned sunk costs into prose for the ages: "From these honored dead we take increased devotion to that cause for which they gave the last full measure of devotion—that we here highly resolve that these dead shall not have died in vain."[38]

Lincoln's words are beautiful and elegiac. But his logic is potentially catastrophic. Fighting for the honored dead may simply swell their ranks. More soldiers could be killed, spurring increased devotion that only prolongs the campaign. "The commonest error in politics," said the British statesman Lord Salisbury, "is sticking to the carcasses of dead policies."[39]

In 1965, George Ball warned against a major commitment in Vietnam. "Once we suffer large casualties, we will have started a well-nigh irreversible process. Our involvement will be so great that we cannot—without national humiliation—stop short of achieving our complete objectives."[40] Just as Ball predicted, the enormous U.S. sacrifice in Vietnam made it hard to even consider quitting. As a rule, we should fight for the living, not the dead.

Another psychological bias can spur escalation after military defeat: overconfidence. People are generally prone to exaggerate their skills, life chances, and ability to control events. A survey of one million high school students found that 70 percent rated themselves as above average in leadership ability. Similarly, around 80 percent of people claim to be above average at driving. It's like we live in Garrison Keillor's fictional Lake Wobegon, where "all the women are strong, all the men are good looking, and all the children are above average."[41]

Overconfidence can be dangerous in wartime if leaders exaggerate the odds that escalation will succeed. Even as the evidence of failure mounts, officials may maintain their belief that victory is just around the corner. During the 1960s, for example, Washington clung to illusions about the effectiveness of more troops and firepower in Vietnam. In 1967, President Johnson said the enemy "knows that he has met his master in the field."[42]

Taken together, loss aversion, sunk costs, and overconfidence are a psychological triple play that can propel leaders toward escalation in wartime. And the effect is reinforced by another hawkish dynamic: the fear of reputational loss. Presidents often worry that retreating from a war will destroy America's image of toughness and resolve, inspire enemies, and cast doubt among friends.

Reputational fears were a siren song that drew the United States further into the Vietnam mire. According to historian Robert McMahon, U.S. officials so often explained the campaign in terms of protecting national credibility that "their statements resemble ritualistic incantations."[43] In 1965, John McNaughton, the assistant secretary of defense, said the war effort was 10 percent about protecting freedom in South Vietnam, 20 percent about preventing Chinese expansion, and 70 percent "to avoid a humiliating U.S. defeat (to our reputation as a guarantor)."[44] In 1968, Kissinger said, "The commitment of five hundred thousand Americans has settled the issue of the importance of Vietnam."[45] Having planted the flag, the nation's image was now on the line. We were fighting in Vietnam because we were fighting in Vietnam.

Isn't America's good name worth protecting? Image is important. The United States doesn't want a reputation for breaching agreements or upping and leaving at the first sign of trouble. Otherwise, allies will question the value of America's word and enemies may be emboldened. After all, if there were no costs to violating a treaty, states wouldn't bother signing them in the first place. Countries that routinely default on their debt pay higher interest rates—and leaders who keep tearing up pacts will find it hard to make new alliances.

Therefore, reputation can be a legitimate reason to stay the course, especially if the stakes are high, we made a cast-iron commitment, allies urge us to see it through, or we're in the early stages of a fight and don't want to signal weakness after just a handful of casualties.

But Washington routinely exaggerates the reputational cost of withdrawing from war. Officials predict apocalyptic consequences for America's image when the true price will probably be much lower. Before fighting for our reputation, we should ask a key question: Whom exactly are we trying to impress by pursuing an endless war? If it's our allies, we should check that they actually want us to keep the campaign going. In Vietnam, for example, many allies and neutrals saw the U.S. war effort as an act of folly and pressed Washington to leave.

What if we're trying to influence the enemy's opinion? The opponent won't necessarily assume we're withdrawing because of a lack of resolve. In private, for example, both the Soviet Union and China recognized that the main reason for America's struggles in Vietnam was the weakness of Saigon. If Washington had headed home earlier, neither Communist country would have automatically seen the United States as lily-livered. Indeed, Moscow was surprised we sacrificed so much when Vietnam mattered so little for our interests.[46]

And fighting in Vietnam to impress the Communists was almost absurd because we privately told China and the Soviet Union this was our plan. The Nixon administration informed Beijing and Moscow that the United States would allow a Communist takeover of South Vietnam after a "decent interval"—to protect America's image. Kissinger advised the Chinese that if South Vietnam "is as unpopular as you seem to think, then the quicker our forces are withdrawn the quicker it will be overthrown...if it is overthrown after we withdraw, we will not intervene."[47] Meanwhile, Kissinger informed the Soviets, "we are prepared to leave so that a Communist victory is not excluded."[48]

In other words, we confessed to the enemy that the exit

strategy was smoke and mirrors designed to create the impression of toughness. As with a magician who reveals his tricks, the illusion loses its power when the logic is outlined to the audience.

It's true that in any crisis, the enemy will weigh the credibility of America's threats and promises. But the opponent is unlikely to base this assessment on a U.S. withdrawal from war that happened, say, five years earlier in time. Instead, the enemy will focus on U.S. interests and power *at that particular moment.* If the stakes are high and Washington has the ability to act, our word will seem reliable. By contrast, if U.S. interests in the crisis are secondary, and we lack the power to achieve much, opponents will rightly question our resolve. Indeed, fighting a war to demonstrate our toughness may only sacrifice American blood and treasure, diminish our power, and reduce the credibility of our next threat.[49]

Presidents shouldn't needlessly squander America's reputation. But withdrawing from a losing venture may not be as damaging for the nation's image as we might think. When we left Vietnam, the predicted geopolitical catastrophe never arose. China didn't dominate Southeast Asia. Instead, Vietnam and China went to war. And fifteen years later, we won the cold war. A quixotic quest for credibility is no substitute for a clear exit strategy designed to achieve national goals.[50]

Of course, the nation's image is not the only reputation that leaders care about. Presidents are also deeply concerned about their party's brand and their personal standing as a guardian of national security. After all, politics doesn't stop at the water's edge. War is a continuation of partisan rancor and electoral maneuvering by other means—especially if the campaign is failing.

Domestic pressures can spur hawkish policies in wartime. Presidents may fear that retreat will prove a personal humiliation, end their career, and destroy their legacy. This dynamic is especially powerful when the leader is personally responsible for initiating the war. Here, there's huge pressure to stick it out, even if the odds of winning are low—one reason why the presidents that started the Korean, Vietnam, Afghanistan, and Iraq wars were unable to finish them.[51]

Democratic presidents are particularly terrified of being labeled weak if they compromise with the enemy. Republicans mercilessly assailed Truman and the Democrats for "losing" China to communism in 1949. And President Johnson thought this was "chickenshit compared to what might happen if we lost Vietnam."[52] He concluded, "I am far more afraid of the right wing than I am of the left wing."[53]

Domestic fears may also have deterred Obama from negotiating with the Taliban. Vali Nasr worked in the administration from

Republican senator Joseph McCarthy attacked Truman for his alleged softness on communism in Korea and elsewhere. "How can we account for our present situation unless we believe that men high in this Government are concerting to deliver us to disaster?" (U.S. Information Agency, National Archives, ARC identifier: 6802721)

2009 to 2011 as a senior advisor to Richard Holbrooke, the U.S. special representative for Afghanistan and Pakistan. From the start, Nasr told me, the White House had its "eyes on 2012." Obama was sensitive to the political optics of negotiation because of his middle name ("Hussein"), the birther issue, and Republican attempts to label him as extreme or weak. The domestic political calculus was simple. There was zero risk in continuing Bush's policy of refusing to negotiate with the enemy. But reaching out to the Taliban was a gamble. The negotiations might fail. They could drag on. And "talking to terrorists is not good politics."[54]

These fears weren't groundless. During the 2012 campaign, Mitt Romney criticized Obama for engaging with the adversary: "We should not negotiate with the Taliban. We should defeat the Taliban."[55] To the question "Who lost Afghanistan?" Republican hawks have a one-word answer ready: "Obama."

In a fiasco, the hawkish pressures don't end there. The U.S. military may also press for escalation. Of course, the Pentagon is not a bunch of gung-ho cowboys that always argue for war. Quite the opposite: Before a conflict starts, generals may be some of the most dovish officials in Washington.[56]

In *peacetime,* that is. Once the flag is committed and the fighting begins, the military tends to be a vocal advocate for using all necessary force to achieve the operational goals. At the core of military culture is a commitment to winning the nation's wars. The idea of cutting losses violates this fundamental mission statement. And admitting defeat may also negatively affect the military's status and budgeting.

One study, for example, found that during the cold war, the military hierarchy was no more hawkish than civilian leaders about going to war. But after American boots were on the ground, military officials were consistently more enthusiastic about escalation than their civilian counterparts.[57]

Similarly, in 2009, U.S. military officials wanted to send an extra forty thousand U.S. troops to Afghanistan and adopt an expansive counterinsurgency campaign—whereas civilian leaders were much more cautious.[58] According to one former Obama administration official, "The White House was convinced that the military had a vested interest in escalating the conflict."[59]

The military's advice is usually influential, partly because of the Pentagon's expertise and partly because of political nervousness. Leon Panetta, the CIA director from 2009 to 2011, said, "No Democratic president can go against military advice, especially if he asked for it."[60]

Human psychology, reputational fears, domestic politics, and the U.S. military are very different kinds of pressures. But they all push in the same hawkish direction—like an unrelenting phalanx. Given these interlocking forces, you might expect presidents to always escalate in a fiasco, ratcheting up the goals, sending more troops, or widening the war. And this was certainly the case in Vietnam.

But it wasn't the full story in Iraq or Afghanistan. As we saw, in Iraq, Washington responded to military failure in 2004 with the disastrous policy of leave-to-win. And when Afghanistan deteriorated sharply in 2006, Washington took its eye off the war effort and was reluctant to send more troops. So what happened in these wars?

The Temptation of the Dove

Following battlefield loss, powerful dovish forces can pull a president in the opposite direction—toward a precipitous exit—in spite of our interests. Most importantly, U.S. leaders and the American public share a visceral dislike of counterinsurgency missions, where we battle guerrillas and engage in nation-building, and usually want to end this kind of stabilization operation as quickly as possible. Americans would much rather fight conventional wars against foreign countries, like in the golden age. The aversion to counterinsurgency is so powerful it can trump all the other hawkish influences combined.[61]

Our distaste for counterinsurgency is partly the result of America's very real struggles against guerrilla opposition. Quite reasonably, we don't want to keep hitting our head against the wall. But counterinsurgency is inherently depressing *even if we somehow succeed.* Interstate wars like the world wars feel like righteous crusades to smite tyrants and spread freedom. By contrast, counterinsurgency is morally murky. We're not sure who the good guys and the bad guys are. Stabilization missions produce few, if any, American heroes. Battling guerrillas dredges up painful memories of Vietnam. And in nation-building operations, negative events like bombings are inherently more newsworthy than positive events like increased electricity production—so if the mission makes the front pages, it's probably for the wrong reasons.[62]

Americans on the left often don't like counterinsurgency because they see it as a form of imperialism: the United States trying to build an empire by force of arms. And many Americans on the right don't like counterinsurgency much, either, because they see it as big-government social engineering. U.S. soldiers should be toppling dictators, not chasing rebels, nation-building, or giving handouts to foreigners.[63]

American support for fighting guerrillas and nation-building is like the sand rushing through an hourglass with an unusually wide neck. Opinion polls soon reveal mounting opposition. Television pundits and newspaper columnists become increasingly skeptical. Congress grows more restless. The center of political gravity invariably shifts toward withdrawal.[64]

How can Congress and public opinion be both hawkish and

dovish? The answer is that Americans hate losing *and* they hate fighting insurgents. In wartime, the public and Congress often support doing whatever it takes to win—unless we're battling guerrillas, where people grow weary of the whole endeavor and want to get out.

In the wake of a military fiasco, skepticism about counterinsurgency and nation-building can trigger an abrupt rush for the exit. The George W. Bush administration saw the whole idea of nation-building as Clinton-style big government do-goodery. "Let me tell you what else I'm worried about," said Bush on the eve of the 2000 election. "I'm worried about an opponent who uses 'nation-building' and 'the military' in the same sentence."[65]

The White House's allergy to stabilization missions produced the disastrous "small footprint" invasions of Afghanistan and Iraq. The Bush administration wanted to swoop in, remove the tyrants, and leave before anyone noticed. In Afghanistan, however, the United States failed to create an effective government in Kabul, allowing the Taliban to recover. And when the mission deteriorated sharply in 2006, officials were reluctant to expand stabilization operations. Ronald Neumann, the former U.S. ambassador to Afghanistan, said that Washington believed it could just hunt terrorists and ignore nation-building: "That was a large mistake."[66]

The same story played out in Iraq. The lack of American troops meant that the country disintegrated and we won the war but lost the peace. When the campaign became a fiasco in 2004, it was critical to stop Iraq from collapsing into a failed state and a base for Al Qaeda. But skepticism about counterinsurgency and nation-building encouraged the failed policy of leave-to-win. The Bush administration was determined to avoid any prolonged stabilization mission in Iraq. Donald Rumsfeld, the secretary of defense, constantly pressed for reducing U.S. troop levels and handing responsibility over to the Iraqis. "If you're not willing to take your hand off the bicycle seat, the person will never learn to ride."[67]

Meanwhile, the public and congressional drumbeat to withdraw from Iraq grew steadily louder. According to Toby Dodge, a British academic and former advisor to David Petraeus, the 2004 presidential election spurred the administration to pursue an overly rapid withdrawal plan: "the needs of Bush's reelection trumped any attempt at sustainable state building in Iraq."[68] By early 2007, 59 percent of Americans opposed sending additional forces to Iraq. The House of Representatives passed a nonbinding resolution critical of any increase in troops.[69] Fortunately, as we will see, Bush overcame these pressures and shifted strategy in 2007 with the surge.

Another powerful force can hasten an American exit: the momentum of withdrawal. Rationally, the White House should be able to escalate and de-escalate a war according to U.S. interests— moving the car into forward or reverse gear as necessary to get out of the ditch. But in the real world, the process of withdrawing from a conflict can develop its own impetus. The car gets stuck in reverse.

Once American troops start leaving, there's pressure to speed up the exit. The boys are coming home. Support for a prolonged commitment starts eroding. Suddenly, it seems unthinkable to send any extra soldiers back. As a result, the president loses flexibility: a large-scale surge of troops can be followed by withdrawal, but a large-scale withdrawal can't be followed by a surge.

In 1969, Nixon's decision to start withdrawing American soldiers from Vietnam proved very popular and created demand for an even quicker exit. The moment the troops began returning, support for sending any more men to Vietnam plummeted.[70] Kissinger said that Americans would become addicted to withdrawal like "salted peanuts...the more U.S. troops come home, the more will be demanded."[71] By 1973, nearly four out of five Americans said the United States shouldn't send soldiers back even if North Vietnam tried to take over the South.[72]

In summary, psychological biases, reputational fears, domestic politics, and pressure from the U.S. military may push the White House toward dangerous escalation. Meanwhile, an aversion to counterinsurgency and nation-building, and the momentum of withdrawal, may pull a president toward a hasty exit. Either set of forces can turn a military fiasco into an outright calamity. And if these hawkish and dovish pressures coexist, with Americans desperate to avoid losing *and* desperate to end the mission, the result may be tortuous anguish and policy paralysis.

Of course, these kinds of pressures are hardly unique to the United States. Dictators also routinely struggle to end a failing conflict, as we saw with the Soviet quagmire in Afghanistan, or the stalemated Iran–Iraq War. Loss aversion, for example, is a universal psychological bias. And autocrats may have even greater cause to worry about the domestic backlash after military retreat. American presidents who walk away from a deteriorating campaign face electoral defeat. By contrast, authoritarian rulers could be looking at a coup, a revolution, or an assassination.

But other dynamics may be particularly powerful in the United States. Since 1945, Washington has obsessed over its credibility more than any other state because of America's superpower status, global alliance commitments, and doctrine of nuclear deterrence. The United States may therefore be especially likely to keep fighting in a bid to protect its image.[73]

The Rules of Disengagement

After a wartime fiasco, the United States has repeatedly pursued a failed exit strategy—at grave cost to American interests. Washington doesn't plan effectively for military reversals, and therefore leaders are forced to improvise amid a treacherous environment of hawkish and dovish pressures. Is it possible to handle battlefield failure more skillfully? Are there principles for marching backward out of a deteriorating war? Like José Raúl Capablanca, can we master the endgame? Or, like Frank Marshall, can we swindle our way out of a difficult position?

Of course, there are few *specific* rules or set formulas. War is not an exact science like physics; it's more of an art or a social science based on probabilities. Fiascos vary greatly in terms of the geographical location, extent of the loss, strength of the enemy, ambition of the goals, and length of the mission. Furthermore, the fog of war creates constant uncertainty that can undo the best-laid plans. If one approach proves successful, the enemy will counter it, often in unexpected ways. When the opponent has three courses of actions available, said German Field Marshal Helmuth von Moltke the Elder, he usually picks the fourth. Tough problems—and they don't come much tougher than ending a failing war—rarely have easy solutions.

But there are *general* rules, or a widely applicable framework for handling loss. Military fiascos don't repeat themselves, but they do rhyme. They're unwinnable wars, or campaigns involving limited U.S. interests, where battlefield failure means that decisive victory is off the table, and we must find an exit strategy. They're domestically unpopular. They usually involve an insurgent enemy. They often trigger prolonged negotiations with adversaries. And time and again, in fiascos, we've faced the same agonizing dilemma: How can we withdraw without seeing our ally collapse?

The next section maps out the core challenges, identifies fundamental principles, and suggests solutions—which should always be adapted to local conditions. The goal is to offer a more useful guide to handling military failure than we have at present, which is essentially nothing. For seventy years, presidents have tried to cobble together a solution in an atmosphere of psychological stress and domestic turmoil: a perfect recipe for failed policies. We must think and prepare before the next fiasco strikes, and get ready to construct our road from perdition.

PART II

THE RIGHT WAY TO LOSE A WAR

CHAPTER 4

Laying the Groundwork

In August 1814, a British force routed the American militia at Bladensburg and captured Washington, DC. George Cockburn, a British admiral, rode around the city on a white mare, identifying targets to be burned. The buildings housing Congress were set ablaze. The White House was put to the torch. Cockburn even ordered that every letter "C" in a newspaper printing office be destroyed—so that he could no longer be personally abused in print.

Everything had looked so different back in 1812, when the United States declared war on Britain. Furious at London's policy of stopping and searching American vessels, and impressing suspected British citizens into the Royal Navy, Washington decided to teach the arrogant empire a lesson about American independence. When the conflict began, the United States held many of the best cards. Britain was three thousand miles away and preoccupied by its death struggle against Napoleon. Thomas Jefferson said that capturing Canada would be "a matter of marching."[1]

By 1814, however, the American war effort was unraveling. The U.S. attempt to conquer Canada had failed. British troops had occupied eastern Maine. New England was threatening to secede from the Union. Nantucket had signed a separate peace

This print from 1820 entitled The Taking of the City of Washington in America *shows British troops attacking the U.S. capital.* (G. Thompson, Library of Congress, LC-DIG-ppmsca-31113)

with Britain. U.S. exports were down by over 90 percent. The U.S. government was almost bankrupt. Nearly 150 American deserters were shot in a single year.

Nothing became the War of 1812 like the leaving of it. President James Madison proved more skillful at peacemaking than war making. Having endured a catalog of debacles on the battlefield, the White House managed to resolve the conflict, defend American interests, and protect the nation's reputation.

In August 1814, the two sides began peace talks in the Netherlands. London dispatched a B team of diplomatic mediocrities (saving its heavy hitters to shape the map of post-Napoleonic Europe at the Congress of Vienna). Washington, however, recruited a formidable outfit, including Henry Clay and John Quincy Adams. The American contingent adeptly met each British demand with diplomatic parries and thrusts, and negotiated the Treaty of Ghent, which returned the combatants to the prewar status quo. Clay concluded that the terms "are undoubtedly not such as our Country expected at the commencement of the War. Judged of however by the actual condition of things, so far as it is known to us, they cannot be pronounced very unfavorable."[2]

The U.S. administration also managed to craft a narrative of the war that averted an image of failure. The popular impression was of a doughty young nation standing up to the might of the British Empire (ignoring the fact that the British already had their hands full battling the French). Americans also celebrated Andrew Jackson's victory in the final battle of New Orleans (even though the encounter was almost irrelevant because it occurred after the peace treaty had already been negotiated). Opponents of the war suffered politically, whereas its supporters prospered—in the case of James Monroe, John Quincy Adams, Andrew Jackson, and William Henry Harrison, by ascending to the newly refurbished White House.[3]

Since 1945, the United States has usually struggled to end failing wars, but there are exceptions. When Dwight Eisenhower won the presidency in 1952, he inherited a deadlocked conflict in Korea. Eisenhower visited Korea, conferred with his generals, and ate C rations with the GIs from his old unit, the Fifteenth Infantry. Taking an observation flight close to the front lines, Eisenhower saw the forbidding mountainous terrain and extensive Chinese defenses, and realized the futility of seeking decisive victory.

Ike was the son of pacifist Mennonites who fretted about his interest in military history. Now Eisenhower needed all his martial and diplomatic skills to end the Korean War. In a speech before the American Society of Newspaper Editors, Eisenhower said, "Every gun that is made, every warship launched, every rocket fired signifies, in the final sense, a theft from those who

This engraving (ca. 1815) entitled Peace of Ghent 1814 and Triumph of America *presents the treaty as a great victory for the United States.* (P. Price Jr., Library of Congress, LC-DIG-ds-01861)

hunger and are not fed, those who are cold and are not clothed." But another path lay open. "A world that begins to witness the rebirth of trust among nations can find its way to a peace that is neither partial nor punitive.... The first great step along this way must be the conclusion of an honorable armistice in Korea."[4]

With great acumen, Eisenhower kept the U.S.-led alliance bound together as he hammered out a truce with the Communist enemy. Hawks in Washington launched scathing attacks on this "last tribute to appeasement."[5] In time, Eisenhower came to seem old and tired. John F. Kennedy declared, "The torch has been passed to a new generation of Americans."[6]

But resolving the Korean War was one of the most important acts of postwar American statecraft. The truce has held for over half a century. A long-term commitment of U.S. troops and aid helped transform South Korea into a prosperous and democratic ally. Ike never forgot what he called "the horror and the lingering sadness of war."[7] During the last seven and a half years of Eisenhower's presidency, only a single U.S. soldier was killed by hostile fire (in Lebanon in 1958). The next generation that grasped the torch would hold a very different record.

Winston Churchill once said that Americans could always be counted on to do the right thing—after they had exhausted all other possibilities. Having pursued a catastrophic leave-to-win withdrawal plan in Iraq from 2004 to 2006, Bush reversed course in 2007 by announcing a surge in American forces, new counterinsurgency tactics, and outreach to Sunni insurgents (known as the Anbar Awakening). The result was a dramatic decline in violence. The Bush and Obama administrations then negotiated a framework for U.S. withdrawal, and the last American soldiers left Iraq in December 2011.

Ideally, Washington would have kept in place a small successor force to train Iraqi troops, provide air defense capability, gather intelligence, and help play a mediating role among Iraqi factions. Whether this was feasible is much disputed. Eric Edelman, a former undersecretary of defense, told me it was widely assumed in Washington and Baghdad that a residual American presence would stay in Iraq. The Obama administration's halfhearted efforts to agree on a successor force amounted to "diplomatic malpractice."[8]

But negotiating a successor force may have been impossible given Iraqi domestic politics. Obama inherited a timetable for withdrawal agreed upon by the Bush administration and the Nouri al-Maliki regime in Baghdad. Washington insisted that any U.S. successor force be granted immunity from prosecution under Iraqi law—but the Iraqi parliament rebuffed this request. John Abizaid, the former head of Central Command, told me that a successor force was "not in the cards at all."[9]

A compromise might have been achieved where Maliki granted

immunity from prosecution via executive memorandum rather than parliamentary approval. It would have been legally murky but potentially workable. Could a U.S. administration that was united and committed to the task have reached a deal with Baghdad? The truth is, we'll never know. The Obama administration was internally divided over the size of a follow-on force, with some officials wanting to leave 16,000 or more troops in place and others favoring a much smaller figure of 3,500. The president was also personally ambivalent about the whole endeavor, given his main goal of bringing a responsible end to the war.

The overall outcome in Iraq was still an American defeat. The cost in blood and treasure from 2003 to 2011 was appalling. But the exit strategy phase from 2007 to 2011 was fairly successful. When American forces withdrew, Iraq was not the complete catastrophe that looked imminent in 2006, when Al Qaeda was running rampant in the country. And this distinction between defeat and catastrophe represents life for thousands of Americans and Iraqis.

The gains made from 2007 to 2011 remain extremely fragile. The Maliki regime in Baghdad proved to be authoritarian and corrupt, and deepened sectarian tensions by cracking down on Sunni opponents. After 2012, the Iraqi state was tested by a new wave of violence caused by spillover from the conflict in neighboring Syria. In 2014, the Sunni extremist group Islamic State swept from Syria into northern Iraq, threatening Baghdad. Iraq could collapse again into full-scale civil war. "Committing murder in Iraq is casual," said one Iraqi official, "like drinking a morning cup of coffee."[10]

Bitter Joy

"In international, as in private, life what counts most is not really what happens to someone but how he bears what happens to him." Diplomat George Kennan penned these words in 1950 after the shock of Chinese intervention in Korea. The United States faced "a major failure and disaster to our national fortunes." If the country accepted this loss "with candor, with dignity, with resolve," it would retain its self-confidence and its allies. But disaster would surely follow "if we try to conceal from our own people or from our allies the full measure of our misfortune, or permit ourselves to seek relief in any reactions of bluster or petulance or hysteria."[11]

Resolving a failing war is perhaps the greatest of all political challenges. Leaders must make critical decisions at a time of stress and incomplete information. They must be wary of the biases that can skew their thinking, from the voices in their head urging escalation to win it all back, to the very real voices from the military pressing for an expansion of objectives. They must accept loss rather than deny it. They must ignore sunk costs and think about future gains and losses. They must assess the true risk of losing credibility. They must be willing to see U.S. soldiers act as nation-builders as well as warriors. They must not allow themselves to be trapped by the momentum of withdrawal (or escalation). They must sustain their own morale and confidence through the dark days of isolation. They must think long-term as well as short-term. They must be willing to withstand enormous domestic pressure, and even sacrifice their own career, to guard the nation's interests and values. They must embrace what Charles de Gaulle called "the bitter joy" of being responsible.[12]

How should the United States end a deteriorating conflict? Can officials extricate the country from a tough campaign with a minimal sacrifice of lives and national reputation? One option is to wait until disaster strikes and then contrive a withdrawal plan. In other words, we build a fire escape after the blaze has already started. But trying to improvise a path out of war in the fierce heat of failure has proven to be extremely difficult and costly.

An alternative approach is to devise an exit strategy ahead of time—before a fiasco strikes. An exit strategy means a plan for using the nation's capabilities efficiently to achieve our goals, as we wind down a conflict and U.S. forces leave. The exit strategy is not a moment but a *process* that can last months or even years.[13]

How can we create an exit strategy that will prove useful in future fiascos? The plan must offer a coherent road map out of the conflict and provide guidance on the key issues that any withdrawal operation will encounter. At the same time, the exit strategy must be flexible enough to take account of widely varying circumstances. War is a collision between hostile forces in conditions of great uncertainty, not an engineering project. The goal is to help officials see the larger strategic picture, not bind their hands with unrealistic fixed policies.

This book proposes an exit strategy for unwinnable major wars called "surge, talk, and leave." It's a loose framework that can be adapted to many different scenarios. Once a campaign becomes a fiasco, Washington should temporarily increase U.S. capabilities, negotiate with the opponent, and find a responsible way to withdraw most American soldiers.

Leaving does not mean abandonment. Instead, the United States should typically stay involved for the long haul, through diplomatic engagement, material aid, or a successor force of American troops and advisors. As Ryan Crocker, the former U.S. ambassador to Iraq and Afghanistan, told me, "The best exit strategy for a country like Iraq or Afghanistan is not to exit."[14]

Surge, talk, and leave is not defeatist—any more than building a fire escape is defeatist. But neither is it triumphalist; the strategy is based on coolly accepting America's recent military struggles. Instead, surge, talk, and leave is pragmatic and realistic. The exit strategy allows the United States to protect its interests and values without fighting indefinitely until exhaustion or surrendering through precipitous withdrawal. The individual elements of surge, talk, and leave are designed to be mutually reinforcing. A surge averts an immediate battlefield crisis and provides room for a negotiated deal. Peace talks in turn smooth America's departure. Leaving in the right way protects the core gains of the mission.

When a war turns into a fiasco, what's the first step? Before we begin the surge phase, we must lay the groundwork by rethinking the goals of the campaign and building support on the home front for the new mission. And this, in turn, requires cutting through the fog of war and getting an accurate picture of the damage.

Where's Wald?

"The night seemed to burst into flower and a rain of red and green blooms fell in front of us," recalled one British bomber crew member in World War II. "Immediately the colored blooms were sprayed with the deadly sparkle of unleashed flak. It was a spectacle of startling beauty."[15] And it was a spectacle of death. Of the 125,000 men who flew in British bombing missions, over half were killed or captured.

To improve these odds, Britain decided to reinforce its planes. This is a basic design problem because more armor means a heavier aircraft and fewer bombs. So where should the extra protection go? British scientists collected data on the location of every bullet hole in the returning planes and worked out where the damage was usually concentrated. Below is a rough sketch that approximates the results they found. The scientists then proposed adding extra armor to the most commonly damaged areas.

Abraham Wald saw things differently. He was a member of the Statistical Research Group (SRG) at Columbia University in

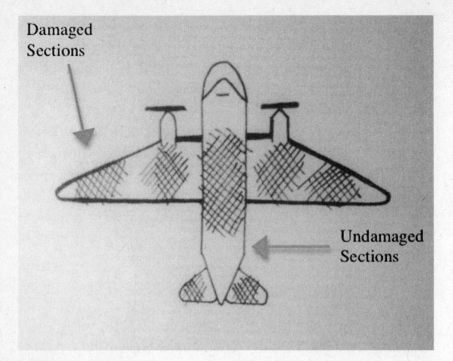

Damaged Sections

Undamaged Sections

New York. The SRG was one of the most distinguished teams of statisticians in history, with Wald, Milton Friedman, Harold Hotelling, and Jacob Wolfowitz (the father of Paul Wolfowitz), supported by a staff of typists, secretaries, and thirty young female mathematicians, recruited from Vassar and Hunter, who did the grunt work of computing. The SRG's mission was to help win the war. Its computations about optimum gun configurations or the best proximity fuses for artillery shells could mean life or death for Allied soldiers.

Wald claimed that the British data on aircraft survivability showed the opposite of what people thought. More armor should be added to the parts of the plane that *weren't* damaged. Wald realized that the untouched areas were the weak spots on the aircraft. Returning bombers showed few hits to these sections because the planes that did take damage here never made it back. This is an example of "survivorship bias," where we get a skewed sample by focusing on the things that survived and ignoring the things that didn't.[16]

Grasping the meaning of damage to aircraft is challenging enough. How much more difficult, therefore, must it be to assess loss on the overall battlefield? And yet, in the wake of a military fiasco, our very first task is to comprehend the wider war effort. The campaign has deteriorated and decisive victory is off the table, but how deep does the rot go? How strong is the enemy? How extensive is its control? Unless we know how bad things really are, we can't create new war aims. And without war aims, there is no exit strategy.

The goal is to distinguish the signal, or the underlying truth about how the war is going, from the noise, or the spurious data and random patterns. Here, more information about the battlefield doesn't always mean more useful information. And it doesn't mean we will analyze this data any more effectively. After 1945, the United States captured more facts and figures about conflicts than ever before—just as it stopped winning wars. One South Vietnamese general told a U.S. official, "*Ah, les statistiques!* Your secretary of defense loves statistics. We Vietnamese can give him all he wants. If you want them to go up, they will go up. If you want them to go down, they will go down."[17]

Let's assume we're fighting against guerrillas. Assessing progress in a counterinsurgency campaign is notoriously difficult. There's often enormous uncertainty about the enemy's strength, its popular backing, its levels of external support, and its potential for future mobilization.

In Vietnam, working out if we were defeating the insurgents turned out to be almost as hard as actually defeating the insurgents. Robert McNamara, the secretary of defense from 1961 to 1968, discussed the problem of choosing metrics in a later interview.

In a conventional war, it's relatively easy. You have front lines; they're either moving forward in the enemy's territory, or you're being forced back further into yours, so you know whether you're winning or not. This was not that kind of a war. The question was: are we winning? What are the proper measures? Are we getting the right information with respect to those measures? We didn't choose the proper measures, and we weren't getting the correct information. That was the problem.[18]

One of the U.S. military's main metrics for measuring progress in Vietnam was the enemy body count. We would force the Communists to concede by removing their soldiers from the battlefield quicker than they could be replaced. The more troops we killed, the closer we were to winning.

But this meat-grinder vision of warfare was deeply misleading. We didn't know how many of the casualties were really insurgents. We couldn't be sure if the deaths inspired others to join the Vietcong insurgency. And most importantly, the core assumption that killing the enemy would force Hanoi to make peace turned out to be wrong.[19]

During the Iraq War, the United States focused on a different metric: the number of insurgent attacks. This data is obviously important, but again its meaning can be deceptive. For one thing, it's hard to know what constitutes an "attack"—which is why different organizations often come up with completely different figures.[20]

Furthermore, the absence of attacks doesn't mean the absence of insurgents. The rebels may be deliberately lying low and conserving their strength. Few bombings in a given region could also mean the insurgents are fully in control of that area. The provinces with the greatest violence are usually the contested zones rather than the territories where either side is strongest. Like the damaged sections on Wald's bombers, the regions that were most shot up in Iraq were not necessarily the most vulnerable.

And we can end up missing the forest for the trees, by focusing on tactical events rather than the overall political situation. After all, guerrillas can endure one battlefield defeat after another and still win if there's a collapse of political will among the counterinsurgents.

Are there more reliable ways of measuring progress against insurgents? If the aim is to win hearts and minds, we should look for signs of popular confidence—especially people's economic choices. How someone spends his money in the midst of war can signal his optimism about the future. If the population believes the U.S.-backed regime will endure and the rule of law will hold, they may invest in legitimate enterprises. By contrast, if people think the rebels will triumph, they may stockpile their resources or turn to crime. From 1966 to 1971, for example, commercial construction in Saigon fell by over half, suggesting that investors didn't have much faith in the future.[21]

Financial markets in Iraq also offered a useful guide to popular confidence about the war effort. When Abu Musab al-Zarqawi, the head of Al Qaeda in Iraq, was killed in June 2006, President Bush said it was a watershed moment. "Zarqawi's death is a severe blow to Al Qaeda. It's a victory in the global war on terror, and it is an opportunity for Iraq's new government to turn the tide of this struggle."[22] But Iraqi financial markets barely moved, suggesting that investors weren't convinced it was such a turning point. And Iraqis were right to be wary, as levels of violence remained high during the summer of 2006.[23]

Other hidden metrics can also reveal much about the reality of the war. You want to know how stable the country is? Check the price of exotic vegetables in the marketplace. The cost of food that must be transported over long distances reflects the risk of attack and the bribes needed to do business. You want to know how secure a region is? Find out if local officials sleep in their district or if they scurry home each night to a faraway haven. Where someone sleeps is a telling sign of perceived safety. You want to understand popular views of the justice system? Look at the number of cases that end up in government courts versus insurgent courts.[24]

Another way to illuminate our knowledge of the battlefield is to examine satellite data on nighttime light levels. In Baghdad, light levels increased from 2003 to 2006, and then dropped off steeply in Sunni areas—vividly revealing the extent of ethnic cleansing as escaping Sunnis literally turned off the lights.[25]

As the indicators of success and failure mount, the problem becomes metric overload. We can end up with a laundry list of military, political, and economic signals. If these metrics all tell the same story, then we have a good idea of what's happening. But what if the data is mixed?

We need to tie the threads together into an overall evaluation of security and governance. John McLaughlin, former acting director of the CIA, told me we should build a province-by-province picture of popular attitudes toward the regime. "There's inevitably a subjective element in weaving together this data." Characterizing the state of the battlefield, he said, is an "inexact science" and "will always be controversial" because particular political or military interest groups are invested in certain policies. The intelligence community, he said, should acknowledge any differences of opinion over the meaning of particular metrics. Leaders want conclusions—but they also want to know the degree of doubt.[26]

To accurately understand the reality on the ground, it's useful to bring in outside analysts like Abraham Wald: people who can offer a fresh perspective, spot flawed conclusions, and, perhaps most crucially, use their imagination.

One person in particular should see the military reality at first hand: the president of the United States. If at all possible, the president should visit the battlefield. Of course, given security requirements, the trip will be carefully stage-managed and the president will only get a snapshot of events. But even a brief tour can reveal core truths about the campaign. In 1952, Ike saw the Chinese defenses in Korea and recognized the mirage of decisive victory. The trip could also help the president build personal relationships with key allies on the ground. Furthermore, a presidential visit signals to domestic and foreign audiences that resolving the war is a top priority. And it may boost the morale of U.S. soldiers—reminding them they are not forgotten.

Why We Fight

By all accounts, Clement Attlee, the British prime minister from 1945 to 1951, was a shy and modest man. Winston Churchill called him a "sheep in sheep's clothing."[27] Attlee may have lacked his famous rival's soaring rhetoric and star power. But in 1950, Attlee played an important role in averting a disastrous escalation of the Korean War.

After China intervened in Korea and U.S. and allied troops retreated south, American commander Douglas MacArthur pressed to broaden the objectives and take the war to Beijing. It was a road that could have led to a military quagmire in China or even World War III.

In December 1950, Attlee flew across the Atlantic to prevent catastrophe. He forged a joint strategy with the Truman administration to limit the war. The goal of rolling back communism in North Korea was abandoned. Instead, the prime minister and the president embraced a more modest objective of defending South

Korea and returning to the prewar status quo through a negotiated truce. Narrowing the war aims was a necessary first step in resolving the Korean War without costly escalation or disastrous retreat.[28]

The United States hasn't always been as pragmatic about rethinking its objectives. In Vietnam, Washington clung for years to the illusory goal of decisive victory: a secure, independent, and non-Communist South Vietnam. Washington underestimated the cost of pursuing this goal, overestimated the odds of success, and exaggerated the importance of this outcome for American security.

In 2003, the United States invaded Iraq with grandiose visions of implanting democracy at the heart of the Arab world and transforming the Middle East. Again, we were slow to adjust these unrealistic goals, even as Jeffersonian democracy proved to be a pipe dream. Finally, in 2007, the Bush administration recalibrated its objectives by aiming for a fairly representative regime and a manageable political order. Emma Sky, a senior political advisor in the Pentagon, said, "We deemed success in a much more modest way as 'sustainable stability.'"[29]

The success of the surge, talk, and leave exit strategy hinges on the ability to rethink war aims. Indeed, the selection of new objectives is the single most critical decision because it guides all future choices. The size of the surge, the role of peace talks, and the timetable for leaving all depend on the goals. Clausewitz said, "No one starts a war—or rather, no one in his senses ought to do so—without first being clear in his mind what he intends to achieve by that war and how he intends to conduct it."[30] This logic also applies to war termination: No one should end a conflict without first being clear what he intends to achieve and how he will achieve it.

The new objectives should be political, meaning they refer to power relations, or who rules a given territory and in what ways.

Clausewitz said that war is not about destruction for its own sake but is, instead, a "political instrument, a continuation of political intercourse, carried on with other means."[31] And the aims should be as clear and concrete as possible. Vague goals like "victory" and "democracy" get people killed. We should have a specific end point in mind, for example, an allied government that can hold off the insurgents, or a power-sharing deal overseen by a United Nations peacekeeping force.

Of course, there's an infinite range of possible military fiascos and an infinite range of possible goals. But all war aims boil down to a question of ambition, or how much political control we seek to exercise over the enemy, our allies, and the contested terrain. In an interstate war, for example, we could pursue fairly narrow objectives (like deterring an enemy from invading a neighbor) or highly expansive aims (such as forcible regime change). Similarly, in a counterinsurgency campaign, we may fight for restricted goals (like eliminating terrorist cells), or broad-ranging aims (such as building a stable and democratic country).

As a general rule, following battlefield loss we should *reduce the ambition of the goals*. A military fiasco implies a disconnection between the means and the ends. We lack sufficient capabilities to achieve our original objectives. The enemy's resistance is greater than expected. The allied regime lacks legitimacy. Our international partners are failing to step up. Since the war involves limited American interests, we can't just write a blank check. Dialing down the goals will bring the ends and means more closely into alignment.

This may be hard for some people to accept. Americans often see the outcome of war in binary terms, as a victory or a defeat. And as MacArthur said: There is no substitute for victory. Dialing down the goals can feel like throwing in the towel. But it's better to achieve a core set of goals and live to fight another day than pursue mission impossible. With the wheels starting to come off the campaign, and American soldiers dying on the battlefield, it's time to get practical and find an end state we can live with. Politics, as Bismarck famously said, is the art of the possible. War as a continuation of politics is therefore also the art of the possible.

Which objectives are essential, and which can be sacrificed? We need to identify the stakes of the war, or the national interests and moral values that are on the line. The psychologist Abraham Maslow argued that individuals exhibit a hierarchy of needs, from the basic physiological requirement for air, food, and water, to a final need for self-actualization, or the realization of one's full individual potential. Similarly, there's a hierarchy of U.S. national needs, or the different kinds of security necessary for American welfare.

The first need is *homeland security,* or ensuring the physical defense of American territory and bordering regions against invading forces, missiles, terrorism, and other threats.

The second need is *great power security,* or maintaining peace between the great powers, and preventing a peer rival from achieving hegemony or forging a hostile alliance against the United States.

The third need is *economic security,* or ensuring American access to markets and strategic resources.

The fourth need is *regional security,* or protecting peace and stability in strategic locations (especially Latin America, Europe, Northeast Asia, and the Persian Gulf) and countering non-great-power threats such as rogue states and terrorists.

The fifth need is *moral security,* or the defense and advancement of American values, including human rights and democracy.

All of these security needs are valuable and worth pursuing. And they're often related and interdependent. The failure to protect regional security, for example, could ultimately erode homeland security if foreign terrorists target American territory. But needs toward the top of the hierarchy take priority. Washington can't deal with a rogue-state challenger on the far side of the world if the United States is directly under threat. Therefore, in a military fiasco, the ambition of the goals hinges on whether there's a clear and present danger to highly ranked security needs.

We must also consider the likely cost of pursuing each objective. Expansive goals will usually stiffen enemy resistance and require a greater commitment of troops and other resources. Can the objectives be realistically achieved given U.S. capabilities in the theater, competing demands elsewhere, third-party support, and public opinion? Which negative consequences could occur? What happens if we pursue the aim and fail? Will any gains we make be sustainable over the long run?

Estimating the probable costs, benefits, and risks of different objectives is easier said than done. It requires a careful calculation of the opponent's strength, our degree of backing from foreign allies, and the level of domestic support—both now and in the future. Here, measuring the enemy's material resources is tricky enough; measuring its will or military skill may be impossible. We also have to consider the role of strategic interaction, in which our best move often depends on the enemy's move. Whether one set of goals is optimal, therefore, may be contingent on how the opponent acts. The adversary knows this, which creates added uncertainty. And as we saw in the last chapter, our beliefs are often skewed by hawkish and dovish biases. These sources of uncertainty provide another reason to err on the side of caution and dial down the goals.

What about moral security or ethical concerns? We have a duty to prevent humanitarian suffering and protect human rights, especially in extreme scenarios like genocide. And America's international reputation may suffer if Washington acts unethically, for example, by abandoning the local people to their fate.

But this duty is not absolute. Rory Stewart and Gerald Knaus drew a useful parallel between humanitarian goals in war and high-altitude mountain rescue operations. When a climber is stranded, there's a moral purpose to save him. But the obligation to the climber doesn't trump everything else. A rescue attempt can easily go wrong and increase the number of deaths. Before launching any mission, rescuers must calculate the risks of intervening. And even after the operation begins, they should look for signs of unexpected danger that could force them to turn back.[32]

This kind of cool-headed assessment of humanitarian goals is doubly important in a military fiasco, where the war effort in unraveling. To continue the metaphor, we're trying to rescue the climber in the midst of a full-blown storm. The risks have increased, and we need to be realistic about what is achievable.

Do we have a moral obligation to the Afghan people? "Absolutely," said Dov Zakheim, who worked as undersecretary of defense in the George W. Bush administration. We can't turn our back on the Afghans like we did in the 1980s, when the United States supported the mujahideen guerrillas against the Soviet Union and then lost interest after Moscow withdrew. If the United States pulls its troops out of Afghanistan precipitously, "do you think we'll be doing any development work there?"[33]

I posed the same question about moral responsibility to Vali Nasr, and his answer surprised me: "I don't think so." Nasr's point was: We don't have a moral responsibility *solely* to the Afghan people. We need to think about the larger ethical picture, including our duty to Americans and our responsibility to people in countries bordering Afghanistan.[34]

Overall, it's tough to make a case for ambitious war aims based mainly on moral security. Our responsibility to the local people must be balanced against other interests and values. America's wider security needs, like those of any country, sometimes clash with its moral values—a tragic but inevitable reality in international affairs.

Let's consider a few simplified illustrations of war-aim scenarios in order of increasing ambition. This is important because the goals we choose will shape the entire trajectory of the surge, talk, and leave exit strategy. Here, we'll assume it's a counterinsurgency campaign, which is the most common type of military fiasco.

#1 Cut and Run

In the first scenario, *cut and run,* Washington reduces its goals dramatically and withdraws as quickly as possible. There's little or no attempt to exercise control over the enemy, our allies, or the contested terrain. Instead, the White House essentially abandons the field. After Afghanistan became a fiasco in 2006, for example, the United States could have washed its hands of the whole morass and just left.

It's tempting to walk away from an unwinnable war. An immediate exit prevents any risk of a quagmire. But cut and run is rarely a realistic option in a major military campaign. For one thing, it will take many months just to physically remove U.S. troops, bases, and equipment from the theater—what the military calls "retrograde." If upping and leaving is a six-to-twelve-month process, it usually makes sense to stay at least somewhat longer and achieve minimal goals.

Furthermore, throwing in the towel could trigger a sudden battlefield collapse for our allies and a rapid enemy victory. It means we give up the possibility of negotiating something in return for America's exit. It could send a dangerous signal about our resolve in the face of loss. And cutting and running may be unethical because it betrays our coalition partners. In summary, the war aims should be reduced—but not given up entirely.

#2 Surgical Strike

In a second scenario, *surgical strike,* Washington chooses quite narrow goals. We don't aim to build a new political order. Instead, we try to neutralize specific threats, for example, by delivering humanitarian supplies to ward off famine, or by targeting terrorists or pirates. In 2006, in Afghanistan, Washington could have dramatically scaled down the goals, abandoned the broader counterinsurgency campaign, and focused solely on fighting Al Qaeda.

The attraction of a *surgical strike* option is that we can achieve our core aims at relatively low cost. Small may be beautiful. The mission will use force with precision and accuracy. America's minimal footprint could avert the kind of massive commitment we saw in Korea, Vietnam, Iraq, and Afghanistan.

But narrow goals can also be risky. After all, there's little prospect of resolving the underlying issues of the war. Raids and drone strikes will rarely be decisive on their own. Therefore, Washington must be willing to tolerate unsavory rulers, massive human rights abuses, and a worsening civil war.

And the failure to exercise broader political control can impede our efforts to combat terrorism or other threats. When the United States and its allies don't control the local territory, it's much harder to find the bad guys. And if the regime becomes actively hostile, for example, following a Taliban takeover in Afghanistan, then America's capacity to pursue a *surgical strike* operation will be further compromised.

Narrowly defined goals are appropriate when the stakes are low, the benefits of expanding control are uncertain, and the costs of establishing a new political order are high.

#3 *Ugly Stability*

In a third scenario, the United States pursues the moderately ambitious goal of *ugly stability,* or a messy but tolerable outcome. We don't try to prohibit the insurgents entirely or build a fully democratic state. Instead, we acknowledge that the rebels will run part of the country, and focus on controlling key strategic locations like the capital or oil production facilities. When Afghanistan became a fiasco in 2006, we could have aimed for *ugly stability,* by seeking to manage the degree of harm, blunt the Taliban advance, and keep the regime playing for the right team—all at an acceptable cost.

In an unwinnable war, *ugly stability* is often a wise goal to pursue. This option allows the United States to shape a minimally acceptable order while avoiding expansive nation-building. We tend to see a civil war as a winner-takes-all clash between the regime and an insurgency. But in many civil wars there are complex and fluid relationships between the government and guerrilla groups. The state may find ways to coexist and even cooperate with some of the insurgents, for example, by making tacit deals to accept the other side's sphere of influence, or by allying with one set of guerrillas to fight a common foe.[35]

Washington may be able to live with a messy result. After all, every year, gangland fighting kills and injures hundreds of people in Chicago. But we don't try to defeat all the criminal gangs. The Chicago Police Department sometimes cracks down through "gang suppression" but usually aims to keep a lid on the shootings rather than eliminate the problem. If we can tolerate violence in Chicago, we can tolerate it in Kabul.[36]

The midrange goal of *ugly stability* does, however, involve some serious risks. Compared to narrower aims, there's likely to be a greater investment of American blood and treasure. And relative to more expansive objectives, the outcome may be untidy and morally challenging. The insurgency will not disappear and the country will not be transformed.

The president should pursue *ugly stability* when the stakes are considerable but not overwhelming, there is some prospect of accommodation with the insurgents, and more expansive control is either unnecessary, too costly, or unlikely to be achieved.

#4 Beacon of Freedom

The most ambitious objective is a *beacon of freedom,* where we seek to suppress the insurgency entirely and build a democratic state. In Afghanistan in 2006, we could have responded to battlefield loss by ratcheting up the aims, trying to crush the Taliban and fashion a truly representative government.

An important point is that even if we manage to construct a beacon of freedom, *it won't be a decisive victory.* Success is about achieving our goals with a favorable cost-benefit analysis. In a fiasco scenario, the costs of war already incurred, and the additional sacrifice required to end the insurgency, are too steep to declare a clear-cut win. Of course, none of the other options, like *surgical strike* or *ugly stability,* will produce decisive victory, either. Since it's at least conceivable that going big by transforming the foreign land is better than the alternative paths available, let's put this option on the table.

What are the pros and cons of aiming for a *beacon of freedom*? This scenario promises to definitively remove the insurgent threat through an extreme makeover of the target country. But the price tag is likely to be extremely high—requiring large numbers of boots on the ground and a long-term commitment. Ambitious war aims will usually provoke bitter resistance from the enemy. If the goals are not achieved and the United States gets bogged down, it may become even harder to withdraw. Given that we're already struggling on the battlefield, do we have the resources and patience to see an expansive mission through? Creating a stable and democratic state hinges on the will and capabilities of the allied regime — but does this regime share U.S. goals? Is the government seen as legitimate, or is it willing to make the reforms necessary to become legitimate? If the answer to these questions is no, ambitious objectives may be a fool's errand.

The goal of a *beacon of freedom* could be justified if the stakes are very high, or the costs are likely to be tolerable because the allied regime has a strong basis of support. But this standard will rarely be met in a military fiasco. Before pursuing grandiose objectives, we should be certain that expansive control is absolutely necessary to protect our core security needs.

Solarium

In the wake of battlefield failure, we must rethink the war aims. We should look at the facts with a cool head and make tough decisions about the costs and benefits of different goals. Typically, we should dial down the objectives and align them with our capabilities. But what if there are competing beliefs about U.S. goals based on different assessments of the stakes and the likely degree of enemy resistance? How can we choose between them? One answer is to take inspiration from Dwight Eisenhower's Project Solarium.

Shortly after his inauguration as president in 1953, Eisenhower had to make a critical decision about America's long-term goals and strategy in the cold war. Ike's closest advisors were divided. Some urged a defensive policy of containing the Soviet Union. Others pressed for a more aggressive approach to undermine Moscow's position in Eastern Europe. The president wanted to make an informed decision after "all the facts are laid out cold and hard."[37] In a meeting at the solarium in the White House, Eisenhower came up with a solution.

Eisenhower picked three of his veteran advisors—diplomat George Kennan, Vice Admiral Richard Conolly, and U.S. Air Force major general James McCormack—and asked them each to recruit a team of specialists from the world of national security. The three teams had to make the best possible case for a different cold war strategy. Team A's job was to champion a plan to contain Soviet expansion and minimize the risk of general war. Team B would argue for drawing a line around the Soviet bloc and threatening massive retaliation if Moscow tried to advance. Team C would make the case for rolling back the Soviet empire—by force, if necessary.

In June 1953, the teams met secretly at the National War College in Washington, DC. For five weeks, they researched the issues and built their respective cases. On July 16, the teams arrived at the White House library for a showdown debate. It was a high-powered gathering. President Eisenhower chaired the meeting. The military chiefs of staff were there, and so was the National Security Council.

Armed with piles of maps and charts, the teams spent the day making their arguments, answering questions, and rebutting objections. Team A claimed that the United States should prioritize political and economic campaigns, negotiation, and the maintenance of alliances. By contrast, Team B pressed for building up preponderant American forces and drawing a clear line in the sand to stop Communist expansion. Finally, Team C rejected containment of the Soviet Union because there was no endgame. Instead, assertive strategies like covert operations and economic coercion could destroy the Soviet empire. "By being too fearful we will lose the contest piecemeal. The game is for high stakes and must be played boldly."[38]

Reproduced at the Dwight D. Eisenhower Presidential Library

TOP SECRET
SECURITY INFORMATION

ANNEX "A"

Personnel Recommendations for Task Force "A":

The exploration and presentation of Alternative "A" requires intimate understanding of the past policies and actions of the United States, the rest of the free world, and of the U.S.S.R., and broad gauge political, military, economic and psychological planning for the future.

The persons recommended to make up this Task Force are:

Chairman: George F. Kennan (Retired Foreign
            Service Political Planner and Russian
            Expert)

Members: Colonel G. A. Lincoln (USA, Military
            Planner and Economist)
            Mr. Paul Nitze (State Department,
            Political Planner and Economist)
            Rear Admiral H. P. Smith (USN, Military
            Planner and Expert on Foreign Military
            Matters)
            Mr. C. Tyler Wood (MSA, Economist and
            Expert on Congressional Relations)

Alternates: Lieutenant General C. P. Cabell (USAF,
            Military Planner and Intelligence Expert)
            Mr. Dean Rusk (Rockefeller Foundation,
            Political and Military Planner and
            Economist)
            Mr. Edward T. Dickinson (NSRB - Economist)
            Mr. Joseph E. Johnson (Carnegie Endowment -
            Historian, Political Planner)

DECLASSIFIED
FRUS, 1952-54, Vol II
Authority ___ p. 350
By ___ ___ 10/27/98

TOP SECRET
SECURITY INFORMATION

This declassified U.S. government document shows the recruitment of George Kennan to head Team A in Project Solarium. (National Archives)

Ike listened attentively to the arguments for hours without taking any notes. After the final presentation, the president spoke for forty-five minutes and summarized the strengths and weaknesses of the various cases. Although Eisenhower found aspects of each analysis useful, Team A won the debate. The president's national security strategy would be based on containment, not rollback.

Project Solarium illustrates the benefits of a "red team, blue team" debate over war aims. Of course, we don't need to copy every detail. In the wake of a fiasco, the president might not have five weeks to respond. But we can gather knowledgeable men and women, place them in teams, give them access to classified data about the war, and ask them to examine different war–aim scenarios—putting rank aside and encouraging free-flowing discussion. Vigorous argument can highlight the opportunities and risks with each set of objectives. And having all the key players in the room will forge unity because everyone takes part in the exercise and signs on to the ultimate decision.[39]

The Home Front

In 1944, the small Nordic democracy of Finland faced the prospect of total destruction. Soviet troops were bearing down on Helsinki. The Finnish leadership needed to end a failing war—but how?

Lodged precariously between the Soviet Union and Nazi Germany, Finland had long maneuvered for survival among the clashing great powers. In 1939, the Soviet Union invaded Finland. Despite brave Finnish resistance, Moscow ultimately seized large portions of Finnish territory. Shortly afterward, in 1941, Germany attacked the Soviet Union and Helsinki made the fateful decision to join the assault and reclaim its land. By launching the Continuation War, Finland hitched its wagon to the Third Reich.

Like their Nazi allies, the Finns assumed that the Soviet regime would quickly collapse. But Moscow defied the invading armies, and Finland faced a prolonged conflict against its more powerful neighbor. By the summer of 1944, with the Soviet Union advancing on all fronts, the prospect of annexation into the Communist sphere loomed. In June 1944, Finnish president Risto Ryti sent a personal letter to Hitler promising that Finland would not sign a separate peace — and in exchange received Nazi weapons. Still the Finnish war effort deteriorated. How could Helsinki break its promise and open negotiations with Moscow?

The answer was new leadership. In August 1944, Ryti resigned. His successor was Carl Gustaf Emil Mannerheim, Finland's national military hero. Mannerheim was born in Finland in 1867 when it was a Russian grand duchy. He fought as a lieutenant general in the Russian army. After Finland became independent in 1917, Mannerheim commanded the non-Communist White army in the Finnish Civil War.

In 1944, Mannerheim, now in his seventies, was entrusted with ending the Continuation War. He had to strike a peace deal at exactly the right moment: late enough that Nazi Germany couldn't invade Finland, but early enough that the Soviet Union wouldn't conquer his country.

Mannerheim wrote to Hitler declaring his intent to sign a separate peace. As the new president, he wasn't bound by his predecessor's private commitment. Whatever happened, he told Hitler, Germany would "live on." But Finland had no such assurance. "If this nation of barely four million be defeated militarily, there can be no doubt that it will be driven into exile or exterminated. I cannot expose my people to such a risk."[40] Germany's wrath was severe: two hundred thousand German troops in Finnish Lapland ravaged the country.

Freed from Ryti's promise, Mannerheim signed an armistice with Moscow in September 1944. The terms were harsh. The Finns had to pay heavy reparations. They were forced to try their leaders as war criminals, and Ryti was sentenced to ten years in prison. But Finland maintained its independence and democratic system.

Carl Gustaf Emil Mannerheim leaves office in 1946 after extricating Finland from a potentially catastrophic war. (Wikimedia Commons, author unknown)

As Finland's experience suggests, a change of leadership can help a country revise its war aims and pursue an effective exit strategy. The leader who started a war is often too invested in the old strategy to shift course. By contrast, a successor is psychologically and politically liberated to pursue a new path.[41]

For the United States, therefore, resolving a dangerous fiasco could require a new commander in chief. The current occupant of the White House may find this advice unappealing. At the very least, in the wake of military loss, the president should shake up the policymaking team. Fresh faces mean new thinking from people who aren't chained to the old failing ways. American strategy in Iraq, for example, only improved after Bush replaced Donald Rumsfeld as secretary of defense in 2006 with the more pragmatic Robert Gates.

In selecting a new team, the president may be tempted to pick a "band of brothers" or a group of party loyalists who speak with one voice. Instead, however, the White House should create a "team of rivals" by tapping figures from across the political aisle as senior officials, diplomats, or informal emissaries. A bipartisan strategy allows the president to draw from the widest pool of talent. It also has the benefit of enlisting outsiders who may ask tough questions, challenge assumptions, and dissent from accepted wisdom.

And reaching across the political aisle can broaden domestic support. In 1814, James Madison deliberately chose a varied group from different parties and regions to negotiate an end to the War of 1812: the Kentucky war hawk Henry Clay; the former ambassador to Russia, John Quincy Adams; the ambassador to Sweden, Jonathan Russell; the Swiss-born former secretary of the Treasury, Albert Gallatin; and Delaware senator James Ashton Bayard. These men had their differences. For one thing, the abstemious Adams grew frustrated with Clay's late-night card playing. But they ended up working as an effective team—and their diversity strengthened Madison's hand back in Washington.[42]

By contrast, partisanship can quickly derail any peace strategy. The checks and balances in the American political system make it easy for an antagonized party to block a settlement. In 1919–20, Woodrow Wilson turned ratification of the Versailles Treaty into a partisan issue by railing against Republican opponents. As a result, the treaty never passed the Senate, and the president destroyed his hope for American global leadership.

Furthermore, a team of rivals can offer political cover for difficult but necessary policies. Democratic presidents are terrified of looking weak on national security if they try to end a war. After Ike made peace in Korea, Truman said, "I would have been crucified for that armistice."[43] Drafting Republicans into the foreign policy lineup can guard Democratic presidents from attack as they withdraw from conflict.

In 1963, John F. Kennedy chose his Republican rival Henry Cabot Lodge Jr. as ambassador to South Vietnam. Lodge was generally hawkish on Vietnam and accepted the logic of the domino theory. Nevertheless, Kennedy could have utilized his appointment to facilitate an American withdrawal. Frederick Nolting, the previous ambassador in Saigon, described Lodge as "Republican asbestos" designed to protect the White House against heat from the right. Secretary of State Dean Rusk believed the selection would blunt conservative calls for further intervention in Vietnam. Privately, JFK talked about de-escalating American involvement after the 1964 election. The president's assassination in 1963, however, means that Vietnam policy in a second Kennedy term remains one of the great unknowns of modern U.S. history.[44]

For Republican presidents, recruiting from across the aisle can pay a different dividend. Bipartisanship may convince skeptical Democrats in Congress to fund long-term economic and military aid to an allied regime or back a residual American force after the bulk of U.S. troops withdraw.

Nixon, for instance, had the opportunity to cooperate with Democrats in Congress during the Vietnam endgame. If the president had treated Congress as a partner, and honestly laid out his negotiation strategy with North Vietnam, including the likely risks and compromises, the White House might have rallied support around a core set of goals. Reaching out to Democratic opponents could also have prevented some of the bitterness and partisan recriminations that followed the collapse of South Vietnam. But Nixon was obsessed with looking tough, centralizing control, and maintaining secrecy. Congress lost confidence in the White House's strategy, and the opportunity for a more united front was gone.[45]

The prospects for bipartisanship hinge, of course, on the degree of division between the parties. Today, a team of rivals approach is hugely complicated by the hyperpartisan political climate. Following battlefield failure, the opposing party may smell blood and go in for the political kill. But even in the current environment, presidents can successfully select figures from across the aisle—as with Obama's choice of Robert Gates as secretary of defense.

When the United States pursues the surge, talk, and leave exit strategy, the president must boldly reach out to opponents through appointments and personal engagement. It shouldn't be Truman's war, LBJ's war, Nixon's war, Bush's war, or Obama's war—it should be *America's war*.

The Afghanistan Conundrum

Given all this, how effectively did Obama rethink the war aims in Afghanistan and lay the groundwork for America's exit?

During the Bush administration, America's objectives in Afghanistan were rarely clear. Washington originally claimed quite narrow goals. In October 2001, for example, Bush said, "These carefully targeted actions are designed to disrupt the use of Afghanistan as a terrorist base of operations and to attack the military capability of the Taliban regime."[46]

But over time the White House signaled a much broader nation-building mission to defeat the Taliban, create a functioning democratic state, and fashion a *beacon of freedom*. George Shultz told me that the goal evolved into "trying to reconstruct Afghanistan into a country it had never been."[47] In 2005, NATO described the objective as "a self-sustaining, moderate, and democratic Afghan government able to exercise its sovereign authority, independently, throughout Afghanistan."[48] In 2006, Bush said, "By standing together in Afghanistan, we'll protect our people, defend our freedom, and send a clear message to the extremists: The forces of freedom and decency will prevail."[49]

Thomas Pickering, the former undersecretary of state for political affairs, told me that in Afghanistan, "we had a failure to define with precision and clarity what our objectives are. The danger is not knowing where we want to go, and seeking to achieve much more than we can possibly achieve."[50] In theory, the Bush administration pursued an ambitious agenda in Afghanistan. In practice, however, few officials believed in these goals, the mission was starved of resources, and attention quickly turned to Iraq.

In 2009, the Obama administration inherited a deteriorating campaign in Afghanistan. Stanley McChrystal, the U.S. commander in Afghanistan from 2009 to 2010, told me that the war was "getting much worse than the administration—or almost anyone—had expected."[51] Obama was personally torn between his long-held view of Afghanistan as a necessary war, and his growing skepticism about the campaign. And he also faced competing demands for time and money from the brewing financial crisis.

The *process* of revising U.S. war aims was commendable. In 2009, the White House engaged in two reviews of the mission: a brief assessment in February and March, and a much longer analysis in the fall. During this second review, Obama personally sat through twenty-five hours of meetings, which covered everything from the lessons of Vietnam and Iraq to the constraints of the budget crisis. Obama asked Joe Biden, the vice president, to deliberately pose tough questions, challenge assumptions, and make the case for a narrower mission focused on counterterrorism (which Biden was, in any case, sympathetic toward). Some accused the president of dithering. But it's better to err on the side of debate. Obama's model of decision making compares favorably to the lack of critical discussion in the Bush administration about the invasion of Iraq.[52]

What about the objectives themselves? Obama gets credit for refocusing on America's core aims in Afghanistan. After all, in difficult wars, desire must be aligned with possibility. "As president," he said, "I refuse to set goals that go beyond our responsibility, our means or our interests."[53] Obama saw U.S. interests in Afghanistan as real but limited. The stakes included a combination of regional security and moral security: combating Al Qaeda, preventing the radicalization or destabilization of Pakistan, avoiding a Taliban victory, and, to a moderate extent, fulfilling our ethical responsibility to the Afghan people.

A goal close to *cut and run* was off the table. Suddenly leaving could trigger the collapse of the Kabul regime. The *surgical strike* option, or a very narrow set of aims focused on counterterrorism, was also rejected because it would effectively hand over much of the country to Taliban rule.

At the other end of the scale, Obama eliminated anything approximating a *beacon of freedom*. Expansive objectives couldn't be justified by America's limited interests and might produce an open-ended commitment, as in Vietnam. In 2011, Obama said, "we won't try to make Afghanistan a perfect place."[54] Robert Gates concluded, "If we set ourselves the objective of creating some sort of central Asian Valhalla over there, we will lose, because nobody in the world has that kind of time, patience and money."[55]

Instead, Obama chose goals closer to *ugly stability*. In March 2009, the president announced an objective "to disrupt, dismantle, and defeat Al Qaeda in Pakistan and Afghanistan and to prevent their return to either country in the future."[56] Building up the Afghan state and pushing back the Taliban were not ends in themselves but a means of combating Al Qaeda. The aim was to make Afghanistan good enough: imperfect but manageable.

Did this require suppressing the Taliban entirely, or merely preventing the Taliban from winning? The answer came during the second review of Afghanistan policy in the fall of 2009. Stanley McChrystal showed a slide that defined the mission: "Defeat the Taliban. Secure the Population." The White House, however, wanted something narrower. A red box was added to the slide, saying the goal was being revised. Eventually "defeat" was replaced with "degrade." It was a wise change because the Taliban were too strong to be militarily crushed at a reasonable cost.[57]

If Washington's review of war aims in 2009 was fairly prudent, the later assessment of objectives was more troubling. As the White House became disillusioned with the pace of change in Afghanistan, it further dialed down the war aims—to a potentially dangerous extent. When Chuck Hagel, the secretary of defense, visited Afghanistan in March 2013, he said that "the goal we have established—to have Afghans assume full responsibility for security by the end of 2014—is clear and achievable."[58] The core objective had narrowed to handing over power. The mission was in danger of becoming a moon-landing operation focused on getting Americans home without regard to what might be left behind.

Did Obama choose an effective decision-making team and build support on the home front for his revised war aims? The fact of a new administration was itself liberating. Obama wasn't invested in the old drifting Afghanistan policy and could pursue a fresh approach. The president also reached across the aisle by retaining Republican Robert Gates as secretary of defense. Gates later criticized senior Obama officials in his memoirs—a warning to some about the perils of mixing political tribes. But overall, Obama gained much from the appointment. Gates shielded the president from domestic hawks as the White House tried to extricate the country from both Iraq and Afghanistan.[59]

The Obama administration was less successful at rallying congressional support around a long-term set of goals in Afghanistan. In the coming years, the United States must make politically difficult choices. We may need to offer painful concessions to the Taliban in negotiations. We could have to pony up aid to Kabul for years or even decades. The White House needs Democratic friends to publicly back these unpalatable options and Republican opponents to avoid criticism and demagoguery.

Building bridges in Congress, however, means spending political capital: lunches with the president, lobbying, horse-trading, and all the rest. The White House must create allies before it has to call on them. As the administration tired of the war, it was reluctant to invest in congressional support—a potentially dangerous misstep as we enter the endgame.[60]

Lay the Groundwork

—Assess the battlefield

—Choose new war aims

—Select a new team

So far, we've laid the foundations for the surge, talk, and leave exit strategy by revising the war aims and building a new decision-making team. But there's another vital opening step: We need to tell a story about the war.

CHAPTER 5

Storytelling

On the evening of Sunday, April 23, 1961, French families gathered anxiously around their television sets to hear an impassioned plea from President Charles de Gaulle. A group of retired generals had launched a putsch to overthrow the French republic and install a military junta. "Frenchwomen, Frenchmen!" said de Gaulle, "help me!"

The catalyst for rebellion was the war in Algeria. For seven years, Paris had battled the *Front de Libération Nationale* (FLN), an Algerian insurgency seeking independence. The rebel French generals feared that de Gaulle was about to sell out the war effort and betray the *pieds-noirs,* or the one million whites of French descent in Algeria. On April 22, the generals made their move, seizing control of Algiers, as *pied-noir* car horns hit a five-note drumbeat: *"Al-gé-rie fran-çaise!"*[1]

The situation in Algiers wasn't the end of de Gaulle's problems. Outside Paris, in the forests of Orléans and Rambouillet, thousands of rebel paratroopers waited to march on the capital. And to top it all off, the French president had a possible loose nuke on his hands. A French atomic bomb was in the Saharan desert ready to be tested. In a nightmare scenario, the rebel generals might seize the weapon as a bargaining chip. How could the president defeat the generals and escape the bleeding wound in Algeria?

First of all, de Gaulle had to outmaneuver his opponents. He took his case directly to the people with a national television appearance. Despite being seventy-one and long retired from the army, de Gaulle dug out his old World War II-era uniform. "A quartet of retired generals" had dishonored the country, he said. "I forbid every Frenchman, and in the first place every soldier, to carry out any of their orders."[2] The force of de Gaulle's personality was irresistible. Across the nation, soldiers, police, and ordinary people rallied around the regime.

The coup soon unraveled. De Gaulle's administration scooped up the rebel leadership on the mainland. The paratroopers were left milling around the forests outside Paris until a few *gendarmes* turned up and ordered them to disband. And de Gaulle defused the atomic threat by bringing forward the date of the test. On April 25, in the midst of the *putsch,* a blinding fireball in the Sahara demonstrated the French Republic's power. With the plot defeated, de Gaulle stepped up his efforts to negotiate Algerian independence. A year later, in March 1962, France and the FLN agreed on terms in the Evian Accords.

De Gaulle knew that negotiating an exit from Algeria was only half the battle. He also had to craft a narrative of the war to unite the French people and avert the impression of catastrophe. The president cared less about the details of Algerian independence and more about the impact of withdrawal on France's image at home and abroad. The retreat from Algeria could prove a crippling blow to the national psyche. France had suffered a string of recent losses—the blitzkrieg in 1940, Indochina, Suez, Morocco, Tunisia, and now Algeria—that could easily meld into a humiliating tale of national malaise. "To lose an empire is to lose yourself," said one Frenchman. "It takes all the meaning away from the life of a man, the life of a pioneer."[3]

Fortunately, as one French general remarked in 1867, "We have a special talent for explaining and justifying our defeats."[4] De Gaulle needed all this national acumen for rationalizing retreat to conjure a positive narrative of the withdrawal.

The first task was to protect France's image as a great power. De Gaulle believed that if the French lost confidence in their global status, the nation would succumb to squabbling and division. "France cannot be France without grandeur."[5] As Paris wound down its imperial project, de Gaulle discounted the importance of colonies as a gauge of prestige. "We do not believe that the interest, honor and future of France is now in the least connected with maintaining domination over populations most of whom do not belong to her people and who are and will increasingly be driven toward emancipation and self-government."[6]

At all costs, France must not seem to be driven out of Algeria by military failure. In other words, there should be no repeat of Dien Bien Phu in Indochina in 1954 (where the French radio operator's final words were, "The enemy has overrun us. We are blowing up everything. *Vive la France!*"). As he negotiated peace in Algeria, de Gaulle carefully cultivated the image of control. He made inevitable concessions to the FLN look like bold exercises of French will. France could accept Algerian independence, he wrote, but only as a magnanimous act initiated by Paris. "France, eternal France, who alone, from the height of her power, in the name of her principles and in accordance with her interests, granted [independence] to the Algerians."[7]

The narrative of withdrawal required a new mission for the French military. The soldiers had lost an empire but not yet found a role. The answer lay with the atom. The French military's sacred duty was now to protect the homeland through nuclear deterrence. The *force de frappe,* or nuclear strike force, allowed Paris to reassert civilian primacy over the military and project an aura of national power.[8]

The president's story also required France to be master of its own destiny and beholden to no one—not even the United States. In 1966, de Gaulle announced that France was withdrawing from full membership in NATO. He told the U.S. secretary of state to remove all American troops from France. The secretary asked acidly if that included the dead ones.[9]

De Gaulle abandoned the dream of an *Algérie française*. But in the process he saved France and forged a new destiny for the country as a modern and prosperous European democracy. At the heart of his exit strategy was storytelling, or the use of rhetoric and optics to cast withdrawal from Algeria as an honorable chapter in the national tale.

When American presidents pursue the surge, talk, and leave exit strategy from a failing war, they must also explain the conflict as a meaningful story and avoid the image of catastrophe.

Gilgamesh

The earliest surviving literature on war is a story. The Epic of Gilgamesh is a collection of poems from Mesopotamia, in modern-day Iraq, carved into clay tablets over four thousand years ago. The poems tell the tale of Gilgamesh, the king of Uruk, who was two-thirds god and one-third man. Gilgamesh sought to slay the terrifying monster Humbaba. With his companion Enkidu, a savage man from the wild lands, Gilgamesh killed Humbaba and carried the monster's head home in triumph. And this was only one of his achievements. Gilgamesh also fought and defeated Akka, the king of Kish, and won independence for the people of Uruk.

The epic was designed to record, inspire, and glorify. Gilgamesh wanted to overcome death but discovered that only through fame could he seize some fragment of immortality. "You will

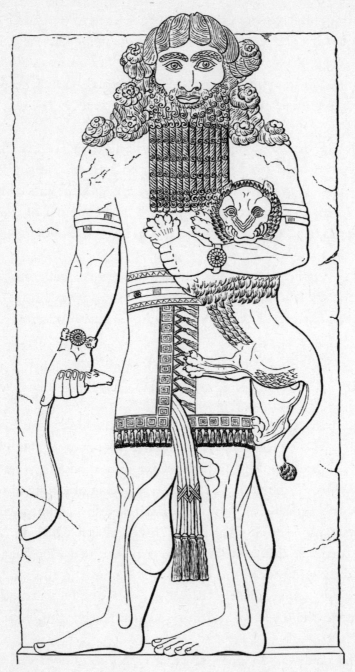

George Smith's illustration of Gilgamesh from The Chaldean Account of Genesis *(1876).*

never find that life for which you are looking. When the gods created man they allotted to him death, but life they retained in their own keeping."[10]

In the millennia since Gilgamesh was written, our appetite for stories has only increased. Every day, we live and breathe stories—not just in novels and movies but also at work and when talking to friends. Narratives of cause and effect are how we make sense of the world. In his bestselling book *Story,* Robert McKee wrote, "The art of story is the dominant cultural force in the world."[11]

People naturally think of war as a story, with a setting, characters, and a narrative arc. The first masterpiece of Western literature is a tale of warfare: Homer's *The Iliad.* The first great Western historians, Herodotus and Thucydides, wrote narratives of war.

Today, we understand American conflicts as stories. Tales of war from the golden age fit a Hollywood script. There's an inciting incident, followed by complications and then ultimately a positive resolution. World War II, for example, is the heroic story of citizen-soldiers storming ashore on D-day and saving the West. It's the modern version of Gilgamesh, with the Japanese surrender documents substituting for Humbaba's head.

Narratives of war from the dark age are more like disorienting art house films. The tale is confusing, there's no obvious meaning or resolution, and the story drifts along in a hallucinogenic haze. The Korean War was a bewildering stalemate: Its national memorial in Washington, DC, is a group of shivering soldiers slogging their way uphill. Vietnam was a destructive quagmire: Its national memorial is a blackened wound cut into the capital's body.

Afghans also understand war in terms of stories. Rural areas of Afghanistan have a predominantly oral culture in which stories are publicly performed. These tales use allegories and metaphors to communicate meaning in a subtle and deniable way—a smart choice in a land of vengeful warlords and insurgents.

In 2008, an American sergeant and his translator approached an elderly Afghan to ask about local Taliban guerrillas. The Afghan replied, "I would like to tell [the Americans] a story. In our country, we grow wheat and we have ants. There is no way we can stop the little ants from stealing the wheat. There are so many little ants it is almost impossible to stop them. I've told this story to help the Americans understand the situation in Afghanistan." In other words, the insurgents had become intermingled with the people.[12]

Why do we think of conflict as a narrative? War itself—*real war*—is too complex to comprehend. The human brain cannot process a vast campaign involving millions of soldiers and civilians on the far side of the globe. We struggle to grasp the exaltation and horror of battle, the moment when life itself hangs in the balance. We cannot compute the rippling geopolitical consequences. "How can I picture it all?" Homer asked in the *Iliad*. "It would take a god to tell the tale." Veterans of war often can't find the words to describe what happened. Oliver Wendell Holmes said his experience in the Civil War was "incommunicable." Or, as Walt Whitman put it, "the real war will never get into the books."[13]

What we can understand is a *story* about the war. A tale of conflict creates order out of an overwhelming mass of information. The narrative is more than just a chronology of incidents. It provides a coherent representation of events that explains why we started the mission, what we achieved, the challenges we overcame, the mistakes we made, how we withdrew, the consequences that followed, and the lessons we should learn.

The story of war is never self-evident. It's a construction fashioned by politicians, journalists, and historians—as well as by ordinary people talking over the watercooler. The tale is not set in stone but is constantly being revised and reinterpreted based on battlefield events, media coverage, and political spin.

Charles Baudelaire, the nineteenth-century French poet, compared human memory to palimpsest, or a type of manuscript on which old writing is erased and replaced with new script. "Everlasting layers of ideas, images, and feelings have fallen upon your brain as softly as light. Each succession has seemed to bury all that went before. And yet, in reality, not one has perished."[14] Similarly, our collective recall of war is continually replaced by novel understandings of the past. The new reminiscence of conflict may seem to obliterate the old, but under-memories remain buried in our culture.

The story of war is always a distortion that highlights certain themes and downplays others. As Drew Gilpin Faust put it, "War struggles and jostles against the artificial structure of narrative... there remains a fundamental un-tellability and unintelligibility about war—in its resistance to language, in its refusal to rest within the bounds and shape of narrative."[15]

Lipstick on a Pig

Should we really encourage the White House to tell stories in wartime? Strategic communication may seem like manipulative spin: a task for Don Draper rather than Dwight Eisenhower. Stories of war can easily become crude and one-dimensional tales of good and evil. In his book *The Black Swan,* Nassim Nicholas Taleb described the "narrative fallacy" or "our predilection for compact stories over raw truth."[16] The Nigerian novelist Chimamanda Adichie talked about "the danger of a single story." A sole dominant narrative is always at least partially false. You need to hear many different tales to understand reality.[17] Furthermore, foreign policy is about serving American interests, not making the president look good. Creating the illusion of success in wartime is dangerous if it prevents us from learning important lessons.

Managing the narrative of war, however, is an essential part of leadership and a critical aspect of any exit strategy. Stories are the language of war, and presidents must speak in this language to be understood. As the Danish author Isak Dinesen said, "All sorrows can be borne if you put them in a story or tell a story about them."[18]

First, the president must tell a story about the war to the American people. If the public can't understand the campaign as a compelling narrative, they won't support it. The White House needs to rally popular backing behind the new war aims by explaining why the conflict started, what went wrong, and how the revised strategy will avert disaster. Obama recognized this responsibility. In 2012, the president told Charlie Rose that he got the big domestic and foreign policy decisions right but failed to "tell a story to the American people that gives them a sense of unity and purpose and optimism, especially during tough times."[19]

Second, the president must tell a story to the Americans who are fighting and dying abroad. The morale of U.S. troops on the battlefield is vital to success in war, and presidents should offer the soldiers a sense of recognition, honor, and purpose.[20]

Third, the president must tell a story to the local population. Crafting a narrative of war that local people can understand is essential for winning hearts and minds. A drone strike in Pakistan may be successful in military terms, but what really counts is how ordinary Pakistanis comprehend this event. It's not about the number of insurgents we kill but the widely accepted narrative of events that emerges.

Fourth, the president must tell a story to the global audience. An effective narrative can boost international support for U.S. foreign policy and mitigate any damage to America's reputation through compromise or retreat. If guns and economic coercion are "hard power," storytelling is a form of "soft power" that enhances the legitimacy of the mission and encourages other countries to voluntarily do what we would like them to do.[21] Here, globalization has dramatically expanded the range of audiences around the world, complicating efforts to manage the strategic narrative.

Fifth, the president must tell a story to the enemy. In one sense, the entire war is about communicating through the medium of violence. Firepower is a language that signals our goals, strength, and commitment. Ideally, we want the opponent to adopt our favored narrative structure. In other words, when we believe we won a battle, the enemy thinks it lost. If the opponent chooses a different narrative structure, we may be in trouble.

According to the American story in Vietnam, the side that lost military engagements would retreat and ultimately give up. According to the Communist narrative, however, each clash of arms was part of a broader political campaign to erode U.S. and South Vietnamese will—and winning or losing a particular battle wasn't the issue. Colonel Harry Summers once told his North Vietnamese counterpart Colonel Tu, "You never beat us on the battlefield." Tu replied, "That may be so, but it is also irrelevant."[22] The entire American strategy was based on the wrong story.

In the end, war is fundamentally a contest to control the narrative. The enemy will certainly propagate its own favored story— most likely a tale of U.S. imperialism, aggression, and brutality. The Taliban, for example, use a range of tools to disseminate their preferred narrative of the Afghanistan War, including websites, an annual Eid message, and traditional forms of communication like poetry and chants. The rebels portray themselves as a heroic Islamic movement and the guardians of Pashtun and Afghan culture. The Taliban also claim to be a more moderate and inclusive movement than in the past—open, for example, to the education of women. With a keen eye on history, the insurgents paint them-selves as heirs to the rebellion against Britain in the 1840s. The Taliban's core membership is made up of Ghilzais, a Pashtun tribe that also formed the heart of the resistance in the 1840s.

Meanwhile, their enemies—that would be us—are depicted as un-believing foreign oppressors. The United States is responsible for the wanton slaughter of civilians, mistreatment of Afghan women, abuse of the Quran, and torture of captives.

This Taliban tale will end in inevitable victory. Just as the Afghan rebels crushed the British Army in the 1840s, just as the mujahideen guerrillas drove out the Soviet Union in the 1980s, so the Taliban will defeat the United States and its allies.[23]

On the unsecured radio in Afghanistan, Taliban insurgents and Afghan police duke it out with rival narratives. The Taliban call the police "American slaves." The police call the Taliban "Pakistani slaves."[24]

A Taliban propaganda video from 2009 featuring captured American soldier Bowe Bergdahl.

We either write the story of war or we end up playing the villain in a drama constructed by the enemy.

Plan for Victory

How can American presidents craft an effective story of war if the campaign will not end in victory? Managing the popular narrative in the United States is extremely challenging. A tarnished war is one of the toughest products to sell. The president may look longingly toward nondemocratic regimes. During World War II, for example, Imperial Japan described the defeat at Midway in 1942 as a triumph, and kept the survivors in the hospital to stop the truth from getting out.

But declaring victory won't get you very far in a freewheeling democracy like the United States, with its rampant partisanship, cynical media, and Wikileaks. The president's message often falls on deaf ears. In a 2005 speech on Iraq, for example, Bush used the word "victory" fifteen times while standing in front of a sign that read "Plan for Victory" and pitching a document called "Our National Strategy for Victory in Iraq." In case you missed it, the message was: *Victory is coming in Iraq*. But given the widespread confusion about what victory in Iraq meant, and the overwhelming evidence of worsening violence, Bush's positive spin didn't work and public support for the war effort continued to erode.[25]

Presidents do, however, have some capacity to shape the popular understanding of war. After all, no one doubts that Washington can *sabotage* its own message through communication blunders. Just think of the negative effect of Bush's 2003 "Mission Accomplished" speech on public confidence about the Iraq War.

The president also has a real—if constrained—ability to positively shape the story of war. The White House usually has more

Bush's "Plan for Victory" speech, November 30, 2005 (Paul Morse, White House photo)

influence over foreign policy than domestic issues. In international crises, Congress and the media often rally around the flag and defer to the president's view (although this advantage diminishes over time and may be limited at the point when an operation turns into a fiasco). The White House also has unique access to the latest intelligence from the field, which can be a powerful tool in the debate over war. Furthermore, presidents enjoy an unparalleled ability to get their message on television through news conferences and prime-time speeches. Theodore Roosevelt famously described the White House as a "bully pulpit," meaning a wonderful platform from which to communicate.

Presidents can't write the entire story of war—but they sometimes get to choose the title. The popular label for a conflict often originates in the White House. Woodrow Wilson said the United States would enter World War I because "the world must be made safe for democracy." FDR described World War II as a struggle for the "Four Freedoms." Bush's "war on terror" frame dominated understanding of the terrorist threat after 9/11, and portrayed the U.S. campaign as a global battle against Islamic extremism.

How can presidents use this influence wisely? As we will see, Washington should pay attention to the narrative at every stage of the surge, talk, and leave exit strategy, from shaping popular expectations as the United States first reels from defeat, to controlling the final imagery when American forces head home. This will be no glorious tale like the Epic of Gilgamesh. Instead, the president must imbue a difficult campaign with meaning.

Let's explore some basic principles of storytelling with a message aimed at quiet Americans.

Silent Majority

In November 1969, Richard Nixon sat at his desk in the Oval Office of the White House and gave his greatest speech. The president wrote much of the language himself on yellow legal pads during long sessions at Camp David. With the nation deeply divided over Vietnam, the president appealed for support from the mainstream population that wasn't protesting in the streets, or the "great silent majority of my fellow Americans."[26]

Nixon's overall exit strategy from Vietnam was a failure. But the "silent majority" speech was certainly an example of skillful storytelling. Polls taken after the speech showed that 77 percent of Americans backed the president. The White House received tens of thousands of positive letters and telegrams. Nixon's approval ratings shot up. Both houses of Congress passed resolutions endorsing Nixon's handling of the war. In 1970, *Time* magazine chose as its "Man of the Year" an abstract image representing the "silent majority."[27] What was the secret of Nixon's wizardry?

Nixon advanced a story of Vietnam that Americans could understand and live with. His exit strategy was a wise middle path between immediate defeat and endless fighting. He had started to bring American troops home. He had tried to negotiate a settlement with Hanoi but faced intransigence at every turn. The United States would not surrender. Instead, the goal was "a just and lasting peace."

Nixon didn't talk down to his audience. Rather, he brought Americans into his confidence by revealing secret U.S. efforts to make peace, including a personal correspondence with Ho Chi Minh. Nixon invited Americans to share the burden of ending the war honorably: "How can *we* win America's peace?" Asking for help is a powerful tool; it empowers listeners, it suggests humility, and it creates a sense of common purpose.

Nixon also described the grim situation he inherited in 1969: four years of war, 30,000 American dead, and no progress in negotiations. By diminishing expectations, he made his own achievements look more impressive.

Aristotle wrote that successful rhetoric combines *logos,* or rational arguments, with *pathos,* or emotional appeals, and *ethos,* or moral assertions.[28] All of these elements are important in storytelling, but *pathos* and *ethos* usually pack the biggest punch. In his book *The Political Brain,* psychologist Drew Westen showed that people weigh political issues based on values and emotions more than dispassionate logic — or, in other words, they "think with their guts."[29]

Nixon didn't explain the Vietnam War solely in terms of rational strategic interests. He first connected emotionally with *pathos* and *ethos* to open up people's minds. The president's target audience — the silent majority — was blue-collar whites and older Americans. Nixon stepped into their shoes and connected with their deepest hopes and fears. He spoke in value-laden terms like freedom, justice, morality, and patriotism. Who are we as a nation? What do we stand for? A precipitous withdrawal from Vietnam would be immoral, triggering Communist atrocities. It would dishonor the United States. "A nation cannot remain great if it betrays its allies and lets down its friends."

Nixon legitimized his Vietnam policy by situating it within the arc of the national story. Two centuries earlier, the United States had been weak and poor. "But even then, America was the hope of millions in the world." Fighting for a just peace in Vietnam would keep the flame alive. Furthermore, Nixon refused to break America's glorious military record by overseeing "this first defeat in our nation's history." Instead, he would fulfill the solemn promise of three previous presidents to protect South Vietnam. And looking ahead, the exit strategy would safeguard America's future as a global power. "I had to think of the effect of my decision on the next generation and on the future of peace and freedom in America and in the world."

Henry Kissinger wrote that the contentious war in Vietnam called for a leader with a nobility of spirit.[30] In the "silent majority" speech, Nixon offered some unifying language. "Honest and patriotic Americans have reached different conclusions as to how peace should be achieved." To America's young people, he said, "I respect your idealism. I share your concern for peace. I want peace as much as you do."

And Nixon outlined the next steps to give people a sense of control. Doctors who have to break bad medical news know that focusing on a course of action can ease people's stress. Similarly, with a tough war, laying out the path ahead can help people handle the exit process. "We have adopted a plan," said Nixon, "which we have worked out in cooperation with the South Vietnamese for the complete withdrawal of all U.S. combat ground forces, and their replacement by South Vietnamese forces on an orderly scheduled timetable."

Overall, Nixon's "silent majority" speech seized the narrative, blunted the antiwar movement, and rallied support behind the Vietnamization plan. Storytelling brought the president some time. Now he had to stick to the script. As communications expert David Gergen put it, "For a narrative to work, a president has to be extremely repetitive."[31]

But Nixon failed to consistently summon a nobility of spirit. Although the "silent majority" speech included some unifying themes, the president couldn't resist discrediting his antiwar opponents by splitting America into two camps: the patriotic real America versus the radicals, naysayers, and leftist elites. And over time, Nixon's rhetoric became increasingly divisive and self-serving. According to Kissinger, Nixon saw a foreign policy debate as a "political battle for survival."[32] The president cast himself as the lone guardian standing against a vast liberal conspiracy. In 1970, he blamed protesters for "mindless attacks on all the great institutions which have been created by free civilizations in the last 500 years."[33]

For Nixon, the media became public enemy number one. In 1972, he said the administration's "major objective over the next few months" would be "the discrediting of the press."[34] The White House tried to tightly control the narrative of war through bullying tactics against the media, wiretaps of reporters, and even burglary.

The story of war is always a distortion but it should still communicate fundamental truth. The president must level with the American people. A credibility gap emerged, however, between Nixon's words and actions. A Gallup poll in January 1973 found that 67 percent of Americans believed Nixon was "not telling the public all they should know about the Vietnam War."[35]

And there was an even deeper problem. Nixon's overall withdrawal plan was a failure, with 20,000 more Americans dying in Vietnam for little benefit. The unraveling position on the battlefield ultimately overwhelmed the White House's ability to control the narrative. Storytelling is part of a successful exit strategy—not an alternative to it.

Nixon's experience reveals how the White House can tell a more effective story about Afghanistan. For years, Washington has struggled to explain the war to Americans in a meaningful way. A campaign that began as a defensive war of necessity turned into a wearying quagmire. It's like we went to sleep after Pearl Harbor and woke up in Vietnam.

The president must offer a coherent narrative about the origins, course, and consequences of the Afghanistan War. We intervened for one reason: We were attacked on 9/11. We came not to conquer but in self-defense. We acted with broad multilateral support. Partly because of the invasion of Iraq, we took our eye off Afghanistan and failed to build a competent regime in Kabul—allowing the Taliban to recover. In 2009, the Obama administration refocused U.S. war aims on the core mission of eliminating Al Qaeda and degrading the insurgency. The surge of American troops has given Kabul a good chance of holding off the Taliban, provided the United States continues to fund the Afghan military in the coming years. The ultimate goal remains a negotiated peace.

The president can lower the bar for success by reminding Americans that Afghanistan was in an utterly ruinous condition when the war began in 2001. He can appeal to *logos* by highlighting the U.S. interest in regional stability, as well as *pathos* and *ethos* by describing the dramatic increase in educational opportunity and life expectancy for ordinary Afghans. He can Americanize the war by placing it in the arc of the national story. Although the goals are more modest, the effort to put Afghanistan on a path to stability echoes the far-sighted commitment to help Germany and Japan after World War II. He can offer a unifying message at home and reach out to both hawks and doves. He can bring Americans into his confidence by explaining the costs and risks of the exit strategy in an honest way. He can ask ordinary people for help in ending America's war—for example, by backing the new plan or by aiding returning veterans. He can map out the next steps and create a feeling of control. He can offer American soldiers a sense of purpose. In 2014, Robert Gates said, "I don't object to the president's speeches about 'exit strategies,' but the troops need their commander in chief to tell them why he is sending them there and why their sacrifice is worthwhile."[36]

Ronald Neumann, the former U.S. ambassador to Afghanistan, told me the war today was a "tough sell." Nevertheless, if Afghanistan can transition successfully to a post-Karzai regime, and the Afghan army holds its ground, "we will have the elements of a story to tell."[37] Although the campaign is not a victory for the United States, Afghans do have a chance at a better future.

Americans are just one of several important audiences for storytelling in wartime. Washington must also craft a narrative for the international community and the local people. This requires tailoring stories to different audiences—but at the same time, keeping these stories cohesive and consistent.[38]

The United States has often failed at strategic communication abroad. One problem is that foreign audiences may be skeptical of American spin. But we've also shot ourselves in the foot. After the cold war ended, Washington failed to invest sufficiently in public diplomacy, including foreign broadcasting and cultural programs. For years, Osama bin Laden seemed to eclipse the United States in getting his message across to key audiences through videos and audio recordings. "How can a man in a cave," wondered diplomat Richard Holbrooke, "out-communicate the world's leading communication society?"[39]

As we pursue an exit strategy in Afghanistan, we must supplant the Taliban narrative with our own rival story. This means understanding the Afghan audience. For ordinary Afghans, the war is confusing. The 9/11 attacks mean little or nothing. Local people may see the fighting not as part of a national struggle but mostly in terms of their family and village.

We need to know which cultural buttons to press and which analogies to draw. We must build trust by providing accurate information on all developments—good and bad. We must highlight the brutality of the Taliban campaign and show that the insurgency's new moderate image is a sham. We must try to align U.S. goals with Afghan nationalism and communicate a message of Afghan reconciliation. We must counter the rumors and conspiracy theories that pervade Afghanistan, such as the belief that the United States is secretly backing the Taliban. We must stress our long-term commitment to the country. We must find credible Afghans to deliver the narrative. And, more than anything, we must create a good product to sell. In other words, the story should reinforce a viable withdrawal plan.[40]

At this point, the opening preparations for the surge, talk, and leave exit strategy are complete. Washington has assessed the battlefield reality, chosen new war aims, shaken up the policy-making team, and started to craft a narrative of the war. Officials can now turn to the next stage: a surge in U.S. forces.

CHAPTER 6

Surge

On January 10, 2007, President George W. Bush addressed the nation about a new strategy in Iraq. His staff thought about holding the speech in the Map Room of the White House. But the backdrop—a ticking grandfather clock—had unfortunate symbolic meaning. So Bush delivered the speech from the library, where he talked with unusual candor about the failing war effort: "The situation in Iraq is unacceptable to the American people, and it is unacceptable to me." The president added, "Where mistakes have been made, the responsibility rests with me."[1]

The speech was the culmination of weeks of discussion in the White House about a change of course in Iraq. The administration looked at a wide range of options and sought critical input from different voices. In other words, it was exactly the kind of vigorous debate that was missing *before* we invaded Iraq.

Bush announced the deployment of over twenty thousand extra American troops and the appointment of a new commander for the war effort, David Petraeus. According to the president, the goal in Iraq was "a functioning democracy that polices its territory, upholds the rule of law, respects fundamental human liberties, and answers to its people."

Bush's surge speech (Eric Draper, White House photo)

The additional American soldiers began arriving in Iraq during the first half of 2007, and U.S. troop levels peaked at 171,000 in October. Petraeus adopted a set of tactics known as population-centric counterinsurgency, or COIN, designed to win hearts and minds. American troops became a more visible presence in Iraq by decamping from large U.S. bases and living and patrolling closer to the people. Firepower was used selectively but effectively to target insurgent strongholds and bomb-making factories on the outskirts of Baghdad. Stanley McChrystal, the head of Joint Special Operations Command from 2003 to 2008, created a lethal covert force that killed or captured numerous Al Qaeda and other insurgent leaders.[2]

In the summer of 2007 the violence began to decline sharply. Iraqi civilian deaths fell from around 3,000 per month in the fall of 2006 to around 300–600 per month a year later. In May 2007, there were 126 U.S. soldiers killed in Iraq. By May 2008, the figure was down to 19. Iraqi economic output and oil production ticked upward. An opportunity was created for political reconciliation—if the Iraqis would seize it.[3]

The arrival of American reinforcements was certainly correlated with the improving security situation in Iraq—but did the new troops *cause* the level of violence to fall? Months before Bush's speech, the underlying political and military terrain was already shifting favorably in Iraq. In the fall of 2006, Sunni tribes began resisting extremist Al Qaeda factions in a process known as the Anbar Awakening. Washington turned poachers into gamekeepers by placing former Sunni insurgents on the U.S. payroll. The brutal ethnic cleansing in Iraq from 2003 to 2007 also had a potential silver lining. The reduced intermingling among Sunnis and Shiites made it easier to reach local cease-fires. In some places, there was no one left to kill.

American reinforcements, however, were an important catalyst for the turnaround. The new troops and tactics boosted security at a critical juncture, helping to facilitate the Anbar Awakening and break the back of Al Qaeda. Indeed, brokering deals with insurgents is itself a key tenet of COIN doctrine. Petraeus personally took Iraqi prime minister Nouri al-Maliki to visit Sunni areas and assess the Awakening. Petraeus believed that outreach to former guerrillas could turn the tide. "We would, in effect, seek to achieve a 'critical mass' of awakenings that would set off a 'chain reaction' as rapidly as was possible—initially up and down the Euphrates River Valley in Anbar Province and then into neighboring Sunni Arab areas of Iraq."[4]

Bush's new strategy in Iraq was known as "the surge." As a synonym for reinforcements, the phrase came out of nowhere. The first use may have been in a *New York Times* article on November 19, 2006, which said that Senator John McCain wanted "a short-term surge in American forces."[5] Two days later, the *Times* quoted unnamed Pentagon officials calling a temporary troop increase in Iraq "the surge option."[6]

The phrase quickly caught on—or *surged*—in popular usage. In 2006, "surge" was a nominee for the American Dialect Society's "word of the year." It lost out to "plutoed," meaning to devalue something (as when the International Astronomical Union determined that Pluto was unworthy of being called a planet). According to the American Dialect Society, "'surge' really didn't emerge until late in the year, so it couldn't be the word for all of 2006."[7] With hindsight, "plutoed" may have been significantly overvalued. "Surge" ended up having a far greater impact on the national lexicon.

Surge Protector

In this chapter, we will look at the *surge* phase—which refers to a temporary increase in U.S. forces—in surge, talk, and leave. Previously, we examined the ends of war, or the choice of political objectives. Now we focus on the means of war, or the employment of U.S. capabilities on the battlefield to achieve national goals.

The word "surge" may give the impression that force exists on a single dimension like electrical power. But in reality a surge can occur in multiple arenas, including ground troops, airpower, and naval vessels. A surge can also vary dramatically in size, from small-scale reinforcements to a doubling or more of American boots on the ground. Here, a surge is defined as a 10 percent or greater increase in U.S. military capabilities, including soldiers and other assets.[8]

In the wake of a military fiasco, is it a smart idea to send reinforcements? A surge may sometimes be impractical—for example, if the United States is fighting multiple major conflicts simultaneously. And even if additional capabilities are available, a surge can carry a high price tag. Deploying a single American soldier in Afghanistan costs about one million dollars per year. In the short run at least, extra U.S. soldiers may translate into more targets and more casualties. Furthermore, an expansion of the war effort could provoke opposition at home, especially if the United States is fighting an unpopular counterinsurgency mission.

At the end of the day, a surge might produce little or no military benefit. The opponent may counter American reinforcements with its own surge of troops, resulting in more devastation but minimal progress. During the 1960s, for example, North Vietnam and its allies, the Soviet Union and China, matched each phase of U.S. escalation with additional infiltration of men and material into South Vietnam. After the first American surge failed, Washington re-surged, and re-surged again—without any clear success. Diplomat George Kennan claimed that America was like a "prehistoric monster" that was slow to be provoked but which, once aggravated, "lays about him with such blind determination that he not only destroys his adversary but largely wrecks his native habitat."[9]

Following battlefield failure, however, a surge is usually required. Whether the enemy is another state like in Korea or an insurgency like in Iraq, the initial response to a military fiasco should be the deployment of additional capabilities.

First, American reinforcements may be necessary to overcome the immediate battlefield crisis and avoid a rout of U.S. and allied troops. A failing conflict can reach a tipping point where the war effort starts unraveling at an accelerating rate. Collapsing morale can suddenly go viral, for example with the Confederacy in 1865, Germany in 1918, or France in 1940. The U.S. Eighth Army that retreated south in Korea in 1950 was badly demoralized by Chinese attacks and, in the eyes of its commander, considered itself defeated.

A tipping point can also occur in a counterinsurgency campaign if the local population believes that the rebels are winning. The mission deteriorates gradually and then suddenly, as investors abandon a sinking ship, civil servants stop coming to work, and fence-sitters jump over to the insurgent side.[10]

Reinforcements can establish a degree of control and prevent mass demoralization or panic. Although the adversary may try to match the American surge with its own additional capabilities, the foe might have stepped up its campaign anyway—and so the United States will be better prepared.

Second, a surge may be necessary to achieve the revised set of war aims. Battlefield defeat implies a mismatch between the mission's goals and capabilities. Washington is fighting for big ends with limited means—a recipe for trouble. Scaling down the objectives and boosting U.S. resources can bring these elements into alignment.

Third, a surge can provide critical new information in an uncertain military environment. We've determined that the war is unwinnable. But there's still probably considerable doubt about the enemy's strength, goals, and commitment.

War is not the only activity where actors make strategic decisions in conditions of uncertainty. Poker players, for example, don't know the value of each other's hands. If the opponent bets and you call, you've put more money at risk but learned little. A classic move is therefore to "raise for information" by throwing extra money in the pot specifically to gain new knowledge. Whatever the opponent does next—folding, calling your raise, or re-raising—tells you something new and potentially useful about the hand. The raise is the main weapon in poker; it can be used when you're dominant, when you're behind, or when you're uncertain about relative strength.

In the same vein, a surge of U.S. forces may produce valuable new information about the war effort. The opponent could prove unexpectedly weak and fold its hand, or de-escalate the war. It's always conceivable that we've miscalculated and the campaign is not unwinnable after all. The fog of war, the unpredictability of battle, and enemy deception can skew assessments of the likely outcome of conflict. The surge could reveal a more positive picture than expected and prompt a shift in strategy.

Alternatively, the adversary may respond to the surge by "calling," or maintaining its war effort. Or the opponent may raise through additional escalation, suggesting unforeseen strength and, again, a need to rethink our approach.

Of course, in wartime, as in poker, raising for information isn't free. And the opponent could try to bluff. The key is to carefully interpret the response. What does the enemy's next move say about its capabilities and intentions? The surge is designed to clear away some of the fog of war. The greater our uncertainty about the battlefield situation, the more valuable this new information is likely to be.

Not surprisingly, great military strategists are often skilled poker players. Dwight Eisenhower paid for his fiancée's wedding dress with the profits from poker. In fact, Ike was so good at poker he had to stop playing because he was winning too much money from his fellow officers.

Fourth, a surge can help with storytelling, by diminishing the sense that the United States is cutting and running. As a result, the surge may co-opt hawks at home into backing the overall withdrawal plan. Going big may lessen the pain of going home.

How can sending more troops be considered part of an *exit* strategy? Because this is a temporary deployment. Reinforcements can facilitate an ultimate withdrawal if they provide security, train local forces, and strengthen our hand in negotiations.

In summary, the best response to a fiasco—like Korea in 1950, Iraq in 2004, and Afghanistan in 2006—is a surge in American forces. Even during Vietnam in 1966, some extra U.S. troops were useful to hold the line. The core problem in Vietnam was not the initial surge but the overly ambitious objective—a secure, non-Communist, and independent South Vietnam, close to a *beacon of freedom*—and the repeated re-surges in pursuit of this illusory goal. As the true nature of the war became clearer in 1966, the United States should have dialed down its objectives and shifted much earlier to negotiation and withdrawal (the second and third parts of surge, talk, and leave).

COIN-Star

How big should the surge be? And how can the reinforcements be used most effectively? The first consideration is the severity of the battlefield crisis. American soldiers may face a desperate predicament, or alternatively, the threat may be slower brewing, allowing additional time to act. Everything held equal, the greater and more immediate the danger, the more troops and other assets should be rushed to the scene.

The second factor shaping the scale of the surge is the ambition of the war aims. The ends determine the means. Washington needs sufficient manpower to achieve the newly defined political goals. As a general rule, the more expansive the objectives, the greater the numbers of troops we need.

Let's consider three scenarios for war aims in a counterinsurgency campaign, starting with the most ambitious option.

Beacon of Freedom

The most grandiose path available is to construct a beacon of freedom by suppressing the insurgency and building a democratic state. It's worth reemphasizing that even if we manage to eliminate the guerrillas, it won't count as a decisive victory. In a fiasco scenario, the costs have risen too high to achieve a clear-cut win. However, the other war-aim scenarios won't deliver victory either, and therefore pursuing a *beacon of freedom* remains an option on the table.

What does this highly ambitious scenario look like? The good news is that there may be a way to transform the foreign land. The bad news is that it's not cheap and it's not easy. The answer is population-centric counterinsurgency, or COIN. Developed in works by David Galula, Robert Thompson, John Nagl, David Petraeus, David Kilcullen, and others, COIN offers the best shot at stabilizing an entire country. COIN is not an end in itself. Rather, it's a set of tactics designed to achieve ambitious political goals. The idea is to turn a conflict-ridden society into a land at peace with itself and its neighbors by engaging in nation-building, securing the population, and winning hearts and minds.[11]

Any guidance on a COIN campaign must start by recognizing the incredible diversity of insurgencies. Each conflict is a unique story of tribal, religious, ideological, and nationalist identities. Guerrilla struggles vary from Maoist people's wars motivated by class-based ideology, to communal civil wars where the divisions lie along ethnic or sectarian lines. Some insurgencies are tightly organized; others are much looser in structure. Therefore, we must avoid seeing the target country as a machine we can fix with simple formulas, a few tools, and a little Yankee know-how. COIN is fundamentally about adapting to local conditions.

Still, COIN does have some general principles. A civil war is a competition between the insurgents and the counterinsurgents over who can govern most effectively. Therefore, COIN is fundamentally not about us; it's about the legitimacy and performance of the allied regime. "We can surge American forces in Afghanistan and train local troops," Richard Myers, chairman of the Joint Chiefs of Staff from 2001 to 2005, told me, "but at some point we need good government agencies. In the end it's up to the Iraqis and Afghans."[12]

American soldiers should isolate the insurgents from the people by living and patrolling close to the population, building local relationships, and developing networks of human intelligence. As nation-builders, U.S. troops may be tasked with duties far beyond a warrior's traditional purview, such as engineering or teaching. The goal is to create a virtuous cycle where diminishing violence strengthens economic growth, which in turn boosts popular backing for the regime and increases the flow of information from the people about the remaining insurgents—further improving security.

The use of force will be necessary. Irreconcilable enemies must be killed, captured, or otherwise marginalized. Large-scale offensives may be necessary to dislodge entrenched guerrilla forces. Decapitation tactics to eliminate rebel leaders can prove effective—especially if the insurgents are led by a charismatic figure who can't easily be replaced.[13]

But U.S. troops should use firepower with discretion. More force may mean less security. Indiscriminate violence can alienate the local people and provoke an antibody response against the American presence. The campaign shouldn't be fought like a conventional war, with the United States chasing guerrillas in futile search-and-destroy missions. Instead, American soldiers should act with restraint and respect toward the people. In other words, knock on doors rather than break them down.[14]

Population-centric counterinsurgency has shown some success in countries as diverse as Malaya, Northern Ireland, and Colombia. And amid the wreckage of Iraq's deteriorating security from 2003 to 2006, there were pockets of relative stability where COIN tactics were used effectively.

During 2003 and 2004, David Petraeus commanded the 101st

Airborne Division in Mosul in northern Iraq. He won hearts and minds by quickly setting up city council elections, building local security forces, and creating an extensive program of public works. Money spent on reconstruction was ammunition, he said.[15]

Meanwhile, in Ramadi in Anbar Province, Colonel Sean MacFarland reached out to local Sunni sheikhs and constructed a coalition against extremist groups like Al Qaeda—successfully curbing the violence.[16]

Maj. Gen. David H. Petraeus (on the right), commander of the 101st Airborne Division, watches as Lt. Gen. William S. Wallace speaks to American soldiers in Kuwait on March 21, 2003. (Joshua Hutcheson, U.S. Army photo)

In Tal Afar in northwest Iraq, Colonel H. R. McMaster gave his troops pocket histories of Iraq to read and instructed them to act respectfully toward the local people. He stationed his troops in small outposts throughout the city and ordered them to patrol on foot rather than in armored convoys. McMaster told me that you must understand war's "human dimension," including the complexities of tribal and ethnic competition. "You can't come in and start talking," he said. "You have to really *listen* to people."[17]

For years, these were exceptions to the rule, as the American military stumbled against the guerrilla opponent in Iraq. Finally, in 2007, the systematic use of COIN tactics as part of the surge contributed to a dramatically improved security situation.

But there are no guarantees that COIN will work. Estimates of the success rate of counterinsurgency campaigns vary from 25 to 70 percent. At best, it will be a long struggle, with many setbacks. After 1945, it took counterinsurgents, on average, around ten to fifteen years to suppress guerrillas. "Making war upon insurgents," said T. E. Lawrence, "is messy and slow, like eating soup with a knife."[18]

And prepare for sticker shock. COIN needs a lot of troops and money to work effectively. According to the conventional wisdom, fully stabilizing an insecure foreign country requires 10-25 U.S., allied, and local counterinsurgents per 1,000 inhabitants. The surge in Iraq brought the total number of security forces to 610,000, reaching the desired ratio. But in the early years of the Afghanistan War, the troop-to-population density was far smaller. Unsurprisingly, the Taliban regained its footing.[19]

The 10–25 per 1,000 ratio is a useful ballpark figure—but nothing more. The French achieved the ratio in Algeria and still lost. One study found a correlation between deploying more counterinsurgents and achieving greater battlefield success, but there's no dramatic tipping point at 10 or 25 troops per 1,000 inhabitants. Instead, the beneficial effect is linear. And other dynamics like the legitimacy of the allied regime may be more important.[20]

How should the United States go about securing the country? Let's look at the core stages in a COIN campaign.

Step one is *safety first*. The United States should begin by protecting strategic sites like the capital, major population centers, oil production facilities, and so on. Security is the greatest vulnerability in a counterinsurgency campaign. The same interdependencies that can spur a virtuous cycle of stabilization may also provoke a vicious cycle of disintegration. During the Vietnam War, Lieutenant Colonel John Paul Vann said, "Security may be ten percent of the problem, or it may be ninety percent, but whichever it is, it's the first ten percent or the first ninety percent....Without security, nothing else we do will last."[21]

Step two is the *mission of mercy*. Washington should address any immediate humanitarian crisis, for example, involving disease or famine. This is about more than just acting morally. A humanitarian crisis could have a wider destabilizing impact by triggering refugee flows.[22]

Step three is the *inkblot*. The United States should consolidate its base of support and then work steadily outward. The inkblot approach, also known as "clear, hold, and build," aims to shore up relatively secure areas, introduce defense forces, win the trust of locals, and then expand control to other regions.[23]

Step four is *effective governance*. The United States should build legitimate institutions and address wider governmental tasks, including law enforcement, education, public health, economic development, and telecommunications. Priorities will likely include creating a central bank to stabilize the local currency, providing jobs for former soldiers, and demobilizing weaponry. A core task is establishing sewer, water, electricity, and trash services—known as SWET operations—which provide for basic human needs and can be instrumental in winning (or losing) hearts and minds.[24]

Here, Washington must decide whether to pursue effective governance through a top-down or a bottom-up approach. The top-down option aims to build a leviathan, or a capable central state. This offers the most direct means of exercising control. But a leviathan may inspire resistance from locals who see new schools, for example, as tools for state indoctrination of language and culture.

By contrast, the bottom-up approach creates effective governance by reaching political bargains at the local level. In theory, local deals may be more enduring than those based on state coercion. The problem is: Who will provide security if there's no strong central regime? The United States must strike the right balance between top-down and bottom-up approaches based on the country's existing culture, institutions, and traditions.[25]

Step five is *striking the center of gravity*. The United States and its allies should take the offensive by targeting the heart of the insurgency. This means discovering what Clausewitz called the "center of gravity," or the locus of the opponent's strength and will, which may be a city, base area, or spiritual heartland.[26] By seizing the initiative, Washington and its allies can signal to fence sitters that the insurgent tide has receded. In principle, controlling the enemy's center of gravity is the quickest path to securing the country, although it may also be the most difficult objective to attain.

Step six is *democratization*. The United States should oversee free and fair elections to legitimize the regime. Democratization is an important stage in a COIN campaign, but it's also a relatively low priority. Premature elections can raise popular expectations, produce corruption and fraud, and exacerbate tensions.[27]

Step seven is *transitional justice*. We should renew civic trust in the aftermath of human rights abuses through tools like war crimes trials and peace and reconciliation tribunals.

There is no one-size-fits-all COIN template. Local conditions vary enormously, and flexibility is required. In a communal civil war, for example, rapid democratization can worsen social divisions, as political parties appeal to sectarian or ethnic loyalties. Furthermore, the above COIN steps are not strictly chronological; instead, they can often be pursued simultaneously. Nevertheless, the steps give a sense of the priorities. We should focus on the later phases only when the earlier stages have been adequately addressed.[28]

In summary, building a *beacon of freedom* through COIN is slow and costly. It takes restraint and patience. But there's no obvious alternative way to suppress an insurgency following military failure in a civil war. Trying to stabilize an entire country on the cheap will very likely end in complete failure.[29] Another tactic—the indiscriminate slaughter of opponents—may have worked for some counterinsurgents in history, but it's not an option for the United States today.

COIN offers the best shot at turning a country racked by civil war into a *beacon of freedom*. The real question is: Do we need to build a *beacon of freedom*?

Ugly Stability

What does the surge look like if we pursue the less ambitious goal of *ugly stability*? Here, we're not aiming for full democratization or nationwide stability. Instead, we seek control over key locations and an accommodation with insurgent groups—or, in other words, a messy but tolerable outcome.

Compared to pursuing a *beacon of freedom,* the goal of *ugly stability* requires fewer troops. The total force may be in the range of 1–10 per 1,000 population rather than 10–25 per 1,000. The composition of the deployment may also vary, with fewer regular soldiers, and more Special Operations Forces and advisory teams to train indigenous troops.

There's no need to complete the full seven-step program above. Instead, we can pursue an abridged path that focuses on security, resolving any humanitarian crisis, and negotiating with the insurgents (the "talk" part of surge, talk, and leave). We may use triage to prioritize key strategic areas where U.S. forces can have the greatest positive impact. We may also alter the approach region by region, creating varying political orders in different provinces. Overall, there will be less nation-building. The United States will work with existing institutions rather than impose Western-style governance — manipulating the local clay rather than importing our own.

Surgical Strike

What if Washington chooses the narrow goal of a *surgical strike* by targeting terrorists, pirates, or a humanitarian crisis? With such modest objectives, do we really need a surge? The answer, oftentimes, is yes. First of all, additional reinforcements may be necessary to avert a battlefield crisis. And given that we failed to achieve the original aims, we may need increased capabilities to move forward with confidence — even if the new goals are limited.

Still, the scale of these forces will be reduced compared to the earlier scenarios. Since there's no serious effort to stabilize the country, the United States can do without many broader nation-building capabilities. For example, a *surgical strike* operation focused on counterterrorism may require additional Special Operations Forces, such as Army Rangers or Navy SEALs, as well as drones and other assets.

How will the new capabilities be used? Again, if the goal is counterterrorism, the operation will prioritize breaking enemy networks through raids, intelligence gathering, and training missions. We'll see a kinetic, strike-oriented operation, with personnel rappelling out of helicopters, kicking down doors, and killing or capturing enemies. U.S. forces may utilize the newly developed targeting system known as "find, fix, finish, exploit, and analyze," or F3EA, designed to locate a target, capture or kill it, extract intelligence, and then examine the new data.

The Afghan Surge

"What I'm looking for is a surge," said Obama to Petraeus in 2009, as the president signaled a major expansion of the war effort in Afghanistan.[30] The Afghan surge actually came in two stages. First, in February 2009, Obama sent seventeen thousand more soldiers to Afghanistan (soon joined by another four thousand troops) to provide security for the upcoming presidential elections, partner with Afghan security forces, and "take the fight to the Taliban in the south and the east" of the country. Obama also pressed for "a dramatic increase in our civilian effort" by sending "agricultural specialists and educators, engineers and lawyers."[31]

Second, in the fall of 2009, the administration engaged in an extensive review of U.S. strategy in Afghanistan. The Pentagon pressed for significant new reinforcements and an expansive COIN campaign to build up the Afghan state. By contrast, Joe Biden favored a narrower counterterrorism mission focused on targeting Al Qaeda. In the end, Obama bridged the gap by choosing a limited COIN campaign as a means of checking the Taliban and defeating Al Qaeda.

Crucially, Obama pushed for both a quick start and a quick end to the deployment. The president agreed to send another thirty-three thousand soldiers—for a total of one hundred thousand U.S. troops—and he wanted these reinforcements in place as fast as possible. But there was also a rapid timetable for with-

On December 1, 2009, Obama visited West Point to announce a surge of troops in Afghanistan. Here, the president is pictured looking at a portrait in the superintendent's quarters. (Pete Souza, White House photo)

drawal. The troops would start coming home in the summer of 2011, barely eighteen months in the future.

On the home front, Obama's surge received a pass. The war was unpopular, but there was little organized opposition in Congress. Here, Obama benefited by having a "(D)" after his name. Democratic presidents may be vulnerable to criticism from the right if they withdraw soldiers. But the flip side is being less susceptible to attack from the left if they increase U.S. troop levels. After all, if a dovish president decides to send more forces, *it really must be necessary.* And liberal antiwar groups tend to pull their punches if their guy's in the White House. This patience has limits, though. "I can't let this be a war without end," said Obama to Senator Lindsey Graham, "and I can't lose the whole Democratic Party."[32]

Was the surge in Afghanistan a success? In other words, did it resolve the immediate crisis and help Washington achieve a revised set of goals?

Obama inherited a very difficult campaign in Afghanistan. The military fiasco began back in 2006. But the Bush administration failed to stem the Taliban advance. By 2009, the Taliban were resurgent, busily creating shadow governors and Sharia courts. Stanley McChrystal, who took over as commander of U.S. forces in Afghanistan in 2009, told me it was a dangerous situation. The insurgents were "perceived to be winning"—and perceptions matter.[33] Leon Panetta, the secretary of defense, said that "Afghanistan faced the real prospect that the Taliban would take over large parts of the country." According to another administration official, "there was a real risk that the mission in Afghanistan might very well fail."[34]

Obama's surge averted a serious battlefield crisis and checked the Taliban's momentum. There was progress in pushing the Taliban out of Marjah and other insurgent strongholds in Helmand Province. Special Operations Forces also eliminated large numbers of mid-level insurgent commanders. The number of Taliban attacks fell slightly from 2010 to 2011—but remained higher than in any previous year in the war.[35] John Allen, the commander in Afghanistan from 2011 to 2013, told me that the surge "really stabilized the situation as everything was trending south. It bought time to develop Afghan troops and build capacity in the Afghan government." He added that the surge "didn't come a moment too early."[36]

The surge, however, came at a high price tag of over $100 billion per year in 2011. American fatalities increased from 317 in

2009 to 499 in 2010 before falling to 418 in 2011 and 310 in 2012. The Taliban continued to benefit from their sanctuaries in Pakistan, and remained in control of many rural areas in the south, east, and west of Afghanistan.[37]

Was the surge appropriately calibrated given the new war aims? As we saw in chapter 4, Obama narrowed the goals in Afghanistan compared to the Bush era by seeking to eliminate Al Qaeda and degrade (not defeat) the Taliban—or, in other words, achieve *ugly stability*. The president recognized the importance of aligning troop levels with these overall objectives. One official said that Obama "didn't just want a number picked out. He wanted the strategy to drive the number."[38]

Given U.S. aims, however, the surge may have been too large and the drawdown too steep. The sharp increase and decrease in troop levels was driven less by strategic logic and more by a compromise between the military's desire for expansive reinforcements and the president's wariness about a long-term commitment. As part of his Spartan work ethic, Stanley McChrystal used to eat only one sit-down meal a day. But it was often a 5,000-calorie monster loaded with burritos and ice cream.[39] McChrystal's gargantuan feasts were a symbol of the American surge in Afghanistan. Washington's brief injection of massive capabilities produced a sugar-high effect.

The surge was outsized for the limited objectives. The goal in Afghanistan was *ugly stability* but the scale of reinforcements was more consistent with creating a *beacon of freedom*. Why was over-resourcing the mission a problem? First of all, it's wasteful—no small issue when every American soldier in Afghanistan has a million-dollar price tag. A mismatch between capabilities and goals can also mean that the surge is unsustainable. The inherent tension between the ends and means may encourage disillusionment and a dramatic correction in force structure—perhaps an overcorrection.

Obama's heart was never in the surge. When progress in Afghanistan proved slow, he rapidly pulled the plug. In 2010, Obama convened a committee known as "Afghan Good Enough" to find a quicker exit. Robert Gates, the secretary of defense, was present at a meeting in 2011. "As I sat there, I thought: The president doesn't trust his commander, can't stand Karzai, doesn't believe in his own strategy and doesn't consider the war to be his. For him, it's all about getting out."[40]

Petraeus, who by then had replaced McChrystal as the U.S. commander in Afghanistan, wanted a minimal reduction of troops in 2011. But Obama pushed for a speedier withdrawal. The president said he would remove ten thousand soldiers by the end of 2011, another twenty-three thousand by the late summer of 2012, and the remaining sixty-eight thousand by 2014. The size of a potential American successor force for training and counterterrorism was revised downward—and there was even talk of a "zero option," or a complete U.S. exit.

On June 22, 2011, Obama announced the plan for a drawdown of U.S. forces in Afghanistan. (Chuck Kennedy, White House photo)

The drawdown may have been too rapid. Obama's strategy provided barely eighteen months for a fully resourced COIN campaign. In many respects, the situation in Afghanistan was even tougher than in Iraq. For example, there was no Afghan equivalent of the Anbar Awakening. And unlike their Iraqi insurgent counterparts, the Taliban enjoyed safe havens in Pakistan. Unsurprisingly, therefore, the gains in Afghanistan sometimes proved transient.

The sharp decline in troop levels created a sense of uncertainty in the region about American intentions. "The president didn't send me over here to seek a graceful exit," said Petraeus.[41] But as Obama stepped up the troop withdrawals, this *did* look like the goal. And the message it sent to the region was: *We're leaving*.

Instead of choosing a single 5,000-calorie feast, Obama could have paced himself with several more modest meals. A smaller but longer surge may have led to a more sustainable payoff.

Another problem was that the surge forces went to the wrong areas of Afghanistan. According to COIN doctrine, soldiers should follow the people. But twenty thousand American marines, including some of the nation's best counterinsurgent forces, were sent to Helmand Province, a largely barren moonscape where less than 4 percent of Afghans live. Just ten thousand U.S. soldiers went to Kandahar, which is the second biggest city in Afghanistan, the spiritual home of the Taliban, and the insurgency's center of gravity. If the war could be turned around, Kandahar was probably the place to do it.

In his book *Little America,* Rajiv Chandrasekaran described how rigid thinking and tribalism in the U.S. military led to a misplaced focus on Helmand. The Marine Corps wanted to demonstrate its autonomy within the U.S. military and showcase its unique talents by managing a single discrete region. Kandahar wasn't attractive because the marines would have to share control with Canadian forces. In Helmand, however, the marines could run the show. The deployment of so many elite counterinsurgents to Helmand may not have made strategic sense but it fit the bill in terms of bureaucratic turf wars. When Chandrasekaran asked a marine general what would happen if the United States won Helmand but lost Afghanistan, the general said, "That would be just fine for the Corps."[42]

Overall, the Afghan surge checked the Taliban advance and helped to stabilize a potentially disastrous situation—a significant achievement. But the curve of escalation and de-escalation was too steep. And the surge forces may have turned up at the wrong address. In the end, Obama's surge turned a faltering campaign into a stalemate; the Taliban were left too weak to win and too strong to lose.

A Few Good Men

With his thin mustache and slicked-back hair, British lieutenant general Gerald Templer looked like an aging film idol. Templer fought in both world wars, competed in the Olympics, and won the British army's bayonet fighting championship. In 1952 he was given the job of suppressing a Communist insurgency in Malaya.

What counts in war, according to Field Marshal Bernard Montgomery, was "the man." These are the leaders "who have the courage to issue the necessary orders, the drive to insist that those orders are carried out, and the determination and willpower to see the thing through to the end."[43]

In Templer, the British found the right man to run the Malayan campaign. With experience in both combat and civil leadership, Templer had the ideal background for counterinsurgency. He sought to win over the "hearts and minds" of the people—a phrase he popularized. Templer employed classic COIN tactics: speeding up the development of the Malayan army, improving the training of police, and expanding intelligence efforts. He granted full citizenship and the right to vote to ethnic Chinese, thereby co-opting the main source of support for the guerrillas. Winning Malayan hearts and minds helped to ultimately end the rebellion.

Templer's experience shows the importance of selecting talented generals during the surge, talk, and leave exit strategy. Compared to the era when Caesar rode into battle wearing a red cape, today military leadership can seem to be less important. Generals don't start America's wars. They're subject to civilian oversight and sometimes micromanagement. And as military operations have grown more complex, generals can look like cogs in a vast machine — at the mercy of an unwieldy organization they can't control.

But military leadership remains vital. Generals advise those higher up, make major decisions on the battlefield, help choose successors, and synchronize different branches of the military. In other words, they become *generalists*. In his book *A Question of Command,* Mark Moyar showed that COIN tactics are not enough to overcome an insurgency. You also need the right men and women to run the campaign — those with a particular skill set that includes initiative, creativity, charisma, flexibility, integrity, and organizational ability.

And generals must be political creatures. It's sometimes suggested that civilian and military officials should neatly divide up their labors. Civilians can decide on the political goals and the overall strategy in war, whereas military leaders ought to be given wide latitude in the tactical realm. The problem is that war is imbued with politics right down to the tactical level. This is especially true in a counterinsurgency campaign where the combatants are competing over who can govern more effectively. Almost every decision — from selecting the overall troop levels to choosing whether to knock on a door or smash it down — has political consequences. Rather than gung-ho warriors, we need generals who are comfortable seeing war and politics as intertwined, are sensitive to foreign cultures, and can negotiate effectively with allies, local people, and insurgents.[44]

As a soldier-scholar, David Petraeus proved highly suited to the complex demands of counterinsurgency. Petraeus had a PhD from Princeton. This was probably a liability in the U.S. military, which sometimes exhibits a pronounced strain of anti-intellectualism. (One Marine Corps general claimed there were "too many intellectuals" in the armed services, when we need "old-fashioned gunslingers.")[45] Fortunately, Petraeus won his fellow officers' respect by outrunning them in five-mile races. Intense, competitive, and sometimes imperious (he was known as "King David"), Petraeus told his men to fasten the top button on their uniforms, the "battle button." It was uncomfortable, but it singled them out.

After successfully leading the 101st Airborne Division in Iraq, Petraeus oversaw the production of the army and Marine Corps field manual, *FM 3-24,* which laid out the tenets of COIN doctrine. Petraeus was lionized in three different *Newsweek* cover stories—one of which said he was "the closest thing to an exit strategy [in Iraq] the United States now has." He became commander of U.S. forces in Iraq, head of U.S. Central Command, commander of the campaign in Afghanistan, and director of the Central Intelligence Agency, until his resignation in November 2012.[46]

Other prominent generals proved less effective at handling the trials of modern war. From 2000 to 2003, Tommy Franks oversaw U.S. Central Command but showed little independence of mind. Franks once told President Bush about his relationship with Donald Rumsfeld: "Sir, I think exactly what my secretary thinks, what he's ever thought, what he will ever think, or whatever he thought he might think."[47]

Franks seemed uninterested in the overarching political goals of the wars in Afghanistan and Iraq. According to an army review: "The lack of a war plan or theater campaign plan [in Afghanistan] has hindered operations and led to a tactical focus that ignores long-term objectives."[48] Franks also helped develop the disastrous small-footprint invasion plan for Iraq and was scornful about the task of postwar occupation. In April 2003, the military needed a name for the new "combined joint task force" that would oversee the stabilization of the country. Franks suggested "CJTF-1369, unlucky cocksuckers."[49]

In his book *The Generals,* Thomas Ricks argues that there's been a decline in the quality of American generals. In World War II, mediocre top brass were quickly removed: "Sixteen Army division commanders were relieved for cause, out of a total of 155 officers who commanded Army divisions in combat during the war. At least five corps commanders also were relieved for cause." But today, generals are rarely relieved because of poor performance on the battlefield. Rising through the ranks has become too easy, and "the vocabulary of accountability has been lost."[50]

Ironically, when the United States struggles at war, it can be harder to remove generals. In the golden age of warfare, few doubted the wisdom of the mission and Washington had a free hand to cut those who failed to perform. But in the dark age of stalemates and losses, civilian leaders are reluctant to fire generals for fear of signaling failure.

The military needs the same tough standards of accountability that apply to CEOs and other leaders. This means a higher bar for promotion and a willingness to reassign or fire generals who don't perform. And it means rewarding generals who push the envelope. Of course, there's much more to finding the right generals than just a Darwinian survival of the fittest. In a world of complex civil wars, anti-intellectualism is dangerous. We must prioritize military education, with more training in counterinsurgency, foreign cultures, and languages—even enrolling a few gunslingers into PhD programs.[51]

Crucially, presidents need to work effectively with generals. Consider an analogy with plane crashes. The author Malcolm Gladwell showed that one of the major causes of air accidents is an overly rigid hierarchy in the cockpit. During a flight, copilots may notice a potential danger on the horizon. At this point, they should issue clear commands. But copilots are sometimes unwilling to challenge a superior who is flying the plane, and so they use vague or evasive language. The result may be an avoidable catastrophe.

This problem is particularly acute in hierarchical cultures like Korea. During the 1980s and 1990s, Korean Air had a dismal safety record in part because the airline's copilots failed to speak up and make their voices heard. The aviation industry has tried to overcome this problem by training people to give assertive instructions—and even telling crew members to call each other by first names. As a result, Korean Air now has one of the best safety records.[52]

In a battlefield crisis, generals must also be willing to challenge their superiors, offer candid advice, and point out looming threats. Unquestioning obedience is disastrous; the chain of command can end up chaining the command. In his book *Dereliction of Duty,* H. R. McMaster described how the Joint Chiefs of Staff became marginalized from key decision making on Vietnam. Divided by internal squabbles, the Chiefs saw the crash coming but failed to provide effective warnings.[53]

It takes courage to tell superiors the plan is wrong. John Abizaid, who took over as head of U.S. Central Command from Franks, told me that "generals don't push up the chain of command hard enough."[54] McChrystal also told me that some generals are too reticent about challenging superiors, believing that "inputs beyond direct military advice are not desired."[55]

For its part, the administration should respect the military's advice and encourage frank and open debate from below. Dissent needs room to breathe. What the White House mustn't do is *Shinseki* any skeptical voices. In 2003, Eric Shinseki, the army chief of staff, suggested that the proposed troop levels for the invasion of Iraq were too low. The Bush administration publicly corrected Shinseki and then replaced him early. This kind of punishment is designed to keep everyone speaking with one voice. As Voltaire wrote in his novel *Candide,* "It is good to kill an admiral from time to time to encourage the others."[56] But such retribution can have a chilling effect on internal debate.

At the same time, presidents must keep all the core policy strands in their own hands by choosing the overarching goals, selecting key generals, and overseeing the war effort. McChrystal told me that some civilian leaders are too hesitant to question generals about military matters, "having a tendency to write a blank check." The answer is what McChrystal called a "partnership" between presidents and generals, or, as Abizaid put it, "a clear conversation both ways."[57]

During the Civil War, Abraham Lincoln oversaw his generals with great skill, mediating disputes between them, and wooing, nudging, or shoving them as required, in pursuit of his objectives. Lincoln sometimes implied humble deference. "The particulars of your plans I neither know, or seek to know," he told General Ulysses S. Grant in 1864. "I wish not to obtrude any constraints or restraints on you."[58] And yet, far from being uninterested, Lincoln sent a personal emissary to report on Grant's movements.

And if there was ever a question of who was really in control, read Lincoln's letter to Joseph Hooker after his appointment to command the Army of the Potomac. Lincoln congratulated Hooker on his bravery and skill before issuing a stark admonishment. "I have heard, in such way as to believe it, of your recently saying that both the Army and the Government needed a Dictator."

Lincoln added, "Only those generals who gain successes, can set up dictators. What I now ask of you is military success, and I will risk the dictatorship."[59]

Lincoln fired generals who failed to deliver results. Joseph Hooker eventually joined Irwin McDowell, George McClellan, John Pope, Ambrose Burnside, and George Meade in passing through the revolving door of the Army of the Potomac.

Robert Gates was critical of the Obama administration's relations with the military. "All too early in the administration, suspicion and distrust of senior military officers by senior White House officials—including the president and vice-president—became a big problem for me as I tried to manage the relationship between the commander in chief and his military leaders."[60] But John Allen told me that his recommendations were always taken seriously. "There's a lot of mythology that this president never listens to his generals. Well, he listened to me."[61]

Speak to the Soul

"A man does not have himself killed for a few half-pence a day or for a petty distinction," said Napoleon Bonaparte. "You must speak to the soul in order to electrify the man."[62] But how do you inspire the soul? In modern history, men and women have died to protect democracy. And they have laid down their lives for communism and fascism. But nothing speaks to the soul like nationalism, or the allure of what Walter Scott called "my own, my native land."[63]

The belief that one's nation, or unique cultural and ethnic group, should possess its own state, free from foreign rule, may be the greatest political motivator in the modern world. Nationalism forged the modern European state system, creating dynamic powers that carved the world up into colonial empires. In turn, nationalism destroyed the European empires from within, and produced new postcolonial states in Africa, Asia, and elsewhere. After World War II, the number of UN member states quadrupled from 51 to almost 200. Today, the power of nationalism can be seen almost everywhere—from Scotland to South Sudan. Lord Mountbatten, the British viceroy of India, once told Gandhi, "If we just leave, there will be chaos." Gandhi replied, "Yes, but it will be *our* chaos."[64]

In the wake of a military fiasco, we must harness popular nationalism or be overrun by it. Understanding the power of nationalism is critical at all stages of the surge, talk, and leave exit strategy. But it can be especially important during the surge phase because American reinforcements may provoke nationalist opposition.

Americans have often struggled to comprehend foreign nationalism. In Vietnam, we couldn't believe that Communists could also be nationalists. After all, communism meant subservience to Moscow. But Hanoi's quest for unification was inspired by Vietnam's two-millennia history as a distinct ethnic and linguistic entity—including independence for almost a thousand years from 939 to 1883, before the French arrived. Standing against the tide of Vietnamese nationalism proved to be a futile endeavor.

In the competition for nationalist hearts and minds, the United States starts out at a major disadvantage. It's all too easy for an insurgency to grasp the banner of resistance against the foreign occupier. The United States can seem to be aping the empires of Britain or Rome. We install puppet regimes. We don't speak the local language or understand the culture. And to top it all off, we've started delivering death from the sky with a fleet of robot drones. In Afghanistan, the Taliban combine religious appeals with nationalist calls to remove the American oppressors.

It's possible, however, for the United States to utilize foreign nationalism in wartime. We must craft a narrative of the campaign that aligns the mission's goals with popular aspirations. There are two sides to this coin. The positive approach is for Washington to become the champion of national self-determination. This is easier in certain wars like Kosovo in 1999, when the United States fights for the autonomy or independence of a group. Today, Kosovo is probably the most pro-American country anywhere outside the United States. (In the capital, Pristina, you can drive down Bill Clinton Boulevard and visit an eleven-foot-high statue of Clinton.)

Washington can also embrace nationalist sentiment by acting respectfully toward the population, adopting local customs and traditions into the new political order, and casting the war effort as a joint endeavor between equal partners. Ryan Crocker stressed the vital importance of understanding local history—especially the country's prior relations with Western powers. He told me that, as ambassador, he sought to ensure that "American policies, action, and rhetoric were supportive of nationalism." The agreements reached with the Iraqis and Afghans represent "a very strong affirmation of the sovereign national identity and the prerogatives of both countries."[65]

In addition, we must credibly pledge to hand over the reins of power. Britain overcame the Communist insurgency in Malaya by endorsing Malayan independence, agreeing to leave after the Communists were defeated, and steadily granting authority to indigenous leaders—effectively neutering the nationalism issue. Templer said that London must offer an attractive path for the Malayan people. "This way of life is not the American way of life. It is not the British way of life. It must be the Malayan way of life."[66] Similarly, we can promise that the surge of American forces is a temporary deployment, and part of an overall strategy to reduce U.S. troop levels and leave.

Meanwhile, the negative means of seizing the nationalist mantle is to label the enemy as a foreign actor. During the surge in Iraq, the United States appealed to Iraqi nationalism by depicting Al Qaeda as an alien entity. The U.S. program that recruited ex-insurgents was called Sons of Iraq. Lieutenant General Ra'ad al-Hamdani, a former commander in Saddam Hussein's Republican Guard, said: "On the ground, it was discovered that [Al Qaeda in Iraq] did not work for the benefit of Iraq. Their objective was to destroy Iraq."[67]

If there's a foreign threat, the local population is more likely to accept the presence of American troops. After 1945, popular resistance to the U.S. nation-building missions in Germany and Japan was diminished by the presence of the Red Army just over the horizon. From a nationalist perspective, the U.S. presence may be an evil—but it's a lesser evil.

Nationalism should be handled with great care. It's tempting to bolster the American surge by stirring up nationalist hatred against the enemy or by embracing a nationalist strongman. But we may end up resolving one conflict and laying the seeds for another. History is rife with examples of unchecked nationalism leading to war.

Great Expectations

In January 1968, the Vietcong launched a major surprise attack during the Tet holiday, a celebration of the Vietnamese New Year when both sides traditionally observed a cease-fire. Targeting dozens of towns and cities across South Vietnam, the Communists aimed to inspire a popular uprising and win the war. But American and South Vietnamese troops struck back in a devastating counteroffensive that killed tens of thousands of Vietcong. In military terms, Tet was a significant reversal for the Communists.

Back at home, however, Americans saw the Tet Offensive as a major defeat for the United States. One reason for public skepticism was Washington's overly optimistic rhetoric about the course of the war. In the weeks before Tet, President Johnson began a "progress campaign" to show that the United States was winning in Vietnam, by churning out masses of data about pacified villages and enemy dead. Relative to these claims, Tet looked like a catastrophe. The White House's narrative of progress disintegrated. "We genuinely thought we were making it," said one of Johnson's aides. "And then boom, forty towns get attacked, and they didn't believe us anymore."[68]

Tet illustrates the vital importance of managing public expectations about the surge. A core part of storytelling is shaping popular beliefs about the future course of the war. After all, people judge the success of a mission relative to what they think will happen. The same outcome for the campaign can look acceptable or disastrous depending on whether expectations are low or high.

The United States is often the victim of overly high expectations. Given the U.S. military's unsurpassed strength, the American public usually anticipates rapid success in war. Images of smart bombs flying down airshafts in the 1991 Gulf War created an exaggerated faith in swift and certain victory. Foreign audiences may also expect miracles—and therefore judge our efforts harshly. The United States put a man on the moon. Therefore, if we fail to provide electricity in Baghdad, it must mean we've chosen to punish the Iraqi people. Audiences at home and abroad don't always recognize the limits of American power. Battling guerrillas in a fractured society like Iraq can quickly level the playing field between the United States and its opponents.

Here, the White House sometimes shoots itself in the foot. The administration knows that Americans get frustrated by the messy business of counterinsurgency and nation-building. And so

Washington is tempted to boost support on the home front with idealistic rhetoric and progress campaigns. But this language only heightens expectations and increases the odds of later skepticism.

In 1993, for example, the United States was involved in a nation-building mission in Somalia. Madeleine Albright, the U.S. ambassador to the United Nations, said the operation was "an unprecedented enterprise aimed at nothing less than the restoration of an entire country as a proud, functioning, and viable member of the community of nations."[69] This was a bold goal when Somalia was completely devastated by war and famine. Given such grandiose objectives, it's no surprise that Americans grew disillusioned when progress proved slow and U.S. soldiers were killed in the infamous Black Hawk Down battle.

The George W. Bush administration made a similar mistake in managing expectations of the Iraq War. Deputy Secretary of Defense Paul Wolfowitz announced shortly before the invasion, "Like the people of France in the 1940s [the Iraqis] view us as their hoped-for liberator."[70] Bush compounded the error by prematurely declaring victory. On May 1, 2003, he landed on an aircraft carrier in a Navy S-3B Viking jet and announced that "major combat operations in Iraq have ended," while a banner behind him read "Mission Accomplished."[71]

Americans assumed the war was over when really it had only just begun. In November 2003, ABC's *World News Tonight* included a shot of an American medic who looked straight at the camera and said, "All major combat operations have ceased," before adding sarcastically, "Right!"[72] One study found that in 2007 the American public was slow to recognize the success of the surge in Iraq. Bush's "Mission Accomplished" speech "later reduced the persuasiveness of his assertions that the U.S. military was making progress in Iraq."[73]

What's the answer? Presidents must pledge that the new strategy will deliver a reasonable outcome while dampening down expectations. This means talking to Americans like adults and avoiding sugarcoated claims about progress on the battlefield. Winston Churchill was the master of this balancing act, giving the impression of confident leadership while promising only "blood, toil, tears, and sweat."[74] In his memoirs, LBJ regretted not being more candid about Vietnam: "If I had forecast the possibilities, the American people would have been better prepared for what was soon to come."[75]

As U.S. surge forces arrive, the president should warn people that the situation might get worse before it gets better. In the short run, new troops could mean more targets. And eliminating irreconcilables may trigger an increase in casualties. In his surge speech in 2007, Bush said, "The year ahead [will be] bloody and violent."[76] The White House should promise blood, toil, tears, and SWET.

In managing expectations of a war like that in Afghanistan, one answer is to focus on the pitiful state of the country *before* Americans arrived. In 2001, civil war and Taliban rule had reduced Afghanistan to an utterly ruinous condition. About one-third of the population had fled the country. Kabul was in ruins. In 2001, the *Economist* gave Afghanistan the award for "worst country."[77] Setting the Taliban era as the benchmark means the president can highlight some improvements without raising unreasonable expectations about the future.

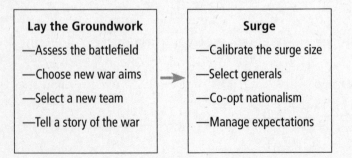

Lay the Groundwork	Surge
—Assess the battlefield	—Calibrate the surge size
—Choose new war aims	—Select generals
—Select a new team	—Co-opt nationalism
—Tell a story of the war	—Manage expectations

In summary, after a fiasco, a surge of U.S. forces is usually necessary to arrest the declining war effort and achieve a revised set of goals. Presidents must carefully calibrate the ends and means of war, select the right generals, align the mission with nationalist sentiment, and manage American and foreign expectations. The next step in the surge, talk, and leave exit strategy is to negotiate with the enemy.

CHAPTER 7

Talk

In December 2010, Richard Holbrooke, the U.S. special representative for Afghanistan and Pakistan, told his wife he had a plan to end the war in Afghanistan. First he needed to tell the president. Before Holbrooke could brief the White House, however, he collapsed and was rushed to the hospital in Washington, DC, for emergency heart surgery.

Holbrooke had a long history as a diplomatic fixer and was known as "the bulldozer" for his brash style. Veteran diplomat Strobe Talbott called him the "unquiet American."[1] During the 1990s, Holbrooke prodded, flattered, and arm-twisted the combatants in the Bosnian Civil War into signing the Dayton Peace Accords.

Over a decade later, Holbrooke pursued the same dream of political reconciliation in Afghanistan. But a deal with the Taliban eluded even this skilled negotiator. Afghan divisions proved insurmountable. And Holbrooke also struggled on the home front. He lacked allies in the Obama administration and found himself shut out from the president by a "Berlin Wall" of staffers and confidants.

Just before Holbrooke was sedated in the hospital, the doctor told him to relax and think of a beach. Holbrooke, half-joking, suggested another calming vision: "Ending the war in Afghanistan."[2] Tragically, Holbrooke died shortly after the heart surgery.

Peace negotiations in Afghanistan have been a wearying tale of frustration and failure. For a decade after the fall of the Taliban in 2001, there were few substantive contacts between Washington or its allies and the senior insurgent leadership. The Taliban were often intransigent, refusing to talk to Kabul and labeling Hamid Karzai as a puppet of the United States. In 2010, Karzai appointed Burhanuddin Rabbani as chair of the High Peace Council, with a mandate to engage the rebels. But the Taliban detested Rabbani, who was president of the Tajik-dominated regime back in the 1990s. The insurgents sent an envoy to meet Rabbani in his home. When the two men embraced, the envoy exploded a bomb hidden in his turban, killing them both.[3]

Kabul also tried to negotiate with a senior Taliban leader named Mullah Akhtar Muhammad Mansour, and handed over tens of thousands of dollars to encourage his participation. Unfortunately, Mansour turned out to be an impostor—a Pakistani shopkeeper. "The Americans and their allies are very stupid," said the Taliban, "and anyone could fool them."[4]

Washington also showed little interest in a negotiated agreement. The Bush administration saw the mission in Afghanistan as part of the war on terror—a battle between good and evil—and refused to entertain a deal. Obama was also reluctant to engage the Taliban. In March 2009, he said the insurgents' core leadership "must be met with force, and they must be defeated."[5] The Saudis tried to broker negotiations between the United States and the Taliban, but Washington declined to pursue the initiative. In the fall of 2009, the wide-ranging American review of Afghan strategy didn't even consider the option of a diplomatic solution. The Pentagon and the CIA wanted to apply military pressure before any negotiations began. Kill first and talk later. In 2010,

Holbrooke asked General Petraeus about reconciliation. Petraeus responded, "Richard, that's a fifteen-second conversation. Yes, eventually. But no. Not now."[6]

Finally, there were glimmers of light. In late 2010, U.S. officials met several times with a senior aide to Taliban head Mullah Omar. A few months later, Hillary Clinton, the secretary of state, publicly endorsed peace talks for the first time. In January 2012, the Taliban agreed to open a liaison office in Qatar. But shortly afterward, the Taliban suspended discussions, describing the United States as "shaky, erratic, and vague."[7] In Qatar, a group of eight or so senior Taliban figures were left milling around, waiting for talks to start. One Afghan diplomat said, "They are just living here enjoying the air-conditioning, driving luxury cars, eating and making babies."[8]

Bernard Bajolet, the French ambassador to Afghanistan, left Kabul in 2013. "I still cannot understand how we, the international community, and the Afghan government have managed to arrive at a situation in which everything is coming together in 2014—elections, new president, economic transition, military transition and all this—whereas the negotiations for the peace process have not really started."[9]

The Parable of Faust

The tortuous path of negotiations in Afghanistan reveals some of the challenges with the second part of the surge, talk, and leave exit strategy: talking to the enemy. This refers to U.S. diplomatic engagement with the adversary, from secret back-channel meetings in Parisian apartments to formal face-to-face talks over the green baize with flags and water bottles. The wars in Korea, Vietnam, Iraq, and Afghanistan all involved prolonged bargaining with the enemy. As George Casey, the U.S. commander in Iraq from 2004 to 2007, told me, "an exit strategy is not just military; it's also political."[10] What's the role of negotiations in a withdrawal plan? Can we parley our way out of a failing war?

Washington usually ends up negotiating after a fiasco—but it does so grudgingly. There's a deeply ingrained skepticism in American culture about talking to evil adversaries. Americans are a moralistic people and often see negotiation in wartime as sullying U.S. values. A golden century of decisive victories from 1846 to 1945 also meant that Americans never had to learn the difficult art of compromising with threatening opponents. Whereas other countries see negotiation as the norm, Americans view face-to-face talks as a prize that the opponent has to earn.[11]

George W. Bush claimed that America's enemies "will not be stopped by negotiation, or concessions, or appeals to reason. In this war, there is only one option—and that is victory."[12] He told the Israeli Knesset, "Some seem to believe that we should negotiate with the terrorists and radicals, as if some ingenious argument will persuade them they have been wrong all along." But this is only "the false comfort of appeasement."[13]

Doubts about the wisdom of negotiating in wartime are easy to understand. In the parable of Doctor Faust, the protagonist makes a pact with the devil and ends up losing his soul. Parleying with military opponents can be similarly unproductive. Peace talks may legitimize the enemy's cause. They could divide our own side. And there may be an ethical price to pay. How can we negotiate with a group like the Taliban that pours acid on the faces of schoolgirls?

We may have to sit down with an enemy that's ruthless, doctrinaire, and cynical. During the Korean War, General Matthew Ridgway described the Communists as "treacherous savages."[14] On one occasion, the opposing negotiators in Korea sat in silence for over two hours. The North Koreans passed the time by exchanging notes among themselves—containing insults about the Americans and South Koreans in large visible letters.

Negotiations may be full of sound and fury, signifying nothing. During the peace talks over the Vietnam War, Hanoi spent much of the time lecturing Americans about imperialism while avoiding any meaningful discussions. Henry Kissinger gave his counterpart, Le Duc Tho, the nickname "Ducky," and called his opponents "tawdry, filthy shits."[15] One French observer described the negotiations in Paris as a *dialogue de sourds,* or a dialogue of the deaf.[16]

Diplomacy can drag on interminably. When negotiations about Vietnam began in 1968, the American diplomatic team made hotel reservations in Paris for a week. The North Vietnamese, however, leased a château for a year and said they would sit in Paris until the chairs rotted. In the end, the talks lasted for half a decade.

Negotiating peace is especially tough in a civil war. Most internal conflicts end in decisive victory for one side—not a peace treaty. When two countries stop fighting, their armies can pull back to recognized borders. But resolving a civil war may require the combatants to live and even govern together. In any deal, one or more sides will usually have to give up its guns. But why would they disarm if they fear the opponent will cheat? Even the basic logistics of talking to insurgents pose a challenge. The enemy may not speak English. It may not have a home address. And its envoy could be a suicide bomber.

What are the odds that Washington can resolve an entrenched civil war like the one in Afghanistan? A chasm exists between American political ideals and the Taliban's commitment to Sharia law, strict Wahhabi ideology, and an Islamic emirate of Afghanistan. Many see the Taliban as a faithless enemy and any peace settlement as an illusion. The Taliban may have little interest in a compromise deal and could be pursuing negotiations only to gain legitimacy on the international stage. American conservatives fear that peace talks will signal U.S. weakness. And liberals worry that we will sacrifice Afghan women's rights in a rush to clinch a deal.

If the Taliban refuse to talk to Kabul, it might be better not to negotiate at all. Ryan Crocker, the U.S. ambassador to Afghanistan from 2011 to 2012, told me that he "always opposed U.S.-Taliban direct negotiations. These talks give legitimacy to the Taliban and take it from the Afghan government." Instead, we should "support Afghan efforts for direct talks with the Taliban, which have been stymied by the Taliban's reluctance to participate."[17] Ronald Neumann, U.S. ambassador to Afghanistan from 2005 to 2007, agreed. "If the Taliban won't talk to the regime, they won't keep any agreement made with the regime." He said that negotiated agreements often take years of effort. Therefore, in Afghanistan, "don't expect this to be quick—and anything you do to make it quick is probably a mistake."[18]

It's enough to make one nostalgic for the golden age of warfare, when we used overwhelming force to achieve decisive victory and diplomatic outreach meant organizing the surrender ceremony.

The Diplomatic Weapon

Abdul Sattar Abu Risha was not a good Muslim. A Sunni tribal sheikh in Iraq, Sattar grew wealthy through extensive smuggling operations. He had an appetite for women, cigarettes, and Scotch, and carried a Walther PPK pistol beneath his white robes. Sattar may have looked more at home in the mob than the mosque, but he helped to alter the course of the Iraq War.

By the fall of 2006, Anbar Province, the heart of Sunni Iraq, was one of the most violent places in the country, with over fifty insurgent attacks per day. An opening developed, however, for the United States. Sunni tribal leaders began to see U.S. forces as less of a threat than other rivals like Shiite death squads and especially Al Qaeda. The jihadist group imposed strict Islamist ideology, banned cigarettes and music, robbed local businesses, forcibly wed the daughters of Sunni families, and murdered prominent Sunnis—including Sattar's father and two brothers.

In September 2006, Sattar formed the Anbar Salvation Council with the goal of expelling Al Qaeda from Anbar. The charismatic Sattar told a meeting of fifty sheikhs: "The coalition forces are friendly forces, not occupying forces."[19] Here was the opportunity for a fundamental realignment in Iraqi politics. For years, the Bush administration had resisted outreach to Sunni insurgents. But now the White House shifted gear. Through extensive

Abdul Sattar Abu Risha pictured in 2007 (Curt Cashour, U.S. Army photo)

negotiations, lubricated by endless cups of tea, the United States brought Sunni tribal leaders into an alliance. Over one hundred thousand Iraqis eventually signed up to fight Al Qaeda and other extremist groups by joining Awakening Councils and the Sons of Iraq program (including over twenty thousand Shiites). The fighters received $300 a month from the U.S. government. The cost amounted to a rounding error in Washington's overall military budget, but it made a decisive difference.

The Awakening removed the majority of Sunni insurgents from the battlefield and broke the cycle of violence. The new recruits were invaluable. They knew where the remaining rebels were and how to beat them. After all, they'd been fighting American soldiers for years. It wasn't a smooth process; Al Qaeda killed Sattar in September 2007. But Anbar came back from the brink of anarchy. In combination with the surge of U.S. forces, the effect was dramatic. By the end of 2007, the number of attacks in Anbar had fallen by over 90 percent.[20]

The Awakening movement is a stark reminder of the value of peace talks during an exit strategy from war. "Many consider negotiations as a sign of weakness," wrote Kissinger. "I always looked at them as a weapon for seizing the moral and psychological high ground.... It is a device to improve one's strategic position."[21]

Negotiations have helped to resolve seemingly intractable civil conflicts, like in El Salvador, Cambodia, Guatemala, Bosnia, South Africa, and Northern Ireland. Over time, many extremist rebel groups have transitioned to normal politics by swapping the Kalashnikov for the teleprompter, including Sinn Féin in Northern Ireland and the Palestine Liberation Organization.

Even if success in peace talks proves elusive, the act of negotiating can provide useful intelligence about the insurgents' organization, capabilities, and goals. If a good-faith effort at diplomacy falters in the face of enemy intransigence, this may boost international and domestic support for a continued war effort. And declaring a willingness to talk is a potentially risky move for the insurgents—undermining their narrative of certain victory.

The ethical price of negotiating must be balanced against the moral cost of not talking. Holbrooke said he had no qualms about bargaining with people who act immorally. "If you can prevent the deaths of people still alive, you're not doing a disservice to those already killed by trying to do so."[22]

Sometimes we shouldn't talk to the enemy, for example, if they're utterly extreme or intransigent. Churchill was right not to negotiate with Hitler. But these are very rare exceptions. Usually, in the wake of a military fiasco, we should aggressively look to make a deal—even an ugly deal—to limit the damage.[23]

After battlefield failure, when should we start talking? Negotiations ought to begin fairly quickly, in parallel with the strengthening of American forces. In other words, the military surge should be accompanied by a diplomatic surge. The idea is to bargain when U.S. force levels are at their peak and Washington has maximum leverage. If we wait until our troops withdraw, the enemy has an incentive to sit on its hands. As Kissinger put it: "You should never be negotiating a peace when the opposing force knows you are leaving."[24] Unfortunately, in Afghanistan, Washington only embraced a diplomatic solution in 2011 when American strength was receding.

In summary, following a military fiasco, peace talks are a difficult but necessary path. With American soldiers fighting and dying in a campaign of limited interests, we can't afford to cling to a good-versus-evil view of the war. We can't afford to wait years to engage the enemy. In Afghanistan, we must embrace negotiations with the Taliban. There's no realistic alternative path to peace or the long-term protection of U.S. interests.

Purpose-Driven Talks

A military fiasco is one of the most challenging negotiation scenarios imaginable. The United States is reeling from battlefield failure. There's little or no trust between our side and the enemy. We're trying to kill each other as we speak. How should we negotiate? Who should talk to whom about what?

Negotiations must be integrated into the overall exit strategy. Therefore, the nature of peace talks hinges on the war aims. If the goal is a *surgical strike,* the United States may seek limited deals with insurgent groups. For example, in a humanitarian operation, Washington may negotiate with warlords to ensure the safe delivery of aid.

If we pursue the mid-range objective of *ugly stability,* we will be looking to reach a workable accommodation between the regime and the insurgents. Washington may create red lines that guerrillas shouldn't cross, such as supporting international terrorism. The result will be messy and ambiguous—but perhaps also cost-effective and tolerable.

If we fight for a *beacon of freedom,* or a stable and democratic society, Washington may pursue expansive negotiating goals to integrate rebels into the new order. The bar will be set high during bargaining, as insurgents are asked to lay down their weapons and accept a free and pluralist political system.

In Afghanistan, the U.S. goal is something close to *ugly stability.* What kind of negotiated deal would help achieve this objective? Diplomats must traverse one obstacle after another, from determining the fate of insurgent leaders to revising the Afghan constitution. An ultimate settlement might include a cease-fire, prisoner exchanges, a verifiable end to Taliban support of Al Qaeda, de facto Taliban control of greater Kandahar, a full withdrawal of international troops, and the Taliban's evolution into a legal political party. Such a deal would protect America's core interests by preventing Afghanistan from becoming a base for international terrorism or a source of instability for neighboring states.[25]

In the midst of conflict, how can we get the negotiation ball rolling?

Communicate Without Talking

In 1994, during the early stages of the Northern Ireland peace process, the British government had a communication problem. London was inching toward talks with Sinn Féin, the political wing of the Irish Republican Army. But the IRA was still engaged in violence, including lobbing mortar bombs at Heathrow Airport in March 1994. London therefore refused any official communication with Sinn *Féin*. At the time, it was even illegal for television and radio to broadcast the voice of Sinn *Féin* leader Gerry Adams. Like a ventriloquist's puppet, Adams was shown speaking on television while actors read his words.

The two sides needed to talk to end the violence, but they couldn't talk until the violence ended. The solution in Northern Ireland was "megaphone diplomacy," where London and Sinn *Féin* negotiated through public speeches, newspaper articles, and press releases. London could send messages to Sinn *Féin* while — technically, at least — not talking to terrorists.

In 1994, megaphone diplomacy worked. The IRA announced a cessation of military operations, and a peace agreement was eventually reached on Good Friday in 1998.[26] But negotiating in public has its downsides. As with shouting at someone from thirty yards away, the message may be misheard. And it requires some common media between the adversaries. The opponents in Northern Ireland shared the same language, television channels, and newspapers — but this isn't true in a country like Afghanistan.

Another way to get the ball rolling is by sending an unofficial agent to meet the adversary. A retired diplomat or a prominent private citizen usually fits the bill. The agent's status means that peace feelers will be taken seriously. But it's still an off-the-record approach and can potentially be disavowed. In 1951, for example, George Kennan talked unofficially to the Soviet Union about a truce in Korea while on leave from the State Department.[27]

Adversaries can also communicate through diplomatic back channels or private contacts between officials. During the endgame in Vietnam, Kissinger met North Vietnam's Le Duc Tho for secret talks in a dingy Parisian apartment at 11, rue Darthé. In scenes straight out of a spy novel, the White House covered its tracks by claiming that Kissinger was at Camp David. Washington gave the participants code names. And Kissinger slouched in the back of a speeding car in Paris to elude journalists. Nixon's chief of staff wrote in his diary: "K all cranked up about his secret trip to Paris.... He loves the intrigue and [Nixon] enjoys it too."[28]

Using diplomatic back channels can be liberating. Freed from public pressure, negotiators may find new ways to move forward. When Israel and the PLO met for highly publicized talks in Madrid in 1991, there was little progress. But secret discussions in Oslo in 1993 produced a breakthrough. If back-channel negotiations are revealed, however, they can be very controversial. After the Oslo Accords were signed, an Israeli extremist gunned down Israel's prime minister Yitzhak Rabin.

Whichever avenue is pursued, we should avoid appearing to move first. Making the opening appeal for negotiations can signal that we're suing for peace—especially if we're on the military back foot. One answer is to claim to be responding to the actions of the other side. During the Korean War, for example, U.S. general Matthew Ridgway broadcast a statement to the enemy: "I am informed that you may wish a meeting to discuss an armistice." The Communists then used the same trick, declaring that because of "grave difficulties" for the United States and its allies on the battlefield, Washington has requested "an immediate ceasefire."[29]

Megaphone diplomacy, unofficial agents, and back-channel talks are all useful ways of breaking the ice, but they probably won't produce much real progress until senior figures sit around the green baize. Where's the best place to talk?

Location, Location, Location

In May 1618, a group of Protestant lords, fearing for their religious liberties, threw two envoys of the Catholic king of Bohemia from the third-floor window of the Royal Palace in Prague. Somehow the envoys survived the fall. The Catholic Church claimed that angels saved them. The Protestants said the envoys landed in a pile of manure.

The Defenestration of Prague (from *fenestra,* the Latin for "window") helped trigger a generation of catastrophic war across Europe. The population of the German states may have fallen by one-fifth or more. Finally, in 1644, peace negotiations began at the Congress of Westphalia.

But six months of negotiations were spent arguing over a seemingly trivial detail: the seating plan for the Congress and the order in which the delegates would enter the room. At the time, rank was all-important. Precedence and hierarchy were forms of power. A final peace deal was reached in 1648. The delay over the seating plan helped give the conflict its name: the Thirty Years' War.

The negotiations at Westphalia illustrate the symbolic importance of the physical setting for peace talks. The choice of location and surroundings can powerfully shape the narrative of war, by signaling victory, defeat, prestige, or humiliation.

Where should the combatants meet? Usually, you need a neutral location, either in no-man's-land between the front lines or in territory controlled by a third party that both sides trust. When truce talks began in Korea in 1951, the United States suggested meeting aboard a Danish hospital ship. The Communists brusquely told Washington to appear at the former Korean capital of Kaesong, thirty-five miles northwest of Seoul. Kaesong was in no-man's-land, and so Washington agreed.

By the time talks began, however, the Communists had seized Kaesong. The Communists proceeded to stage-manage the entrance of the American negotiators to make it look like Washington was suing for peace. The Communist jeeps were out in front and the U.S. convoy followed, flying large white flags. Communist cameramen snapped photos for widespread distribution. Soon wising up, Washington insisted the talks move to Panmunjom, which was also in no-man's-land—but this time less likely to fall under Communist control.[30]

The psychological one-upmanship continued inside the negotiating room. The Communists gave the U.S. representative a shorter chair, which the American swapped for a chair of normal height. When the Americans built modest latrines for their team, the Communists constructed larger and more brightly painted latrines for their side. When the United States planted scrub pines, the Communists planted flowering plants. When the chief U.S. negotiator arrived in a sedan, the Communists imported a similarly prestigious vehicle from the Soviet Union.[31]

At one point, the American negotiators brought a small UN flag to the talks and placed it on the table. The Communists pushed the flag to the side. The Americans casually moved it back to its original position. This game continued until a recess, when the Communists returned with a larger North Korean flag. The two sides were on the verge of a pennant arms race—until the Americans decided the issue wasn't worth pursuing.

A decade later, talks over Vietnam stalled for weeks because of arguments about the shape of the negotiating table. This seemingly absurd debate over furniture actually reflected a profound underlying question: Was the Vietcong, or the South Vietnamese insurgency, an independent actor in the conflict, or a lackey of Hanoi? North Vietnam said the Vietcong was a popular uprising and an autonomous group. South Vietnam said it was a puppet of the North.

Washington suggested a rectangular table with the United States and South Vietnam on one side, and North Vietnam and the Vietcong on the other—emphasizing the two-sided nature of the fight.

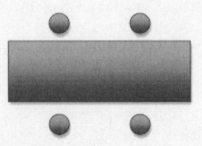

North Vietnam, however, wanted the Vietcong recognized as an independent and equal participant and favored a square table, with Saigon facing the Vietcong and the United States facing Hanoi.

In the end, North Vietnam agreed to a round table.

But now South Vietnam refused to sit next to the Vietcong. And so two small tables were placed between the adversaries for tape recorders and secretaries "at a distance of 45 centimeters, or 18 inches, from the round table."[32]

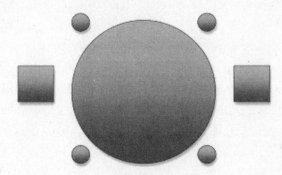

In 2013, negotiations over the Afghanistan War were immediately derailed by disputes about the physical setting. The Taliban tried to make their office in Qatar look like the embassy of a government-in-waiting. They hoisted a white-and-black Taliban flag and added a nameplate that read, "Political Office of the Islamic Emirate of Afghanistan"—the same title they used when they were in power. After complaints, the Taliban changed the nameplate to "Political Office of the Taliban" and placed the flag on a shortened pole. Kabul still felt tricked and announced a suspension of bilateral security discussions with the United States.

Opening Salvos

The location is chosen. The green baize is laid out. Senior figures enter the room for serious discussion. During the early rounds of negotiations, all sides may be intransigent, and progress can seem impossible. At this point, there's still great uncertainty. The combatants don't understand each other's capabilities, resolve, confidence in military victory, bargaining positions, or underlying interests. Opponents fear that any concessions they offer will just be pocketed—and, even worse, communicate weakness. As a result, each side tends to open with their maximum demands and ask for more than they can possibly receive.

Negotiators shouldn't give up. As the combatants sound each other out, there's usually a narrowing of differences. Both sides start looking at the same basic set of facts. Illusions are stripped away. Expectations about the future of the war begin to converge. As a result, more extreme requests are quietly abandoned. And, crucially, once concessions are made, they're hard to take back. The willingness to yield on a point sends a signal about resolve and interests.

In Afghanistan, the Taliban and the United States have both softened their positions. The current Taliban are actually the (slightly) kinder and gentler version. The insurgents have given up—at least temporarily—their campaign against music and have embraced what they call "modern education."[33] The Taliban originally said they would only negotiate after foreign troops left, but this position has been shelved. In 2013, a Taliban spokesman claimed that the insurgents' political and military goals "are limited to Afghanistan" and that the group "would not allow anyone to threaten the security of other countries from the soil of Afghanistan"—a signal the Taliban may end their support for international terrorism.[34]

Meanwhile, the United States has also quietly made concessions. At first, Washington implied that the Taliban had to concede on "red-line" issues—such as accepting the Afghan constitution and breaking ties with Al Qaeda—before talks could even begin. Only later did Washington say these red lines were a necessary outcome of talks.[35]

During the early sparring rounds, it's useful to look past the other side's bargaining *positions* and focus on their underlying *interests*. The gap between the respective positions can seem impossible to bridge. But interests may be more compatible. The United States and the Taliban both suffer from the costs of war. They are both concerned about Iranian influence in Afghanistan. They both want to see U.S. troops leave—although they have very different views about *how* this should happen. The American vision of a representative regime in Kabul also includes a political voice for the Taliban's Pashtun constituency.[36]

And other Taliban interests suggest possible opportunities for leverage. The Taliban resent what they see as manipulation by Pakistan. They fear a powerful anti-Taliban coalition of non-Pashtuns. And they crave domestic and international legitimacy. These underlying interests provide a reason to talk and hope for ending the war.

Deal or No Deal

Once bargaining starts in earnest, how can we negotiate successfully? An effective tactic is to prepare simultaneously for two very different scenarios. The first scenario is where we manage to reach a diplomatic settlement. Let's call it the *deal world*. In Afghanistan, for example, this would mean an agreement with the Taliban. The second scenario is where peace talks fail and violence continues. Let's call it the *no-deal world*. In Afghanistan, this would mean the conflict dragging on indefinitely. Understanding and manipulating these two rival futures may hold the key to successful negotiations.[37]

First of all, comprehending the no-deal world helps determine our bottom line in negotiations. We should never accept an agreement that's worse than our no-deal world. It would be better to keep fighting.

And it's also critical to actively improve our no-deal world. Planning for a scenario where peace talks collapse provides an insurance policy. The sky won't fall in if we fail to reach a settlement. In Afghanistan, for example, we should assume that negotiations unravel and develop a program of long-term aid to Kabul.

Preparing for the no-deal world has another benefit: It enhances our leverage in negotiations. Imagine you're buying a car. One way to bargain more effectively with the seller is to strengthen your no-deal world by finding alternative vehicles available on the market. Showing the seller you have other viable options means you can credibly threaten to walk away, and may be able to drive a lower price.

Similarly, in wartime, improving our no-deal world makes it easier to stop talking, which can reinforce our hand in negotiations, help us reach a tolerable agreement—and actually avert the scenario of continued conflict. In other words, if you want peace, prepare for war. Ryan Crocker told me that if the Taliban "see a commitment to maintain well-equipped, armed, and trained Afghan security forces, it may change their calculus."[38] By contrast, if Washington intends to quickly leave Afghanistan, we have a weak no-deal world, and the Taliban have few incentives to make concessions. Why take half a loaf when you can grab the whole bakery?

Washington can also try to make the no-deal world look worse from the opponent's point of view. As a global power, the

United States has many resources and allies that can make life difficult for the enemy if it refuses to play ball. We can threaten an intransigent enemy with America's focused enmity long into the future, including international ostracism, sanctions, and support for opposition groups.[39]

But manipulating the opponent's no-deal world is easier said than done. Simply telling the enemy how grim life will be without an agreement may fail, given our obvious incentives to deceive. We may therefore have to pay a fairly steep price in terms of additional military and economic commitments to alter the opponent's calculus.

Isn't there a simpler option: Why not threaten to bomb the enemy back to the Stone Age?

Rolling Thunder

At the height of Rolling Thunder, the U.S. bombing campaign in Vietnam, President Johnson couldn't sleep. He kept picturing his "boys" flying into enemy territory and getting shot down, or accidentally killing some Russians and sparking World War III. In the middle of the night, the president grabbed his flashlight and descended into the hubbub of the Situation Room, where he pored over maps and tracked the incoming bombing reports.[40]

Johnson saw airpower as one of America's major coercive tools in Vietnam. He would turn the heat up or down to compel North Vietnam to negotiate on U.S. terms and end its support for the insurgency. Massive strikes would punish Hanoi. Bombing pauses would reward good behavior. From 1966 to 1968, Washington dropped more tonnage of bombs on Southeast Asia than Allied forces delivered in both theaters of World War II. As Kissinger put it: "I can't believe that a fourth-rate power like North Vietnam doesn't have a breaking point."[41]

U.S. B-66 Destroyer and F-105 Thunderchief aircraft bomb North Vietnam in 1966. (Cecil J. Poss, U.S. Air Force)

Rolling Thunder didn't work. Three years of bombing produced a great deal of destruction but little if any political payoff—as Hanoi refused to submit. This failure illustrates the challenges in trying to bludgeon the enemy into making concessions at the negotiating table.

Unsurprisingly, if the use of force is ineffective, it won't reap a diplomatic dividend. Rolling Thunder failed to stem the flow of supplies to the Vietcong guerrillas in the South because the insurgents didn't need much material to maintain their campaign. North Vietnam adapted to the bombing by using portable electricity generators, submersible pontoon bridges, and a vast network of tunnels. Dud American bombs even provided the raw materials for Communist booby traps. Rolling Thunder killed thousands of North Vietnamese civilians, but the Communists were willing to take this punishment in their sacred quest for unification.[42]

Military coercion may also be ineffective because it heightens the pain for both sides. During Rolling Thunder, the United States lost almost one thousand aircraft. By 1967, Washington estimated it was spending ten dollars to cause one dollar of damage. The United States was coercing itself into ending the war.

And even if the punishment is one-sided, the enemy may still refuse to budge. The opponent will avoid caving for fear of inviting further attack. The enemy may even *raise* its demands to compensate for losses. "The more brutal your methods," wrote the British strategist Basil Liddell Hart, "the more bitter you will make your opponents, with the natural result of hardening the resistance you are trying to overcome."[43]

Does firepower ever produce political concessions? Of course, the answer is yes. Military capabilities stop the opponent from seizing everything it wants. And negotiations occur when both sides lose confidence that they can win a decisive victory anytime soon. "Diplomacy without arms," said Frederick the Great, "is like music without instruments."

Overall, airpower failed as a coercive tool in Vietnam—but there's an important exception. In March 1972, North Vietnam launched a massive conventional invasion of South Vietnam known as the Easter Offensive. Instead of relying on guerrillas, the North attacked with hundreds of tanks in a bid to capture territory and deliver a hammer blow to South Vietnamese forces.

The United States responded with a sustained bombing campaign known as Linebacker I. Washington struck a range of targets in North and South Vietnam, including transportation hubs, storage facilities, and air defenses. Nixon said, "The bastards have never been bombed like they're going to be bombed this time."[44]

North Vietnam's conventional campaign was far more vulnerable to American airpower than the Vietcong insurgency. Hanoi's attempt to capture and hold fixed positions placed its forces in the U.S. target sights. Linebacker I interrupted Communist supply lines and caused shortages of vital material including fuel. Backed by American airpower, South Vietnamese resistance stiffened. In the end, Hanoi gained some additional territory but suffered one hundred thousand casualties and lost most of its tanks.[45]

After the Easter Offensive stalled, North Vietnam softened its negotiating position. Hanoi dropped its long-standing demand that a coalition government replace the Nguyen Van Thieu regime in South Vietnam, and instead accepted a national commission to oversee elections. For sure, the extent of this concession is debatable. Hanoi could tolerate Thieu's temporary continuation in office because it knew the United States was leaving and believed that victory was inevitable. And the United States offered an even greater concession by agreeing that North Vietnam's troops could remain in South Vietnam, whereas American soldiers would withdraw. Still, the U.S. bombing campaign allowed the Nixon administration to leave Vietnam without a clear-cut and immediate defeat.[46]

Coercing an enemy into changing its negotiating stance usually requires targeting its military capabilities and denying its ability to achieve core goals. In 1972, Hanoi realized that the expected territorial gains would no longer be possible. The path to victory had lengthened, and so Hanoi compromised to get the Americans out.[47]

To be effective, the use of force should change the opponent's no-deal world. The adversary will be least willing to talk if it suffers failure today but expects success tomorrow. And it will be most willing to talk if it wins on the battlefield today but fears defeat tomorrow. Therefore, firepower works best when it signals that *still greater injury lies ahead.*[48]

The use of force must also be of unexpected duration or intensity. Even a destructive assault won't have much effect if the enemy has already factored the pain into its calculations. Linebacker I forced a rethink in North Vietnam because Hanoi didn't anticipate the extent of U.S. and South Vietnamese resistance.

Given this experience in Vietnam, can we bludgeon our way to success in Afghanistan? Leon Panetta concluded: "Unless [the Taliban are] convinced the United States is going to win and that they're going to be defeated, I think it's very difficult to proceed with a reconciliation that's going to be meaningful."[49]

The use of force has an essential role to play in Afghanistan. But the key is not the number of insurgents we remove from the battlefield today. What matters is the Taliban's perception of the likely situation tomorrow. The least effective option is to kill guerrillas while signaling that we're about to leave. A rational enemy will just ride out the storm. The most effective option is to communicate that more force will be employed in the coming years than the Taliban currently expect.

To really impact negotiations, the use of force should be a game changer that targets the enemy's military capabilities and changes its expectations about the future. But achieving this kind of result may be so costly in military and political terms that the payoff isn't worth it—which is why the club is such a challenging negotiating tool.

The Wedge Shot

In 2003, Darryl Worley released his third country music album, *Have You Forgotten?* The title track, which spent seven weeks at the top of *Billboard* magazine's Hot Country Songs chart, included the lines: "Some say this country's just out looking for a fight/ After 9/11, man, I'd have to say that's right." One radio show host played "Have You Forgotten?" every hour in the buildup to the war in Iraq. He was asked about the lack of evidence connecting Saddam Hussein to Al Qaeda: "The audience is so wrapped up in the emotion of what it's about, I don't think they're nitpicking at this point....Everybody's viewing all the bad guys in a big bucket."[50]

We're often tempted to lump adversaries together into a "big bucket" or view them as a single entity. But this is usually a mistake. An effective negotiator sees the opposing side as a coalition of different groups, each of which pursues its own agenda. This coalition should be cajoled, threatened, and assisted into reaching an acceptable deal.

In Afghanistan, the Taliban present themselves as a unified movement. But in truth the insurgents are more of a decentralized "network of networks." There's the Taliban proper, which are directly under the control of the Quetta Shura, or the leadership council led by Mullah Omar. There's also Hezb-e-Islami Gulbuddin, headed by Gulbuddin Hekmatyar, which fought against the Soviets in the 1980s and reemerged after 2001 as a militant anti-Kabul force. There's the Haqqani Network, established by mujahideen commander Jalaluddin Haqqani, which operates in the southeast of Afghanistan and is closely connected to the Pakistani intelligence services. And there are also local tribal groups, drug gangs, and foreign jihadists like Al Qaeda.

Some insurgents fight because they believe the United States seeks to dominate Afghanistan and destroy Islam. Others oppose the corruption and misrule in Kabul. And still others have more personal motivations such as individual gain, vengeance, or a yearning for excitement. Different insurgent networks act with considerable autonomy: pursuing turf wars, quarreling, and even selling suicide bombers to each other.[51]

Given these divisions, it's tempting to drive a wedge into the insurgency. Fostering dissent, or playing one faction against another, could undercut the enemy's war effort or even shatter the rebellion. We might negotiate separately with different elements of the insurgency, try to peel away certain factions, or target the use of force against specific leaders and groups.

But the placement of the wedge is critical. The rebel leadership is hypersensitive to internal cohesion. If negotiations threaten to fragment the insurgency, the opponent will just walk away. And sometimes it's better to keep the insurgency unified so we can bargain with a cohesive actor. Splintering an insurgency may be like blowing up an asteroid headed to Earth: We swap one big threat for many smaller threats. Even if the rebel leadership wants to make peace, spoilers will continue to use violence.

In Afghanistan, trying to drive a wedge into the core Taliban may be counterproductive. Even if we somehow succeed, we might create rejectionist factions that continue the fight whatever deal is reached. The United States could even have an interest in maintaining Mullah Omar's control over the Taliban. Omar may be an extreme ideologue but he's also the one man with the moral authority to convince most Taliban fighters to lay down their arms. A coherent Taliban are more capable of making war, and more capable of making peace.

So where should we drive the wedge? Often the sweet spot lies between local insurgents and groups linked to international terrorism. David Kilcullen described the alliance of convenience between "accidental guerrillas," meaning the local rebels who resist Western intervention, and the hard-core jihadists who seek global revolution. The language of a "war on terror" only serves to fuse together this enemy coalition. By contrast, a combination of targeted firepower and diplomatic outreach can break the ties between accidental guerrillas and international terrorists—for example, with the Awakening in Iraq.[52]

In Afghanistan, we should drive a wedge between the Taliban and Al Qaeda. For years, we failed to differentiate between these groups—a major strategic blunder. But they have very different goals. The Taliban's horizons are mainly limited to Afghanistan and Pakistan, whereas Al Qaeda seeks an international caliphate. The Taliban want to be recognized as a legitimate actor in Afghan politics rather than a terrorist group and have signaled a willingness to distance themselves from Al Qaeda. Indeed, by 2011, there were perhaps fewer than 100 Al Qaeda members left in Afghanistan.

The Taliban and Al Qaeda were originally connected in the same UN sanctions program, but in 2011 the UN Security Council distinguished between the two groups. U.S. ambassador to the United Nations Susan Rice said the move "sends a clear message to the Taliban that there is a future for those who separate from Al Qaeda."[53]

The Heart of Joseph

On the morning of March 1, 1953, there was no sign of Stalin. After a night drinking Georgian wine at his dacha outside Moscow, Stalin went to bed and never reemerged. For hours, his bodyguards were too terrified to enter the bedroom. Finally, they plucked up the courage and found the dictator lying semiconscious on the floor. Officially, Stalin suffered a massive stroke. Many think he was poisoned.

The Soviet high command delayed getting medical attention, probably because they were negotiating the political succession. The doctor didn't arrive until the next morning, and was visibly shaking as he examined the dictator. Finally, after three days of futile treatment, Stalin passed away. According to the new rulers: "The heart of the comrade and inspired continuer of Lenin's will, the wise leader and teacher of the Communist Party and the Soviet people—Joseph Vissarionovich Stalin—has stopped beating."[54]

Stalin's death had dramatic consequences thousands of miles away, in Korea. The Soviet dictator was an architect of the Korean War. He gave Pyongyang the green light to invade the South and pushed for a tough stance during negotiations—hoping to tie down American forces in an Asian quagmire. Within weeks of Stalin's death, the new leadership in Moscow decided to make concessions and end the fighting.[55]

As Stalin's demise reveals, no war is fought in isolation. Regional players and distant great powers can powerfully impact the success of U.S. negotiations. Peacemaking therefore requires a wide-angle lens, a broad international strategy, and an understanding of the ripple effects of far-off events.

As a general rule, outside countries can't resolve a conflict on their own—but they can prolong it. In other words, external powers can stop the peace more easily than they can stop the war.

Neighboring states and great powers usually lack the will or capacity to force belligerents to lay down their arms. Attempting to end a conflict "from without" will rarely work. For example, Nixon thought the road to peace in Vietnam lay through Moscow and Beijing. During great-power diplomacy, Washington tried to wring concessions in Vietnam via "linkage." Nixon made progress on issues like trade and arms control contingent on the Communist giants pressuring Hanoi to play ball.

In the end, however, the results were disappointing. From the Soviet and Chinese perspective, linkage looked like bribery or intimidation. Neither country was willing to accept the loss of prestige from publicly betraying its ally. And Hanoi skillfully played Moscow and Beijing against each other to keep the aid flowing, by leaning first one way and then the other.[56]

Outside countries may not be able to deliver peace, but they can sabotage a negotiated deal. It's difficult or impossible to resolve a conflict when neighbors are determined to frustrate progress. Regional players have an extensive toolbox to foster discord. They can pressure allies to take a hard line, step up aid to extremist groups, or offer a sanctuary for rejectionist factions. The key, therefore, is to stop outside countries from acting as spoilers.

Afghanistan's neighbors, as well as distant great powers, have a long history of interfering in the country. In recent decades, India, Iran, Pakistan, Russia, Saudi Arabia, Turkey, the Central Asian republics, and the United States have all supported different insurgent groups. One of the major players is Pakistan, which is simultaneously the Taliban's sanctuary, sponsor, and victim. Pakistani intelligence provides support to the Afghan Taliban as part of a broader strategy to prevent Pakistan's encirclement in a hostile Afghan-Indian alliance. Meanwhile, since 2004, around 5,000 Pakistani soldiers have died fighting the Pakistani Taliban (political cousins of the Afghan Taliban)—more than the 3,500 international troops killed in Afghanistan.

For the United States, Pakistan is an ally from hell: a "frenemy" that received $40 billion in U.S. economic and military aid since the 1940s and responded with a covert nuclear weapons program and backing for Afghan insurgents.

For Pakistan, the United States is an ally from hell: a bullying superpower that killed its troops in an accidental air strike in 2011 and humiliated its military by taking out Osama bin Laden on Pakistani territory. Ronald Neumann told me, "Westerners with big resources think of foreign policy issues in terms of 'what do I want?'" By contrast, weaker countries like Pakistan start with, "what do I have to deal with?" and "how do I protect myself?"[57]

Does the road to peace in Afghanistan lie through Pakistan?

Islamabad can positively affect negotiations by marginalizing hardliners among the Taliban leadership. But Pakistan can't deliver peace on its own. Instead, the main goal is to stop Pakistan from sabotaging the reconciliation process.

The obvious tactic is to use carrots and sticks to cajole Pakistan into playing for the right team. As an incentive, we might try to curb Indian involvement in Afghanistan, for example, by limiting the number of Indian consulates in the country. We could also pressure Kabul to accept the Durand Line between Afghanistan and Pakistan as a permanent border—a goal that Islamabad seeks but Kabul has historically resisted. Meanwhile, as a stick, we could threaten to punish Pakistan by reducing U.S. aid if it undermines negotiations.

But talk of carrots and sticks implies that Pakistan is an exasperating mule we can cajole into following the right path. The language itself is inherently patronizing. How would we feel if an ally said it was using carrots and sticks to guide our behavior? The truth is, we have less leverage over Pakistan than we might think. John McLaughlin, the former acting director of the CIA, told me, "It's hard to make carrots and sticks work. The stick is rarely enough if the country strongly believes in its own interests."[58] The Afghan establishment is not going to accept the Durand Line anytime soon. Neither can we force India to reduce its diplomatic presence in Afghanistan. And Pakistan will not bend to our whims on core interests simply to safeguard American aid.

So what can we do to stop Pakistan from playing spoiler? First of all, we should give Pakistan a seat at the table. Diplomatic outreach can keep Pakistan in the loop as we draw down U.S. forces and begin the process of negotiations. The surest path is an appeal to Pakistan's self-interest. Marc Grossman, Obama's special representative for Afghanistan and Pakistan from 2011-2012, told me, "The Pakistanis are beginning to realize that the Pakistani Taliban is an existential threat to Pakistan." If Afghanistan stabilizes, there could be a new silk road of trade and economic development in the region. But if Afghanistan spirals further into civil war, the "Pakistani Taliban would benefit."[59]

Pakistan is determined to prevent an encircling Afghan–Indian alliance. But Pakistan is not committed to a Taliban takeover of Afghanistan. Islamabad can live with the Taliban as a player rather than a ruler in Afghanistan: a proxy force with regional sway as opposed to a government-in-waiting.

Can we alter Pakistan's calculation of its own interests? Yes, to some extent. For example, we can boost Pakistan's economic payoff from a positive relationship with the United States. Reducing tariffs on Pakistani textile exports to the United States, and ultimately negotiating a U.S.-Pakistan Free Trade Agreement, would shift the economic relationship from aid to trade.[60] But we can't fundamentally change Pakistan's core hopes and fears in Afghanistan. A deal that is intolerable in Islamabad won't work.

Hell Is Other People

In June 1953, the end of the Korean War was finally within sight as the combatants hammered out the final issues at the negotiating table. Suddenly, South Korea's president and U.S. ally, Syngman Rhee, became a clear and present danger to American interests. Rhee had long been a fierce critic of truce negotiations and wanted to use atomic weapons to force decisive victory and unify the country. The South Korean president organized hostile public demonstrations against a settlement. He threatened to expel American troops from the peninsula and fight on alone. And he jeopardized the armistice by unilaterally releasing captured POWs into South Korea (the United States and the Communists had agreed that prisoners would be handed over to a neutral-nation commission, which would determine whether they preferred to stay in the South or return home). As the U.S. president's son, John Eisenhower, put it, "I guess Syngman Rhee pretty well scuttled the truce."[61]

Ike needed all his diplomatic skills to keep the alliance together. First, he told Rhee that "unless you are prepared immediately and unequivocally to accept the authority of the U.N. Command to conduct the present hostilities and to bring them to a close, it will be necessary to effect another arrangement."[62] This was a polite way of saying the United States would abandon South Korea to its fate. Washington even developed a secret plan—Operation Everready—to launch a coup and topple Rhee by force.

But another path lay open to Rhee, which Eisenhower made as enticing as possible. If South Korea accepted the peace deal, Washington offered a defense pact and economic aid in return. This formula allowed Rhee to retreat without losing face, and an armistice was signed on July 27, 1953.

Rhee's rebellion reveals the vital importance of keeping our own side united as we bargain with the enemy. Time and again, allies have complicated America's exit strategy. In the critical final stages of negotiation, as war or peace hangs in the balance, we may find that the enemy shooting at us is less frustrating than the ally sharing our foxhole.

The interests of the United States and its allies overlap significantly but not perfectly. Americans are probably looking to leave after a treaty is signed, whereas our partner has to live in the neighborhood. As the U.S. exit approaches, and all parties start maneuvering for the post-American era, the glue binding our coalition together can quickly come unstuck.

Afghan president Hamid Karzai can charitably be called a difficult ally. The chicly dressed moderate Pashtun somehow evolved into an associate of known crooks—like Nelson Mandela morphing into Tony Soprano. A mercurial and theatrical man, Karzai publicly compared the United States to the Taliban and threatened to throw his hand in with the insurgency. In 2014, Karzai refused to sign a long-term security pact with Washington that he himself negotiated and released several Taliban militants from jail. Over the years, U.S. intelligence reports claimed that Karzai was "delusional," while other descriptions included "off his meds" and high on "weed."[63]

Afghan peace talks have also strained relations with non-Pashtun northern groups that fought the Taliban and oppose bringing them into the government. Amrullah Saleh, an Afghan politician and ethnic Tajik, led a rally of ten thousand people in Kabul against a deal—his "anti-Taliban constituency." Saleh signaled that any peace settlement might be followed by the remobilization of northern forces: "Don't push me to take a gun."[64]

What's the solution? First of all, we need patience and pragmatism. It's certainly frustrating when weaker countries refuse to play ball. (After Bill Clinton first met Israeli prime minister Benjamin Netanyahu, Clinton privately wondered, "Who's the fucking superpower here?")[65] But Washington's goal in wartime is to create a sovereign regime rather than an American lackey—and we should expect the allied government to pursue its own agenda. We can't blame partners for doggedly fighting for their interests or trying to slow down America's withdrawal. They're playing for all the chips: their nation's destiny, their political future, and their personal survival.

Karzai may have had in mind the fate of Mohammad Najibullah, the Soviet-backed ruler of Afghanistan. After the Taliban captured Kabul in 1996, Najibullah was castrated, shot, and hanged in Ariana Square. American commanders sometimes speak of entering unstable regions in Afghanistan and bringing "government in a box." But the government in a box that Karzai probably worries about is his own corpse lying in a coffin.

We also need to be realistic about governance in a country where the economy is based on drugs and foreign aid, and power is exercised through patronage networks. The Karzai administration was simultaneously one of the most venal regimes in the world—and also the best Afghan government in a generation. By the standards of the region, his administration wasn't especially illegitimate or brutal. Karzai easily won the 2004 elections, receiving over three times as many votes as the nearest challenger. The 2009 election was marred by fraud, but Karzai probably received most of the legitimate votes. As Marc Grossman told me, "Karzai has promised Obama he will leave office and has said he wants to raise his children in Afghanistan—which would represent the first peaceful political transition in Afghanistan's history."[66]

Karzai's rhetoric was designed to boost his domestic standing and avert the impression of being a foreign puppet. Alliances are like marriage; it can pay to be a little deaf. Sometimes it's best to pretend we didn't hear.

An obvious way to influence allies, in theory at least, is to brandish carrots and sticks. Washington can woo its partners with aid and diplomatic commitments or threaten to cut support or withdraw entirely from the war effort—as with Rhee in 1953. John Hillen, the assistant secretary of state for political-military affairs from 2005 to 2007, told me he used "every trick in the book" to keep allies on board during his time in office, "from the highest appeal to moral principle, to eating a lot of bad foreign delicacies, to presenting a two-star Korean general with a signed picture of Condoleezza Rice as a personal thank you."[67]

In Afghanistan, we can promise financial support if Kabul and non-Pashtun northern groups play ball. And we can threaten to sideline factions that act as spoilers, or in extremis, leave the country altogether. But once again, carrots and sticks often turn out to be unwieldy tools. If our ally is strong, then we can't readily push them around. If our ally is weak, we can't easily threaten to punish them by withholding aid—their collapse would complicate our exit. Hillen found that the most reliable lever was usually an appeal to self-interest. A stable region will advance our goals—and the ally's goals.[68]

The Bargainer's Dilemma

In November 1861, shortly after the Civil War began, the *San Jacinto,* a Union naval vessel, sighted the *Trent,* a British mail packet, steaming through the Caribbean. The commander of the U.S. ship was Charles Wilkes, a headstrong man and self-described expert in international law, who was about to bring the United States and Britain to the brink of war.

In Wilkes's target sights were a pair of Confederate diplomats, aboard the *Trent* and headed for Europe. After firing warning shots, Union forces boarded the *Trent* and apprehended the diplomats as contraband of war. In the North, Wilkes was feted as a hero for scooping up the Confederates and thumbing America's nose at the British Empire. But London was outraged and demanded the release of the men and an apology.

Abraham Lincoln was desperate to avoid conflict with Britain. "One war at a time," he said.[69] But the president faced the bargainer's dilemma: How can you offer a concession without looking weak and seeming to bend before a rival's will? Is it possible to break the connection between an opponent's pressure and your own decision to yield? Overcoming the bargainer's dilemma isn't just superficial spin. It's an essential part of telling a story about compromise, and averting or ending war.[70]

This montage of photographs published in 1862 is entitled "The Great Surrender" and depicts the outcome of the Trent Affair as a retreat by all sides with no clear winner. Text on the reverse side says: "America surrenders the great commissioners—England surrenders her great pretensions—Jeff. Davis surrenders his great expectations." (E. Anthony, Library of Congress)

Lincoln's solution was to *act on principle,* or offer a concession based on a rule rather than the adversary's coercion. It's much easier to compromise in pursuit of an objective standard—such as past precedent, international law, or notions of fairness—than to bow before the intimidation of an opponent.[71]

Washington claimed that Wilkes acted without orders and failed to follow the correct legal path: bringing the *Trent* to port for adjudication as a prize. Releasing the Confederate diplomats would therefore uphold a principle, and "do to the British nation just what we have always insisted all nations ought to do to us."[72] As a result, war was averted, Anglo-American relations entered calmer seas, and Lincoln was left to focus on the main conflict at hand.

A second way to overcome the bargainer's dilemma is *leaving from behind,* or using other countries, outside mediators, and international organizations to mask a retreat from war. A particular peace plan, for example, may be unacceptable if suggested by the enemy, but tolerable if recommended by an ally, a neutral country, or the United Nations, because saying yes doesn't imply weakness to the same extent. *We can live with this UN-proposed solution.*

It's also much less painful to yield as part of a group than on our own. Concessions don't cause the same loss of face if allies share responsibility because there's uncertainty about which country was pushing a conciliatory line. *Our friends wanted us to do this and we went along.*

Leaving from behind could have been America's ticket out of Vietnam. One of the major barriers to withdrawal from Vietnam was the fear of reputational loss. The United States could have saved face by using an international conference as a fig leaf to cover an exit. A poll in 1969 found that 55 percent of Americans thought the United States had placed its credibility on the line and couldn't leave South Vietnam without guaranteeing the country's independence. But Americans changed their tune if the United Nations was involved in any exit. In 1967, 60 percent of Americans favored a "United Nations solution even if it includes United States withdrawal." A "United Nations solution" didn't trigger the same sense of defeat.[73]

Washington has used this tactic in Afghanistan by stressing that our allies are pushing for negotiations—thereby distancing the United States from conciliatory moves. In 2012, the State Department announced, "If this is part of an Afghan-led, Afghan-supported process and the Afghan Government itself believes it can play a constructive role, and it is also supported by the host country, then we will play a role in that as well."[74]

A third idea is the *blame game*. In other words, we gave it our best shot but foreign allies sabotaged the war effort. In 1966, John

McNaughton, the assistant secretary of defense, wrote in his diary, "It is clear to me that the ground beneath us [in Vietnam] is mush....the war cannot be won without a political base in South Vietnam and the base is not and will not be there....Since the big issue is U.S. reputation, the time to disengage is when the blame is on someone else—in this case on the South Vietnamese Government, whose total incapacity to behave themselves should amount to at least a minimum justification for our dumping them."[75]

A fourth way out of the bargainer's dilemma is *waiting for success,* where we break the connection between military failure and an American concession by delaying the shift in policy until we achieve some gains on the battlefield. Early in the Korean War, for example, neutral states like India offered peace feelers. But Washington said that negotiations had to wait until the military situation improved.

We can also sever the tie between a battlefield defeat and our subsequent yielding with a fifth tactic, *keeping control,* or claiming that retreat was the plan all along. As we saw earlier, de Gaulle tried this trick in Algeria by making the French exit seem like a free-willed choice. The French weren't being driven out. It was their decision to leave.

Similarly, in 1984, the Reagan administration withdrew marines from a peacekeeping mission in Lebanon, just a few months after a suicide bomber killed 241 Americans. The White House said the withdrawal had long been in the works. "Even before the latest outbreak of violence, we had been considering ways of re-concentrating our forces and the nature of our support in order to take the initiative away from the terrorists."[76]

A sixth tactic is *plutoing,* or diminishing the value of something to make the loss look more tolerable. For example, we can claim to be retreating (or "re-concentrating our forces") because the broader strategic picture has changed in a positive way. The decline of Al Qaeda's strength in Afghanistan, for example, has *plutoed* the U.S. war effort in the country, reducing its importance for American security.

A seventh idea is *pivoting,* or claiming that extrication from war will refocus American resources on a bigger and more important threat. Obama was able to withdraw from Iraq without looking weak by arguing that the real fight against Al Qaeda was in Afghanistan. In turn, the administration described the departure of U.S. troops from Afghanistan as part of a pivot to address wider regional dangers, as well as a rising China. "As we move to a train-and-advise mission in Afghanistan," said Obama in 2014, "our reduced presence allows us to more effectively address emerging threats in the Middle East and North Africa."[77]

Help the Other Side Look Good

To maneuver out of a failing war, we may need to help the opponent save face. This might seem like an odd suggestion. Why should we aid the other guy? Can't they deal with their own optics?

But put yourself in the counterpart's shoes. They're deeply concerned with their image. They face their own bargainer's dilemma. If the adversary thinks the deal even hints at capitulation, they won't sign on. The enemy leader needs a victory speech to show that the war ended in an honorable way—and we can help them.

The opposing side can overcome the bargainer's dilemma by using the same toolbox described above. They can claim that concessions resulted from objective standards of fairness and law, proposals from neutrals or coalition partners, their allies' weakness, long-established plans, a changed strategic situation, or the need to pivot to a different threat. The Taliban, for example, will require a strong Islamic justification for any peace deal, evidence that the settlement addresses their practical grievances, and no trace of surrender.[78]

We may need to give the adversary a face-saving path. This means avoiding bluster that makes it look like the opponent is retreating before American might. U.S. negotiations with the Soviet Union at the end of the cold war involved plenty of hard bargaining. But Washington also deliberately tried not to complicate Soviet leader Mikhail Gorbachev's life. After the Berlin Wall fell, George H. W. Bush refused to publicly declare a win—to avoid embarrassing his counterpart. Gorbachev appreciated this act of American restraint.[79]

We can also use conciliatory language. During the Iraq War, one of the major opposing factions was the Shiite Mahdi army led by Muqtada al-Sadr. General David Petraeus began describing Sadr as a legitimate figure in Iraqi politics, and even referred to Sadr using the honorific "Seyed," which is a term used for descendants of the Prophet Muhammad.[80] The tactic reaped a dividend. In August 2008, Sadr announced a permanent cease-fire and presented himself as a national leader seeking reconciliation. By contrast, when U.S. officials like Paul Wolfowitz describe the enemy as "Nazis," it makes negotiation difficult or impossible.

Washington can help the opponent frame a loss as a win. The British prime minister Benjamin Disraeli once received a request from a colleague for a noble title. Disraeli was unable to honor the wish, but offered a face-saving formulation. "You know I cannot give you a baronetcy, but you can tell your friends I offered you a baronetcy and that you refused it. That's far better."[81]

The United States can also employ what statesman Dean Acheson called "Humpty Dumpty words," or deliberately vague language. In Lewis Carroll's *Alice's Adventures in Wonderland*, Humpty Dumpty said that when he used a word, "it means just what I choose it to mean, neither more nor less."[82] In delicate negotiations, the United States may choose phrases with maximum ambiguity.

During the Vietnam War, for example, North Vietnam refused to recognize the "puppet regime" in Saigon. In turn, South Vietnam balked at recognizing the Vietcong. To break this impasse, Washington engineered an "our-side, your-side" arrangement for the talks. The makeup of each rival coalition was left purposefully vague. Since the adversaries could interpret the composition of the other side as they saw fit, everyone was willing to sit down.

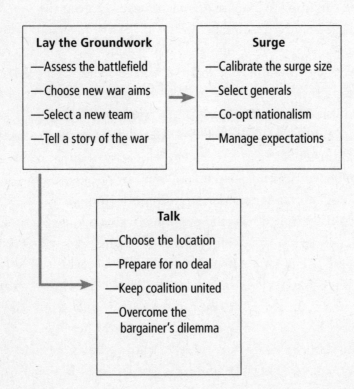

In summary, as the above chart shows, the talk phase should begin in parallel with the surge. The ultimate purpose of negotiating is to reach a deal that allows the United States to withdraw the bulk of its troops. This brings us to the third stage of our exit strategy: leaving.

CHAPTER 8

Leave

In the summer of 2013, I stood at the entrance to the Gaza Strip, the Middle East's political leper colony. Gaza is a rectangular parcel of land lodged between Egypt and Israel, with 1.7 million Palestinians crammed into 140 square miles. The Gazans are impoverished outcasts, ruled by the Islamist group Hamas, and living under an Israeli and Egyptian quarantine.

The Israeli-controlled crossing point of Kerem Shalom sits at the southern edge of the Gaza Strip where Egypt, Israel, and Gaza meet. It's one of the main freight routes into Gaza. With great piles of boxed goods surrounded by concrete blast walls, barbed wire, and drifting observation balloons, Kerem Shalom looks like a cross between IKEA and Guantanamo Bay. The entry point is periodically under attack by Palestinian militants. I nearly stepped in a pothole—which turned out to be a mortar bomb crater. Here, in 2006, Hamas kidnapped the Israeli soldier Gilad Shalit. His release became a cause célèbre in Israel and took five years to negotiate.

Israel has devised an elaborate system to deliver goods into Gaza and avoid contact with the Hamas regime. Essentially, Israelis drop the stuff and run. Several hundred trucks rumble into

A mortar bomb crater at Kerem Shalom (Author's collection)

Kerem Shalom every day, carrying everything from water and food to air conditioners and forty-two-inch flat screen televisions. The contents are first unloaded and inspected by Israeli forces. Then the goods are put onto a second set of vehicles, which transports them a few yards past concrete barriers, where they're unloaded for a second time. Finally, a third set of Palestinian trucks appears and takes the shipment into Gaza. Israel says these elaborate controls are vital for its security. The Palestinians see it as a humiliating siege.

How did we end up here? In 1994, Israel partially withdrew

from Gaza in line with the Oslo Peace Accords. A decade later, in 2005, Ariel Sharon's Israeli government decided to unilaterally remove all Israeli troops and settlers from Gaza—while retaining control (with Egypt) of Gaza's borders, power, and airspace.

Sharon's motives are hotly debated. His supporters depict the move as a bold bid for peace and the first step in a broader strategy of disengaging from Palestinian territory, including most of the West Bank. Critics see a more Machiavellian calculation to reduce international pressure on Israel and strengthen Israel's long-term hold over major settlements in the West Bank. Sharon certainly sold the disengagement to the Israeli right as a hawkish policy—either because it was politically necessary to do so or because he meant what he said.[1] In the end, Sharon's strategy may never be fully understood. He slipped into a coma in 2006 and passed away in 2014.

For many Israelis and Palestinians, the exit from Gaza ended in regret. The withdrawal was a wrenching experience for Israeli society. Around eight thousand Israeli settlers were uprooted. Some of the settlers threatened to set themselves on fire, or symbolically wore the Star of David badge to draw a parallel with Nazi persecution.

The Israeli disengagement didn't end the violence in Gaza. Within weeks of the withdrawal, dozens of rockets were being fired from the territory. In 2006, Israel responded with a large-scale intervention, in which hundreds of Palestinians and a handful of Israelis were killed.

In 2007, Hamas launched a bloody coup that purged its rival Fatah from Gaza. Hamas fighters physically threw a senior Fatah member from the top of the tallest building in Gaza—a fifteen-story apartment complex. Fatah fighters then threw a Hamas militant from a twelve-story building. The Palestinian people were now cleaved into two, with Hamas ruling in Gaza and Fatah governing in the West Bank.

The following years were punctuated by three major Israeli incursions into Gaza to suppress rocket fire: Operation Cast Lead in 2008, Operation Pillar of Defense in 2012, and the longest and bloodiest of all, Operation Protective Edge in 2014. These interventions led to the deaths of dozens of Israelis, as well as over three thousand Palestinians.

Some hoped that the Israeli departure might invigorate the Gazan economy and create a "Dubai on the Mediterranean." But today, youth unemployment in Gaza runs at over 50 percent. The Gazan people survive on goods delivered through a handful of crossing points or smuggled through an elaborate network of illicit tunnels. (A twelve-piece bucket of KFC chicken can be delivered from Egypt to Gaza in four hours at a cost of about $27 via multiple taxi drivers, couriers, and underground traffickers.)

The Black Arrow memorial overlooks Gaza and commemorates the Israeli soldiers who died in raids against Egypt in the 1950s. Here, I asked a colonel from the Israeli Defense Force's southern command about the exit strategy from Gaza. The withdrawal, he said, was the most difficult operation he had been involved in. "We ruined people's lives" — by which he meant the lives of Israeli settlers. As a result, "a terror organization is the government." Hamas chose the path of violence and would now reap the consequences of Israeli firepower. "They had their chance," he said.

The elegant majesty of the King David Hotel in Jerusalem is barely fifty miles away from Gaza but it feels like another universe. The hotel wasn't always an oasis from the fighting. In 1946, when the King David was the British headquarters in Palestine, the militant Zionist Irgun group set off a massive bomb in the hotel that killed ninety people. But as I sipped coffee in the Jaffa Room at the hotel, the Kerem Shalom crossing point may as well have been in Somalia.

Here I met Brigadier General Udi Dekel, the former head of

the Israeli Defense Force's strategic planning division and a former chief of the Israeli negotiating team with the Palestinians. Was the exit strategy from Gaza a success? Yes, he said, in one sense: Almost no Israeli wants to go back to the days of controlling over 1.5 million Palestinians in Gaza.

But the forcible removal of the settlers, and the subsequent Hamas takeover, cast a shadow over the withdrawal. Gilead Sher, a former Israeli negotiator, told me the disengagement was an "excellent strategic decision, lousily managed." There was little dialogue with the settlers. The Israeli government failed to plan for their relocation and compensation. Some of the former settlers are still struggling to find work. And the simultaneous departure of the Israeli military and Israeli civilians created a dangerous security vacuum.

Many Palestinians aren't happy with the withdrawal either. In Ramallah I met with Saeb Erekat, the chief Palestinian negotiator. Erekat is an effervescent performer—the kind of man who laughs heartily and then suddenly turns deadly serious. He earned his PhD in negotiation. "That was my mistake. Now I'm stuck with this job."

What was the lesson of Israel's withdrawal from Gaza? His answer: "Unilateralism fails." In 2005, Israel maintained minimal contact with the Palestinians during the pullout. As Erekat saw it, unilateral withdrawals like Gaza (or the Israeli pullout from southern Lebanon in 2000) triggered more bloodshed, whereas the negotiated Israeli departure from Egyptian territory in the 1970s created stability. An exit strategy needs to be bilateral—a lesson the Israelis should "get through their thick heads."

In the wake of the Gaza withdrawal and a stalled peace process, the Palestinians "don't have a partner." Israel controls all aspects of the Palestinians' lives, down to whether Palestinian Authority president Mahmoud Abbas can take two or three cars

Saeb Erekat explaining to my group the dangers of unilateral Israeli withdrawal. (Author's collection)

into Israel. "Time is running out on me" to negotiate a peace, said Erekat. "I'm looking for my exit strategy."

Mohammed Shtayyeh, the president of the Palestinian Economic Council for Development and Reconstruction, also felt that time was not on the Palestinians' side. The Israeli settlements in the West Bank are growing. And unable to deliver peace, "the authority of the Authority is shrinking." But time may not be working for the Israelis either. The situation is drifting toward a one-state reality, with a minority of Jews governing a majority of Arabs, threatening Israel's existence as a Jewish democracy.

Back at the King David Hotel, Israel's former negotiators said that everyone knows what the political endgame looks like — but we can't get there. This fatalism might be hard for Americans to understand. Tal Becker, the deputy legal advisor for the Israeli

Ministry of Foreign Affairs, told me that Americans are naturally optimistic with a can-do spirit, whereas Israelis tend to be more pessimistic. American movies are upbeat stories with a positive narrative arc. By contrast, Israeli movies are about complex and dysfunctional families—and the audience argues about the meaning of the film on the way home.

The Israelis and Palestinians do agree on one thing: They're not going anywhere. Erekat said the Israelis are "stuck with me as a neighbor." The Israeli guide at Kerem Shalom also told me, "At the end of the movie, we'll still be neighbors."[2]

The Israeli withdrawal from Gaza reveals some of the challenges with the third phase of our exit strategy: *leaving.* This refers to the departure of most U.S. soldiers from the military theater and the shifting of responsibility to local troops, allies, or an international peacekeeping force. Leaving doesn't mean the end of American involvement in the war. A residual force of U.S. troops may remain and Washington can also continue to provide aid and other forms of assistance.

Leaving is a necessary step following a military fiasco. Since the campaign involves limited U.S. interests, we can't justify an endless war effort. Ultimately, we need to wind down the mission and pass the baton over to the local people. The goal is to withdraw while ensuring a smooth handover to a successor regime and continuing to exercise some influence at a reduced cost.

Leaving is a campaign all by itself. "Retrograde," or shipping out the little America of bases, airfields, and fast-food restaurants, is a logistical nightmare—especially under fire. After all, the information age "has not suspended the laws of physics," as H. R. McMaster told me.[3] Equipment must be boxed up, handed over to allies, or destroyed. Exit routes must be plotted. Great convoys must set out for the border. It can take weeks to remove a single brigade from a combat zone. A large-scale presence may take months or years to extricate.

During the endgame in Iraq, the United States shipped out over two million items from ninety-two bases in around twenty thousand truckloads. But Iraq was relatively easy because of an extensive road system and a nearby port in Kuwait. In Afghanistan, the terrain is forbidding and there's no Kuwait next door. The enormous inventory of Humvees, mine-resistant vehicles, Blackhawk helicopters, air conditioners, TGI Fridays, and other flotsam and jetsam of war must be sent by plane, train, and automobile, south through Pakistan or north via the former Soviet Union, in a vast operation costing around $5–7 billion.

Leaving is also a performance. As American soldiers depart, the United States and its opponents compete to control the storyline. Washington must choreograph the optics of withdrawal and avoid a narrative of surrender.

What practical steps can we follow?

Deadline Pressure

After World War I, the British Empire reached its apogee. With territory seized from the collapsed German and Ottoman empires, London controlled almost one quarter of the globe's land surface. But like a distant dying star, the empire's bright luster represented a long lost glory. Weakened by four years of debilitating conflict, Britain governed more territory than it could handle.

One of the newly acquired colonies—or *mandates,* as they were termed—was Iraq. In 1921, Britain installed Faisal I as king of Iraq and hoped to set the country on a path toward stable rule and independence. London created ambitious benchmarks to measure progress toward "a healthy body politic, guided and controlled by healthy public opinion."[4]

Over time, however, there was increasing domestic pressure to withdraw from Iraq, or Quit Mesopotamia, as the campaign

The coronation of Faisal I as king of Iraq in 1921

was known. The British public was weary of committing scarce resources to a backwater in the Middle East. London therefore scaled back its goals and sought indirect control over Iraq through local allies. High Commissioner Henry Dobbs hoped that Iraq "may be able to rub along in a corrupt, inefficient, oriental sort of way."[5] Britain relied on the air force as a punitive tool; the biplane was the drone of its day. In one of his un-finest hours, Winston Churchill suggested dropping mustard gas to "inflict punishment upon recalcitrant natives without inflicting grave injury upon them."[6]

The benchmarks for stabilizing Iraq proved difficult to achieve, and the pressure to leave only grew stronger. London decided to fudge the issue by exaggerating the degree of progress, and then announced a fixed deadline in 1932 for British withdrawal and Iraq's entry into the League of Nations as an independent state.

By setting a firm exit date, London abandoned any hope of creating a modern liberal country. Iraq was left as a quasi state, unable to maintain its territorial integrity or protect domestic order, and dependent on British finance and airplanes. After British forces left, Iraq succumbed to a series of military coups. Finally, in 1941, the Golden Square movement seized power in Baghdad. The new regime espoused virulent nationalism and anti-Semitism and sought an alliance with Hitler. Britain was forced to reoccupy Iraq from 1941 to 1947.

During a power vacuum before British troops reentered Baghdad in 1941, anti-Semitic Iraqis launched a pogrom against the country's Jewish community—which was 130,000 strong and had been present in Babylon for over 2,500 years. In an echo of the European Holocaust, hundreds of Jews were murdered. Over the subsequent years, almost the entire Jewish community left Iraq. By 2008, there were only about half a dozen mostly elderly Jews still in the country—too few to read the Torah in public. Soon there will be none.[7]

London's decision to depart in 1932, come hell or high water, allowed Britain to exit the Iraqi quagmire. But a decade later it was back. This experience suggests a fundamental dilemma for the United States today. How quickly can we withdraw without seeing the entire military campaign crumble into ashes? We want to achieve our goals and get out—but which takes priority? In other words, should the exit be guided by *benchmarks* or *deadlines*?

Benchmarks are tests that must be passed before Washington can exit. Therefore, the timetable for withdrawal depends on the ambition of the aims. Achieving the benchmarks for a *beacon of freedom* will typically mean a prolonged intervention. According to one RAND study, for example, creating an enduring transition to stable democracy usually takes a minimum of five years, "while staying long does not guarantee success, leaving early ensures failure."[8] Add guerrillas to the mix, and the vision of a *beacon of freedom* may recede even further into the distance. A counterinsurgency campaign can take a decade or more to suppress the enemy.[9] By contrast, with more modest goals like a *surgical strike* or *ugly stability,* the benchmarks may be easier to achieve and the timescale could be measured in months rather than years.

Benchmarks have one major attraction: They maximize the chance of achieving our goals. We can verify the degree of progress, make sure the new strategy is proceeding on schedule, and take necessary steps if we fall behind.

But as the British discovered in Iraq, benchmarks can slow or prevent an exit. If they're not achieved, we're looking at an open-ended commitment. It can also be hard to know whether the benchmarks have been accomplished, especially with ambiguous goals like establishing the rule of law or overseeing free and fair elections. Set the bar too high and we stay indefinitely. Set the bar too low and we end up fudging the issue to allow an escape.

Benchmarks are appropriate when the war impacts vital American security needs, and Washington is confident the goals can be achieved. "If you feel that the mission is worthy enough to make the commitment," said Senator William Cohen, "then you shouldn't put a time frame to it."[10] Benchmarks can also work when an operation is inherently open-ended—such as a peace-keeping mission—and the likely costs of staying a little longer than planned are modest.

The alternative option is to withdraw based on a fixed deadline. In other words, we pick a date when the United States will depart—whether or not our goals have been achieved. Setting a deadline has one huge advantage: There's no prolonged quagmire. The United States really will leave, come what may. Our allies on the ground have a window of opportunity to create a better future. If they fall short, we exit stage right.

But deadlines can raise the odds of failure. Time pressure may produce a shoddy job. Deadlines are also rigid and difficult to alter if conditions change. And local spoilers will be tempted to bide their time, knowing that U.S. troops will soon be gone. Setting a deadline means that American soldiers can become an army of lame ducks, constantly looking at their watches.[11]

Deadlines are best if the campaign involves few U.S. interests and there's considerable risk in staying indefinitely. A fixed time horizon may also be necessary if American public support collapses, or if the local regime insists on a quicker exit. Deadlines rarely work if the goal is a *beacon of freedom*. If we're tempted to set an alarm clock on such a grandiose endeavor, it's best to scale down the objectives and shoot for *ugly stability*.

Was it smart to announce a 2014 deadline for the withdrawal of U.S. forces from Afghanistan? During the 2012 election campaign, Vice President Joe Biden said, "We are leaving [Afghanistan] in 2014. Period."[12]

There was logic to the deadline. The war was increasingly unpopular among Americans and allies alike. Stanley McChrystal told me that a fixed date in Afghanistan could provide a "forcing function" and give "impetus" to the local actors.

But according to McChrystal, the 2014 date didn't need to be "so declarative."[13] Once an exit is set in stone, we may stop pushing as hard to achieve our goals—and start *hoping* things are good enough by the time we leave. The fixed timetable was also inflexible. What if hell or high water actually happened—like terrorists threatening to seize Pakistani nuclear weapons? Would we still leave? And crucially, if we had started negotiating with the insurgents earlier, we might have received something in return for an exit date. The Taliban's major goal is the withdrawal of foreign troops. *But we gave away this bargaining chip for free.*

It Is Their War

In 2012, Mahmoud was a twenty-two-year-old Afghan government soldier. Hearing stories of Americans killing Afghans and insulting Muhammad "strengthened my desire to kill Americans with my own fingers." Mahmoud contacted the Taliban and told them about his plan to attack U.S. troops. The insurgents doubted he would follow through. But Mahmoud killed one American and wounded two, before escaping to join the rebels.[14]

Insider strikes by Afghan soldiers and police against U.S. and allied troops—"green-on-blue" attacks—became one of the Taliban's signature moves. "I urge all Afghans who perform duties in the ranks of the enemy," said Mullah Omar in an Eid message, "to turn barrels of their guns against the infidel invaders and their allies instead of martyring their Muslim Afghans."[15] In 2012, fifty-seven coalition troops died in green-on-blue incidents.[16]

Insider attacks reveal some of the challenges with training local soldiers. Creating indigenous security forces is often seen as the ticket out of war. We can leave without losing by equipping local military units and letting them handle the insurgency. Nixon tried Vietnamization, or the expansion and modernization of South Vietnam's military, to the point where we handed out more than one million M16 rifles. Bush pursued what we might call "Iraqization," saying, "As the Iraqis stand up, we will stand down."[17] And today, what could be termed "Afghanization," or the training of four hundred thousand Afghan soldiers and police, is central to America's withdrawal plan. In 2013, Afghan security forces took the lead in providing security across the whole country.[18]

As part of an exit strategy, the logic of training and advising is compelling. American boys shouldn't be doing what South Vietnamese boys—or Iraqi boys or Afghan boys—can do. Handing over responsibility may dramatically reduce America's outlay in blood and treasure. We can pay for fifty or more Afghan troops for the price of a single American service-member (Afghan soldiers cost $10,000 to $20,000 per year, whereas U.S. soldiers cost

$1,000,000 per year).[19] Local troops may have stronger language skills and cultural knowledge. De-Americanizing the war effort also respects local sovereignty and averts the impression of U.S. imperialism. According to the official U.S. counterinsurgency manual, "the host nation doing something tolerably is normally better than us doing it well."[20]

George Casey, the U.S. commander in Iraq from 2004 to 2007, told me that the only responsible exit strategy "is to train indigenous forces to the point where they can maintain domestic order and keep terrorists out." Building up allied capabilities means, "you can look yourself in the mirror and say you gave these guys a fighting chance."[21]

Unfortunately, training and mentoring is not a magic solution in a military fiasco. For one thing, training and advising doesn't always work. North Vietnam's chief negotiator once cut right to the chase. If Washington couldn't win the Vietnam War with half a million Americans soldiers on the ground, "how can you expect to succeed when you let your puppet troops do the fighting?" Kissinger admitted the question "torments me."[22] Vietnamization turned South Vietnam's air force into the fourth largest in the world—and the country still lost the war. Poor leadership and high desertion rates plagued Saigon's military. In 1975, a North Vietnamese assault routed South Vietnam's forces in fifty-five days.

During the early years of the Iraq War, David Petraeus oversaw a crash program to train thousands of Iraqi security forces in the midst of a deteriorating security situation. Petraeus said it was like constructing an aircraft in flight while under fire. The recruits weren't properly vetted. Iraqi soldiers sometimes refused to fight or defected to the insurgency. Shiite troops moonlighted as death squads that targeted Sunnis.[23] A decade later, in the summer of 2014, Iraqi security forces crumbled in the face of the Islamic

State's advance into northern Iraq, and left behind hundreds of millions of dollars of U.S-supplied equipment as spoils of war for the extremists.

Meanwhile, Afghan troops have improved since 2009 and oversaw security for the 2014 elections quite effectively. But many critics predict disaster once American troops depart. "You will fail," said Pakistani general Ashfaq Parvez Kayani. "Then you will leave and that half-trained army will break into militias that will be a problem for Pakistan."[24]

Training and advising is a highly vulnerable process. It can break down for reasons largely beyond our control, such as sectarian tensions, endemic corruption, or the poor quality of available recruits. Some U.S. military capabilities are highly technical and difficult for poor countries to replicate, including intelligence gathering, medical evacuations, and air support. The allied regime also has to *want* to learn and change. But the local government may view a strong army trained by the United States as a threat to its rule more than a national salvation, and seek to "coup-proof" the military through political appointments rather than create an effective fighting force.

Furthermore, green-on-blue attacks, like the one carried out by Mahmoud, can drive a wedge between the United States and the host country, slow the growth of indigenous forces, and imperil combined operations. In 2012, Washington temporarily suspended joint combat missions between Americans and Afghans.

In communal civil wars, training government forces may actually worsen the violence. If the fighting is between ethnic groups and the regime is identified with one particular faction, boosting regime capabilities can throw "gasoline on the fire," in Stephen Biddle's words, and provoke rival factions to step up resistance.[25]

Another problem is that we often get serious about training indigenous forces far too late in the game. The U.S. military traditionally sees advising as a low-status occupation—not something for an ambitious officer to touch. And Washington has also repeatedly failed to devote the necessary resources to training programs.

In Afghanistan after 2001 we decided to rely on local warlords rather than create an effective national military—losing valuable time. In 2006, after five years of limited U.S. and allied training programs, the Afghan National Army numbered fewer than twenty thousand deployable men. The failure to develop capable indigenous forces aided the Taliban's resurgence and produced today's desperate efforts to catch up.[26]

In Iraq, there was overoptimism about the speed with which we could prepare local forces. "The first lesson from Iraq," George Casey told me, "is that everything is going to take longer than you think. People honestly believed we could get all this done in eighteen months."[27] In truth, it would take more like five years.

Given their central importance to America's exit strategy, training and advising programs require an appropriate degree of investment. We should start early. We can't wait until we're already halfway offstage before trying to patch together an indigenous military. We need some of our best men and women on the job—which means improving the career incentives for U.S. officers to become educators.

We should focus on getting the basics right. It's less about teaching allies how to fly F-16s and more about creating infantry units that can fight and resupply at the company and battalion levels (80–1,200 troops). We should prioritize the sharing of intelligence between the United States and indigenous troops. We should create communally mixed forces with significant representation from all ethnic groups.

To minimize the risk of green-on-blue attacks, we must intensify the screening of local security forces. Setting up a system for anonymous reporting of suspicious behavior can flag potential threats. And controlling the supply and distribution of army uniforms makes it harder for infiltrators to strike from within.

Passing the Baton

Next up is a critical issue: planning for the successor regime. The nature of the new government hinges on the war aims. If the goal is a *beacon of freedom,* the bar is set pretty high. The successor regime should be stable and democratic. With *ugly stability* as the objective, we're looking for a workable order based on an accommodation between the regime and insurgents. And in a *surgical strike* operation, we don't particularly care about the makeup of the regime, so long as the specific threat—terrorism, piracy, or humanitarian disaster—doesn't reemerge.

If the fighting is ongoing when U.S. forces withdraw, Washington may leave in place a follow-on force of American troops for a transitional period. This requires negotiating a status of forces agreement (SOFA) to regulate the legal position of U.S. soldiers—covering everything from the use of radio frequencies to the distribution of driver's licenses.

The size of an American successor force will vary greatly depending on the ambition of the objectives, the capacity of the regime, and the extent of the threat. Compared to the main wartime deployment, it will likely include proportionately more trainers and Special Operations Forces and fewer regular soldiers. We may also need to leave in place highly technical capabilities like airpower that the allied regime can't easily replicate.

Obama stated that U.S. forces would remain engaged in Afghanistan after 2014 in "two long-term tasks," which were "very specific and very narrow." The first was "training and assisting Afghan forces," and the second was "targeted counterterrorism missions against Al Qaeda and its affiliates."[28] The follow-on troops would number around ten thousand in early 2015 and then be steadily withdrawn over the subsequent two years.

McChrystal told me that the effectiveness of a successor force in Afghanistan depends on establishing "in clear terms our objectives," or, in other words, "what we're willing to live with." The Afghan security forces can fight, he said. What they need is a "guarantee they have an ally." This doesn't necessarily mean a large number of American troops but instead a "confidence building guarantee."[29]

What if there's a negotiated peace deal when we leave? Here, any settlement requires trust—and also verification. As Ronald Neumann told me, "we talk about agreements in the West as if they mean closure, but agreements in Afghanistan often hold until one side is strong enough to break them. Any deal needs validation and enforcement."[30]

One option is to hand the reins over to an international peacekeeping force. Peacekeeping operations certainly have their share of problems. Participating countries may pursue their own private agendas. And Blue Helmets have limited capabilities. They can handle a small number of spoilers but will struggle against any major opposition.

In recent years, however, peacekeeping has a fairly successful record at preventing civil wars from restarting in places like Bosnia and Kosovo—if, crucially, there's actually a peace to keep and the combatants consent to the arrival of international troops. One of the major barriers to ending a civil war is mutual distrust and the fear that the other side will renege on any deal. A third-party force can help overcome this hurdle by providing security guarantees. It's also easier for armed groups to hand weapons over to a neutral party like the United Nations rather than the hated enemy. In addition, an international peacekeeping force can inject a lot of money into the local economy and offer juicy contracts to keep key players in line.[31]

Different international organizations bring varying assets to the peacekeeping table. The United Nations offers the most legitimacy as well as extensive experience at peacekeeping—but is sometimes hobbled by political gridlock. NATO has the greatest military capability, but its troops are more expensive and it doesn't carry the same degree of legitimacy in much of the world. The European Union is effective in civilian areas like election monitoring and setting up court systems—but it's far less proficient militarily. In some situations, an African Union force may be more politically acceptable than the alternatives, but it's the least capable organization and often depends on rich Western countries to pay the bills.[32]

If a negotiated deal is brokered with the Taliban in Afghanistan, a United Nations peacekeeping force could oversee a new transitional regime, with the troops probably coming from relatively distant Islamic countries.[33]

Prisoner Dilemmas

Francis Dodd may be the most naïve brigadier general in American history. In May 1952, Dodd commanded the POW camp on Koje-do Island in South Korea. One day, the Communist prisoners invited him to visit their compound and discuss their grievances. Dodd graciously agreed, whereupon the prisoners seized him and threatened his safety if their demands were not met.

U.S. general Mark Clark had a suggestion: "Let them keep that dumb son of a bitch Dodd, and then go in and level the place."[34] But the ranking U.S. officer at Koje-do chose a more tactful line. He secured Dodd's release by signing a statement admitting that the United States had committed atrocities, which the Communists then gleefully distributed for propaganda purposes. U.S. reinforcements eventually restored order on Koje-do, but not before bloody clashes killed and injured dozens of POWs and a handful of American soldiers. The prison camps were another front in the war.

In Korea, the fate of captives was a central part of the exit strategy equation. By early 1952, truce negotiations had resolved almost every question, including the borders between North and South Korea. Only one major issue remained: the future of the POWs. The Communists demanded an "all for all" swap of prisoners, in line with the customs of war and the Geneva Conventions.

But U.S. president Harry Truman decided that Communist prisoners must be allowed to defect. There were powerful humanitarian reasons to resist forcible repatriation. Many POWs were South Koreans who had been impressed into service when the Communists marched down the Peninsula. Some of the Chinese POWs claimed to be Nationalists and wanted to go to Taiwan. There was also considerable guilt in the United States over the forcible return of liberated Soviet prisoners back to Stalin's mercies at the end of World War II. Many of these men disappeared into the Gulag archipelago, never to be seen again.

In his diary, Truman suggested that American negotiators take the ethical high road with the Communists. "Read Confucius on morals to them. Read Buddha's code to them. Read the Declaration of Independence to them. Read the French declaration, Liberty & Fraternity. Read the Bill of Rights to them. Read the 5th, 6th, & 7th Chapters of St. Matthew to them."[35]

But Washington's resistance to forcible repatriation wasn't just about morals. The Truman administration also saw the propaganda value of thousands of North Koreans and Chinese preferring to stay in the "free world."

At first, the issue seemed resolvable. The United States thought that around 16,000 of the 132,000 Communist POWs might reject repatriation. North Korea and China hinted they could live with this. The screening process, however, produced a shocking result. Almost half the prisoners refused to be repatriated.

This figure was inflated by systematic violence and coercion. Anti-Communist prisoners controlled many of the prison barracks and ran the repatriation screenings. At one mock screening, the POWs were asked who wanted to return to mainland China. Those who stepped forward were beaten or killed. When they were asked the question again, terrified prisoners kept repeating the same word: "Taiwan."[36]

Communist negotiators were outraged by the idea of half their men defecting to the West. It was now an issue of national honor and ideological prestige. For Truman, there was no going back. "To agree to forced repatriation would be unthinkable," he told the American people. "We will not buy an armistice by turning over human beings for slaughter or slavery."[37] Truman had drawn a line in the sand. Voluntary repatriation was the hill on which American soldiers would die. It was not until Stalin's death in the spring of 1953 that the Communists conceded on the issue of voluntary repatriation, and a neutral commission was created to process the prisoners.

What was the balance sheet from Truman's repatriation policy? On the positive side of the ledger, 22,600 Communist prisoners ultimately chose to defect. (And 23 American POWs decided to stay in the Communist world, producing allegations of brainwashing that inspired the novel and movie *The Manchurian Candidate*.)

On the negative side of the ledger, the single issue of repatriation prolonged the war for an extra fifteen months. During this time, over 100,000 allied troops were killed, including 9,000 Americans, billions of dollars were spent, and every major North Korean city was carpet-bombed, with hundreds of thousands of civilian deaths. Fighting for voluntary repatriation also lengthened the brutal captivity of 3,600 American prisoners.[38]

Truman's hard-line policy on POWs was a trap. He decided on voluntary repatriation without thinking through the consequences and elevated a single ethical principle over a broader calculus about the moral effects of the war. Less high-minded rhetoric, and more dexterous diplomacy, might have produced a compromise.[39]

During the Vietnam War, the fate of prisoners also became a highly emotive issue that overshadowed broader U.S. war aims. In this case, public attention was focused on the five hundred American captives. The families of American prisoners and of those missing in action (POW/MIA) began an unprecedented public campaign to heighten awareness of the men by organizing petitions and setting up public displays of North Vietnamese prison cages. In a grim war, Americans saw the prisoners as sanctified martyrs. For many Americans, the fate of the POWs was more important than the future of South Vietnam.

Nixon encouraged the POW/MIA campaign, partly because of genuine concern for the men and partly as a way to boost support for the war. The White House began talking as if the United States had intervened in Vietnam to rescue the POWs—or "hostages," as Vice President Spiro Agnew described them. Washington would fight, said Nixon, "as long as there is one American prisoner being held prisoner by North Vietnam."[40]

Unfortunately, Washington's fixation on the prisoners weakened its leverage in negotiations by handing North Vietnam a powerful bargaining chip. Hanoi had an obvious solution: Leave and the men will be released.[41]

Captives also loom large in Afghanistan. Kabul and Washington hold hundreds of Taliban prisoners. Meanwhile, in 2009, the Taliban captured their sole American POW, Bowe Bergdahl, who wandered off his base in circumstances that remain mysterious.

One of the insurgency's major objectives is to free their detainees. In a statement announcing the creation of a political office in Qatar, the Taliban "asked for the release of its prisoners from the

American POWs cheer as they return home from North Vietnam in 1973. (U.S. Navy, Department of Defense, National Archives, ARC identifier: 532510)

Guantanamo prison in exchange basis."[42] In 2014, after months of negotiations, Obama announced that a handful of senior Taliban leaders would be transferred from Guantanamo Bay to Qatar in return for Bergdahl.

The trade was politically explosive. Critics alleged that Washington had violated its policy of not negotiating with terrorists. The swap might encourage America's enemies to capture more soldiers. And the former Taliban captives could rejoin the struggle. Was all this worth it to return a soldier who some see as a deserter? John McCain said the swap "poses a great threat to the lives and well-being of American servicemen and women in the future."[43]

The trade may be morally troubling, but this is what ending an unwinnable war looks like. Even if Bergdahl was partly responsible for his own capture, we still needed to try to free him. It's true, of course, that the Taliban have committed many evil acts, including harboring Al Qaeda terrorists. But the State Department does not officially designate the Taliban as a terrorist organization. Rather, they are an organized insurgency and a political faction—and one we've been negotiating with for years. The prisoner exchange could help pave the way for more expansive peace talks down the line. The Taliban's political office in Qatar coordinated the trade, demonstrating that the office does indeed speak for the rebels.

Korea, Vietnam, and Afghanistan all reveal the centrality of prisoners to the conflict endgame. Indeed, the fate of POWs can easily derail an entire exit strategy. The POW issue is emotional and symbolic dynamite and can become bound up with national reputation and honor. Washington should avoid moralistic rhetoric or publicly fixating on captives—and instead use careful and quiet diplomacy to secure a rapid and safe exchange of prisoners.

The Last Rites

When the United States toppled the leftist government of Grenada in 1983, the American public and Congress weren't initially sure what to make of it. Was Grenada really a grave Communist threat that required regime change? During the mission, 19 U.S. troops were killed and 116 were wounded. The UN General Assembly condemned the invasion by a vote of 108 to 9.

And then, for Americans at least, one image changed everything. The media showed pictures of rescued American medical students returning home from Grenada and joyfully kissing American soil. "With that simple gesture," noted the attorney general, "the debate over Grenada was effectively over." Ronald Reagan's press secretary said, "When we saw how happy they were to be home, we started cheering and pounding the table. 'That's it! We won!'"[44]

Grenada shows the power of the final act in shaping the overall story of war. Psychologists have found that people evaluate painful experiences based on how they end and whether they

An American student kisses the ground after being evacuated from Grenada. (Department of Defense, American Forces Information Service, Defense Visual Information Center, National Archives, ARC identifier: 6376109)

improved or not—even marginally. In one experiment, for example, subjects placed their hand in ice water for sixty seconds. (It's quite painful and I wouldn't recommend it.) The subjects then repeated the same experience, but this time followed by an additional thirty seconds of holding their hand in water that was slightly warmed up—but still cold and unpleasant. Interestingly, when the subjects were given the choice of which experiment to repeat (for money), they preferred the second experiment. It may have produced more overall pain, but it got better at the end.[45]

In the same vein, when people judge a military campaign, they don't always assess the overall costs and benefits. Instead, they're strongly influenced by the final act and whether things improved.

The Korean War ended in a symbolically dismal manner. In 1953, the armistice was signed in a specially constructed bamboo-and-wood structure. The negotiators barely registered each other's presence. The London *Times* noted: "There was no pretense at an exchange of courtesies, or even of civility."[46] The armistice allowed twelve hours of further warfare, so the two sides blasted away at each other for another half a day. The *New York Times* reported from the truce site. "Outside the thin wooden walls there was the mutter of artillery fire—a grim reminder that even as the truce was being signed men were still dying on near-by hills."[47]

Among the most searing images of Vietnam are the desperate scenes in 1975 when Americans and South Vietnamese escaped in helicopters from the rooftops of Saigon. (The famous staircase that stood atop the American embassy is now on display at the Gerald R. Ford Museum in Grand Rapids, Michigan.) Ironically, the rescue mission was one of the more successful American undertakings in the Vietnam War. Improvising in tough circumstances, U.S. pilots saved 1,373 Americans and 5,595 Vietnamese.[48] But it looked like the capstone of catastrophe.

We remember the U.S. intervention in Somalia in 1992–94 as a failure in large part because of the closing act. Almost no one recalls the first phase (1992–93), known as Operation Restore Hope, when American troops delivered humanitarian supplies and saved one hundred thousand Somali lives. Instead, people recollect the Black Hawk Down battle in Mogadishu in October 1993, pictures of American corpses being dragged through the streets, and Clinton's decision to effectively cut and run.[49]

In 2004, Paul Bremer's tenure as the chief administrator in Iraq didn't end well. To avoid being blown up by terrorists, Bremer created an elaborate ruse for his departure. He seemed to leave on one aircraft but was secretly whisked by helicopter to a different plane. "This was embarrassing," said one member of the Coalition Provisional Authority. "He left Iraq in such an appropriate way, running out of town."[50]

U.S. policymakers should pay close attention to the optics of the final withdrawal. The last days and hours have an outsized impact on how domestic and international audiences perceive

A helicopter is pushed over the side of the USS Okinawa *to allow more helicopters to land during the evacuation of Saigon in April 1975.* (U.S. Marine Corps)

the war. When the United States withdrew from Iraq in December 2011, Washington wisely chose a low-key approach. There was minimal fanfare or public attention. Coffee shops, bowling alleys, and movie theaters were quietly disassembled. American bases were shut down or handed over to the Iraqis. Armored trucks rumbled back into Kuwait. Where there had once been shock and awe, now there was only a subdued procession of ghosts. It was no triumph—but at least people weren't desperately clambering onto helicopters.

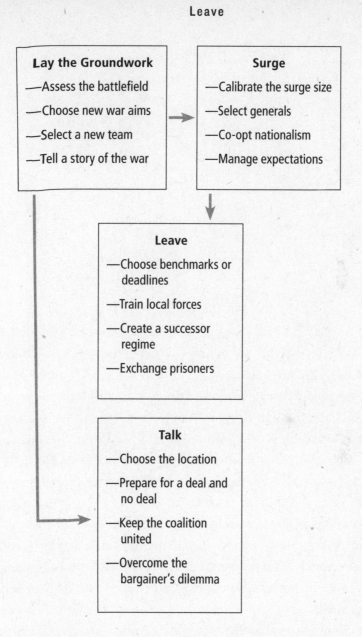

At this point, we have laid the groundwork for the U.S. exit, sent additional surge forces, negotiated with the opponent, and withdrawn the bulk of American troops. Now we must handle the aftermath of a difficult war.

CHAPTER 9

Aftermath

In December 1979, a force of seven hundred elite Soviet soldiers seized control of Kabul. Moscow's target sights were locked on the Afghan president, Hafizullah Amin. He was a Communist— but also an incompetent Communist. Amin couldn't rule effectively. Leftist factions in Afghanistan were at each other's throats. There was a full-blown jihadist insurgency. The USSR decided enough was enough and launched Operation Storm-333.

Amin heard that his palace was under assault but remained confident of survival. The Soviets, he said, would dispatch a rescue mission. Then Amin was told the Soviets were the ones attacking. Moscow's forces overcame stiff resistance and killed the Afghan president. The tempest in Kabul was just the beginning, as one hundred thousand Soviet troops rumbled into Afghanistan from the north.

The United States saw the invasion of Afghanistan as a carefully orchestrated act of Soviet expansion. But there was no master plan. The sclerotic Politburo improvised the whole adventure. Moscow hoped that a quick and decisive show of force would create a stable and friendly regime on the border. Hungary in 1956, Czechoslovakia in 1968, and Afghanistan in 1979: three-for-three.

Washington, however, had a different historical parallel in mind. On the day of the invasion, Zbigniew Brzezinski, Jimmy Carter's national security advisor, told the president, "We now have the opportunity of giving to the USSR its Vietnam War."[1]

Like many countries that invade Afghanistan, the Soviet Union didn't get the war it expected. The alien Soviet presence provoked an antibody response in the form of the mujahideen insurgency. Moscow responded with a brutal campaign of repression. At the first sign of resistance, entire villages were destroyed. Afghanistan became an empire of graveyards.

The mujahideen received aid from a diverse coalition, including China, Pakistan, Saudi Arabia, Osama bin Laden and his legion of Arab fighters, and the United States. Charismatic Texas congressman Charlie Wilson pressed Washington to step up arms supplies to the Afghan rebels, including, most famously, the Stinger ground-to-air missile.

The Soviets were adrift in a war they didn't understand. But one man saw things clearly: Mikhail Gorbachev. In 1985, Gorbachev rose to power in Moscow intent on revitalizing the USSR through economic and political reform. Change at home required suturing what Gorbachev called the "bleeding wound" in Afghanistan.[2] "We have been fighting already for six years," declared Gorbachev at a Politburo meeting in 1986. "If we don't change our approach we will fight for another twenty to thirty years. Are we going to fight forever, knowing that our military can't handle the situation?"[3]

Gorbachev broadly followed a surge, talk, and leave exit strategy. He initially sent reinforcements to buttress the Soviet position. Then he "Afghanized" the war effort by stepping up the training of local forces. And he also pursued peace negotiations with the United States. In 1988, Afghanistan and Pakistan signed the Geneva Accords, with Washington and Moscow as guarantors. The accords laid out a road map for the Red Army's exit by 1989. The withdrawal took only nine months and Moscow's troops left in good order.

Gorbachev tried to tell a positive story about the campaign. Soviet soldiers had achieved their goal of Afghan reconciliation and could leave with their heads held high (the rhetorical tactic of *keeping control*). Gorbachev also deliberately emphasized the role of the United Nations in the withdrawal and portrayed the departure as an effort to revitalize the international organization (a classic example of *leaving from behind*).[4]

Moscow attempted to end the mission on a high note. On February 15, 1989, General Boris Gromov was officially the last Soviet soldier to leave Afghanistan. Under a media glare, Gromov walked across the Friendship Bridge between Afghanistan and the USSR, embraced his young son, and received a bouquet of red carnations. It was all a charade. Gromov had been living on the Soviet side of the border and only traveled to Afghanistan for this moment of theater.

The last Soviet troops leave Afghanistan in a stage-managed exit. (RIA Novosti archive, A. Solomonov, CC-BY-SA 3.0, Wikimedia Commons)

Another Soviet soldier left Afghanistan on February 15. It was the dead body of a paratrooper, carried across the Friendship Bridge in a blanket with little fanfare. He was the last of fourteen thousand official Soviet fatalities in the Afghanistan War (the real figure may be several times as high). The harvest of war also included tens of thousands of wounded Soviet soldiers; hundreds of thousands of sick Soviet troops who succumbed to hepatitis, typhoid, and other illnesses; one million dead Afghans; and five million Afghan refugees.

Charlie Wilson watched Gromov cross the bridge on television, then opened a bottle of Dom Pérignon and toasted the Soviet general: "Here's to you, you motherfucker."[5]

Gromov's red carnations didn't signal the end of Moscow's exit strategy in Afghanistan. Instead, the Red Army's departure triggered a new phase in Soviet-Afghan relations, as Moscow sought cheaper ways to exercise influence. The cornerstone of Gorbachev's policy was the creation of a viable successor regime in Kabul under Afghan president Mohammad Najibullah.

Without Soviet troops, few gave Najibullah much hope for survival. But Moscow's withdrawal removed the glue that bound the insurgency together. No longer seeing red, mujahideen factions turned on each other with a vengeance. Najibullah skillfully exploited these divisions and cut deals with local mujahideen commanders. The Afghan president also tried to broaden the regime's support by downplaying communism, adopting more Islamic customs, and appealing to Afghan nationalism.

To help Najibullah weather the jihadist assault, the Soviet Union left behind huge quantities of ammunition, fuel, and food—topped up by a weekly convoy of six hundred trucks. Backed by Soviet largesse, the Afghan regime proved unexpectedly resilient. Indeed, Najibullah survived longer than the Soviet Union itself. His regime only collapsed in 1992, when Moscow switched off the aid supply.

Najibullah clung on to power, but Afghanistan was left a devastated land with little hope for peace and reconciliation. Two decades later, Afghan hillsides remain littered with rusted Soviet tanks—fossils of a lost dominion.

As Moscow's experience suggests, the aftermath of withdrawal is a critical part of the surge, talk, and leave exit strategy. The aftermath is no mere epilogue to the main drama. Rather, this is the phase when the political effects of war are consolidated, revised, or entirely overthrown. As the bulk of American soldiers leave the war zone, there's still much—and perhaps everything—to play for.

Having endured a difficult conflict, Washington may approach the postwar era with trepidation. After all, the consequences of military failure present a litany of challenges, from uniting the American people to helping veterans recover.

But the aftermath of war is not always a time of triumph for the winner—or further decline for the loser. Battlefield success can sometimes be a curse. It may trigger "victory disease," wherein the winning side sees itself as invincible and pursues ever more ambitious conquests, until disaster ensues. After Japan's early victories in World War II, for example, Tokyo broadened its horizons across East Asia and became dangerously overextended. Alternatively, battlefield success can represent a Pyrrhic victory at such high cost that it amounts to a loss. When the Greek king Pyrrhus defeated the Romans in 280 BC, he sacrificed so many men he said one more victory would ruin him.

America's golden-age triumphs sometimes spurred dangerous long-term consequences. Washington's seizure of territory in the Mexican-American War ultimately deepened sectional divisions in the United States. The capture of the Philippines in the Spanish-American War triggered a bloody counterinsurgency campaign against Filipino nationalists.

Meanwhile, military failure can offer unexpected opportunities for strategic gain. The enemy's ranks may thin as the winning coalition quarrels over the spoils. And the losing side is often more open to innovation. The searing experience of defeat can overcome entrenched interests, spur creativity, and produce badly needed reform. In the end, stalemate and loss may prove to be just as Pyrrhic as victory.

Let's look at four different aspects of the aftermath of tough wars: handling enemies, dealing with allies, healing veterans, and shaping historical memory. The thread that ties them together is a search for national *renewal*. After difficult campaigns, Americans should recover, reflect, and seek to emerge stronger than before.

Making Friends

Nguyen Tan Dung was born in southern Vietnam in 1949. At age twelve, he joined the Vietcong, worked in a medical unit, and was wounded four times. In 1968, not yet twenty years old, Dung served in the Mekong Delta. Fighting on the opposite side in the Mekong Delta at the time was Chuck Hagel, who volunteered for the U.S. Army and won two Purple Hearts.

Half a century later, in 2013, Dung's and Hagel's paths crossed again, this time at a conference on security in Singapore. Dung, the prime minister of Vietnam, and Hagel, the U.S. secretary of defense, exchanged war stories. The Vietnamese Communists who once railed against American imperialism now favored a strong U.S. presence in the region to balance a rising China. The American military that once obliterated much of Vietnam now sought a partnership with its former adversary.

How should the United States handle relations with enemies in the aftermath of loss? One answer is what I call *divide and woo*.

First of all, Washington can exploit fractures in the enemy camp. Indeed, the United States can often foster dissension among adversaries simply by leaving. The Soviet withdrawal from Afghanistan in 1989 triggered divisions among the mujahideen that enabled the Kabul regime to stay in power. In the same vein, the presence of the American military may be the only thing binding the enemy alliance together. The exit of U.S. forces may therefore cause underlying discord to emerge.

During the Vietnam War, the U.S. incursion into Cambodia in 1970 helped forge an alliance between North Vietnam and Cambodia's leftist insurgency, the Khmer Rouge. But after American troops withdrew from Vietnam and the Khmer Rouge seized power in Cambodia, tensions quickly emerged between the Indochina leftists. In 1978, Vietnam invaded Cambodia and toppled the Khmer Rouge regime. The conflict in Cambodia became Vietnam's Vietnam War, a counterinsurgency quagmire that lasted over a decade until Hanoi withdrew in 1989.

A similar story played out with China and Vietnam. One of the major reasons for U.S. intervention in the region was the fear that a Communist Vietnam would become a Chinese pawn. But such alarm betrayed a lack of understanding of East Asian history. Vietnam has resisted Chinese influence for two millennia—a narrative celebrated in Hanoi's National Museum of Vietnamese History. In his book on modern Vietnam, *Shadows and Wind,* Robert Templer wrote that the fear of Chinese domination "has been constant and has crossed every ideological gap, it has created the brittle sense of anxiety and defensiveness about Vietnamese identity."[6] As one Vietnamese historian put it, "China is always just there, and it will always be dangerous."[7]

The American presence in Southeast Asia spurred the very outcome it was designed to avert, an alliance between China and Vietnam. Once American troops left, Communist divisions came to the fore, culminating in China's invasion of Vietnam in 1979. The Vietnamese fought China with equipment inherited from the United States—ironically fulfilling the weaponry's original purpose.

As well as splintering its opponents, the United States can also seek to woo them. Reconciliation with enemies is not always possible. Truly extreme adversaries like Al Qaeda may need to be contained or destroyed. But with most opponents, a modus vivendi or even a durable peace is possible. After all, many of Washington's closest allies were once enemies, like Britain, Mexico, Spain, Italy, Germany, and Japan—not to mention the southern states.

How can enemies become friends? According to political scientist Charles Kupchan, the diplomatic dance begins with a peace offering. Egyptian president Anwar Sadat's dramatic visit to Jerusalem in 1977, for example, catalyzed the reconciliation process between Egypt and Israel. Next, the former opponents make concessions, and political, economic, and cultural contacts start to grow. Finally, the two sides write new narratives to tell a more positive story about their relationship. Instead of holding the other country responsible for every past conflict, the former enemies place the blame on tragic forces like arms races or mutual misunderstandings.[8]

Reconciliation between the United States and Vietnam proved to be a hard road. Flush with victory after 1975, Hanoi bungled the process of rapprochement by demanding billions of dollars in "reparations." Meanwhile, motivated by a mixture of humanitarianism, self-promotion, or material profit, influential Americans propagated the myth that Vietnam was secretly holding U.S. prisoners of war. Finally, in 1995, with the support of Vietnam veterans like John Kerry and John McCain, President Clinton established full diplomatic relations with Hanoi.[9]

In the twenty-first century, the United States and Vietnam may become close allies. Vietnam fears the colossus to the north far more than the distant United States. China's population is fifteen times greater than that of Vietnam, and the two countries have a number of maritime border disputes. The United States has only intervened in Vietnam once: China has invaded Vietnam seventeen times. By the 1990s, according to Templer, the American war in Vietnam "was no longer a central feature of life."[10] Three-quarters of Vietnam's population was born after U.S. soldiers left. And Hanoi has no fear that closer relations will make Vietnam look subservient to Washington. After all, they defeated us.[11]

The emerging strategic partnership between Washington and Hanoi is founded on a shared interest in checking a rising China. But Vietnam is an increasingly influential player in its own right, with the world's thirteenth largest population, a rapidly developing economy, and a location close to the South China Sea—the route for nearly 60 percent of Japan's and Taiwan's energy supplies and about 80 percent of China's crude oil imports.

In 2010, Secretary of State Hillary Clinton visited an ASEAN conference in Vietnam and announced that the United States had a "national interest" in the South China Sea and would participate in multilateral efforts to resolve maritime disputes. The United States and Vietnam began joint naval training exercises for the first time since the Vietnam War.[12]

Tensions remain between Washington and Hanoi over issues like human rights. And both sides are wary of antagonizing China. But the shift in relations is unmistakable. During the 1960s and 1970s, the Vietnam War felt all-consuming. But in the long run, we may see Washington's conflict with Hanoi as a temporary rivalry that disguised a powerful underlying symmetry of interests.

In 2010, the diplomat Richard Holbrooke recalled visiting Vietnam and being struck by the high-rise buildings named after Western corporations. "A subversive, ironic thought crept into my mind: If General Westmoreland, who had died before these dramatic changes became apparent, were to be suddenly brought back to that very spot, he'd look around and say, 'By God, we won.' "[13]

If our enemies can be divided or wooed, how should we deal with our allies?

Sesame Garden

One of the all-time great *New York Times* corrections appeared in 2013. "An earlier version of this article misidentified the 'Sesame Street' character with whom Ryan C. Crocker, the former United States ambassador, was photographed in Kabul. It was Grover, not Cookie Monster."[14]

What was Ambassador Crocker—once labeled by George W. Bush as "America's 'Lawrence of Arabia' "—doing in a photo op with Grover? Crocker told me that the State Department wanted

Ambassador Crocker pictured with Grover from the Afghan version of Sesame Street *in 2011.* (U.S. Department of State)

to see if any American television shows could be adapted for an Afghan audience, especially for Afghan kids. After some research, it turned out that the Afghans loved *Sesame Street*. The State Department helped pay for Dari and Pashto versions of the show, which was called *Sesame Garden* and given an Afghan flavor. The Count character, for example, was cut because Afghan kids hadn't heard of Dracula and couldn't understand the fangs. "The new show turned out to be very popular with Afghan kids," Crocker told me, before stressing *"and their parents."*[15]

Sesame Garden launched in 2011 and symbolized the boom days of the war effort in Afghanistan, when the United States was spending over $100 billion per year. For a while, no expense was too great. Washington tried to win Afghan hearts and minds with a "stealth rock concert" featuring Australian musician Travis Beard, and a fashion show designed for female empowerment. "At one point," said a former embassy aide, "we were throwing money at anything with a pulse and a proposal. It was out of control."[16]

Once U.S. troops began leaving, the party was over. War weariness and donor fatigue set in, and economic aid to Kabul became a much tougher sell. The American narrative focused on getting the boys home, and Afghans began disappearing from the story. The same administration that tripled U.S. troop levels in 2009 began seriously considering a "zero option" for the American presence after 2014.

The White House eventually settled on a successor force of ten thousand. But these soldiers were given a very narrow mission to train Afghans and hunt Al Qaeda—even though Al Qaeda barely exists in the country. (In November 2014, Obama bowed to military reality by announcing that the successor force could also fight the Taliban, which very much does exist.)

The American successor force will be steadily withdrawn by 2016. Why is this date significant? The answer is not strategic but political: the end of the Obama presidency. The proposed timeline will enable Obama to say he concluded the war before leaving office. However, it may be better for a few thousand troops to stay and train Afghans beyond 2016—even if it complicates Obama's narrative. In early 2015, Afghan president Ashraf Ghani said that the withdrawal date may need to be reexamined: "Deadlines should not be dogmas."[17]

Iraq offers a similar story of declining attention. As long as U.S. soldiers were fighting and dying in Iraq, Washington concentrated intensely on the country. During the surge phase, Iraq was the Bush administration's top foreign policy issue. In the early months of the Obama administration, the White House continued to prioritize Iraq. Vice President Joe Biden visited Baghdad seven times from 2009 to 2011 and built close relationships with Iraqi leaders. According to one U.S. general, Biden came so frequently he was eligible for Iraqi citizenship.

But when American forces left Iraq in 2011, the country slipped down the White House agenda. The period from 2010 to 2014 was a critical phase in Iraqi politics as the violence worsened dramatically and the gains made during the surge were put at risk. Fighting in Syria seeped into northern Iraq, first in a drip feed of refugees and rebels, and then in a torrent of Islamic State extremists. Meanwhile, efforts to craft a power-sharing deal in Baghdad fell apart, as Prime Minister Maliki pursued a highly sectarian agenda that marginalized Sunnis.

The White House thought the war was over and focused on other issues. From 2011 through early 2015, Biden didn't visit Iraq. The administration refused to publicly criticize the Iraqi leader. Political commentator Peter Beinart summed up Obama's policy: "Let Maliki do whatever he wants so long as he keeps Iraq off the front page."[18] A Sunni tribal leader asked, "Where are the Americans? They abandoned us."[19]

As these experiences in Afghanistan and Iraq reveal, the United States can act in wartime like a capricious paramour whose interest in the fate of its partner lurches from obsession to neglect. During the escalation phase, we may seek to transform our ally into a dream companion, by writing blank checks for a massive and even disproportionate war effort. But when American soldiers depart, our interest in the ally's fate dissipates like a fading romance. We look at our watches desperate to leave. We become almost narcissistic, overwhelmingly concerned with getting U.S. troops home. The locals are now objects that we maneuver around to withdraw. We start nickel-and-diming the mission. Congress would rather spend $100 billion funding American troops than $10 billion paying for indigenous soldiers. *It's not our problem anymore.*

We need to replace these dramatic swings in American attention with a smoother arc of intervention. This means fighting for less expansive goals early on and pursuing an enduring strategic partnership later on. After all, withdrawal is about removing the bulk of U.S. troops, not abjuring responsibility.

What should our relationship with allies look like in the aftermath of war? Of course, if most U.S. soldiers leave the war zone, our leverage is much reduced. We couldn't force Baghdad to reconcile with Sunni opponents when 150,000 American troops occupied Iraq, and we can't impose a settlement with almost zero boots on the ground. Still, we can at least avoid switching off attention. And as opportunities arise, we can use our influence to encourage political compromise and the creation of effective and nonsectarian institutions.[20]

One of our key tools is economic and military aid. The international community, for example, has made a number of commitments to Afghanistan. At Chicago in 2012, NATO countries pledged to help Kabul pay the estimated $4.1 billion annual cost of the Afghan National Security Forces. And at Tokyo in 2012, the United States and its allies pledged $16 billion in civilian aid over four years.

Is it smart to continue channeling assistance to Kabul? Money for development projects can end up enriching a local elite, spurring more corruption, or lining the pockets of Western expatriates—just look at the fleets of Land Rovers in Kabul. Over the last decade, Western governments and private philanthropists have poured tens of billions of dollars into Afghanistan but the country remains one of the five or so poorest states in the world.

You can count former assistant secretary of state John Hillen among the critics. "So much of it is a waste," he told me. "We didn't even put the Buddhas back together." In 2001, the Taliban spent weeks systematically destroying the huge carved Buddhas of Bamiyan using dynamite, artillery, anti-aircraft guns, and anti-tank mines. After a decade of talk about rebuilding the statues, the reconstruction project has barely got off the ground. For Hillen, it's a symbolic failure: The return on investment from most aid programs is unimpressive.[21]

Dov Zakheim worked as the Pentagon's coordinator for civilian reconstruction in Afghanistan during the Bush administration. Much of the foreign aid effort, he told me, was woefully mismanaged. "We know it's stupid," but we keep spending big on complex systems that can't be maintained and end up rotting.[22] The Kajaki Dam in Helmand Province is the dam to nowhere. An ambitious project to rebuild the turbines was designed to win hearts and minds in the Taliban homeland. But the enterprise is years behind schedule due to mismanagement and insurgent attacks.[23]

Economic aid, however, can play an important role after American troops leave. Although Afghanistan remains one of the most impoverished countries, the last decade has seen a major improvement in the health and education of ordinary Afghans.[24] Rather than waste money on big-name projects, we should think small. Carter Malkasian, an advisor to the U.S. military on counterinsurgency, described the National Solidarity Program as "the crown jewel of development in Afghanistan."[25] The program gives relatively modest grants to local village councils to create schools and other infrastructure. We can also step up aid for Afghan agriculture. Most Afghan men of working age are small-scale farmers. They need high-quality seeds and agricultural equipment, advice on yields, and new roads. In all these cases, we should carefully evaluate the efficacy of programs and monitor contracts to reduce corruption.[26]

In the long run, the answer is trade rather than aid. At the moment, Afghanistan's biggest export is illegal opium. Indeed, opium production reached a record high in 2013. There are many challenges in extricating the United States from the Afghanistan War, but the most Sisyphean is trying to end opium production. Eradication programs run headlong into market forces; poppies produce far more revenue than other crops like wheat. Fighting a drug war while simultaneously fighting the Taliban is a fool's errand, which will only serve to lose the support of rural Afghans.

Reducing opium production will take decades of development. We should encourage international investment in Afghanistan and lift trade barriers for Afghan goods to enter the U.S. market. Stepping up U.S. imports of Afghan pomegranates and pistachios might do more good than simply opening the American checkbook. The economic future of Afghanistan could hinge on exploiting the one trillion dollars or more of natural resources in the country, including gold, copper, lithium, coal, gemstones, oil, and gas.

What about military aid? As we saw with Najibullah's fate after 1989, military assistance can have a big impact on regime survival in a country like Afghanistan. We need clarity about U.S. commitments in Afghanistan until the end of the decade. In a counterinsurgency war, uncertainty about foreign support can be deadly because it saps confidence. This means building on the pledges made at Chicago and guaranteeing funding for the Afghan army for at least the next five years. The Taliban today are weaker than the Soviet-era mujahideen. If we pay for the Afghan army, Kabul can probably hold most of the country. But Kabul's own revenues can only sustain a small fraction of the Afghan security forces. If funding is slashed, the Afghan army may wither on the vine and the country could descend into chaos—shifting the entire war effort from stalemate to defeat.[27]

Homeward Bound

War changes people. In 2010, the British photographer Lalage Snow spent eight months taking portraits of British soldiers before, during, and after their deployments in Afghanistan. In a project called We Are The Not Dead, these portraits formed striking triptychs that captured a grueling tour of duty. Men's and women's faces became toughened, gaunt, and worn by the hot sun. The secret is in their eyes: sometimes lost, sometimes fixed and intense.[28]

Handling the aftermath of war requires dealing with the psychological as well as the physical wreckage of conflict. It means caring for veterans, or "for him who shall have borne the battle and for his widow and his orphan," as Lincoln put it in his second inaugural address.[29] Helping returning soldiers is an essential part of the surge, talk, and leave exit strategy. It's the moral thing to do—and it's also good policy. A veteran's struggle to readjust to the home front can ripple outward into the lives of friends and family. Positive treatment of veterans can also help manage the narrative of war and soften the impression of complete failure.

Most of the nation's 22 million veterans (including more than 2.5 million men and women who served in Iraq, Afghanistan, and other battlefields in the war on terror) reacclimatized successfully to civilian life. But many veterans face a painful struggle, which psychiatrist Jonathan Shay compared to Odysseus's journey home after the Trojan War.[30] Male veterans, for example, are about twice as likely to die of suicide as their civilian counterparts.[31]

Veterans from dark-age wars may encounter particular challenges in returning home. The U.S. military was not configured for prolonged counterinsurgency campaigns in Afghanistan and Iraq. The result was extended deployments, multiple tours, and shorter rest periods. Soldiers had to deal with mass graves, improvised explosive devices, and pulling their injured buddies out of Humvees.[32]

In recent wars, veterans have rarely enjoyed the solace of victory. After a military fiasco, it may be more difficult to readjust to civilian life because the public sees the war as a mistake. *What did I fight for?*

And veterans from dark-age wars can also feel isolated. Wars of national survival mobilize the whole population. In World War II, about 9 percent of Americans were on active military duty at any one time. But the figure for Afghanistan and Iraq is less than 1 percent. The vast majority of Americans haven't served and can't fully relate to the veterans' experiences.

Chris Kyle was one of America's top snipers in Iraq, with 160 confirmed kills. The Iraqi insurgents called him the Devil of Ramadi. In 2013, Kyle took a fellow Iraq War veteran, Eddie Ray Routh, to a gun range in Texas to help him deal with symptoms associated with post-traumatic stress disorder (PTSD). Kyle was shot dead and Routh later confessed to the killing. Routh's dad said the Iraq War changed his son: "When he gets back I ain't got my son no more. I got a body that looks like my son."[33]

PTSD is the signature affliction of the dark age of American warfare (along with traumatic brain injury). It's an anxiety disorder caused by traumatic events involving injury or death. Symptoms may include sleep deprivation, flashbacks, withdrawal from emotional attachment, diminished trust in others, a sense of purposelessness, and hypervigilance. PTSD can impair work prospects, destroy relationships, and raise the risk of alcohol or drug abuse and suicide.[34]

PTSD is probably as old as war itself. It used to go by many names: combat stress, shell shock, soldier's heart, or battle fatigue. In 1980, the American Psychiatric Association formally recognized PTSD as a disorder. According to RAND, 14 percent of Afghanistan and Iraq War veterans suffered from PTSD (other estimates range from 5 to 15 percent).[35]

The disorder symbolizes America's struggles in the new era of civil wars. Just as counterinsurgency is a battle against an enemy we can't see, so PTSD is a fight to overcome invisible wounds: a shadow illness for a shadow war.

As a country, we're failing to deal with the problem of PTSD. There's a gap between our bumper-sticker "support the troops" mentality and our willingness to face up to the true price of war. RAND found that "the majority of individuals with a need for services had not received minimally adequate care."[36]

Veterans may be reluctant to seek help for mental health issues, for example, because of fears about confidentiality. Other problems lie with health care provision. The Veterans Affairs medical system, a vast network of 171 medical centers and 350 clinics, does a great deal of good work. In larger metropolitan areas, the VA is at the forefront of treatment for PTSD. But the VA system has come under strain from recent wars. Around fifty thousand Americans were wounded in Iraq and Afghanistan but the VA has treated over two hundred thousand people for PTSD. The VA is also famously slow and bureaucratic in deciding whether to cover a particular claim. And the quality of treatment is inconsistent. Routh, for example, didn't receive appropriate care in the weeks before he shot Kyle. In May 2014, Eric Shinseki, the secretary of the Department of Veterans Affairs, resigned following a scandal over chronic waiting times at VA hospitals.

There are no easy answers. PTSD is a complex condition that depends on an individual's psychological makeup and experiences. Each soldier needs a personal exit strategy from war. Several treatments have proven to be consistently effective. Exposure therapy, for example, habituates veterans to the experience of trauma by recounting past events in great detail, helping to adjust people's emotional response. Meanwhile, cognitive processing therapy enables veterans to become more aware of their thoughts and feelings, which reduces cognitive errors (like the belief that all people are essentially evil) and encourages a more balanced view of the world.[37] According to psychiatrist Matthew Friedman, with these evidence-based practices, "complete remission can be achieved in 30–50 percent of cases of PTSD, and partial improvement can be expected with most patients."[38]

We need an increased number of trained mental health professionals to provide these treatments in a timely and effective manner. Therapy is expensive but it quickly pays for itself through improved productivity and a reduced risk of suicide and other problems.

We must also enhance funding for wider kinds of distress. PTSD has captured the national limelight, but other psychological problems are also part of the wreckage of war. Depression, for example, affects 2–10 percent of returning veterans. Indeed, the focus on PTSD means that some veterans end up being misdiagnosed and given the wrong treatment.[39]

By definition, veterans are the lucky ones: the not dead. But some of them return from the darkness, not to a civilian light, but into a kind of twilight world, still bearing the visible and invisible wounds of war. Many soldiers feel isolated after severing the deep bond they had with their buddies and their unit. As David Finkel wrote in his book *Thank You for Your Service,* "It is such a lonely life, this life afterward."[40] Much of the healing comes from the fellowship of other veterans—from those who really understand and can help find new ways of contributing to society. "Recovery happens only in community," Jonathan Shay wrote of the veteran's odyssey.[41]

That July Afternoon

"For every Southern boy fourteen years old," wrote William Faulkner, "not once but whenever he wants it, there is the instant when it's still not yet two o'clock on that July afternoon in 1863."[42] The moments before Major General George Pickett's futile charge on Union lines at Gettysburg, when Confederate victory was still possible, are seared into Southern memory and folklore.

The century from 1846 to 1945 was the golden age of American warfare—but this wasn't true for all Americans. Southerners knew the meaning of loss. In 1865, the Confederacy was a devastated land. The entire slave society had collapsed. Half the Southern white men of military age were dead or maimed.

As Southerners tried to make sense of this cataclysm, they discovered the trauma of remembrance. For decades, Southerners found that historical loss has a wounding presentness. One of Faulkner's characters says in *Requiem for a Nun,* "The past is never dead. It's not even past."[43] After the initial shock of defeat subsided, the unbearable question remained: Why had this catastrophe been inflicted on God's people?

After 1945, the experience of loss became a national, rather than just a regional, phenomenon. Now all Americans were forced to sift through the ashes of failure and deal with painful memories of military fiascos. For a democracy like the United States, the recollection of past debacles cuts particularly close to the bone. We can't write off battlefield loss as the folly of a misguided Caesar. The fault is in ourselves.

Yesterday's war is a story we tell each other. Through speeches, books, films, and memorials, we assemble, disassemble, reassemble, and dissemble history. Narratives of conflict are constantly in flux as new information emerges, and we view old facts in the light of present-day concerns.[44]

Our collective memory of war is critical because it shapes the lessons we draw for future policy. And how we recall military *loss* is especially important because we usually learn much more from past failures than from successes. Psychologists have identified a "negativity bias" in the human mind where "bad is stronger than good." According to psychologist Roy Baumeister and colleagues, "bad things will produce larger, more consistent, more multifaceted, or more lasting effects than good things."[45] People process memories of failure in more complex ways than memories of success and reflect more carefully on the causes of negative events. "Prosperity is easily received as our due, and few questions are asked concerning its cause or author," observed philosopher David Hume. "On the other hand, every disastrous accident alarms us, and sets us on enquiries concerning the principles whence it arose."[46]

The experience of military loss is often burned into a nation's consciousness. One of the major cultural touchstones for Serbs today is their defeat in the battle of Kosovo—even though it happened in 1389. Meanwhile, the foundational event in modern German and Japanese identity is the Götterdämmerung of 1945.

How should we recall difficult wars? In the wake of battlefield failure, the United States can fall prey to a kind of national posttraumatic stress disorder, with significant impairment to functioning. Americans may adopt unhealthy forms of remembrance, including amnesia, phobia, and dangerous myths—and sometimes all three maladies at the same time.

The first hazard is *amnesia,* when we repress memories of loss and fail to learn the tough lessons about war. We sign on to a national pact of forgetting. Following an intense focus on violence and bloodshed, people often want to think about anything other than the conflict. It's precisely because failure looms so large in our minds that we try to avoid painful memories.

Korea is often called the "forgotten war"—although it's not clear if Americans ever really understood what the conflict was about. Journalist David Halberstam said that Americans "preferred to know as little as possible" about the campaign.[47] The complex nature of the struggle as both a superpower proxy conflict and a civil war between Koreans, the attritional fighting, and Washington's decision not to strive for victory proved confusing for a generation of Americans used to winning decisive good-versus-evil contests. "The Korean War, more than any other war in modern times," wrote historian Bruce Cumings, "is surrounded by residues and slippages of memory.... There is less a presence than an absence."[48]

Many Americans also preferred to forget about the Vietnam War. After the fall of Saigon, President Ford urged his fellow citizens to avoid "refighting a war that is finished—as far as America is concerned."[49] Henry Kissinger, the secretary of state, said, "We should never have been there at all. But it's history."[50] According to journalist Martha Gellhorn, "consensual amnesia was the American reaction, an almost instant reaction, to the Vietnam War."[51]

The U.S. military tried especially hard to put Vietnam out of its mind. Chasing the Vietcong was a terrible mistake never to be repeated. Rather than institutionalize the hard-won lessons of guerrilla war, the U.S. Army destroyed all the material on counterinsurgency held at the special warfare school at Fort Bragg. As a result, the military was unprepared for stabilizing Afghanistan and Iraq.[52]

The Iraq War also slipped from memory. In 2013, the ten-year anniversary of the beginning of the conflict was greeted mainly by silence. Obama rose to the presidency in large part because of his opposition to the Iraq War. But he marked the anniversary by issuing a brief 275-word statement, of which 240 words praised American veterans and a total of 35 words were about Iraq and the Iraqi people.[53]

Afghanistan is already being labeled a "forgotten war." Many Americans have mentally checked out. Tough questions are being ignored. Will we leave behind a deeply dysfunctional state? Is the best outcome a military stalemate or a deal with those who once harbored Al Qaeda? What does the deterioration of the war effort say about the future of American global leadership?

Amnesia can be a useful coping strategy. Nietzsche said that forgetting allows us "to close the doors and windows of consciousness for a time." Putting events out of our mind is "like a doorkeeper, a preserver of psychic order, repose, and etiquette."[54]

But expunging a negative experience of American conflict is not a long-term solution. We need to reckon with the bleak side of our nation's past. Otherwise, we will repeat our mistakes.

The second risk is *phobia,* where we fixate on past events and try to avoid copying the experience at all costs. Traumatic occurrences can burn a "never again" syndrome into the national psyche. This is the opposite response to amnesia: hyperlearning rather than forgetting.

Phobia can produce a knee-jerk opposition to anything resembling the painful experience. Mark Twain said of a cat that sits on a hot stove top, "She will never sit down on a hot stove-lid again—and that is well; but also she will never sit down on a cold one anymore."[55]

Having been burned once in war, the United States may refuse to engage in any similar experience—even if it's necessary to protect our interests and values. We may also see everything associated with the bad war as tainted, when some aspects of the campaign were actually quite successful and should be copied.

A phobia means we won't make the same mistake; instead, we could make the opposite mistake. During the humanitarian intervention in Somalia in 1992–94, forty-three Americans died. It was a fairly minor tally by historical standards. And the overall mission succeeded in saving tens of thousands of Somali lives. But for many Americans, Somalia encouraged a phobia about humanitarian intervention. Memories of Somalia were a critical reason why the United States failed to stop the Rwandan genocide in 1994. The ghosts of Mogadishu ensured the rescuer was nowhere in sight.[56]

Today, Americans are desperate to avoid a repeat of the scarring experience in Iraq and Afghanistan. The dictate "no more Iraqs and Afghanistans" has shaped almost every aspect of Obama's foreign policy, from the narrative of extrication from Middle Eastern wars to the "pivot" to the Pacific; from the preference for multilateralism in conflicts like Libya in 2011 to the repugnance for nation-building.

The desire not to copy past errors could spur a healthy concern about wading into foreign civil wars. But the siren song of "not Iraq" could also lead the United States into a damaging retreat from global leadership. The scholar Lawrence Freedman described the Iraq syndrome as a "renewed, nagging and sometimes paralyzing belief that any large-scale U.S. military intervention abroad is doomed to practical failure and moral iniquity."[57]

If we have a phobic reaction to bad wars, why does the United States end up repeating the experience—like counterinsurgency in Vietnam, Afghanistan, and Iraq? Psychological dread can actually trigger a recurrence of the negative events. The George W. Bush administration was extremely hostile to prolonged Vietnam-style nation-building and invaded Iraq with a small footprint designed to allow a speedy exit. But the lack of American troops produced chronic insecurity and exactly the kind of drawn-out quagmire that Bush sought to avoid.

The third harmful memory of loss is *dangerous myths,* where we learn pernicious lessons about the past. After the American Civil War, Southerners embraced the myth of the "Lost Cause" to make sense of their catastrophic defeat. According to this legend, the South won a moral victory through superior gallantry, heroism, and skill, but was ultimately ground down by greater numbers, industrial might, and brutal warfare. Although the South deserved to win, so the myth goes, its defeat was ultimately for the good of mankind.

The Lost Cause narrative helped reconcile the South to defeat and reunion. "*Because* I love the South," said Woodrow Wilson in 1880, "I rejoice in the failure of the Confederacy."[58] But the story of national rapprochement excluded blacks. The Lost Cause was a white man's tale. Memories of the Civil War highlighted glory and sacrifice rather than emancipation and race. Black human rights became another lost cause as a new apartheid system emerged in the Southern states. In 1913, during the fiftieth anniversary of Gettysburg, white Union and Confederate veterans joined hands in friendship, but black veterans were not allowed to participate.

Another dangerous myth is the "stab in the back"—or blaming domestic opponents for the military loss. Following the fall of Saigon, Nixon held liberals, Congress, and the media responsible for snatching defeat from the jaws of victory. Scapegoating the enemy within deepened the social divisions from the war.[59]

The answer is not amnesia, phobia, or dangerous myths; it's *renewal.* Americans should craft a narrative of the past that confronts the hard truths of war while ultimately helping the country come to terms with its experience.

After all, failure is a priceless opportunity to learn and adapt. People, institutions, and countries are often averse to change. To

White Northern and Southern veterans reconcile in 1913 during the 50th anniversary of Gettysburg. (Library of Congress, LC-DIG-ppmsca-32660)

alter the system, you need a shock to the system—and the most powerful shock is losing.

In the 1980s, sportswriter Bill James found that baseball teams that improved in one year tended to decline in subsequent years, whereas teams that did poorly often made a comeback. Failing sides were more willing to innovate. "There develop over time separate and unequal strategies adopted by winners and losers; the balance of those strategies favors the losers, and thus serves constantly to narrow the difference between the two."[60]

In the same vein, winners in war may succumb to enervation and complacency, whereas losers are more open to creative thinking. The experience of stalemate or defeat can overcome vested interests and produce necessary change. During the decades after World War I, for example, the victorious powers of Britain and France believed that the next war would be much like the last and developed a defensive doctrine based on fortifications like the ill-fated Maginot Line. By contrast, the losing country, Germany, embraced reform. Berlin engaged in a root-and-branch critique of its failure in the Great War and ultimately developed a new doctrine of armored warfare known as blitzkrieg.

Winning sports teams accept their losses and study the game tapes to avoid a repeat performance. We should approach past failure with a similar spirit of confidence and humility. This means not gilding the war effort, but instead taking responsibility for our actions, including war crimes and other abuses. It means identifying the things we got right—even if the overall campaign was a failure. And it means accepting the complexity of past wars, the context-specific nature of historical "lessons," and the danger of simplistic instruction.

In the next chapter, we'll look more closely at Korea, Vietnam, Iraq, and Afghanistan as teachable moments and discover how to start winning wars again. But before we do that, let's take a step back and summarize what we've learned so far.

Surge, Talk, and Leave

We live in the dark age of American warfare when most major conflicts end in regret. After 1945, the collision between U.S. power and a changed battlefield environment triggered seven decades of stalemate and loss. The nation's newfound strength encouraged an interventionist impulse, just as the locus of conflict shifted from interstate war to civil war, throwing the U.S. military off balance.

The United States began battling in distant lands against culturally alien foes it didn't understand. And the enemy usually had much more at stake in the fight. Washington was stuck using a golden-age playbook of conventional warfare and failed to adapt to the new era of counterinsurgency. By contrast, guerrillas raised their game by seizing the banner of nationalism, adapting to American weaknesses, and seeking outside sources of support. As a result, U.S. wars repeatedly degenerated into fiascos, or unwinnable conflicts where victory was no longer realistic.

Time and again, in the face of battlefield loss, the United States miscalculated and made a poor situation even worse. Sometimes we waded further into the mire like in Vietnam. In other conflicts, we tried to exit too hastily like in Iraq. We failed to revise our war aims effectively. We waited too long to talk to the adversary and then adopted an intransigent stance in negotiations. As the U.S. war effort peaked and declined, we tended to lurch from an obsessive concern with the ally's fate to a narcissistic focus on getting Americans home. Presidents were not always candid with Congress or the American people, deepening divisions on the home front.

What's the answer? First of all, we must realize that the outcome of war is not a binary like victory or defeat—where only victory is tolerable. Instead, the result lies on a spectrum with many gradations of success and failure. Achieving a draw rather than a catastrophic loss may be a profile in courage that saves thousands of American and allied lives.

When a war becomes unwinnable, we need an exit strategy rather than exit tactics. We must step back, assess the terrain, and craft a long-term plan, rather than putting out fires one by one. The exit strategy should be surge, talk, and leave. Washington sends additional forces, negotiates with the adversary, and then withdraws the bulk of American troops. The surge averts immediate battlefield disaster and helps the United States achieve a revised set of goals. Diplomacy delivers a tolerable negotiated deal. And U.S. forces leave with a clear plan for the political succession. Then, in the aftermath of war, we divide and woo adversaries, optimize the level of aid to allies, heal veterans, and foster national renewal.

Meanwhile, the president should tell a story of the war to rally support at home and abroad. The White House must keep expectations in check, pay attention to the symbolism of peace talks, overcome the bargainer's dilemma, manage the optics of the final act, and shape the way we remember and learn from war.

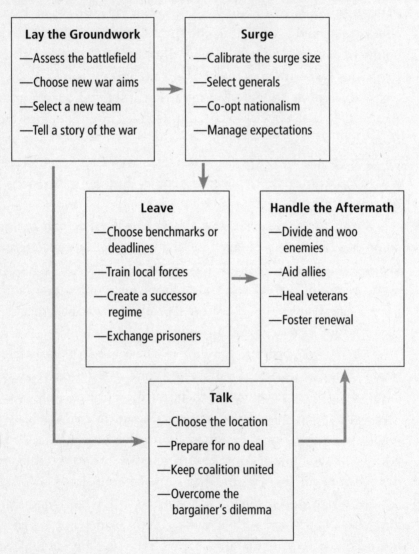

Surge, talk, and leave creates a bell curve of U.S. troop strength that rises and declines. The shape of the curve will vary greatly depending on the overall objectives. If the United States pursues limited *surgical strike* aims, the arc may feature a relatively small surge and a quick withdrawal. By contrast, if Washington seeks to build a *beacon of freedom,* the curve may show a significant escalation followed by a slow drawdown of troops over many years.

Other dynamics can also shape the curve. If the United States faces a severe immediate crisis but pursues restricted goals, there could be a sharp increase in troop levels followed by a rapid decrease. Alternatively, if the battlefield crisis is contained, but training local soldiers will be time consuming, the curve may be flatter and longer, with a smaller expansion of force strength and a more prolonged withdrawal.[61]

The different elements of the surge, talk, and leave exit strategy are designed to be mutually reinforcing. First, a military fiasco implies that Washington has too few capabilities to achieve its objectives. Dialing down the goals and surging the resources can bring the ends and means into alignment—which is necessary for a successful strategy. During the surge phase in Iraq, for example, Washington scaled down its aims to "sustainable stability" and boosted U.S. troop levels, producing a much closer match between the aims and the capabilities.

Second, the surge can help the United States talk more effectively to the enemy. By eroding the opponent's military strength, we may make gains at the diplomatic table. U.S. reinforcements can also boost America's no-deal world and weaken the enemy's no-deal world, thereby improving our bargaining leverage. And new soldiers can protect rebels who want to defect.

Third, the surge can aid the process of leaving by facilitating efforts to train and advise indigenous forces. These programs often require large numbers of American soldiers to live and work with local allies. As part of the surge in Iraq, for example, Washington significantly expanded its training programs for Iraqi army and police forces.[62]

There are potential vulnerabilities, however, with surge, talk, and leave. For one thing, the act of leaving may undermine the narrative of the campaign. The answer is to tell a story that moderates expectations, solves the bargainer's dilemma, and controls the symbolism of the final acts.

Unless we're careful, the process of leaving can also diminish the chance of successful talks. If American troops are heading home anyway, why will the opponent bargain? In 1969, American diplomat Henry Cabot Lodge wrote, "To be in a hurry when your opponent is not puts one in a very weak negotiating position."[63]

It all depends on *how* we leave. Training indigenous forces can improve our no-deal world, and therefore our negotiating leverage. And the act of withdrawing can itself be a powerful bargaining chip. The speed of the drawdown and the size of any successor force are all potentially on the table for discussion in peace talks. This is one reason why it's best to start negotiating with the enemy in parallel with the surge and before a fixed deadline for withdrawal is set.

The surge, talk, and leave exit strategy should be implemented immediately after a fiasco. But what happens if the United States fails to act and the situation gets even worse? Presidents may inherit a war that became a fiasco long before, like Eisenhower in 1953, Nixon in 1969, or Obama in 2009. What happens now?

Just like getting sick and failing to receive appropriate medical attention, waiting too long to address a fiasco complicates the response. There could be further deterioration on the battlefield, more American casualties, deepening domestic division, and additional alliance strains. We may therefore have to adjust the surge, talk, and leave exit strategy and look at starker options of damage limitation. At some point, a surge of American troops may no longer be feasible. By 1969, when Nixon came to power, the time for U.S. reinforcements in Vietnam had long since passed. The onus was now on talking and leaving.

We should also alter the surge, talk, and leave exit strategy mid-course because of changes in the military, political, and economic environment. The withdrawal plan needs a feedback loop. As new information emerges about the military balance and political context, we can reconsider our objectives and alter the troop levels, negotiation strategy, and speed of departure. In other words, we should repeatedly return to the very first task— measuring progress.

Surge, talk, and leave can help the United States limit the damage after battlefield loss. But like any exit strategy from a difficult campaign, it's tough, painful, and carries a degree of risk. Stumbling from a fiasco, there are no easy choices. Indeed, resolving a failing war may be the single greatest challenge in all of politics—one that proved beyond such skillful leaders as Harry Truman and Lyndon Johnson.

Today, American patience with the war in Afghanistan is almost exhausted. In just four years we went from tripling U.S. troop levels to an unsustainable figure of one hundred thousand to contemplating a minimal successor force or a zero option of complete withdrawal. As U.S. forces leave, we must remain focused on our core goals: preventing a Taliban victory, stopping the return of Al Qaeda, and averting the destabilization of neighboring Pakistan. We should continue to fund the Afghan army, support efforts at a negotiated deal, and tell a meaningful story of the withdrawal for Americans and Afghans.

Looking ahead, future American wars are likely to turn into military fiascos. The combination of U.S. power and a prevalence of civil wars is a recipe for unwinnable conflicts, as Washington is lured into tough foreign campaigns. Are we doomed to a generation of quagmires? Or is it possible to avoid some of these wars, and win those campaigns we do fight?

PART III

THE RIGHT WAY TO WIN A WAR

CHAPTER 10

No More Fiascos

Harold Smith, Darwin Judge, Charles McMahon, and David Hickman were the last Americans fatalities in Korea, Vietnam, and Iraq, respectively. They stand at the head of three single-file columns of Americans dead from these wars, arranged in the order they fell in battle. These martial corteges reveal the human value of resolving a failing war. If we had ended the fighting sooner, the first lives to be spared would have been those of Smith, Judge, McMahon, and Hickman. And as we halt the violence a day, a week, or a year earlier, we move down the line, saving more and more of these men and women.

Eventually, as we work down the column, we reach a turning point: the first American soldier to die in an unwinnable cause. It's a GI killed by a Chinese grenade in the icy wastes of North Korea in 1950. It's a marine shot by an insurgent sniper in Iraq in 2004. It's an army private blown up by a Taliban IED in Afghanistan in 2006. Every combatant standing behind this soldier was killed when victory was still possible. Every man ahead fell when a decisive triumph was no longer possible. The goal of losing the right way is to shorten the forward portion of this line.

But there's another way to save American lives. What if we

stopped the war from ever becoming a fiasco? What if we eliminated the turning point and ensured that victory remained on the
table? Rather than just losing the right way, can we start winning
again?

And if we continue moving down the line, we come to the
very first casualty of the war, which begs an even more fundamental question. Can we save this man, and all who stand ahead
of him, by avoiding the conflict at all?

To turn America's military experience around, we must maneuver more skillfully through the terrain of modern warfare. We
need a set of guiding ideas for an era defined by American power,
global interstate peace, internal conflict, and an interconnected
globe. Here, we can briefly outline six core principles.

Prepare for the Age of Civil Wars

Sun-tzu wrote that victory in war comes before the fight is joined,
by creating the proper conditions for success. How can Washington prepare more effectively for future campaigns?

The answer is to ensure adequate training for the kind of wars
we're actually going to face: nation-building and counterinsurgency missions. Stabilization operations are tough and wearying
work, but in some shape or form they're inevitable. In 2007, Robert Gates said that unconventional wars were "the ones most likely
to be fought in the years ahead."[1] The following year, Gates
remarked, "Think of where our forces have been sent and have
been engaged over the last forty-plus years. Vietnam, Lebanon,
Grenada, Panama, Somalia, Haiti, Bosnia, Kosovo, Afghanistan,
Iraq, the Horn of Africa, and more. In fact, the first Gulf War
stands alone in over two generations of constant military engagement as a more or less traditional conventional conflict from
beginning to end."[2]

It's really a question of math. We live in a world where nine out of ten wars are civil wars. Since Vietnam, enemy states have killed barely three hundred Americans, whereas insurgents and terrorists have killed over ten thousand Americans. In this conflict environment, almost every conceivable military path leads to a stabilization operation, whether we're battling terrorist networks in a foreign civil war, launching a humanitarian intervention, or contributing U.S. soldiers to an international peacekeeping mission.

Even the rare exceptions—conventional interstate wars—often turn into stabilization missions. The campaigns in Afghanistan and Iraq both evolved from regime change operations into extended nation-building campaigns. As the so-called Pottery Barn Rule holds, *you break it, you own it.*

We're also likely to engage in irregular conflicts because the enemy gets a vote. Given our dominance at conventional war and our struggles at counterinsurgency, adversaries will gravitate toward guerrilla tactics.

For better or worse, this is the world we live in. Therefore, we must prepare for the reality of modern war. It means forging the U.S. military into a tool with a full spectrum of capabilities—less like a rapier and more like a Swiss Army Knife. It means creating an adaptable institution that can out-innovate insurgents and terrorists. It means investing in engineers, Special Operations Forces, and foreign advisory teams. It means readying soldiers for the human dimension of war, from language training to lessons on how to dine with a sheikh.[3]

These capabilities aren't cheap. But they're less expensive than purchasing big-ticket hardware designed for battling enemy countries, like the F-35 warplane—the most expensive defense program in history with a lifetime price tag of over one trillion dollars.

How well has Washington adapted to modern conflict? In the

fierce crucible of war in Afghanistan and Iraq, the U.S. military was forged into a more effective counterinsurgency force. The landmark 2006 U.S. Army and Marine Corps field manual, *FM 3-24,* placed stability operations at the heart of the armed forces' mission.[4] The army also created the Irregular Warfare Center at Fort Leavenworth, in Kansas, to institutionalize the lessons of Afghanistan and Iraq. The military even practiced counterinsurgency by hiring hundreds of Iraqi Americans through the Screen Actors Guild to play the part of Iraqi civilians and rebels. These efforts paid a dividend. By 2007, Iraqi insurgents needed to use six times as many bombs to kill one American soldier compared to when IEDs first appeared.[5]

But today this progress is at risk because of a powerful backlash in the United States against the whole idea of nation-building and counterinsurgency. The U.S. military and the American people are traditionally skeptical about stabilization missions and see a soldier's true vocation as fighting and winning the nation's wars — meaning conventional interstate wars. In the wake of exhausting guerrilla conflicts in Afghanistan and Iraq, there's a strong desire to return to our comfort zone by shifting the focus of training,

A member of the Irregular Warfare Center teaches the principles of counterinsurgency. (U.S. Army photo)

preparation, and weapon procurement to campaigns against enemy countries.

In 2012, the Pentagon announced, "U.S. forces will no longer be sized to conduct large-scale, prolonged stability operations."[6] The Obama administration's famous pivot from the Middle East to the Pacific is really a turn from nation-building in places like Iraq toward interstate competition against opponents like China.

The pivot to interstate war is a seductive pirouette. After all, the last decade has starkly revealed the challenges of nation-building. Creating an effective state in a divided society like Iraq or Afghanistan is a long and grueling business, and the arrival of Americans for a few years doesn't offer a simple shortcut. *So let's train for something we're actually good at—smashing tyrants.*

Another argument for the pivot is that failure in a major conventional war could be more costly than receiving a bloody nose from guerrillas. Therefore, the focus on counterinsurgency in Iraq and Afghanistan may have distracted the U.S. military from its core mission of interstate campaigns. Colonel Gian Gentile, a professor at West Point, argued that a "hyper-emphasis on counterinsurgency puts the American Army in a perilous condition. Its ability to fight wars consisting of head-on battles using tanks and mechanized infantry is in danger of atrophy."[7]

But the pivot to conventional interstate fighting is the real peril. By neglecting our readiness for nation-building operations, we're raising the odds of future fiascos. Looking ahead, stabilization missions are virtually inevitable. Indeed, the more we signal our distaste for counterinsurgency, the more likely an opponent is to play the insurgent card. Nation-building is certainly challenging, but the answer is to prepare as effectively as possible rather than hamstring ourselves by deliberately eroding our capabilities.

And while it's true that failure in a major interstate campaign would be costly, it's also unlikely. After decades of investment in conventional war, the United States has a massive advantage over its rivals, and this edge won't disappear any time soon. By contrast, debacles in future counterinsurgency campaigns are all too easy to imagine and, as we saw in Iraq and Afghanistan, potentially carry a very high price in blood and treasure.[8]

The backlash means that the United States is in danger of losing its proficiency at nation-building. During a time of budget pressures, the ax may fall disproportionately on stabilization capabilities. In 2014 the army decided to close the Irregular Warfare Center, *even though irregular warfare is the dominant kind of global conflict.*

The pivot toward conventional war is laying the groundwork for another military debacle. If American troops fought tank battles or aerial dogfights with defective equipment, there would be an outcry. Sending soldiers into stabilization missions without adequate preparation is just as scandalous. Visit section 60 of Arlington National Cemetery, where the graves of many Afghanistan and Iraq War casualties lie.

Fight Fewer Wars

Washington must ensure the U.S. military is ready for modern war, and then employ this tool with greater discretion. Put simply, we're too quick to seize the sword. There have been five major American wars since 1945, and two of them should never have been fought: Vietnam and Iraq.

The answer is greater restraint, or setting a higher bar for the use of force. This is not an excuse for inaction or a retreat into isolation. American leadership helps underpin global order. It does mean casting aside chimerical nightmares, like the fall of Vietnam triggering a domino effect of Communist gains across East Asia. And it means discarding alluring dreams, like regime change in Iraq causing a cascade of freedom in the Middle East.

How should we pick our fights in the dark age of American

warfare? Of course, there's no simple formula for determining when to act. In the end, war is always a gamble. Fortunately, we do have some control over the odds.

Decisions to use force should be based on a careful calculation of the stakes in terms of U.S. interests and values, as well as the relevant military and political costs, benefits, and risks. How big is the upside of war and are these gains worth the potential dangers? Have alternative nonviolent avenues been fully explored, such as diplomacy, covert action, or passing the buck to local allies? Is the plan to use force feasible? Are the political goals clearly understood? Have we considered the potential for unanticipated consequences? Which weak links could derail the plan?[9]

Campaigns involving clear-cut enemy aggression and threats to core American security needs would pass the test—including the Korean War, the Gulf War, and the Afghanistan War. By contrast, the Vietnam War was based on illusions about the strength and resolve of North Vietnam, the legitimacy of South Vietnam, and the negative consequences of allowing unification on Hanoi's terms. And the Iraq War was an entirely avoidable misadventure, where the threat was distant and the use of force was far from a last resort.

Given America's recent experience, we should rarely, if ever, willingly start a major counterinsurgency campaign. But other kinds of stabilization operations may be appropriate, provided the likely costs and risks are tolerable. In some cases, nation-building could be essential, for example, after a regime change operation. Washington should also be ready to contribute to peacekeeping missions, where international forces oversee a peace agreement reached by the combatants. Peacekeeping has a fairly successful recent record. Indeed, it's precisely because entrenched insurgencies are so intractable that it can be worth deploying troops to prevent a civil war from breaking out, or to stop it from restarting. During the 1990s, the U.S.-led peacekeeping operations in

Bosnia and Kosovo stabilized the war-torn Balkan provinces with zero American casualties.

The United States should also be ready to intervene in egregious cases of genocide or mass killing. Although Washington has often been too eager to fight, there are occasions where we didn't act but should have. In 1994, hundreds of thousands of Rwandans could have been saved from genocide at modest risk.

Identifying the questions to pose before using force is the relatively easy part. What really matters is how these questions are assessed. We should reform the structure of decision-making to encourage an open and critical debate about war—especially a war of choice like Vietnam or Iraq.

One option is to create a devil's advocate by picking a member of the foreign policy team to deliberately offer a skeptical view of the likely fortunes of war. An even better idea may be to form a murder board, or a committee of notables tasked with finding flaws in a military plan and killing the idea. A single devil's advocate can be ignored; a whole array of devils is harder to dismiss.

Of course, reforming institutions is one thing: Lower-ranked officials must also be empowered to offer criticism, and the top brass should be ready to listen. In chapter 6, we saw the dangers of an overly hierarchical culture when life-and-death decisions are being made—either in the cockpit or the Oval Office. The White House can't be the Korean Air of governing bodies, where officials are unwilling to point out looming threats for fear of committing professional suicide. Instead, presidents must set the tone by signaling a willingness to hear dissent. A truly confident leader can accept criticism without projecting the image of an administration in disarray.

Another useful way of sobering up hawks is to conduct a thought exercise before the war begins, where officials imagine what would happen if the campaign fails and we need to withdraw. In other words, leaders can think through the challenges involved with the surge, talk, and leave exit strategy before pulling the trigger. What will the world look like if the war becomes unwinnable? How will we dial down the goals and give up cherished dreams? How will we negotiate with a hated enemy, rally a divided home front, and craft a narrative of withdrawal?

Before heading to Vegas for a quick-fire wedding, it's wise to spend some time sitting in the divorce courts, watching the marital exit strategies unfold. In a similar vein, contemplating the difficulties of withdrawing the United States from a tough campaign may cause even the most bellicose leader to think twice.

Legalize the War

Let's assume the military is prepared for an era of civil wars, and the proposed use of force has passed the murder board. What next? We need to legalize the war effort by fighting according to domestic, international, and local rules. Employing force legally involves an inherent trade-off: more legitimacy in return for less freedom of maneuver. But in the dark age of civil wars, when conflicts are often prolonged, unpredictable, and politically divisive, the cost-benefit analysis tilts decisively in favor of playing by the rules.

First, dark-age wars should be legal *domestically*, which means securing congressional approval. Legal scholars debate whether the president is constitutionally obliged to receive the blessing of Congress before using force.[10] Whether or not such an injunction exists, there are powerful wider incentives to build support down Pennsylvania Avenue. For a start, reaching out for legislative approval may encourage a healthy debate about the costs, benefits, and risks of going to war.[11] In addition, seeking legislative support can forge political consensus around the prospective military campaign and signal unity and resolve to foreign allies and enemies.

The dark age is no time to go to war with an uncertain country. Missions involving nation-building and counterinsurgency often test the public's patience. If the glue binding the war effort together comes unstuck before we've even started fighting, we risk a debilitating political rift—especially if unexpected problems arise.

Second, dark-age wars should be legal *internationally*, with multilateral backing and UN Security Council authorization. Constructing a broad international coalition involves a great many headaches. Allies may demand a quid pro quo in exchange for their support. Weaker partners can even actively hinder the war effort. More than three dozen countries provided troops in Afghanistan, and they each had their own rules of engagement. Some states restricted their forces to the relatively peaceful north of the country—marching away from the sound of the guns.

Broadening the international coalition for war may feel like herding cats, but it's usually worth the effort. For one thing, the degree of allied support is a useful barometer of the wisdom of the mission. If a close ally like Britain refuses to fight—as in Vietnam—it's a stark warning about the prudence of the campaign. *What do they know that we don't?*

And there are also practical benefits to fighting a multilateral war. Allies can share the burden by providing troops, money, intelligence, and bases. Multilateralism may also help us compete more effectively with the insurgents for global legitimacy. Guerrillas usually need outside backing to win. The rebels' degree of external support—and perhaps the course of the war—will wax or wane depending on international beliefs about the justice of America's campaign.

To illustrate the value of multilateralism, we can contrast Washington's two major wars against Iraq. In the 1991 Gulf War, the United States fought with UN authorization and a broad coalition of support. Saudi Arabia and Japan bankrolled the war effort to the tune of tens of billions of dollars, and Washington may even have turned a profit.

In 2003, however, the White House invaded Iraq with no UN approval and limited international support. When the insurgency emerged, the United States was left to face the gathering storm almost alone. John Abizaid, the former head of Central Command, told me, "There was plenty of time to build a solid international coalition if we had more patience. The military is your last resort; building a coalition is your first resort."[12]

Third, dark-age wars should be legal *locally,* by prioritizing the rule of law during stabilization missions. One of the main principles of COIN doctrine is to win hearts and minds by out-governing the guerrillas. This means using force with restraint. And it means creating a justice system that can operate more effectively than insurgent courts. In a world of globalization and camera phones, abuses can quickly go viral, magnifying the damage. When pictures emerged of the Abu Ghraib scandal in Iraq, one U.S. corporal said, "Some assholes have just lost the war for us."[13]

Start at the End

How should we plan for victory? Washington often begins wars by focusing on the initial blows and neglecting the ultimate political goals. The architects of the Iraq invasion, for example, saw regime change as the main objective and postwar stabilization as a secondary concern—partly because they assumed it would be easy. As a result, the United States achieved tactical success and strategic defeat.

Achieving victory in the dark age requires thinking through the military endgame, and making extensive preparations for the postwar order. Clausewitz advised against taking the first step in war "without considering the last."[14] Or, as Petraeus asked about Iraq in 2003, "Tell me, how does this end?"[15]

The traditional approach to military planning is to *engineer victory* by identifying our objectives and then creating a road map that works toward this end state. In a regime-change mission, for example, we can move through what the military terms Phase I (deterrence and engagement), Phase II (initial operations to seize the initiative), Phase III (major combat operations), and Phase IV (postcombat stabilization).

An alternative approach is to *reverse engineer victory,* or work backward from the endgame. Reverse engineering means examining an intact product with a known function, and then taking it apart to see how it was created. Reverse engineering victory means starting with the end result in war, "taking it apart," and seeing how we got there.

We should begin by visualizing the desired finale in as much detail as possible. How much territory does America control? What does the target country's political system and economy look like? What is the timeframe for achieving these goals? Before invading Iraq, for example, we might have outlined a plausible conception of the country as a fairly stable and representative state by, say, 2006.

We can then work backward from this future vision. What's the final step before reaching the end state? What's the second-to-last step? What will be required one month before the target date? How about six months or one year? This path can be broken down into short-term actions and milestones. With Iraq, for example, we could have worked backward from a stable country in 2006 through the intermediate stages, such as overseeing elections, creating effective security forces, and so on.

Reverse engineering victory offers several valuable benefits.

First of all, it's an antidote to short-termism. If we plan ahead, today's world is cast in bright light, whereas the finale is usually murky. We're therefore tempted to focus on the first steps we can clearly identify and hope that everything somehow works out. By contrast, starting at the end forces officials to illuminate the denouement by imagining this outcome in detail.

Furthermore, reverse engineering victory provides a reality check. If the exercise of creating a plausible path from the end state is too hard, we may need to rethink the whole endeavor. Working backward can therefore mitigate the overconfidence that often infects wartime planning. We tend to underestimate the time, blood, and treasure required to stabilize a foreign land. Abizaid told me, "Some of the assumptions behind the invasion of Iraq, like it would be similar to the liberation of France, suggest naïveté."[16]

Reverse engineering victory can also reveal unexpected obstacles, challenges, or opportunities. Working backward may show that certain steps in the plan are fairly straightforward to map out—for example, a plausible timetable for elections during the stabilization phase. *If Baghdad has a representative regime in 2006, we need national elections in 2005.* But other aspects of the plan may be extremely hard to project, such as building regional backing for the new government. These uncertainties should then be factored into the decision whether or not to wage war.

Reverse engineering victory may also show that a seemingly minor move early in the war could turn out to be critical later on. Capablanca used to work backward from checkmate. By thinking through the second-to-last move, the third-to-last move, and so on, he discovered that a small positional edge at the start would ultimately prove decisive. The same possibility exists with war. By starting at the end and working backward, we may find that an apparently trivial move at the beginning—say, allying with a minor local leader—could eventually prove invaluable as the political arena opens up.

How speculative is this exercise? The proposed path backward will be more or less tentative depending on the length, complexity, and difficulty of the military campaign. In a relatively straightforward operation, officials may be able to follow the proposed road map with some confidence. When fighting more powerful enemies or in conflicts involving extensive postwar stabilization, these steps will be more difficult to map out. But here the exercise remains valuable—indeed it may be *more* valuable—as a creative thought exercise to identify challenges, opportunities, and uncertainties.

Engineering victory and reverse engineering victory are complementary tools. We can end up with two paths: from the origin to the destination and from the destination to the origin. Comparing and integrating the two routes may reveal the optimum course.

Use Decisive Forces

We can further improve the odds of success by employing sufficient capabilities to achieve the mission. Clausewitz wrote, "A short jump is certainly easier than a long one, but no one wanting to get across a wide ditch would begin by jumping halfway."[17] Similarly, when going to war, we shouldn't begin by jumping halfway or using too few troops. Instead, the means must be matched with the ends. According to political scientist Richard Betts, American leaders "liked to use force frequently but not intensely, when the reverse combination would have been wiser."[18]

Stabilizing foreign territory is not about decisive *force* in the sense of massive firepower. Indiscriminate violence may simply alienate the population and recruit more insurgents. Rather, the answer is decisive *forces,* or sending enough soldiers to take control. In the rare circumstances where we need to occupy an entire country, we shouldn't intervene on the cheap. Instead, we should accept responsibility and go in big right away, by deploying sufficient troops to create order. If we had invaded Iraq with a larger military footprint, we might have prevented the vicious cycle of sectarian violence that spiraled downward.[19]

Won't a large footprint inspire a nationalist backlash? Intervention in a culturally alien society can provoke an antibody response from local traditionalists. But attacking with fewer troops will do little to diminish this resistance. After all, we're still occupying the country. A smaller force may, however, produce a very real reduction in security. Therefore, trying to sidestep a nationalist backlash with a small footprint can produce the worst of all worlds: enough Americans soldiers to inspire opposition but too few to provide stability.[20]

The foreign public may accept the presence of American forces on a temporary basis if they bring order. Despite Afghanistan's history as the graveyard of empires, the majority of Afghan people initially welcomed international troops. Similarly, during the Iraq War, polls showed that residents of Baghdad didn't like the presence of coalition soldiers—but they were also wary of an immediate withdrawal given the lack of security.[21]

Beware of Crusades

Americans often go to war with crusading fervor and a moralistic view of the campaign as good against evil. Compared to other rich democracies, Americans are unusually religious and sometimes see U.S. soldiers as spiritual warriors engaged in a sacred quest. Americans are also committed to the founding creed of freedom, democracy, and individual rights, which encourages a missionary impulse to spread our values. And after suffering traumatic attacks like Pearl Harbor or 9/11, moralism can take a more wrathful tone as we look to exact righteous vengeance. Seeing conflict as good against evil shapes how we fight — sometimes in dangerous ways. The answer is not to adopt an unprincipled view of war but instead to temper our moralism with hardheaded pragmatism.[22]

When the United States fights a foreign country, Americans usually want the campaign to end with the tyrant's overthrow and a surrender ceremony, as in Tokyo Bay in 1945. Any lesser result seems unworthy of our nation's ideals.[23]

But it's often wise to fight for more limited goals. We can still win a campaign even if the enemy dictator stays in power. After all, America's sole victory in major war after 1945 was achieved with restricted aims. During the 1991 Gulf War, George H. W. Bush freed Kuwait but decided against marching on Baghdad to overthrow Saddam Hussein.

It was a smart call. U.S. allies opposed expanding the war, and toppling Saddam would have destroyed the coalition. Regime change in Iraq would also have been illegal under international law, because the United Nations mandate only covered the liberation of Kuwait. And occupying Baghdad would have burdened the United States with the task of stabilizing postwar Iraq.

U.S. strategic interests favored keeping the war limited. But that's not how most Americans saw it. When the Gulf War began, a crusading spirit gripped the country. Americans rallied around the flag, and Lee Greenwood's song "God Bless the USA" became the theme tune of the campaign. The public saw Saddam Hussein as a demon and the second coming of Hitler. Over 70 percent of Americans wanted to overthrow the Iraqi dictator.[24]

Fighting for restricted goals in the Gulf was the correct decision but it cut against the grain of American culture. In the end, Bush received remarkably little credit for the Gulf War. The following year, he lost his bid for reelection—a result that Saddam greeted with massive celebrations in Baghdad.

Pragmatism about war aims is also critical in a stabilization mission. When creating order in a foreign country, we should think very carefully before trying to construct a *beacon of freedom*. Fashioning a representative government and suppressing an entire insurgency usually require a huge investment of time, money, and manpower. In an impoverished society like Afghanistan— which has a literacy rate lower than that of America in the 1600s—creating Western liberal democracy in one generation is an impossible dream.[25] As John Allen, the U.S. commander in Afghanistan from 2011 to 2013, told me: "Campaign objectives must be aligned with the realities you can achieve in a country that is tied for dead last as most corrupt."[26]

Instead, we may be able to protect our core interests and values by pursuing the more limited goal of *ugly stability*. The allied regime may be able to coexist with, or even cooperate with, some of the guerrilla groups through formal or informal spheres of influence. This kind of messy outcome is not ideal, but it could be tolerable and cost-effective.

A moralistic view of war can also make it hard to negotiate with enemies. The best time to pursue peace talks is often when the adversary is on the run and we have maximum leverage. But this is exactly when Americans are least willing to bargain. Imbued with a sense of righteousness and with the military wind at our back, we resist outreach to evildoers. Instead, we wait until the war effort starts spiraling downward before reluctantly embracing diplomacy.

It took almost a decade before we began serious negotiations with the Taliban. As Stanley McChrystal told me, "We should have started talking in 2003."[27] The insurgents' fortunes were then at a low ebb, and they might have offered major concessions.[28] At the same time, the Taliban were unlikely to disappear anytime soon. They enjoyed sanctuaries in Pakistan and a base of support among Pashtuns. And, in addition, international forces in Afghanistan were few and far between. Sooner or later we would have to deal with the insurgents. So why not talk when we still held the best cards?

It's true, as McChrystal told me, that the Taliban were disorganized in 2003, and it's not clear if they yet represented a coherent partner. But at the very least, we could have outlined an inclusive vision for Afghanistan's future, with a place for the Taliban and its Pashtun constituency and a rehabilitation program for former Taliban.

Back in 2003, however, the diplomatic option was never even considered. The hawkish American mood after 9/11, the moralism of the Bush administration, and the tendency to lump the Taliban and Al Qaeda together as the epitome of evil meant the idea of negotiating with the enemy was dismissed out of hand. Overly confident and overly wrathful, the United States missed its chance.

The Pity of War

The single-file columns of American dead from Korea, Vietnam, and Iraq take their place among all the lines of wartime fatalities in history—forming a vast echelon of parallel rows. Here are the fallen warriors from Gilgamesh's epic adventures in ancient Mesopotamia, the Roman struggles against the Germanic tribes, the War of 1812, the First Anglo-Afghan War, the world wars, the French war in Algeria, the Soviet quagmire in Afghanistan, the Israeli-Palestinian conflict, and a thousand other campaigns.

At the head of the American column from World War I is Private Henry N. Gunther, from East Baltimore. On the last day of the war, November 11, 1918, he fixed his bayonet and dashed toward the German lines, shouting, "Let's get those SOBs." Gunther may have had a death wish. He was gunned down at 10:59 a.m.—one minute before the war ended at the eleventh hour of the eleventh day of the eleventh month.[29]

Augustin Trébuchon stands at the head of the French line of dead from the Great War. He was the final French soldier to fall on November 11, killed fifteen minutes before the war ended. Paris was so ashamed that some of its soldiers died on the last day of the fighting, when the armistice had already been agreed, that it backdated their headstones to say that they were killed on November 10. Even today, the French Defense Ministry's website of war casualties claims, quite wrongly, that Trébuchon *"Mort pour la France le 10-11-1918."*[30]

The line of British dead from World War I is over seven hundred thousand strong. The column includes my great-grandmother's first husband, John Margerison, who died in April 1918, just a few months before the armistice. He stands nearly nine-tenths of the way toward the front of the line. Yet the final tenth of casualties arrayed ahead of Margerison—this British decimation—is thirty miles long.

Some of these processions of men and women fell in the course of winning a great victory. But many of the columns stretch far into the distance because countries became trapped in a failing war and couldn't find a way out. True leaders know how to win, and they also know the right way to lose.

Acknowledgments

In the course of writing this book, I became indebted to a great many people.

Several of my colleagues offered excellent comments on the manuscript: Michael Boyle, Richard Caplan, David Danelo, David Edelstein, Christopher Fettweis, Ryan Grauer, Samuel Helfont, Tally Helfont, Ayse Kaya, Lou Klarevas, James Lebovic, Austin Long, Dominic Johnson, Daniel Moran, Michael Noonan, Amy Oakes, Michael Patrick O'Hara, and Andrew Polsky.

I am grateful to the interviewees who gave generously of their time: John Abizaid, John Allen, Stephen Biddle, Zbigniew Brzezinski, George Casey, Ryan Crocker, Ivo Daalder, Toby Dodge, Eric Edelman, Robert Gallucci, Marc Grossman, John Hillen, Thomas Keaney, Graeme Lamb, Stanley McChrystal, John McLaughlin, H. R. McMaster, Mary Alice Mills, Robert Mnookin, Richard Myers, John Nagl, Vali Nasr, Ronald Neumann, Thomas Pickering, George Schultz, James G. Stavridis, Bernard Trainor, Joshua White, and Dov Zakheim.

The political science department at Swarthmore College has been an exceptional environment in which to work. I would like to thank my wonderful colleagues and students. Several students offered helpful comments and research assistance: Gabriella Capone, Sara Fitzpatrick, Caleb Jones, Susana Medeiros, Kathleen Naccarato, Emma Saarel, Fredrick Toohey—and, especially, Lorand

Acknowledgments

Laskai, Sara Morell, Stuart Russell, and Chloe Wittenberg. Swarthmore College also provided funding for a sabbatical leave, which was invaluable in finishing the book.

The Foreign Policy Research Institute helped the book in a number of important ways, including setting up interviews and facilitating valuable conversations. I would especially like to thank: David Danelo, Samuel Helfont, Tally Helfont, Alan Luxenberg, and Michael Noonan.

Part of the book was completed when I was a visiting fellow at the Arnold A. Saltzman Institute of War and Peace Studies at Columbia University, and I would like to thank Richard Betts, Robert Jervis, and Tonya Putnam.

The Academic Exchange program and the Yitzhak Rabin Center in Tel Aviv organized a highly productive trip to Israel, and I am grateful to Nachum Braverman, Charles Kupchan, and Fufi Sedaka.

For help with family history, I am grateful to Dorothy Jones, Sally Shepherd, and Angela Tracy-Smith.

My friend Will Lippincott cemented his status as the best agent in New York and proved a wonderful guide throughout the process. I was fortunate to work with two highly talented editors, Geoff Shandler and Asya Muchnick, who offered superb input and mentorship at every stage of the project. For terrific copyediting, I want to thank Peggy Freudenthal and Janet Byrne.

Most of all, I would like to thank my family: John, Angela, Ben, Sam, Dylan, Christian, Vuokko, Sienna, and Mila.

Notes

Preface

1. Strachan, *The First World War,* 253–54.

Chapter 1: The Dark Age

1. "Mail Call," *VFW Magazine* (August 2003), 6–7.
2. Richard K. Kolb, "Last to Die: Final KIAs of the Korean War," *VFW Magazine* (June/July 2003), 34–35.
3. "Buddies, Hometowns Honor Last Two Marines Killed in Vietnam War," available at: http://www.cnn.com/2010/US/04/29/vietnam.last.killed/.
4. Bissell, *The Father of All Things,* 57.
5. J. Freedom du Lac, "In Iraq, the Last to Fall: David Hickman, the 4,474th U.S. Service Member Killed," *Washington Post,* December 17, 2011.
6. http://www.fallofsaigon.org/iframe.php?id=3.
7. Tucker, ed., *The Encyclopedia of the Vietnam War,* 1631.
8. http://www.cbsnews.com/news/23-year-old-david-hickman-was-last-iraq-casualty/.
9. Mark Landler, "U.S. Troops to Leave Afghanistan by End of 2016," *New York Times,* May 27, 2014.
10. Torricelli and Carroll, eds., *In Our Own Words,* 139–44.
11. For more on the definition of victory in war, see Johnson and Tierney, *Failing to Win.* Here, victory and success, and defeat and failure, are used interchangeably.
12. Defining "major war" solely based on U.S. casualties is problematic because Washington may suffer steep costs in a small-scale mission or few casualties in a large-scale intervention. Similar numbers of Americans died during the peacekeeping operation in Lebanon in 1982–1984 and in the Gulf War in 1991, but the Gulf War was a far larger endeavor. Defining major war solely in terms of total casualties is also problematic because the United States may intervene briefly in a bloody foreign struggle. Consider U.S. intervention in

the Russian Civil War in 1918–1920. This was a major war for the Russians — but not for the Americans.

13. Abraham Lincoln, "Second Annual Message," December 1, 1862, available at: http://www.presidency.ucsb.edu/ws/?pid=29503. The Civil War was a de facto interstate war in which the Union effectively fought against another country, and most of the fighting was conventional. See Tierney, *How We Fight*.

14. McPherson, *What They Fought For*, 30.

15. Goodwin, *The Bully Pulpit*, 230.

16. Linn, *The Philippine War*. The United States also fought a series of engagements against Native American populations from the founding of the country until the 1890s. U.S. troops lost individual battles, but the overall outcome was the destruction and removal of the native peoples.

17. Torricelli and Carroll, eds., *In Our Own Words*, 139–44.

18. "A Doctor at Nagasaki, August 1945," in Freedman, ed., *War*, 41–43.

19. Hacker, "A Census-Based Count of the Civil War Dead."

20. Bierce, *A Sole Survivor*, 19.

21. Jenkins, *Churchill*, 621.

22. Hess, *Presidential Decisions for War*, 4.

23. Huebner, *The Warrior Image*, 126. Later on, Americans became somewhat more positive about the Korean War. By 1956, a plurality, although not a majority, of the public thought it was worthwhile. For the polling data, see Khong, *Analogies at War*, 114.

24. Gian P. Gentile, "Vietnam: Ending the Lost War," in Moten, ed., *Between War and Peace*, 263.

25. Kalb and Kalb, *Haunting Legacy*, 1.

26. Hess, *Vietnam and the United States*, 137.

27. Scales, *Certain Victory*, 5.

28. Tierney, *How We Fight*, 212–14.

29. Martel, *Victory in War*, 193.

30. Rory Stewart, "Lessons from Afghanistan," *New York Review of Books*, August 16, 2012.

31. United Nations Assistance Mission in Afghanistan, "Afghanistan: Midyear Report 2014," July 2014, available via: http://unama.unmissions.org/.

32. CNN poll, December 16–19, 2013. For the evidence of success, see Miller, "Finish the Job."

33. George W. Bush, "Address to the Nation on Iraq," March 19, 2003, available at: http://www.presidency.ucsb.edu/ws/index.php?pid=63368.

34. Powers, *The Yellow Birds*, 91.

35. Interview with Zbigniew Brzezinski, January 15, 2014.

36. If we turn to recent small-scale operations like Grenada, Lebanon, or Somalia, the success rate is only moderately better. The U.S. intervention in the Dominican Republic in 1965–66 led to the creation of a non-Communist

regime under Joaquín Balaguer—and stable if mildly authoritarian rule. But in 1974, only 10 percent of Americans recalled the mission as a "proud moment" in American history. The United States won a couple of minor league trophies in Grenada and Panama during the 1980s. The intervention in Lebanon in 1982–1984, however, turned into a debacle when 241 Americans died in a suicide terrorist attack on the marine barracks—the bloodiest single day for the Marine Corps since Iwo Jima in World War II. A decade later, in 1992, Washington launched a humanitarian intervention in Somalia that saved around 100,000 Somali lives. But over time the wheels started to come off the mission, and in October 1993, Somali insurgents killed 18 Americans in the Black Hawk Down battle in Mogadishu. The United States quickly withdrew, eroding any gains from the mission. Washington achieved mixed results in Haiti and greater success in Bosnia and Kosovo in the 1990s—although these operations weren't very popular among Americans. The U.S. intervention in Libya in 2011 initially looked successful as the regime was toppled at low cost (for the United States). But the Libyan state remains extremely weak, and on September 11, 2012, a mob attacked a U.S. diplomatic compound in Benghazi, killing the U.S. ambassador and three other Americans. For details on these cases see Tierney, *How We Fight.*

37. The quote comes from Walter Cronkite's CBS broadcast about Vietnam on February 27, 1968: "To say that we are closer to victory today is to believe, in the face of the evidence, the optimists who have been wrong in the past. To suggest we are on the edge of defeat is to yield to unreasonable pessimism. To say that we are mired in stalemate seems the only realistic, yet unsatisfactory, conclusion."

38. Cassius, *Roman History,* 43.

39. Spielvogel, *Western Civilization,* 168.

40. Henry R. Luce, "The American Century," *Life,* February 17, 1941, 61–65.

41. Kagan, *Of Paradise and Power,* 31.

42. Westad, *The Global Cold War;* Leffler, *For the Soul of Mankind.*

43. John F. Kennedy, "Inaugural Address," January 20, 1961, available at: http://www.presidency.ucsb.edu/ws/index.php?pid=8032.

44. Ron Suskind, "Faith, Certainty and the Presidency of George W. Bush," *New York Times,* October 17, 2004.

45. Gaddis, *The Long Peace.*

46. Morris, *The Rise of Theodore Roosevelt,* 594.

47. Mexico, Spain, Germany, Italy, and Japan all spend less than 2 percent of their GDP on the military and have national cultures that are skeptical about the use of force. Sheehan, *Where Have All the Soldiers Gone,* xvi, 216–17; Zenko and Cohen, "Clear and Present Safety"; Pinker, *The Better Angels of our Nature;* Mueller, *The Remnants of War;* Goldstein, *Winning the War on War.*

48. Kalyvas defines civil war as "armed combat within the boundaries of a recognized sovereign entity between parties subject to a common authority at the

outset of hostilities." Before World War II, civil wars often involved conventional fighting between armed columns—for example, in the United States and Spain. But since 1945, civil wars have mainly featured guerrilla warfare. Kalyvas, "The Changing Character of Civil Wars, 1800–2009," 203. See also Boot, "The Evolution of Irregular War"; Van Creveld, *The Transformation of War.*

49. Vasquez, ed., *What Do We Know About War?,* 263.

50. Smith, *The Utility of Force;* Hammes, *The Sling and the Stone.*

51. *The National Security Strategy of the United States of America* (September 2002), 1, available at: http://www.state.gov/documents/organization/63562.pdf; Ghani and Lockhart, *Fixing Failed States.*

52. Gompert et al., *War by Other Means,* 354; Simpson, "The Perils of Third-Party Counterinsurgency Campaigns"; Lyall and Wilson, "Rage Against the Machines," 69.

53. Kaplan, *The Insurgents,* 206.

54. Kilcullen, *The Accidental Guerrilla.*

55. After World War II, Ho Chi Minh told a French representative, "You will kill ten of our men and we will kill one of yours, and in the end it will be you who tire of it." Record, *Beating Goliath,* 5; Betts, *American Force,* 153; Mack, "Why Big Nations Lose Small Wars"; Lebovic, *The Limits of U.S. Military Capability,* chapter 4; Arreguin-Toft, "How the Weak Win Wars."

56. Sanger, *Confront and Conceal,* 20.

57. Boot, *Invisible Armies,* 418. General William Depuy reportedly said the answer in Vietnam was "more bombs, more shells, more napalm...'til the other side cracks and gives up." Ucko, *The New Counterinsurgency Era,* 35, 43.

58. Kocher, Pepinsky, and Kalyvas, "Aerial Bombing and Counterinsurgency in the Vietnam War."

59. Krepinevich, *The Army and Vietnam.* One study found that when militaries become more mechanized they tend to lose against insurgents because the force structure prevents soldiers from collecting information from the population. Lyall and Wilson, "Rage Against the Machines."

60. Weigley, *The American Way of War,* 36.

61. Fitzgerald, *Learning to Forget.*

62. "Making Sense of the Mission," *New York Times,* April 11, 2004.

63. Rotmann, Tohn, and Wharton, "Learning Under Fire." One of the most important pieces of equipment in the dark age is the Mine-Resistant Ambush-Protected vehicle (MRAP). The army resisted purchasing MRAPs because they wanted sleeker vehicles designed for the next interstate war. Kaplan, *The Insurgents,* 272–74.

64. Robert Gates, speech in Washington, DC, October 10, 2007, available at: http://www.defense.gov/speeches/speech.aspx?speechid=1181.

65. Kilcullen, *Counterinsurgency,* 8; Mao, *On Guerrilla Warfare;* Hammes, *The Sling and the Stone.*

66. Giustozzi, *Negotiating with the Taliban,* 12.

67. Jones, "The Rise of Afghanistan's Insurgency," 35–36.
68. Kalyvas, "The Changing Character of Civil Wars, 1800–2009," 203.
69. Connable and Libicki, *How Insurgencies End,* xiii; Record, *Beating Goliath.*
70. Templer, *Shadows and Wind,* 295.
71. Caplan, "Devising Exit Strategies," 111.
72. Clausewitz, *On War,* 254.
73. Rosen, *War and Human Nature,* chapter 4.
74. For a discussion, see Angos, *You Move . . . I Win!*
75. Kaplan, *The Insurgents,* 224–25. For the transcript, see: http://www.washington post.com/wp-dyn/content/article/2006/08/03/AR2006080300802.html.
76. On exit strategies, see Iklé, *Every War Must End;* Rose, *How Wars End;* Caplan, ed., *Exit Strategies and State Building;* Record "Exit Strategy Delusions"; Edelstein, "Exit Lessons"; Walt, "Cutting Losses in Wars of Choice"; Moten, ed., *Between War and Peace;* Gleis, *Withdrawing Under Fire.* On war termination, see Stanley, *Paths to Peace;* Goemans, *War and Punishment;* Cimbala and Waldman, eds., *Controlling and Ending Conflict;* Fox "The Causes of War and Conditions of Peace"; Croco, "Peace at What Price?" On the causes of military failure, see Cohen and Gooch, *Military Misfortunes.* On the experience of losing, see Schivelbusch, *The Culture of Defeat;* Fettweis, *Losing Hurts Twice as Bad.*
77. Tocqueville, *Democracy in America,* 97.
78. Ashley Merryman, "Losing Is Good for You," *New York Times,* September 24, 2013.
79. Foot, *A Substitute for Victory,* 2.
80. Schweikart, *America's Victories.*

Chapter 2: Fiasco

1. Brydon appeared to be the sole survivor of the march—although a handful of Indian troops eventually straggled back in. Grant, ed., *1001 Battles that Changed the Course of World History,* 557. For the history of the First Anglo-Afghan War, see Macrony, *Retreat from Kabul*; Preston, *The Dark Defile;* Dalrymple, *The Return of a King.*
2. Dalrymple, *The Return of a King,* 126.
3. Ibid., 145.
4. Boot, *Invisible Armies,* 164.
5. Preston, *The Dark Defile,* 218.
6. Macrory, *Retreat from Kabul,* 209; Rory Stewart, "Lessons from Afghanistan," *The New York Review of Books,* August 16, 2012.
7. Dalrymple, *The Return of a King,* 346.
8. Ibid., 437.
9. Rose, *The Literary Churchill,* 293–94.
10. "Winning by Losing: The (un)American Way?" BBC, June 27, 2014, available at: http://www.bbc.com/news/blogs-echochambers-28065500.
11. Rose, "The Exit Strategy Delusion."

12. The memoir is available at: http://www.koreanwar-educator.org/memoirs/ dixon_gene/index.htm. See also Cohen and Gooch, *Military Misfortunes,* chapter 7; Hastings, *The Korean War;* Millett, *The War for Korea;* Hogan, *A Cross of Iron;* Cummings, *The Korean War;* Stueck, *Rethinking the Korean War,* chapter 6; Ridgway, *The Korean War.*

13. O'Donnell, *Give Me Tomorrow,* 111.

14. Russ, *Breakout,* 124.

15. http://www.koreanwar-educator.org/memoirs/dixon_gene/index.htm.

16. Stueck, *Rethinking the Korean War,* 93.

17. Ridgway, *The Korean War,* 102–3.

18. Stanley, *Paths to Peace,* 68; Foot, *A Substitute for Victory,* 17.

19. Stueck, *Rethinking the Korean War,* chapter 6; Ridgway, *The Korean War.*

20. Stanley, *Paths to Peace,* 6, 70; Stueck, *Rethinking the Korean War,* chapter 6.

21. Logevall, *Choosing War.*

22. Bostdorff, *The Presidency and the Rhetoric of Foreign Crisis,* 61.

23. Logevall, "What Really Happened in Vietnam"; Berman, *Lyndon Johnson's War;* Young, *The Vietnam Wars.*

24. Boot, *Invisible Armies,* 420; Berman, *Lyndon Johnson's War,* 22.

25. Berman, *Lyndon Johnson's War,* 13–16; Hess, *Vietnam;* Harrison and Mosher, "The Secret Diary of McNamara's Dove," 522–23.

26. Asselin, "We Don't Want a Munich."

27. "Rescuing a Vietnam Casualty: Johnson's Legacy," *New York Times,* February 15, 2014.

28. Vandiver, *Lyndon Johnson's Wars,* 167; Krepinevich, "Recovery from Defeat: The U.S. Army and Vietnam," in Andreopoulos and Selesky, eds., *The Aftermath of Defeat,* 124–42; Hixson, *George F. Kennan,* 228.

29. Johnson's decision was influenced by the degree of opposition he faced in the 1968 Democratic primary. On March 12, 1968, LBJ only narrowly won the New Hampshire primary against Senator Eugene McCarthy. Four days later, Senator Robert Kennedy entered the race.

30. Hughes, "Fatal Politics," 498.

31. Polsky, *Elusive Victories,* 253; Kimball, *Nixon's Vietnam War;* Hoff, *Nixon Reconsidered;* Asselin, *A Bitter Peace;* Langguth, *Our Vietnam;* Hunt, *Pacification.*

32. Richard Nixon, "Address to the Nation Announcing Conclusion of an Agreement on Ending the War and Restoring Peace in Vietnam," January 23, 1973, available at: http://www.presidency.ucsb.edu/ws/?pid=3808.

33. Kimball, *Nixon's Vietnam War,* 340.

34. Kimball, *Nixon's Vietnam War;* McMahon, "The Politics, and Geopolitics, of American Troop Withdrawals from Vietnam, 1968–1972"; Langguth, *Our Vietnam,* 546.

35. Hughes, "Fatal Politics," 501; Rose, *How Wars End,* 191–93. In the margins of Kissinger's briefing book for his first trip to China in July 1971, he wrote, "We need a decent interval." Kimball, "The Case of the 'Decent Interval.' "

36. Rose, *How Wars End,* 193; Nguyen, *Hanoi's War.*
37. Hughes, "Fatal Politics," 503.
38. Ibid., 505.
39. Berman, *No Peace, No Honor,* 8; Gian P. Gentile, "Vietnam: Ending the Lost War," in Moten, ed., *Between War and Peace,* 271.
40. Berman, *No Peace, No Honor,* 3.
41. Kaiser, *American Tragedy,* 427; Logevall, *The Origins of the Vietnam War,* 2; Berman, *No Peace, No Honor;* Kimball, *Nixon's Vietnam War.*
42. Kissinger, *White House Years,* 227–28; Isaacson, *Kissinger,* 165.
43. Hixson, *George F. Kennan,* 229.
44. Galbraith, *How to Get Out of Vietnam;* McNamara et al., *Argument Without End.*
45. Interview with Graeme Lamb, September 11, 2013. See also "How a 'Good War' in Afghanistan Went Bad," *New York Times,* August 12, 2007; Barfield, *Afghanistan.*
46. Jones, "The Rise of Afghanistan's Insurgency"; Jones, *In the Graveyard of Empires;* West, *The Wrong War;* Tomsen, *The Wars of Afghanistan;* Malkasian, *War Comes to Garmser,* chapter 5.
47. Woodward, *Obama's Wars;* Rashid, *Descent into Chaos.*
48. Interview with Ronald Neumann, October 9, 2013.
49. Barack Obama, "Address Before a Joint Session of Congress on the State of the Union," February 12, 2013, available at: http://www.presidency.ucsb.edu/ws/?pid=102826.
50. Nasr, *Dispensable Nation,* 12.
51. During the 1990s, Washington in theory sought regime change in Iraq. But despite some covert efforts to destabilize Saddam Hussein's administration, there was little will for a U.S.-led invasion. Containment was the de facto policy. Gordon and Trainor, *Cobra II;* Gordon and Trainor, *The Endgame.*
52. Interview with George Shultz, September 27, 2013.
53. Diamond, *Squandered Victory,* 293–94; Rose, *How Wars End,* 239–40, 261–62; Gordon and Trainor, *The Endgame,* 9; Lebovic, *The Limits of U.S. Military Capability,* 43.
54. Polsky, *Elusive Victories;* Kaplan, *The Insurgents,* 59; Dyson, "What Really Happened in Planning for Postwar Iraq?"
55. Hess, *Presidential Decisions for War,* 269; http://icasualties.org; http://www.brookings.edu/about/centers/saban/iraq-index; Ricks, *Fiasco.*
56. George W. Bush, "Address to the Nation on the War on Terror from Fort Bragg, North Carolina," June 28, 2005, available at: http://www.presidency.ucsb.edu/ws/index.php?pid=64989
57. In 2004, the U.S. ambassador to Iraq, John Negroponte, told Bush that the United States was "in a deep hole with the Iraqi people" and would need five years to right the ship. Bush replied: "We don't have that much time." Gordon and Trainor, "The Iraq War that Might have Been." Toby Dodge, "Iraq,"

in Caplan, ed., *Exit Strategies and State Building,* 246–50; Ricks, "General Failure"; Ricks, *The Gamble,* 52.

58. http://www.brookings.edu/about/centers/saban/iraq-index.

59. Perry, *Talking to Terrorists,* 10.

60. Interview with John Abizaid, August 8, 2013. Abizaid recognized there were significant challenges, including Shiite and Kurdish wariness about letting the Sunnis back into power.

61. Kaplan, *The Insurgents,* 82.

62. Donald Rumsfeld, press conference, July 24, 2003, available at: http://www .defense.gov/transcripts/transcript.aspx?transcriptid=2894.

63. Ucko, *The New Counterinsurgency Era,* 61; Boot, *Invisible Armies,* 538.

64. Caroline Alexander, "U.S. Has No Exit Strategy for Iraq, Rumsfeld Says," April 12, 2005, available at: http://www.bloomberg.com/apps/news?pid=ne wsarchive&sid=a8sZejFz9ssI.

65. Ricks, *The Gamble;* Anderson, *Bush's Wars.*

66. Logevall, *Choosing War,* 244; Kaiser, *American Tragedy,* 349–51; Staw and Ross, "Understanding Behavior in Escalation Situations," 216.

67. Kaiser, *American Tragedy,* 407.

Chapter 3: The Landscape of Loss

1. Hitler, *Hitler's Table Talk,* 21.

2. Evans, *The Third Reich at War,* 187.

3. Overy, *The Dictators,* 94; Montefiore, *Stalin,* 374–77.

4. Shirer, *The Rise and Fall of the Third Reich,* 1108–9.

5. Paul K. Davis, "Behavioral Factors in Terminating Superpower War," in Cimbala and Waldman, eds., *Controlling and Ending Conflict,* 165–82; Rosen, *War and Human Nature,* chapter 4.

6. Iklé, *Every War Must End,* 102.

7. Chernev, *Capablanca's Best Chess Endings,* v. This section draws on Tierney, "Mastering the Endgame of War."

8. Iklé, *Every War Must End,* 1.

9. Ibid., 4.

10. Kershaw, *Fateful Choices,* 352–53.

11. U.S. military doctrine talks about "termination criteria" and "end states," or the conditions that mean success has been attained and we can go home. But the trigger for leaving is often extremely hazy. Richard Caplan, "Exit Strategies and State Building," in Caplan, ed., *Exit Strategies and State Building,* 7; Johnson, "Exit Strategy," 5.

12 Rose, *How Wars End.*

13. "Desert Crossing Seminar: After Action Report," June 28–30, 1999, available at: http://www2.gwu.edu/~nsarchiv/NSAEBB/NSAEBB207/Desert% 20Crossing%20After%20Action%20Report_1999-06-28.pdf.

14. "Straight Talk from General Anthony Zinni," available at: http://www.international.ucla.edu/article.asp?parentid=11162.

15. Ibid. See also Roger Strother, "Post-Saddam Iraq: The War Game," November 4, 2006, available at: http://www2.gwu.edu/~nsarchiv/NSAEBB/NSAEBB207/index.htm.

16. Wass de Czege, "Wargaming Insights"; Kaplan, *Daydream Believers,* 47–48; Kaplan, *The Insurgents,* 59–60.

17. Rose, *How Wars End,* 2.

18. Franks, *American Soldier,* 440–41; Rose, *How Wars End,* 3; Woodward, *Plan of Attack;* Dyson, "What Really Happened in Planning for Postwar Iraq?"

19. Interview with Thomas Pickering, January 3, 2014.

20. Marshall, *Marshall's Chess "Swindles."*

21. Soltis, *Frank Marshall, United States Chess Champion,* 168.

22. Schivelbusch, *The Culture of Defeat,* 6.

23. Interview with James Stavridis, September 16, 2013.

24. Cohen and Gooch, *Military Misfortunes,* 38.

25. Wass de Czege, "Wargaming Insights."

26. Sean D. Naylor, "War Game Rigged?" *Army Times,* August 16, 2002; Fred Kaplan, "War-Gamed," March 28, 2003, available at: http://www.slate.com/articles/news_and_politics/war_stories/2003/03/wargamed.html.

27. Packer, *The Assassin's Gate,* 117.

28. Special Inspector General for Iraq Reconstruction, *Hard Lessons,* 323–24; Gordon and Trainor, *Cobra II,* 142–50.

29. Interview with John Abizaid, August 8, 2013.

30. Interview with Richard Myers, January 17, 2014.

31. Bernard Weinraub with Thom Shanker, "A Nation At War: Under Fire," *New York Times,* April 1, 2003.

32. Interview with James Stavridis, September 16, 2013.

33. Cohen and Gooch, *Military Misfortunes,* 38.

34. Kahneman and Renshon, "Why Hawks Win"; Kahneman and Renshon, "Hawkish Biases"; Kahneman, *Thinking, Fast and Slow.*

35. Taliaferro, *Balancing Risks.*

36. Craig and Logevall, *America's Cold War,* 238. Loss aversion also makes peace negotiations in wartime much harder. Even if both sides offer equal sacrifices our loss *feels* worse. Kahneman, *Thinking, Fast and Slow,* 284; Jervis, "Political Implications of Loss Aversion"; Milburn and Christie, "Effort Justification as a Motive for Continuing War," 244.

37. Kahneman, *Thinking, Fast and Slow,* 345; Kahneman and Renshon, "Hawkish Biases"; Bazerman, "Why Negotiations Go Wrong," 221.

38. Abraham Lincoln, "Address at the Dedication of the National Cemetery at Gettysburg, Pennsylvania," November 19, 1863, available at: http://www.presidency.ucsb.edu/ws/?pid=73959.

39. Steele, *Lord Salisbury,* 121.

40. Anderson, *The Columbia Guide to the Vietnam War,* 266–67; Glad and Rosenberg, "Bargaining Under Fire"; Stanley, *Paths to Peace,* 46–47; Downs, "The Lessons of Disengagement"; Staw and Ross, "Understanding Behavior in Escalation Situations."

41. Colman, *A Dictionary of Psychology,* 411; Bazerman, "Why Negotiations Go Wrong"; Kahneman and Renshon, "Hawkish Biases," 81; Kahneman, *Thinking, Fast and Slow,* part 3.

42. In 1968, Townsend Hoopes, undersecretary of the air force, found "repeated miscalculations as to the force and time required to 'defeat the aggression,' pacify the countryside, and make [South Vietnam's government and military] viable without massive US support. Each fresh increment of American power has been justified as the last one needed to do the job." Berman, *Lyndon Johnson's War,* 201; Polsky, *Elusive Victories,* 232, 242; Johnson and Tierney, *Failing to Win,* 147; Milburn and Christie, "Effort Justification as a Motive for Continuing War," 241–43.

43. McMahon, "Credibility and World Power," 466; Welch, *Painful Choices,* 127.

44. Young, *The Vietnam Wars,* 135. Nixon said that if the chips were down, and the most powerful country acted like "a pitiful, helpless giant," totalitarianism would threaten free nations. McMahon, "Credibility and World Power," 467.

45. McMahon, "Credibility and World Power," 467.

46. There's often a revealing double standard. Presidents are sure that an American retreat will destroy our reputation for toughness. But presidents don't think that an opponent's retreat necessarily signals its weakness. When the Soviet Union pulled out of Afghanistan, for example, Washington didn't assume that further withdrawals would occur. We're usually cautious about reading too much into an opponent's concession, just as other countries are wary of reading too much into our concession. For a discussion of reputation, see Logevall, *Choosing War,* xviii; Hopf, *Peripheral Visions;* Mercer, *Reputation in International Politics.*

47. Rose, *How Wars End,* 192.

48. Ibid.

49. Press, *Calculating Credibility;* Mercer, *Reputation and International Politics.*

50. Iklé, *Every War Must End,* x. The flip side is that using force will not necessarily establish a reputation for toughness that deters aggressors. For example, U.S. intervention in Panama in 1989 didn't deter Saddam Hussein from invading Kuwait the following year. Similarly, American intervention in Afghanistan and Iraq in 2001–2003 didn't stop Russia from intervening in Georgia in 2008.

51. Croco, "Peace at What Price?"

52. Welch, *Painful Choices,* 141; Logevall, *Choosing War,* 77; Stanley, "Ending the Korean War"; Tierney, *How We Fight;* Goemans, *War and Punishment.*

53. VanDeMark, *Into the Quagmire,* 75.

54. Interview with Vali Nasr, July 24, 2013.

55. John Vinocur, "The Unmentionable War," *New York Times,* September 20, 2012.

56. Madeleine Albright, U.S. ambassador to the UN, once pressed Colin Powell to intervene in Bosnia: "What's the point of having this superb military that you're always talking about if we can't use it?" As Powell put it, "I thought I would have an aneurysm." Powell, *My American Journey,* 576.

57. Betts, *Soldiers, Statesmen, and Cold War Crises;* Betts, *American Force,* 206.

58. Chandrasekaran, *Little America,* 117–18; Walt, "Cutting Losses in Wars of Choice." An exception is Iraq, where many senior U.S. military officials were skeptical of the surge policy.

59. Rosa Brooks, "Obama vs. the Generals," available at: http://www.politico.com/magazine/story/2013/11/obama-vs-the-generals-99379.html.

60. Woodward, *Obama's Wars,* 247. Military officials, like all bureaucrats, like to deal in threes, by presenting their favored policy sandwiched between two utterly unpalatable options. Henry Kissinger once said that bureaucrats always gave him three choices: "war, surrender, and present policy." Rose, *How Wars End,* 176.

61. For a longer discussion of this point, see Tierney, *How We Fight.*

62. As the violence fell in Iraq from 2007 to 2008, U.S. media coverage of the conflict also declined sharply. Ricks, *The Gamble,* 254.

63. For popular attitudes toward counterinsurgency and nation-building, see Tierney, *How We Fight.*

64. In Vietnam, American public support was fairly resilient until 1968, even though it was a counterinsurgency war. But there were really two Vietnam wars: an interstate war between the United States and North Vietnam, and a counterinsurgency mission inside South Vietnam against the Vietcong. Interestingly, Americans who primarily saw Vietnam as an interstate war tended to back the war effort. Americans who saw the conflict mainly as a civil war in South Vietnam tended to be more skeptical. Support for the counterinsurgency and nation-building campaign in Afghanistan also held up for several years after 2001 because of the lingering rally-around-the-flag effect of 9/11. But by 2014 some polls suggested that Afghanistan was the least popular war in American history. See Tierney, *How We Fight,* 172–80.

65. Terry M. Neal, "Bush Backs into Nation Building," *Washington Post,* February 26, 2003.

66. David Rohde and David E. Sanger, "How a 'Good War' in Afghanistan Went Bad," *New York Times,* August 12, 2007.

67. Rumsfeld, *Known and Unknown,* 667; Daniel Serwer, "Statebuilding in Iraq: An American Failure, Lately Redeemed," in McMahon and Western, eds., *The International Community and Statebuilding,* 169–83.

68. Toby Dodge, "Iraq," in Caplan, ed., *Exit Strategies and State Building,* 248.

69. *USA Today*/Gallup poll, January 12–14, 2007. Congressional opposition can have the benefit of signaling to foreign allies that American patience is not unlimited.

70. Rose, *How Wars End,* 181.

71. Kissinger, *Diplomacy,* 682.

72. Roselle, *Media and the Politics of Failure,* 59–60; Polsky, *Elusive Victories,* 264. Similarly, U.S. withdrawal from Iraq created its own momentum. Polls in 2011 showed that 78 percent of the public approved of withdrawing all troops by the end of the year. If Iraq had suddenly collapsed and U.S. interests required sending troops back, this option would have been politically difficult or impossible. Parasiliti, "Leaving Iraq," 129.

73. McMahon, "Credibility and World Power," 471; Morgan, "Saving Face for the Sake of Deterrence," 142.

Chapter 4: Laying the Groundwork

1. Stephen Burgess-Whiting and Spencer C. Tucker, "Declaration of War, U.S.," in Tucker, ed., *The Encyclopedia of the War of 1812,* 186.

2. Wayne E. Lee, "Plattsburgh 1814: Warring for Bargaining Chips," in Moten, ed., *Between War and Peace,* 58; Robert D. Schulzinger, "American Presidents and their Negotiators, 1776–2009," in Solomon and Quinney, *American Negotiating Behavior,* 162.

3. Johnson and Tierney, *Failing to Win,* 6–7.

4. Dwight D. Eisenhower, "Address Delivered Before the American Society of Newspaper Editors," available at: http://www.presidency.ucsb.edu/ws/index.php?pid=9819.

5. Stephen J. Whitfield, "Korea, the Cold War, and American Democracy," in McCann and Strauss, eds., *War and Democracy,* 216.

6. John F. Kennedy, "Inaugural Address," January 20, 1961, available at: http://www.presidency.ucsb.edu/ws/index.php?pid=8032.

7. Dwight D. Eisenhower, "Farewell Radio and Television Address to the American People," January 17, 1961, available at: http://www.presidency.ucsb.edu/ws/index.php?pid=12086. Ike's judgment was not always impressive, however. After his retirement in 1961, Eisenhower became a strong hawk on Vietnam and urged LBJ to escalate U.S. involvement in the war.

8. Interview with Eric Edelman, September 27, 2013.

9. Interview with John Abizaid, August 8, 2013. Toby Dodge, who worked as an advisor to David Petraeus in Iraq, concurred that "it was never going to happen." Interview with Toby Dodge, August 7, 2013. A few hundred U.S. service members stayed behind to handle the sale of military equipment and coordinate training.

10. Parker, "The Iraq We Left Behind." See also Dodge, "The U.S. and Iraq"; Sky, "Iraq, From Surge to Sovereignty"; Ricks, *The Gamble.*

11. Stueck, *The Korean War,* 134–35.

12. Anne Saadah, "Sovereignty and Citizenship: The Old France and the New Europe," in Miller and Smith, eds., *Ideas & Ideals,* 339.

13. Caplan, "Devising Exit Strategies," 113; Strachan, "The Lost Meaning of Strategy"; Betts, *American Force,* chapter 10; "Statement of Catherine Dale on Transition in Afghanistan," February 27, 2013, available at: http://docs.house .gov/meetings/AS/AS00/20130227/100315/HHRG-113-AS00-Wstate -DaleC-20130227.pdf.

14. Interview with Ryan Crocker, September 27, 2013.

15. "Bombing Duisburg, October 1944," in Freedman, ed., *War,* 40.

16. The original memo is at: http://cna.org/sites/default/files/research/0204320000 .pdf. See also Mangel and Samaniego, "Abraham Wald's Work on Aircraft Survivability"; Wallis, "The Statistical Research Group, 1942–1945."

17. Gaddis, *Strategies of Containment,* 256.

18. Robert McNamara interview, George Washington University National Security Archives, December 6, 1998, available at http://www.gwu.edu/~nsarchiv/ coldwar/interviews/episode-11/mcnamara1.html.

19. Kapstein, "Measuring Progress in Modern Warfare"; Daddis, *No Sure Victory;* Lebovic, *The Limits of U.S. Military Capability.*

20. Kapstein, "Measuring Progress in Modern Warfare."

21. Kapstein, "Measuring Progress in Modern Warfare," 150; Connable and Libicki, *How Insurgencies End,* 18.

22. George W. Bush, "Remarks on the Death of Senior Al Qaida Associate Abu Musab Al Zarqawi," June 8, 2006, available at: http://www.presidency.ucsb .edu/ws/index.php?pid=92.

23. Chaney, "Assessing Pacification Policy in Iraq."

24. Kilcullen, *Counterinsurgency,* 59–76.

25. Agnew et al., "Baghdad Nights."

26. Interview with John McLaughlin, August 27, 2013. See also Kapstein, "Measuring Progress in Modern Warfare"; Cordesman, "Afghanistan: The Failed Metrics of Ten Years of War."

27. Thomas-Symonds, *Attlee,* 270.

28. Stueck, *The Korean War,* 136–37.

29. Ricks, *The Gamble,* 9, 155.

30. Clausewitz, *On War,* 579.

31. Ibid., 87.

32. Stewart and Knaus, *Can Intervention Work?* See also Pape, "When Duty Calls."

33. Interview with Dov Zackheim, July 19, 2013.

34. Interview with Vali Nasr, July 24, 2013.

35. Staniland, "States, Insurgents, and Wartime Political Orders," 243; Simpson, *War from the Ground Up.*

36. When Stanley McChrystal described the complex allegiances in Kandahar, Afghanistan, Obama said, "This reminds me of Chicago politics....You're

asking me to understand the interrelationships and interconnections between ward bosses and district chiefs and the tribes of Chicago like the tribes of Kandahar." Woodward, *Obama's Wars*, 350. On Chicago's gangs, see Venkatesh, *American Project*.

37. Bowie and Immerman, *Waging Peace*, 123.
38. Krebs, *Dueling Visions*, 49.
39. Watkins and Rosegrant, *Breakthrough International Negotiation*, 70.
40. Iklé, *Every War Must End*, 26, 66–68.
41. Croco, "Peace at What Price?"; Stanley, *Paths to Peace*.
42. Robert D. Schulzinger, "American Presidents and Their Negotiators, 1776–2009," in Solomon and Quinney, *American Negotiating Behavior*, 162.
43. Stephen J. Whitfield, "Korea, the Cold War, and American Democracy," in McCann and Strauss, eds., *War and Democracy*, 216.
44. Interview with Frederick Nolting, November 11, 1982, available at: http://lcweb2.loc.gov/service/mss/mfdip/2005%20txt%20files/2004nol01.txt; Johns, *Vietnam's Second Front*, 32–33.
45. Jervis, "The Politics of Troop Withdrawal," 515–16.
46. George W. Bush, "Address to the Nation Announcing Strikes Against Al Qaida Training Camps and Taliban Military Installations in Afghanistan," October 7, 2001, available at: http://www.presidency.ucsb.edu/ws/index.php?pid=65088.
47. Interview with George Shultz, September 27, 2013.
48. Simpson, *War from the Ground Up*, 123–24.
49. George W. Bush, "Remarks at Latvia University in Riga," November 28, 2006, available at: http://www.presidency.ucsb.edu/ws/index.php?pid=24325.
50. Interview with Thomas Pickering, January 3, 2014.
51. Interview with Stanley McChrystal, August 5, 2013.
52. Chandrasekaran, *Little America*.
53. Barack Obama, "Remarks at the United States Military Academy at West Point, New York," December 1, 2009, available at: http://www.presidency.ucsb.edu/ws/index.php?pid=86948. See also Simpson, *War from the Ground Up*.
54. Barack Obama, "Address to the Nation on the Drawdown of United States Military Personnel in Afghanistan," June 22, 2011, available at: http://www.presidency.ucsb.edu/ws/index.php?pid=90556.
55. "Gates Predicts 'Slog' in Afghanistan," *Washington Post*, January 28, 2009.
56. Barack Obama, "Remarks on United States Military and Diplomatic Strategies for Afghanistan and Pakistan," March 27, 2009, available at: http://www.presidency.ucsb.edu/ws/index.php?pid=85924.
57. Anne E. Kornblut, Scott Wilson, and Karen DeYoung, "During Marathon Review of Afghanistan Strategy, Obama Held Out for Faster Troop Surge," *Washington Post*, December 6, 2009.
58. Chuck Hagel, "Message to ISAF Personnel from Secretary of Defense Chuck Hagel," March 08, 2013, available at: http://www.defense.gov/speeches/speech.aspx?speechid=1756.

59. Gates, *Duty*; Thom Shanker, "Bipartisan Critic Turns His Gaze Toward Obama," *New York Times*, January 7, 2014.

60. Interview with Stephen Biddle, September 16, 2013; Biddle, "Ending the War in Afghanistan."

Chapter 5: Storytelling

1. Horne, *A Savage War of Peace*; Wall, *France, the United States, and the Algerian War*; Smith, *Stopping Wars*, 84.

2. Bernstein, *The Republic of De Gaulle*, 50.

3. Stephen Tyre, "The Memory of French Military Defeat at Dien Bien Phu and the Defense of French Algeria," in MacLeod, ed., *Defeat and Memory*, 214.

4. Gildea, *The Past in French History*, 113.

5. Ibid., 112.

6. Ibid., 113.

7. De Gaulle, *Memoirs of Hope*, 46. See also Pillar, *Negotiating Peace*, 219.

8. Martin S. Alexander and Philip C. F. Bankwitz, "From Politiques en Képi to Military Technocrats: De Gaulle and the Recovery of the French Army after Indochina and Algeria," in Andreopoulos and Selesky, eds., *The Aftermath of Defeat*, 79–102.

9. Schoenbaum, *Waging Peace and War*, 421.

10. Sandars, *The Epic of Gilgamesh*, 102.

11. McKee, *Story*, 15.

12. Vanessa M. Gezari, "How to Read Afghanistan," *New York Times*, August 10, 2013.

13. These quotes are from Drew Gilpin Faust, "Telling War Stories: Reflections of a Civil War Historian," available at: http://www.neh.gov/about/awards/jefferson-lecture/drew-gilpin-faust-lecture.

14. Baudelaire, *Artificial Paradises*, 147.

15. Drew Gilpin Faust, "Telling War Stories: Reflections of a Civil War Historian," available at: http://www.neh.gov/about/awards/jefferson-lecture/drew-gilpin-faust-lecture

16. Taleb, *Black Swan*, 63; Roselle, *Media and the Politics of Failure*, 59–60.

17. http://www.ted.com/talks/chimamanda_adichie_the_danger_of_a_single_story.html.

18. Anna Fels, "Great Betrayals," *New York Times*, October 5, 2013.

19. "Obama Reflects on His Biggest Mistake as President," CBS News, available at: http://www.cbsnews.com/news/obama-reflects-on-his-biggest-mistake-as-president/. Of course, claiming to have got the substance right but the style wrong is itself a form of storytelling—no president would argue the opposite.

20. David M. Barnes, C. Kevin Banks, Michael Albanese, and Michael F. Steger, "Meaning-Making: The Search for Meaning in Dangerous Contexts," in

Notes

Sweeney, Matthews, and Lester, eds., *Leadership in Dangerous Situations,* 139–60.

21. Nye, *Soft Power.*
22. Simpson, *War from the Ground Up,* 36.
23. Thomas H. Johnson and Kevin L. Steele, "The Taliban Narrative: Understanding the Group's Messages, Actions and Clues to Their Endgame," in Corman, ed., *Narrating the Exit from Afghanistan,* 71–98; William Dalrymple, "The Ghosts of Afghanistan's Past," *New York Times,* April 13, 2013.
24. Simpson, *War from the Ground Up,* 215.
25. For the challenges faced by the president in shaping political opinion, see Edwards, *The Strategic President.*
26. The speech is available at: http://watergate.info/1969/11/03/nixons-silent -majority-speech.html.
27. Bochin, *Richard Nixon,* 62; Johns, *Vietnam's Second Front,* 273.
28. For a discussion, see Simpson, *War from the Ground Up.*
29. Westen, *The Political Brain,* xv; Entman, *Projections of Power.*
30. Kimball, *Nixon's Vietnam War,* 168.
31. Matt Bai, "Still Waiting for the Narrator in Chief," *New York Times,* October 30, 2012.
32. Kimball, *Nixon's Vietnam War,* 168.
33. Dallek, *Nixon and Kissinger,* 199.
34. Small, *The Presidency of Richard Nixon,* 227.
35. Gallup poll, January 12–15, 1973, available at http://www.ropercenter.uconn.edu.
36. http://www.politico.com/story/2014/01/robert-gates-harry-reid-book-criti cism-102295.html.
37. Interview with Ronald Neumann, October 9, 2013.
38. David M. Barnes, C. Kevin Banks, Michael Albanese, and Michael F. Steger. "Meaning-Making: The Search for Meaning in Dangerous Contexts," in Sweeney, Matthews, and Lester, eds., *Leadership in Dangerous Situations,* 139–62.
39. Walt, *Taming American Power,* 230.
40. Thomas H. Johnson and Kevin L. Steele, "The Taliban Narrative: Understanding the Group's Messages, Actions and Clues to Their Endgame," in Corman, ed., *Narrating the Exit from Afghanistan,* 71–98.

Chapter 6: Surge

1. George W. Bush, "Address to the Nation on Military Operations in Iraq," January 10, 2007, available at: http://www.presidency.ucsb.edu/ws/index.php ?pid=24432.
2. Ucko, *The New Counterinsurgency Era,* chapter 6; Gordon and Trainor, *The Endgame*; interview with Toby Dodge, August 7, 2013.
3. Ucko, *The New Counterinsurgency Era,* 125. See also: http://icasualties.org.

Notes

4. Petraeus, "How We Won in Iraq"; Biddle, Friedman, and Shapiro, "Testing the Surge"; Feaver, "The Right to Be Right"; Hagan et al., "Correspondence: Assessing the Synergy Thesis in Iraq"; Betts, Desch, and Feaver, "Correspondence: Civilians, Soldiers, and the Iraq Surge Decision"; Simon, "The Price of the Surge"; Lynch, "Explaining the Awakening."

5. Brian Knowlton, "Kissinger Says Victory in Iraq Is Not Possible," *New York Times,* November 19, 2006.

6. David S. Cloud, "U.S. Considers Large, Temporary Troop Increase in Iraq," *New York Times,* November 21, 2006.

7. Paul Farhi, "Surge (Surj) N. 1. A Sudden Increase…in Political Parlance," *Washington Post,* January 10, 2007.

8. The deployment of civilian administrators may be part of the surge, but an increase in military capabilities is usually necessary. Iklé, *Every War Must End,* 39.

9. Kennan, *American Diplomacy,* 66.

10. Connable and Libicki, *How Insurgencies End;* Rosen, *War and Human Nature,* chapter 4.

11. This discussion of COIN draws on Galula, *Counterinsurgency Warfare*; Nagl, *Learning to Eat Soup with a Knife;* U.S. Army and Marine Corps, *The U.S. Army/ Marine Corps Counterinsurgency Field Manual;* Dobbins et al., *The Beginner's Guide to Nation-Building;* Kilcullen, *The Accidental Guerrilla;* Kilcullen, *Counterinsurgency;* William J. Durch, "Exit and Peace Support Operations," in Caplan, ed., *Exit Strategies and State Building,* 79–99; Hammes, *The Sling and the Stone;* Paris, *At War's End;* Sepp, "Best Practices in Counterinsurgency"; Ghani and Lockhart, *Fixing Failed States;* Paul et al., *Paths to Victory.*

12. Interview with Richard Myers, January 17, 2014.

13. Johnston, "Does Decapitation Work?"; Price, "Targeting Top Terrorists."

14. One study of the Iraq War found that both insurgents and counterinsurgents suffer costs if they kill civilians. When counterinsurgents were responsible for the death of noncombatants, insurgent attacks rose. When rebels did the same, insurgent attacks declined. Condra and Shapiro, "Who Takes the Blame?"

15. Gordon and Trainor, *The Endgame,* 25; Robinson, *Tell Me How This Ends.*

16. Gordon and Trainor, *The Endgame,* 243–50.

17. Interview with H. R. McMaster, July 19, 2013; George Packer, "The Lesson of Tal Afar," *New Yorker,* April 10, 2006. The U.S. military eventually improved efforts at cultural training by giving American soldiers "smart cards" with basic information on Islam, Iraqi culture, and Arabic phrases, together with CDs and online training programs.

18. Nagl, *Learning to Eat Soup with a Knife;* Biddle, "Is there a Middle Way?"; Jones, *Counterinsurgency in Afghanistan;* Connable and Libicki, *How Insurgencies End;* Paul et al., *Paths to Victory,* xxxi–xxxiii.

19. According to the U.S. Army and Marine Corps's *Counterinsurgency Field Manual,* "Most density recommendations fall within a range of 20 to 25

counterinsurgents for every 1000 residents in an [area of operations]. Twenty counterinsurgents per 1000 residents is often considered the minimum troop density required for effective COIN operations; however as with any fixed ratio, such calculations remain very dependent upon the situation." U.S. Army and Marine Corps, *The U.S. Army/Marine Corps Counterinsurgency Field Manual,* 1–13. See also Dobbins et al., *The Beginner's Guide to Nation-Building,* xxxvi, 37–41; Betts, *American Force.*

20. Friedman, "Manpower and Counterinsurgency"; Paul et al., *Paths to Victory,* 120–22.

21. Sheehan, *A Bright Shining Lie,* 67.

22. One RAND study estimates that humanitarian challenges require an average commitment of $34 per member of the local population. Dobbins et al., *The Beginner's Guide to Nation-Building,* 134.

23. Kilcullen, *Counterinsurgency,* 37; O'Neill, *Insurgency & Terrorism,* 162; Boot, "The Evolution of Irregular War"; Krepinevich, "How to Win in Iraq."

24. One study found that spending on education, health, and social security, especially through small-scale projects, won hearts and minds and reduced insurgent violence. Berman, Eli, Shapiro, and Felter, "Can Hearts and Minds Be Bought?"

25. Staniland, "States, Insurgents, and Wartime Political Orders," 256–57; Kilcullen, *Counterinsurgency,* 156–57.

26. Clausewitz, *On War,* 29.

27. Connable and Libicki, *How Insurgencies End,* 127; Paris, *At War's End.*

28. Gorka and Kilcullen, "An Actor-centric Theory of War."

29. Connable and Libicki, *How Insurgencies End.*

30. Kornblut, Wilson, and DeYoung, "During Marathon Review of Afghanistan Strategy, Obama Held Out for Faster Troop Surge."

31. Barack Obama, "Remarks on United States Military and Diplomatic Strategies for Afghanistan and Pakistan," March 27, 2009, available at: http://www.presidency.ucsb.edu/ws/index.php?pid=85924.

32. Woodward, *Obama's Wars,* 336.

33. Interview with Stanley McChrystal, August 5, 2013.

34. David E. Sanger and Thom Shanker, "Two Campaigns Skirt Talk of Tough Choices in Afghanistan," *New York Times,* October 21, 2012.

35. Livingston and O'Hanlon, "Afghanistan Index."

36. Interview with John Allen, December 10, 2013.

37. Livingston and O'Hanlon, "Afghanistan Index"; Biddle, "Ending the War in Afghanistan." See also: http://icasualties.org/oef/.

38. Kornblut, Wilson, and DeYoung, "During Marathon Review of Afghanistan Strategy, Obama Held Out for Faster Troop Surge."

39. Chandrasekaran, *Little America,* 59.

40. Shanker, "Bipartisan Critic Turns His Gaze Toward Obama."

41. Kalb and Kalb, *Haunting Legacy,* 293.

42. Chandrasekaran, *Little America,* 345; Nasr, *Dispensable Nation,* 25.

43. Moyar, *A Question of Command,* 120–21; Hack, "'Iron Claws on Malaya.'"

44. Desch, "Bush and the Generals."

45. Lloyd J. Matthews, "The Uniformed Intellectual and His Place in American Arms," *Army,* August 2002, 31–40, available at: http://www.ausa.org/publications/armymagazine/archive/2002/8/Documents/Matthews_0802.pdf.

46. Ricks, *The Gamble,* 15–23; Kalb and Kalb, *Haunting Legacy,* 217.

47. Woodward, *Bush at War,* 251.

48. Ricks, *The Generals,* 400–401.

49. Rose, *How Wars End,* 247, 268; Ricks, "General Failure."

50. Ricks, *The Generals,* 7, 421; Ricks, "General Failure"; Bacevich, *The Limits of Power,* 147.

51. Scales, "The Quality of Command." Presidents can't summarily fire a general, but they can recall him or her from an assigned position, which usually triggers voluntary retirement because the general has few prospects for career advancement. Removing a general from the armed services requires a court-martial or an administrative separation board hearing.

52. Gladwell, *Outliers,* chapter 7.

53. McMaster, *Dereliction of Duty.*

54. Interview with John Abizaid, August 8, 2013.

55. Interview with Stanley McChrystal, August 5, 2013.

56. *"Il est bon de tuer de temps en temps un amiral pour encourager les autres."*

57. Interview with Stanley McChrystal, August 5, 2013; interview with John Abizaid, August 8, 2013.

58. Cohen, *Supreme Command,* 15–17. An image of the original letter can be seen at www.gutenberg.org/files/3253/3253-h/files/8110/8110-h/8110-h.htm.

59. McPherson, *Battle Cry of Freedom,* 585.

60. Shanker, "Bipartisan Critic Turns His Gaze Toward Obama."

61. Interview with John Allen, December 10, 2013.

62. Chandler, *The Campaigns of Napoleon,* 155.

63. The Scott quote is from his 1805 poem "The Lay of the Last Minstrel."

64. Zakaria, *The Post-American World,* 33; Hutchinson, *Modern Nationalism.*

65. Interview with Ryan Crocker, September 27, 2013.

66. Richard Stubbs, "From Search and Destroy to Hearts and Minds: The Evolution of British Strategy in Malaya, 1948–1960," in Marston and Malkasian, eds., *Counterinsurgency in Modern Warfare,* 109; Edelstein, "Occupational Hazards."

67. Lindsay and Petersen, *CIWAG Case Study of Irregular Warfare and Armed Groups,* 16.

68. Johnson and Tierney, *Failing to Win,* 149.

69. Larson and Savych, *American Public Support for U.S. Military Operations,* 30.

70. Paul Wolfowitz, "Veterans of Foreign Wars Remarks," March 11, 2003, available at: http://www.defense.gov/speeches/speech.aspx?speechid=359.

71. George W. Bush, "Address to the Nation on Iraq from the U.S.S. Abraham Lincoln," May 1, 2003, available at: http://www.presidency.ucsb.edu/ws/index.php?pid=68675.

72. "Pfc. Jessica Lynch Isn't Rambo Anymore," *New York Times,* November 9, 2003.

73. Baum and Groeling, "Reality Asserts Itself," 475.

74. Langworth, ed., *Churchill by Himself,* 591.

75. Johnson, *The Vantage Point,* 380.

76. George W. Bush, "Address to the Nation on Military Operations in Iraq," January 10, 2007, available at: http://www.presidency.ucsb.edu/ws/index.php?pid=24432.

77. http://www.economist.com/blogs/theworldin2009/2008/10/the_worst_country_of_2009.

Chapter 7: Talk

1. Strobe Talbott, "Remembering the Unquiet American," available at: http://www.foreignpolicy.com/articles/2011/11/01/remembering_a_happy_warrior; Chollet and Power, eds., *The Unquiet American.*

2. Rajiv Chandrasekaran, "Richard Holbrooke Dies, Veteran U.S. Diplomat Brokered Dayton Peace Accords," *Washington Post,* December 14, 2010; Chollet and Power, eds., *The Unquiet American;* Nasr, *Dispensable Nation.*

3. Bew et al., *Talking to the Taliban.*

4. Matthew Rosenberg and Adam Entous, "Sign of War Gains Proves False," *Wall Street Journal,* November 24, 2010; Dexter Filkins and Carlota Gall, "Taliban Leader in Secret Talks Was an Impostor," *New York Times,* November 22, 2010; Joshua Partlow, "British Faulted for Taliban Impostor," *Washington Post,* November 26, 2010.

5. Barack Obama, "Remarks on United States Military and Diplomatic Strategies for Afghanistan and Pakistan," March 27, 2009, available at: http://www.presidency.ucsb.edu/ws/index.php?pid=85924.

6. Chandrasekaran, *Little America,* 231–35; Nasr, *Dispensable Nation,* 25.

7. Semple et al., "Taliban Perspectives on Reconciliation."

8. Rod Nordland, "Peace Envoys from Taliban at Loose End in Qatar," *New York Times,* April 9, 2013.

9. Alissa J. Rubin, "Departing French Envoy Has Frank Words on Afghanistan," *New York Times,* April 27, 2013; Bew et al., *Talking to the Taliban.*

10. Interview with George Casey, September 23, 2013.

11. Foot, *A Substitute for Victory,* 15; Tierney, *How We Fight.*

12. George W. Bush, "Commencement Address at the United States Naval Academy in Annapolis, Maryland," May 27, 2005, available at: http://www.presidency.ucsb.edu/ws/index.php?pid=63919.

13. George W. Bush, "Address to Members of the Knesset in Jerusalem," May 15, 2008, available at: http://www.presidency.ucsb.edu/ws/index.php?pid=77330.

14. Stueck, *Rethinking the Korean War*, 146–47.
15. Marilyn Young, "Fighting While Negotiating," in Gardner and Gittinger, eds., *The Search for Peace in Vietnam, 1964–1968*, 36–37.
16. Asselin, "We Don't Want a Munich," 578.
17. Interview with Ryan Crocker, September 27, 2013.
18. Interview with Ronald Neumann, October 9, 2013.
19. Bergen, *The Longest War*, 267.
20. Biddle, Friedman, and Shapiro, "Testing the Surge"; Lynch, "Explaining the Awakening"; Ricks, *The Gamble*.
21. Kissinger, *Ending the Vietnam War*, 293.
22. Matthew Lee, "Veteran Diplomat Holbrooke Dies at Age 69," *Washington Times*, December 13, 2010.
23. Mnookin, *Bargaining with the Devil*.
24. Sanger, *Confront and Conceal*, 123.
25. Biddle, "Ending the War in Afghanistan"; Anatol Lieven, "Afghanistan: The Best Way to Peace," *The New York Review of Books*, February 9, 2012; Brahimi and Pickering, *Afghanistan;* Bew et al., *Talking to the Taliban.*
26. Sparre, "Megaphone Diplomacy in the Northern Irish Peace Process."
27. Pillar, "Ending Limited War," 254–55. In Afghanistan, the Taliban may have adopted the same strategy. During the Obama administration, the United States met with a Taliban agent, Tayyab Aga. The Taliban didn't publicly affirm Aga's status as an official negotiator, but he established his bona fides by promising that a coded message would appear on a Taliban-affiliated website—which duly occurred.
28. Haldeman, *The Haldeman Diaries*, 154.
29. Xia, *Negotiating with the Enemy*, 50–51.
30. Stueck, *Rethinking the Korean War*, 147; Seidel, "The Use of the Physical Environment in Peace Negotiations"; Joy, *How Communists Negotiate;* Salacuse and Rubin, "Your Place or Mine?"
31. Sandler, ed., *The Korean War*, 25; Seidel, "The Use of the Physical Environment in Peace Negotiations"; Holmes, "Zero-Sum Game."
32. Seidel, "The Use of the Physical Environment in Peace Negotiations"; Mayo, "The Manifestation of Politics in Architectural Practice"; Langguth, *Our Vietnam*, 530.
33. See Mullah Omar's 2013 Eid Message, available at: http://shahamat-english .com/index.php/paighamoona/35234.
34. Matthew Rosenberg and Alissa J. Rubin, "Taliban Step Toward Afghan Peace Talks Is Hailed by U.S.," *New York Times*, June 18, 2013; Semple et al., "Taliban Perspectives on Reconciliation."
35. Hillary Clinton, "Remarks at the Launch of the Asia Society's Series of Richard C. Holbrooke Memorial Addresses," February 18, 2011, available at: www.state.gov/secretary/rm/2011/02/156815.htm.
36. Fisher, Ury, and Patton, *Getting to Yes*, chapter 3; Watkins and Rosegrant, *Breakthrough International Negotiation*, 22.

Notes

37. The no-deal world is sometimes called a BATNA, or the Best Alternative to a Negotiated Agreement. Fisher, Ury, and Patton, *Getting to Yes*. See also Lebow, *The Art of Bargaining;* Sebenius and Singh, "Is a Nuclear Deal with Iran Possible?"

38. Interview with Ryan Crocker, September 27, 2013.

39. Shinn and Dobbins, *Afghan Peace Talks: A Primer.*

40. Bernstein, *Guns or Butter*, 489; Sherry, *In the Shadow of War*, 254.

41. Isaacson, *Kissinger*, 246.

42. Pape, "Coercive Air Power in the Vietnam War"; Lebovic, *The Limits of U.S. Military Capability*, 27.

43. Liddell Hart, *Strategy*, 357. The use of force is designed to send a message, but will this message be heard? President Johnson was too clever by half. He wanted Rolling Thunder to communicate a subtle mixture of resolve and restraint. *We're committed to this war, so forget about winning. But we're not destroying as much of your country as we could, so let's talk.* These mixed messages, however, were lost in translation. Hanoi saw any American bombing as punitive and any pause in the bombing as an ultimatum. Lebovic, *The Limits of U.S. Military Capability,* chapter 4.

44. Berman, "From Intervention to Disengagement," 54.

45. Pape, *Bombing to Win*, 199–200; Langguth, *Our Vietnam*, 602.

46. Pape, "Coercive Air Power in the Vietnam War"; Pillar, *Negotiating Peace*, 168; Quester, "The Psychological Effect of Bombing on Civilian Populations."

47. Pape, *Bombing to Win*; Kimball, *Nixon's Vietnam War*; Nguyen, *Hanoi's War*, 298.

48. For a wider discussion, see Schelling, *The Strategy of Conflict.*

49. Shinn and Dobbins, *Afghan Peace Talks*, 5–6.

50. Brian Mansfield, "Country Anthem Plays a Drumbeat for War," *USA Today*, February 26, 2003.

51. Byman, "Talking with Insurgents"; Connable and Libicki, *How Insurgencies End*, xvi.

52. Kilcullen, *The Accidental Guerrilla.*

53. Susan E. Rice, "Statement by Ambassador Susan Rice," June 17, 2011, available at: http://usun.state.gov/briefing/statements/2011/166468.htm.

54. "Moscow's Formal Announcement of Stalin's Death," *New York Times*, March 6, 1953.

55. Kathryn Weathersby, "The Soviet Role in the Korean War: The State of Historical Knowledge," in Stueck, ed., *The Korean War in World History*, 84–85; Stanley, "Ending the Korean War," 63–65, 74–76.

56. Kimball, *Nixon's Vietnam War.*

57. Interview with Ronald Neumann, October 9, 2013.

58. Interview with John McLaughlin, August 27, 2013.

59. Interview with Marc Grossman, October 30, 2013.

60. Bergen, "After the Withdrawal," 19–20.

61. Newton, *Eisenhower*, 100.

62. Stueck, *The Korean War*, 333.

63. Woodward, *Obama's Wars*, 128; William Dalrymple, "The Ghosts of Afghanistan's Past," *New York Times*, April 13, 2013.

64. "Glimmers of Hope," *The Economist*, May 12, 2011.

65. Miller, *The Much Too Promised Land*, 273.

66. Interview with Marc Grossman, October 30, 2013.

67. Interview with John Hillen, July 23, 2013.

68. Ibid.

69. McPherson, *Battle Cry of Freedom*, 390.

70. Smith, *Stopping Wars*, 62.

71. Fisher, Ury, and Patton, *Getting to Yes*.

72. Symonds, *Lincoln and His Admirals*, 93.

73. Larson, *Casualties and Consensus*, 25; Mueller, *War, Presidents and Public Opinion*, 90.

74. State Department press briefing, January 3, 2012, available at: http://www .state.gov/r/pa/prs/dpb/2012/01/180088.htm.

75. Harrison and Mosher, "The Secret Diary of McNamara's Dove," 521.

76. Ronald Reagan, "Statement on the Situation in Lebanon," February 7, 1984, available at: http://www.presidency.ucsb.edu/ws/index.php?pid=39433.

77. Barack Obama, "Remarks by the President at the United States Military Academy Commencement Ceremony," May 28, 2014, available at: http:// www.whitehouse.gov/the-press-office/2014/05/28/remarks-president -west-point-academy-commencement-ceremony.

78. Semple et al., "Taliban Perspectives on Reconciliation."

79. Solomon and Quinney, *American Negotiating Behavior*, 50.

80. Ucko, *The New Counterinsurgency Era*, 129–30.

81. Macdonagh, "The Prime Minister," 194.

82. Solomon and Quinney, *American Negotiating Behavior*, 79.

Chapter 8: Leave

1. Dov Weissglass, Sharon's chief of staff, claimed that the exit from Gaza was a "bottle of formaldehyde" that would freeze movement on the American peace plan until the Palestinians abandoned terrorism. "There is a decision here to do the minimum possible in order to maintain our political situation." Sharon told supporters: "We cannot fulfill all our dreams but through the means of disengagement we can achieve most of them." Joel Peters, "Gaza," in Peters and Newman, eds., *The Routledge Handbook of the Israeli-Palestinian Conflict*, 199.

2. These meetings occurred in July 2013. I am grateful to the Yitzhak Rabin Center for setting them up. See also Joel Peters, "Gaza," in Caplan, ed., *Exit Strategies and State Building*, 224–41.

Notes

3. Interview with H. R. McMaster, July 19, 2013.

4. Rayburn, "The Last Exit from Iraq," 33.

5. Dodge, *Inventing Iraq,* 38.

6. Gilbert, *Churchill,* 424–25.

7. Rayburn, "The Last Exit from Iraq"; Sluglett, *Britain in Iraq;* Dodge, *Inventing Iraq;* Stephen Farrell, "Baghdad Jews Have Become a Fearful Few," *New York Times,* June 1, 2008.

8. Dobbins et al., *America's Role in Nation-Building,* 164.

9. Gorka and Kilcullen, "An Actor-centric Theory of War," 17.

10. Rose, "The Exit Strategy Delusion," 67.

11. Rose, "The Exit Strategy Delusion"; Record, "Exit Strategy Delusions."

12. Barack Obama, "The President's News Conference in Lisbon, Portugal," November 10, 2010, available at: http://www.presidency.ucsb.edu/ws/index.php?pid=88758; "The Vice-Presidential Debate," October 11, 2012, available at: http://www.debates.org/index.php?page=october-11-2012-the-biden-romney-vice-presidential-debate.

13. Interview with Stanley McChrystal, August 5, 2013.

14. Matthew Rosenberg, "An Afghan Soldier's Journey from Ally to Enemy of America," *New York Times,* January 3, 2013.

15. Mullah Omar's 2013 Eid Message is available at: http://shahamat-english.com/index.php/paighamoona/35234. The term "green-on-blue" is modeled on the phrase "blue-on-blue," which means friendly fire incidents where soldiers on the same side accidentally attack each other. The colors refer to the standard military symbols on maps, where blue designates friendly forces, red refers to the enemy, and green represents neutral actors.

16. Livingston and O'Hanlon, "Afghanistan Index."

17. George W. Bush, "Address to the Nation on the War on Terror from Fort Bragg, North Carolina," June 28, 2005, available at: http://www.presidency.ucsb.edu/ws/index.php?pid=64989.

18. O'Hanlon and Riedel, "Plan A-Minus for Afghanistan," 129; McMahon, "The Politics, and Geopolitics, of American Troop Withdrawals from Vietnam, 1968–1972," 476–77.

19. U.S. forces also have a long support "tail," which reduces the number of frontline troops. When you factor in headquarters, logistics, maintenance, and rotations, twenty thousand Americans troops can become five thousand soldiers on the front lines at any one time.

20. U.S. Army and Marine Corps, *The U.S. Army/Marine Corps Counterinsurgency Field Manual,* 1–23. One study found that "indigenous counterinsurgents are on balance more effective, but also less consistent, than their foreign counterparts." Friedman, "Manpower and Counterinsurgency," 576.

21. Interview with George Casey, September 23, 2013.

22. Record, "Leaving Vietnam: Insights for Iraq?," 573.

23. Lebovic, *The Limits of U.S. Military Capability,* 176; Kilcullen, *Counterinsurgency,* 20; Gordon and Trainor, *The Endgame,* 146–47.

24. Nasr, *The Dispensable Nation,* 11.

25. Biddle, "Seeing Baghdad, Thinking Saigon," 8.

26. Rashid, *Descent into Chaos;* Betts, *American Force,* 157; Nagl, "Let's Win the Wars We're In," 23.

27. Interview with George Casey, September 23, 2013.

28. Barack Obama, "The President's News Conference with President Hamid Karzai of Afghanistan," January 11, 2013, available at: http://www.presidency .ucsb.edu/ws/index.php?pid=102831.

29. Interview with Stanley McChrystal, August 5, 2013.

30. Interview with Ronald Neumann, October 9, 2013.

31. Walter, *Committing to Peace;* Dobbins et al., *The Beginner's Guide to Nation-Building;* Fortna, *Does Peacekeeping Work?*

32. Dobbins et al., *The Beginner's Guide to Nation-Building,* xxvi.

33. Brahimi and Pickering, *Afghanistan: Negotiating Peace,* 45–47.

34. Doyle, *The Enemy in Our Hands,* 259.

35. Rose, *How Wars End,* 143; Stanley, "Ending the Korean War," 69; Boose, "Fighting While Talking," 25–29; Foot, *A Substitute for Victory,* 53, 74–76.

36. Joy, *Negotiating While Fighting,* 355; Rose, *How Wars End,* 147–48.

37. Stanley, *Paths to Peace,* 158; Stanley, "Ending the Korean War," 65.

38. Stanley, *Paths to Peace.*

39. Foot, *A Substitute for Victory,* 217–18.

40. Allen, *Until the Last Man Comes Home,* 50; Franklin, *M.I.A., or Mythmaking in America,* 63.

41. Franklin, *M.I.A., or Mythmaking in America,* 61; Schell, *The Time of Illusion,* 231; Marilyn Young, "Fighting While Negotiating," in Gardner and Gittinger, eds., *The Search for Peace in Vietnam, 1964–1968,* 41; Kimball, *Nixon's Vietnam War;* Hoff, *Nixon Reconsidered,* 222–27.

42. http://www.longwarjournal.org/threat-matrix/archives/2012/01/taliban _release_statement_on_n.php.

43. http://www.politico.com/story/2014/06/john-mccain-bowe-berghdal -107331.html.

44. Johnson and Tierney, *Failing to Win,* 63–64.

45. Kahneman et al., "When More Pain Is Preferred to Less"; Ezekiel J. Emanuel, "How Colonoscopies Are Like Home Renovations," *New York Times,* May 6, 2013.

46. Stueck, *Rethinking the Korean War,* 179.

47. "Truce Is Signed, Ending the Fighting in Korea," *New York Times,* July 27, 1953.

48. Kalb and Kalb, *Haunting Legacy,* 27.

49. Johnson and Tierney, *Failing to Win;* Weiss, *Military-Civilian Interactions,* 66–69.

50. Hess, *Presidential Decisions for War,* 269.

Notes

Notes

Chapter 9: Aftermath

1. Kalb and Kalb, *Haunting Legacy,* 75. See also Boot, *Invisible Armies;* Borer, *Superpowers Defeated;* Farrell, Osinga, and Russell, eds., *Military Adaptation in Afghanistan;* Grau, "The Soviet-Afghan War"; Braithwaite, *Afgantsy;* Barfield, *Afghanistan;* Kalinovsky, *A Long Goodbye;* Feifer, *The Great Gamble;* Lester W. Grau, "Breaking Contact Without Leaving Chaos: The Soviet Withdrawal from Afghanistan," in Corman, ed., *Narrating the Exit from Afghanistan,* 38–70.

2. Roselle, *Media and the Politics of Failure,* 90.

3. Cordovez and Harrison, *Out of Afghanistan,* 207.

4. Roselle, *Media and the Politics of Failure.*

5. Crile, *Charlie Wilson's War,* 506.

6. Templer, *Shadows and Wind,* 298.

7. Ibid., 308; Kaplan, "The Vietnam Solution."

8. Kupchan, *How Enemies Become Friends;* Lind, "Apologies in International Politics."

9. Schulzinger *A Time for Peace;* Entman, *Projections of Power,* 159; Keating, *Prisoners of Hope.*

10. Templer, *Shadows and Wind,* 1.

11. Kaplan, "The Vietnam Solution."

12. Hillary Clinton, "Remarks at Press Availability," Hanoi, Vietnam, July 23, 2010, available at: http://www.state.gov/secretary/rm/2010/07/145095.htm.

13. Dumbrell, *Rethinking the Vietnam War,* 239.

14. Rod Nordland, "Foreign Projects Give Afghans Fashion, Skate Park and Now 10,000 Balloons," *New York Times,* May 25, 2013.

15. Interview with Ryan Crocker, September 27, 2013. For the "Lawrence of Arabia" quote, see George W. Bush, "Remarks on Presenting the Presidential Medal of Freedom at the Department of State," January 15, 2009, available at: http://www.presidency.ucsb.edu/ws/index.php?pid=85426.

16. Nordland, "Foreign Projects Give Afghans Fashion, Skate Park and Now 10,000 Balloons."

17. http://www.bbc.com/news/world-asia-30676581.

18. Peter Beinart, "Obama's Disastrous Iraq Policy: An Autopsy," June 23, 2014, available at: http://www.theatlantic.com/international/archive/2014/06/obamas-disastrous-iraq-policy-an-autopsy/373225/.

19. "Biden in Iraq to Prepare for Postwar Relations," *New York Times,* November 29, 2011; Ned Parker, "Who Lost Iraq? It's Complicated," January 9, 2014, available at: http://www.politico.com/magazine/story/2014/01/iraq-barack-obama-george-bush-101996.html.

20. Parasiliti, "Leaving Iraq"; Sky, "Iraq, from Surge to Sovereignty."

21. Interview with John Hillen, July 23, 2013. For mismanagement in Iraq, see Van Buren, *We Meant Well.*

22. Interview with Dov Zakheim, July 19, 2013.

23. See also the January 2014 quarterly report of the Special Inspector General for Afghanistan Reconstruction, which highlights a number of problems with U.S. aid programs in Afghanistan, available at: http://www.sigar.mil/pdf/quarterlyreports/2014Jan30QR.pdf.

24. Afghan Public Health Institute et al., *Afghanistan Mortality Survey 2010;* Livingston and O'Hanlon, "Afghanistan Index," 23.

25. Malkasian, *War Comes to Garmser,* 78.

26. Aid is especially useful if the conflict has ended and there is a peace process. Economists Paul Collier and Anke Hoeffler found that following a civil war there's a window of opportunity where economic assistance can have an unusually positive impact. "Aid is considerably more effective in augmenting growth in post-conflict situations than in other situations." Collier and Hoeffler, "Aid, Policy, and Growth in Post-Conflict Societies," 13. See also Dobbins et al., *The Beginner's Guide to Nation-Building;* Berdal and Zaum, eds., *Political Economy of Statebuilding;* Paris and Sisk, eds., *The Dilemmas of Statebuilding.*

27. Biddle, "Ending the War in Afghanistan."

28. http://lalagesnow.photoshelter.com/gallery/We-Are-The-Not-Dead/G0000_eT5QooYacY.

29. Abraham Lincoln, "Inaugural Address," March 4, 1865, available at: http://www.presidency.ucsb.edu/ws/index.php?pid=25819.

30. Shay, *Odysseus in America.* Interview with Mary Alice Mills, September 20, 2013.

31. Kaplan et al., "Suicide Among Male Veterans"; Boehmer et al., "Postservice Mortality in Vietnam Veterans"; James Dao, "As Suicides Rise in U.S., Veterans are Less of Total," *New York Times,* February 1, 2013.

32. Tanielian and Jaycox, eds., *Invisible Wounds of War.*

33. Nicholas Schmidle, "In the Crosshairs," *New Yorker,* June 3, 2013, 45.

34. Tanielian and Jaycox, eds., *Invisible Wounds of War,* 12.

35. Ibid., xxi.

36. Ibid., 101.

37. Ibid., 340–41.

38. Friedman, "Posttraumatic Stress Disorder Among Military Returnees from Afghanistan and Iraq," 592.

39. Tanielian and Jaycox, eds., *Invisible Wounds of War,* 54.

40. Finkel, *Thank You for Your Service,* 86; Shay, *Odysseus in America;* Schulzinger, *A Time for Peace.*

41. Shay, *Odysseus in America,* 4.

42. Faulkner, *Intruder in the Dust,* 190.

43. Faulkner, *Requiem for a Nun,* 73; MacLeod, ed., *Defeat and Memory.*

44. Drew Gilpin Faust, "Telling War Stories: Reflections of a Civil War Historian," lecture available at: http://www.neh.gov/about/awards/jefferson-lecture/drew-gilpin-faust-lecture.

45. Baumeister et al., "Bad Is Stronger Than Good," 325.

46. Hume, *Dialogues and Natural History of Religion,* 143; Gilovich, "Biased Evaluation and Persistence in Gambling"; Peeters and Czapinski, "Positive-Negative Asymmetry in Evaluations."

47. Halberstam, *The Coldest Winter,* 2.

48. Cumings, *The Korean War,* 62.

49. McMahon, "Contested Memory," 164.

50. Hess, *Vietnam and the United States,* 137.

51. Cumings, *The Korean War,* 63; Herring, *America's Longest War.*

52. Fitzgerald, *Learning to Forget;* Nagl, *Learning to Eat Soup with a Knife.*

53. Barack Obama, "Statement on the 10th Anniversary of the Iraq War," March 19, 2013, available at: http://www.presidency.ucsb.edu/ws/index.php?pid=103380. Sometimes the amnesia about war is selective. Hawks like to recall the relatively successful surge phase in Iraq and forget the original disastrous decision to invade. By contrast, doves want to damn everything about the war, and often downplay the role of the surge in helping to cut America's losses. But rarely is a war all good or all bad.

54. Nietzsche, *Basic Writings of Nietzsche,* 493–94. In 2001, reports emerged that Bob Kerrey, a former senator from Nebraska, had participated in a mission in Vietnam in 1969 that killed civilians. "There's a part of me that wants to say to you all the memories that I've got are my memories, and I'm not going to talk about them," he responded. "Part of living with the memory, some of those memories, is to forget them." Gregory L. Vistica, "One Awful Night in Thanh Phong," *New York Times,* April 25, 2001.

55. Twain, *The Wit and Wisdom of Mark Twain,* 6.

56. Seybolt, *Humanitarian Military Intervention,* 21; DiPrizio. *Armed Humanitarians,* 71, 148–49; Power, *"A Problem from Hell,"* 366.

57. Lawrence Freedman, "Rumsfeld's Legacy: The Iraq Syndrome?" *Washington Post,* January 9, 2005.

58. McPherson, *Battle Cry of Freedom,* 854.

59. Jeffrey Kimball, "The Enduring Paradigm of the 'Lost Cause': Defeat in Vietnam, the Stab-in-the-Back Legend, and the Construction of a Myth," in MacLeod, ed., *Defeat and Memory,* 233–50.

60. Kaiser, "Strategy in War and Sports," 28.

61. Surge, talk, and leave is designed to extricate the United States from major war. But can it be applied to small-scale peacekeeping or humanitarian missions? The answer is *possibly.* If a small-scale mission turns into a fiasco, the United States may choose to boost its capabilities, negotiate with adversaries, and look to withdraw. Much of the advice in this book, such as calibrating goals, overcoming the bargainer's dilemma, and so on, could still apply. But given the limited stakes, Washington may move more rapidly toward withdrawal, or, in some cases, skip the surge phase entirely.

62. Biddle, "Is there a Middle Way?"; Petraeus, "How We Won in Iraq."

63. McMahon, "The Politics, and Geopolitics, of American Troop Withdrawals from Vietnam, 1968–1972," 474.

Chapter 10: No More Fiascos

1. "Gates: Relief on Way as Army Resets, Reshapes Force," Department of Defense News, October 10, 2007, available at: http://www.defense.gov/News/NewsArticle.aspx?ID=47744. For more on this argument, see Tierney, "The Backlash Against Nation-Building."

2. Robert Gates, speech at the National Defense University, September 29, 2008, available at: http://www.defense.gov/qdr/gates-article.html. Since Gates spoke, Washington has begun a variety of new stabilization missions—not counting the massive operations in Afghanistan and Iraq. American military personnel have been dispatched to help allied regimes in central Africa fight the Lord's Resistance Army, assist Jordan with the consequences of civil war in Syria, and train Libyan commandos in counterterrorism in the wake of the 2012 Benghazi attacks.

3. Nagl, "Let's Win the Wars We're In"; Hammes, *The Sling and the Stone;* Ucko, *The New Counterinsurgency Era.*

4. "Soldiers and Marines are expected to be nation-builders as well as warriors." U.S. Army and Marine Corps, *The U.S. Army/Marine Corps Counterinsurgency Field Manual,* xlvi. For the latest version, see: http://www.defenseinnovationmarketplace.mil/resources/CounterinsurgencyJointPublication.pdf.

5. Sepp, "From 'Shock and Awe' to 'Hearts and Minds,'" 299; Lebovic, *The Limits of U.S. Military Capability,* 62.

6. Department of Defense, "Sustaining U.S. Global Leadership: Priorities for 21st Century Defense," January 2012, available at: http://www.defense.gov/news/defense_strategic_guidance.pdf.

7. Gian P. Gentile, "Misreading the Surge Threatens U.S. Army's Conventional Capabilities," *World Politics Review,* March 4, 2008, available at: www.worldpoliticsreview.com/article.aspx?id=1715.

8. It's sometimes argued that training the U.S. military at counterinsurgency is dangerous because it may tempt presidents to wade into distant civil wars. If the military is incapable of stabilizing foreign lands, then it won't be asked to carry out these missions. But deliberately hamstringing ourselves won't save us from nation-building. It will only raise the odds of failure. After Vietnam, the U.S. Army tried to forget everything it had learned about counterinsurgency. But in the subsequent years, the army found itself engaged in a variety of nation-building missions—including major operations in Iraq and Afghanistan—and wasn't prepared. Benjamin H. Friedman, Harvey M. Sapolsky, and Christopher A. Preble, "Learning the Right Lessons from Iraq," February 13, 2008, available at: http://www.cato.org/publications/policy-analysis/learning-right-lessons-iraq.

9. These questions partly build on the Weinberger-Powell Doctrine, outlined by Caspar Weinberger and Colin Powell in the 1980s and early 1990s. According to the Weinberger-Powell Doctrine, the United States should

only go to war if vital U.S. interests are threatened, the objectives are clear and achievable, the risks and costs are fully assessed, alternative nonviolent remedies are exhausted, the consequences of using force are fully understood, the American people support the war, and we have broad international backing. Once the United States has decided on war, all necessary force should be used to ensure a swift victory. The model is the Gulf War of 1991. There's much common sense here, and we can only wish these tests had been applied before the invasion of Iraq, when Powell was secretary of state. But there are also some dangers with the Weinberger-Powell Doctrine. First, fighting only for vital interests is too narrow. The use of force should be justified based on threats to America's hierarchy of security needs. A major threat to a secondary security need may still justify intervention. Second, the implicit purpose of the tests is to filter out operations other than interstate war. But stabilization operations can be appropriate even if U.S. interests are limited and public support is lukewarm—provided the costs and risks are tolerable. Third, counterinsurgency or nation-building operations may not be amenable to the use of overwhelming force, at least in the sense of massive firepower. See Powell, "U.S. Forces."

10. The Founders granted Congress the right to declare war and sustain or end war through the power of the purse. Congress no longer declares war—part of a wider international trend where countries have ceased declaring war on each other. In 1973, Congress passed the War Powers Resolution, which limited the use of force to sixty days (followed by an extra thirty days to withdraw American forces) without congressional approval. Presidents have denied the constitutionality of the War Powers Resolution, claiming that it infringes on their constitutional powers as commander in chief.

11. Congress voted in favor of invading Iraq, illustrating that congressional authorization does not always equate to due oversight, especially if the president controls key intelligence. Still, going to Congress improves the odds of critical discussion.

12. Interview with John Abizaid, August 8, 2013.

13. Anderson, *Bush's Wars,* 177.

14. Clausewitz, *On War,* 584; Rose, *How Wars End.* This section draws on Tierney, "Mastering the Endgame of War."

15. Gordon and Trainor, *The Endgame,* 689.

16. Interview with John Abizaid, August 8, 2013.

17. Clausewitz, *On War,* 598.

18. Betts, *American Force,* 4.

19. For evidence of the importance of boots on the ground when fighting insurgents, see Paul et al., *Paths to Victory.*

20. Betts, *American Force.*

21. Biddle, "Is There a Middle Way?"

22. Tierney, *How We Fight,* 20–30.

Notes

23. Ibid., 14.
24. Ibid., chapter 8.
25. Today, about 30 percent of the Afghan adult population can read and write. The figure for adult white Americans in 1650 was about 45 percent.
26. Interview with John Allen, December 10, 2013.
27. Interview with Stanley McChrystal, August 5, 2013.
28. Gopal, *No Good Men Among the Living*.
29. Richard K. Kolb, "Last KIA on the Western Front," *VFW Magazine* (November/December 2005), 40.
30. http://www.memoiredeshommes.sga.defense.gouv.fr/en/arkotheque/client/mdh/base_morts_pour_la_france_premiere_guerre/index.php.

Bibliography

Afghan Public Health Institute, Ministry of Public Health, Central Statistics Organization, ICF Macro, Indian Institute of Health Management Research, and World Health Organization Regional Office for the Eastern Mediterranean. *Afghanistan Mortality Survey 2010*. Calverton, MD: APHI/MoPH, CSO, ICF Macro, IIHMR, and WHO/EMRO, 2011.

Agnew, John, Thomas W. Gillespie, Jorge Gonzalez, and Brian Min. "Baghdad Nights: Evaluating the U.S. Military 'Surge' Using Nighttime Light Signatures." *Environment and Planning* A40, no. 10 (2008): 2285–95.

Allen, Michael J. *Until the Last Man Comes Home: POWs, MIAs, and the Unending Vietnam War*. Chapel Hill: University of North Carolina Press, 2009.

Anderson, David L. *The Columbia Guide to the Vietnam War*. New York: Columbia University Press, 2002.

Anderson, Terry H. *Bush's Wars*. New York: Oxford University Press, 2011.

Andreopoulos, George J., and Harold E. Selesky, eds. *The Aftermath of Defeat: Societies, Armed Forces, and the Challenge of Recovery*. New Haven, CT: Yale University Press, 1994.

Angos, Alex. *You Move…I Win!* Davenport, IA: Thinkers' Press, 2005.

Arreguín-Toft, Ivan. "How the Weak Win Wars: A Theory of Asymmetric Conflict." *International Security* 26, no. 1 (2001): 93–128.

Asselin, Pierre. *A Bitter Peace: Washington, Hanoi, and the Making of the Paris Agreement*. Chapel Hill: University of North Carolina Press, 2002.

———. "We Don't Want a Munich: Hanoi's Diplomatic Strategy, 1965–1968." *Diplomatic History* 36, no. 3 (June 2012): 547–81.

Bacevich, Andrew J. *The Limits of Power: The End of American Exceptionalism*. New York: Metropolitan Books, 2008.

Barfield, Thomas. *Afghanistan: A Cultural and Political History*. Princeton, NJ: Princeton University Press, 2010.

Baudelaire, Charles. *Artificial Paradises*. Translated by Stacy Diamond. New York: Citadel Press, 1996.

Bibliography

Baum, Matthew A., and Tim Groeling. "Reality Asserts Itself: Public Opinion on Iraq and the Elasticity of Reality." *International Organization* 64, no. 3 (Summer 2010): 443–79.

Baumeister, Roy F., Ellen Bratslavsky, Catrin Finkenauer, and Kathleen D. Vohs. "Bad Is Stronger Than Good." *Review of General Psychology* 5, no. 4 (2001): 323–70.

Bazerman, Max H. "Why Negotiations Go Wrong." In *The Negotiation Sourcebook,* edited by Ira Asherman and Sandy Asherman, 219–24. Amherst, MA: HRD Press, 2001.

Berdal, Mats, and Dominik Zaum, eds. *Political Economy of Statebuilding: Power After Peace.* New York: Routledge, 2013.

Bergen, Peter L. *The Longest War: The Enduring Conflict Between America and Al-Qaeda.* New York: Free Press, 2011.

———. Statement to the House, Committee on Foreign Affairs. "After the Withdrawal: The Way Forward in Afghanistan and Pakistan." Hearing, March 19, 2013. Available at: http://docs.house.gov/meetings/FA/FA13/20130319/100524/HHRG-113-FA13-Wstate-BergenP-20130319.pdf.

Berman, Eli, Jacob N. Shapiro, and Joseph H. Felter. "Can Hearts and Minds Be Bought? The Economics of Counterinsurgency in Iraq." *Journal of Political Economy* 119, no. 4 (August 2011): 766–819.

Berman, Larry. *Lyndon Johnson's War: The Road to Stalemate in Vietnam.* New York: W. W. Norton & Company, 1989.

———. "From Intervention to Disengagement: The United States in Vietnam." In *Foreign Military Intervention: The Dynamics of Protracted Conflict*, edited by Ariel E. Levite, Bruce W. Jentleson, and Larry Berman, 23–64. New York: Columbia University Press, 1992.

———. *No Peace, No Honor: Nixon, Kissinger, and Betrayal in Vietnam.* New York: Free Press, 2001.

Bernstein, Irving. *Guns or Butter: The Presidency of Lyndon Johnson.* New York: Oxford University Press, 1996.

Bernstein, Serge. *The Republic of De Gaulle, 1958–1969.* Cambridge: Cambridge University Press, 1993.

Betts, Richard K. *Soldiers, Statesmen, and Cold War Crises.* Cambridge, MA: Harvard University Press, 1977.

———. *American Force: Dangers, Delusions, and Dilemmas in National Security.* New York: Columbia University Press, 2012.

Betts, Richard K., Michael C. Desch, and Peter D. Feaver. "Correspondence: Civilians, Soldiers, and the Iraq Surge Decision." *International Security* 36, no. 3 (Winter 2011/2012): 179–99.

Bew, John, Ryan Evans, Martyn Frampton, Peter Neumann, and Marisa Porges. "Talking to the Taliban: Hope Over History?" *The International Centre for the Study of Radicalisation and Political Violence* (2013). Available at: http://icsr .info/2013/06/icsr-insight-talking-to-the-taliban-hope-over-history/.

Bibliography

Biddle, Stephen. "Seeing Baghdad, Thinking Saigon." *Foreign Affairs* 85, no. 2 (March/April 2006): 2–14.

———. "Is There a Middle Way? The Problem with Half-Measures in Afghanistan." *The New Republic,* October 20, 2009. Available at: http://www.new republic.com/article/world/there-middle-way.

———. "Ending the War in Afghanistan: How to Avoid Failure on the Installment Plan." *Foreign Affairs* 92, no. 5 (September/October 2013): 49–58.

Biddle, Stephen, Jeffrey A. Friedman, and Jacob N. Shapiro, "Testing the Surge: Why Did Violence Decline in Iraq in 2007?" *International Security* 37, no. 1 (Summer 2012): 7–40.

Bierce, Ambrose. *A Sole Survivor: Bits of Autobiography.* Edited by S. T. Joshi and David E. Schultz. Knoxville, TN: University of Tennessee Press, 1998.

Bissell, Tom. *The Father of All Things: A Marine, His Son, and the Legacy of Vietnam.* New York: Pantheon, 2007.

Bochim, Hal W. *Richard Nixon: Rhetorical Strategist.* Westport, CT: Greenwood Press, 1990.

Boehmer, Tegan K. Catlin, W. Dana Flanders, Michael A. McGeehin, Coleen Boyle, and Drue H. Barrett. "Postservice Mortality in Vietnam Veterans: 30-year Follow-up." *Archives of Internal Medicine* 164, no. 17 (2004): 1908–16.

Boose, Donald W. Jr. "Fighting While Talking: The Korean War Truce Talks," *OAH Magazine of History* 14, no. 3 (Spring 2000): 25–29.

Boot, Max. *Invisible Armies: An Epic History of Guerrilla Warfare from Ancient Times to the Present.* New York: Liveright, 2013.

———. "The Evolution of Irregular War." *Foreign Affairs* 92, no. 2 (March/April 2013): 100–114.

Borer, Douglas A. *Superpowers Defeated: Vietnam and Afghanistan Compared.* London: Frank Cass, 1999.

Bostdorff, Denise M. *The Presidency and the Rhetoric of Foreign Crisis.* Columbia: University of South Carolina Press, 1994.

Bowie, Robert R., and Richard H. Immerman. *Waging Peace: How Eisenhower Shaped an Enduring Cold War Strategy.* New York: Oxford University Press, 1998.

Brahimi, Lakhdar, and Thomas R. Pickering. *Afghanistan: Negotiating Peace, The Report of The Century Foundation International Task Force on Afghanistan in Its Regional and Multilateral Dimensions.* New York: The Century Foundation, 2011.

Braithwaite, Rodric. *Afgantsy: The Russians in Afghanistan, 1979–1989.* London: Profile Books, 2011.

Brewer, Susan A. *Why America Fights: Patriotism and War Propaganda from the Philippines to Iraq.* New York: Oxford University Press, 2009.

Byman, Daniel. "Talking with Insurgents: A Guide for the Perplexed." *Washington Quarterly* 32, no. 2 (April 2009): 125–37.

Caplan, Richard. "Devising Exit Strategies." *Survival* 54, no. 3 (June/July 2012): 111–26.

Bibliography

Caplan, Richard, ed. *Exit Strategies and State Building.* New York: Oxford University Press, 2012.

Dio Cassius, *Roman History.* Vol. 7. Translated by Earnest Cary. Bury St. Edmunds, UK: St. Edmundsbury Press, 2000.

Chandler, David G. *The Campaigns of Napoleon: The Mind and Method of History's Greatest Soldier.* New York: Scribner, 1966.

Chandrasekaran. Rajiv. *Little America: The War Within the War for Afghanistan.* New York: Alfred A. Knopf, 2012.

Chaney, Eric. "Assessing Pacification Policy in Iraq: Evidence from Iraqi Financial Markets." *Journal of Comparative Economics* 36, no. 1 (March 2008): 1–16.

Cherney, Irving. *Capablanca's Best Chess Endings.* Oxford: Oxford University Press, 1978.

Chollet, Derek, and Samantha Power, eds. *The Unquiet American: Richard Holbrooke in the World.* New York: PublicAffairs, 2011.

Cimbala, Stephen J., and Sidney R. Waldman, eds. *Controlling and Ending Conflict: Issues Before and After the Cold War.* New York: Greenwood Press, 1992.

Clausewitz, Carl von. *On War.* Edited and translated by Michael Howard and Peter Paret. Princeton, NJ: Princeton University Press, 1989.

Cohen, Eliot A. *Supreme Command: Soldiers, Statesmen, and Leadership in Wartime.* New York: Free Press, 2002.

Cohen, Eliot A., and John Gooch. *Military Misfortunes: The Anatomy of Failure in War.* New York: Free Press, 2006.

Collier, Paul, and Anke Hoeffler. "Aid, Policy, and Growth in Post-Conflict Societies." *The World Bank Development Research Group,* Policy Research Working Paper 2902 (October 2002).

Colman, Andrew M. *A Dictionary of Psychology.* 3rd ed. New York: Oxford University Press, 2009.

Condra, Luke N., and Jacob N. Shapiro. "Who Takes the Blame? The Strategic Effects of Collateral Damage." *American Journal of Political Science* 56, no. 1 (2012): 167–87.

Connable, Ben, and Martin C. Libicki. *How Insurgencies End.* Santa Monica: RAND, 2010.

Cordesman, Anthony H. "Afghanistan: The Failed Metrics of Ten Years of War." *Center for Strategic and International Studies* (February 9, 2012). Available at: http://csis.org/files/publication/120209_Afghanistan_Failed_Metrics.pdf.

Cordovez, Diego, and Selig S. Harrison. *Out of Afghanistan: The Inside Story of the Soviet Withdrawal.* New York: Oxford University Press, 1995.

Corman, Steven R., ed. *Narrating the Exit from Afghanistan.* Tempe, AZ: Center for Strategic Communication, 2013.

Craig, Campbell, and Fredrik Logevall. *America's Cold War: The Politics of Insecurity.* Cambridge, MA: Harvard University Press, 2009.

Crile, George. *Charlie Wilson's War: The Extraordinary Story of How the Wildest Man in Congress and a Rogue CIA Agent Changed the History of Our Times.* New York: Grove Press, 2003.

Bibliography

Croco, Sarah E. "Peace at What Price? Domestic Politics, Settlement Costs and War Termination." PhD diss., University of Michigan, 2008.

Cumings, Bruce. *The Korean War: A History.* New York: Modern Library, 2011.

Czege, Huba Wass de. "Wargaming Insights." *Army* (March 2003): 36–44.

Daddis, Gregory A. *No Sure Victory: Measuring U.S. Army Effectiveness and Progress in the Vietnam War.* New York: Oxford University Press, 2011.

Dallek, Robert. *Nixon and Kissinger: Partners in Power.* New York: HarperCollins, 2007.

Dalrymple, William. *The Return of a King: The Battle for Afghanistan, 1839–1842.* New York: Alfred A. Knopf, 2013.

———. *Memoirs of Hope: Renewal and Endeavor.* Translated by Terence Kilmartin. New York: Simon & Schuster, 1971.

de Gaulle, Charles. *The Edge of the Sword.* Westport, CT: Greenwood Press, 1975.

Desch, Michael C. "Bush and the Generals." *Foreign Affairs* 86, no. 3 (May/June 2007): 97–108.

Diamond, Larry. *Squandered Victory: The American Occupation and the Bungled Effort to Bring Democracy to Iraq.* New York: Henry Holt and Company, 2005.

DiPrizio, Robert C. *Armed Humanitarians: U.S. Interventions from Northern Iraq to Kosovo.* Baltimore: Johns Hopkins University Press, 2002.

Dobbins, James, Seth G. Jones, Keith Crane, and Beth Cole DeGrasse. *The Beginner's Guide to Nation-Building.* Santa Monica: RAND, 2007.

Dobbins, James, John G. McGinn, Keith Crane, Seth G. Jones, Rollie Lal, Andrew Rathmell, Rachel M. Swanger, and Anga R. Timilsina. *America's Role in Nation-Building: From Germany to Iraq.* Santa Monica: RAND, 2003.

Dodge, Toby. *Inventing Iraq: The Failure of Nation Building and a History Denied.* New York: Columbia University Press, 2003.

———. "The US and Iraq: Time to Go Home." *Survival* 52, no. 2 (2010): 129–40.

Downs, George W. "The Lessons of Disengagement." In *Foreign Military Intervention: The Dynamics of Protracted Conflict,* edited by Ariel E. Levite, Bruce W. Jentleson, and Larry Berman, 285–300. New York: Columbia University Press, 1992.

Doyle, Robert C. *The Enemy in Our Hands: America's Treatment of Prisoners of War from the Revolution to the War on Terror.* Lexington: The University Press of Kentucky, 2010.

Drury, Bob, and Tom Clavin. *Last Men Out: The True Story of America's Heroic Final Hours in Vietnam.* New York: Free Press, 2011.

Dumbrell, John. *Rethinking the Vietnam War.* London: Palgrave Macmillan, 2012.

Dyson, Stephen Benedict. "What Really Happened in Planning for Postwar Iraq?" *Political Science Quarterly* 128, no. 3 (2013): 455–88.

Edelstein, David M. "Occupational Hazards: Why Military Occupations Succeed or Fail." *International Security* 29, no. 1 (Summer 2004): 49–91.

———. "Exit Lessons," *The Wilson Quarterly* 33, no. 4 (2009): 34–39.

Edwards, George C., III. *The Strategic President: Persuasion and Opportunity in Presidential Leadership.* Princeton, NJ: Princeton University Press, 2009.

Bibliography

Entman, Robert. *Projections of Power: Framing News, Public Opinion, and U.S. Foreign Policy.* Chicago: University of Chicago Press, 2004.

Evans, Richard J. *The Third Reich at War: 1939–1945.* New York: Penguin Books, 2009.

Farrell, Theo, Frans Osinga, and James A. Russell, eds. *Military Adaptation in Afghanistan.* Stanford: Stanford University Press, 2013.

Faulkner, William. *Intruder in the Dust.* New York: Vintage, 1991.

———. *Requiem for a Nun.* New York: Vintage, 2011.

Feaver, Peter D. "The Right to Be Right: Civil-Military Relations and the Iraq Surge Decision." *International Security* 35, no. 4 (Spring 2011): 87–125.

Feifer, Gregory. *The Great Gamble: The Soviet War in Afghanistan.* New York: HarperCollins, 2009.

Finkel, David. *Thank You for Your Service.* New York: Farrar, Straus and Giroux, 2013.

Fisher, Roger, William Ury, and Bruce Patton. *Getting to Yes: Negotiating Agreement Without Giving In.* New York: Penguin Books, 2011.

Fitzgerald, David. *Learning to Forget: US Army Counterinsurgency Doctrine and Practice from Vietnam to Iraq.* Stanford: Stanford University Press, 2013.

Foot, Rosemary. *A Substitute for Victory: The Politics of Peacemaking at the Korean Armistice Talks.* Ithaca, NY: Cornell University Press, 1990.

Fortna, Virginia Page. *Does Peacekeeping Work? Shaping Belligerents' Choices after Civil War.* Princeton, NJ: Princeton University Press, 2008.

Fox, William T. R. "The Causes of War and Conditions of Peace." *Annals of the American Academy of Political and Social Science* 392 (November 1970): 1–13.

Franklin, H. Bruce. *M.I.A., or Mythmaking in America.* Brooklyn: Lawrence Hill, 1992.

Franks, Tommy. *American Soldier.* New York: HarperCollins, 2004.

Freedman, Lawrence, ed. *War.* New York: Oxford University Press, 1994.

Friedman, Jeffrey A. "Manpower and Counterinsurgency: Empirical Foundations for Theory and Doctrine." *Security Studies* 20, no. 4 (December 2011): 556–91.

Friedman, Matthew J. "Posttraumatic Stress Disorder Among Military Returnees from Afghanistan and Iraq." *The American Journal of Psychiatry* 163, no. 4 (April 2006): 586–93.

Gaddis, John Lewis. *Strategies of Containment: A Critical Appraisal of American National Security Strategy During the Cold War.* New York: Oxford University Press, 1982.

———. *The Long Peace: Inquiries into the History of the Cold War.* New York: Oxford University Press, 1987.

Galbraith, John Kenneth. *How to Get Out of Vietnam: A Workable Solution to the Worst Problem of Our Time.* New York: Signet, 1967.

Galula, David. *Counterinsurgency Warfare: Theory and Practice.* Westport, CT: Praeger, 2006.

Gardner, Lloyd C., and Ted Gittinger, eds. *The Search for Peace in Vietnam, 1964–1968.* College Station: Texas A&M University Press Consortium, 2004.

Bibliography

Gates, Robert M. *Duty: Memoirs of a Secretary at War*. New York: Alfred A. Knopf, 2014.

Ghani, Ashraf, and Clare Lockhart. *Fixing Failed States: A Framework for Rebuilding a Fractured World*. New York: Oxford University Press, 2009.

Gilbert, Martin. *Churchill: A Life*. New York: Owl Books, 1992.

Gildea, Robert. *The Past in French History*. New Haven, CT: Yale University Press, 1994.

Gilovich, Thomas. "Biased Evaluation and Persistence in Gambling." *Journal of Personality and Social Psychology* 44, no. 6 (1983): 1110–26.

Giustozzi, Antonio. *Negotiating with the Taliban: Issues and Prospects*. Washington, DC: Century Foundation, 2010. Available at: http://tcf.org/publications/pdfs/pb716/Giustozzi.pdf.

Glad, Betty, and J. Philipp Rosenberg. "Bargaining Under Fire: Limit Setting and Maintenance During the Korean War." In *Psychological Dimensions of War*, edited by Betty Glad, 181–200. Newbury Park, CA: Sage, 1990.

Gladwell, Malcolm. *Outliers: The Story of Success*. New York: Little, Brown and Company, 2008.

Gleis, Joshua L. *Withdrawing Under Fire: Lessons Learned from Islamist Insurgencies*. Washington, DC: Potomac Books, 2011.

Goemans, H. E. *War and Punishment: The Causes of War Termination and the First World War*. Princeton, NJ: Princeton University Press, 2000.

Goldstein, Joshua S. *Winning the War on War: The Decline of Armed Conflict Worldwide*. New York: Penguin Books, 2011.

Gompert, David C., John Gordon IV, Adam Grissom, David R. Frelinger, Seth G. Jones, Martin C. Libicki, Edward O'Connell, Brooke Stearns Lawson, and Robert E. Hunter. *War by Other Means: Building Complete and Balanced Capabilities for Counterinsurgency*. Santa Monica: RAND, 2008.

Goodwin, Doris Kearns. *The Bully Pulpit: Theodore Roosevelt, William Howard Taft, and the Golden Age of Journalism*. New York: Simon & Schuster, 2013.

Gopal, Anand. *No Good Men Among the Living*. New York: Metropolitan Books, 2014.

Gordon, Michael R., and Bernard E. Trainor. *Cobra II: The Inside Story of the Invasion and Occupation of Iraq*. New York: Pantheon, 2006.

———. "The Iraq War That Might Have Been." *Foreign Policy,* March 12, 2013. Available at: http://www.foreignpolicy.com/articles/2013/03/12/the_iraq_war_that_might_have_been.

———. *The Endgame: The Inside Story of the Struggle for Iraq, from George W. Bush to Barack Obama*. New York: Vintage, 2013.

Gorka, Sebastian L.v., and David Kilcullen. "An Actor-centric Theory of War: Understanding the Difference Between *COIN* and *Counterinsurgency*." *Joint Forces Quarterly* 60 (1st Quarter 2011): 14–18.

Grant, Reg G., ed. *1001 Battles that Changed the Course of World History*. New York: Universe, 2011.

Bibliography

Grau, Lester W. "The Soviet-Afghan War: A Superpower Mired in the Mountains." In *Conflict and Insurgency in the Contemporary Middle East,* edited by Barry Rubin, 187–208. New York: Routledge, 2009.

Hack, Karl. "'Iron Claws on Malaya': The Historiography of the Malayan Emergency." *Journal of Southeast Asian Studies* 30, no. 1 (March 1999): 99–125.

Hacker, J. David. "A Census-Based Count of the Civil War Dead." *Civil War History* 57, no. 4 (December 2011): 307–48.

Hagan, John, Joshua Kaiser, Anna Hanson, Jon R. Lindsay, Austin G. Long, Stephen Biddle, Jeffrey A. Friedman, and Jacob N. Shapiro. "Correspondence: Assessing the Synergy Thesis in Iraq." *International Security* 37, no. 4 (Spring 2013): 173–98.

Halberstam, David. *The Coldest Winter: America and the Korean War.* New York: Hyperion, 2008.

Haldeman, H. R. *The Haldeman Diaries: Inside the Nixon White House.* New York: Berkley Books, 1995.

Hammes, Thomas X. *The Sling and the Stone: On War in the 21st Century.* St. Paul: Zenith Press, 2006.

Hampson, Fen Osler, and Tod Lindberg. "'No Exit' Strategy." *Policy Review* 176 (December 2012/January 2013): 15–33.

Harrison, Benjamin T., and Christopher L. Mosher. "The Secret Diary of McNamara's Dove: The Long-Lost Story of John T. McNaughton's Opposition to the Vietnam War." *Diplomatic History* 35, no. 3 (June 2011): 505–34.

Hart, B. H. Liddell. *Strategy.* 2nd ed. New York: Meridian, 1991.

Hastings, Max. *The Korean War.* New York: Simon & Schuster, 1987.

Herring, George C. *America's Longest War: The United States and Vietnam, 1950–1975.* New York: John Wiley & Sons, 1979.

Hess, Gary R. *Vietnam and the United States: Origins and Legacy of War.* New York: Twayne, 1998.

———. *Vietnam: Explaining America's Lost War.* Malden, MA: Blackwell, 2009.

———. *Presidential Decisions for War: Korea, Vietnam, the Persian Gulf, and Iraq.* Baltimore: Johns Hopkins University Press, 2009.

Hitler, Adolf. *Hitler's Table Talk, 1941–1944.* New York: Enigma Books, 2000.

Hixson, Walter L. *George F. Kennan: Cold War Iconoclast.* New York: Columbia University Press, 1989.

Hoff, Joan. *Nixon Reconsidered.* New York: Basic Books, 1994.

Hogan, Michael J. *A Cross of Iron: Harry S. Truman and the Origins of the National Security State.* Cambridge, MA: Cambridge University Press, 1998.

Holmes, James. "Zero-Sum Game: Armistice Negotiations in Korea, 1951–1953." Master's thesis, Tufts University, 2003. Available at: http://dl.tufts.edu/catalog/tufts:UA015.012.DO.00023.

Hopf, Ted. *Peripheral Visions: Deterrence Theory and American Foreign Policy in the Third World, 1965–1990.* Ann Arbor: University of Michigan Press, 1994.

Horne, Alistair. *A Savage War of Peace: Algeria 1954–1962.* New York: New York Review of Books, 2006.

Bibliography

Huebner, Andrew J. *The Warrior Image: Soldiers in American Culture from the Second World War to the Vietnam Era.* Chapel Hill: University of North Carolina Press, 2008.

Hughes, Ken. "Fatal Politics: Nixon's Political Timetable for Withdrawing from Vietnam." *Diplomatic History* 34, no. 3 (June 2010): 497–506.

Hume, David. *Dialogues and Natural History of Religion.* New York: Oxford University Press, 1998.

Hunt, Richard A. *Pacification: The American Struggle for Vietnam's Hearts and Minds.* Boulder: Westview Press, 1995.

Hutchinson, John. *Modern Nationalism.* London: Fontana Press, 1994.

Iklé, Fred Charles. *Every War Must End*, rev. ed. New York: Columbia University Press, 2005.

Isaacson, Walter. *Kissinger: A Biography.* New York: Simon & Schuster, 2005.

Jenkins, Roy. *Churchill.* Oxford: Pan, 2002.

Jervis, Robert. *The Logic of Images in International Relations.* New York: Columbia University Press, 1989.

———. "Political Implications of Loss Aversion." In *Avoiding Losses / Taking Risks: Prospect Theory and International Conflict,* edited by Barbara Farnham, 23–40. Ann Arbor: University of Michigan Press, 1994.

———. "The Politics of Troop Withdrawal: Salted Peanuts, the Commitment Trap, and Buying Time." *Diplomatic History* 34, no. 3 (June 2010): 507–16.

Johns, Andrew L. *Vietnam's Second Front: Domestic Politics, the Republican Party, and the War.* Lexington: University Press of Kentucky, 2010.

Johnson, Dominic, and Dominic Tierney. *Failing to Win: Perceptions of Victory and Defeat in International Politics.* Cambridge, MA: Harvard University Press, 2006.

Johnson, Gregory C. "Exit Strategy: Where Does It Fit into Operational Planning?" Unpublished paper, Naval War College, 2002.

Johnson, Kirk W. *To Be a Friend Is Fatal: The Fight to Save the Iraqis America Left Behind.* New York: Scribner, 2013.

Johnson, Lyndon B. *The Vantage Point: Perspectives of the Presidency, 1963–1969.* New York: Holt, Rinehart and Winston, 1971.

Johnston, Patrick B. "Does Decapitation Work? Assessing the Effectiveness of Leadership Targeting in Counterinsurgency Campaigns." *International Security* 36, no. 4 (Spring 2012): 47–79.

Joint Chiefs of Staff. *Joint Publication 3-0: Joint Operations.* Washington, DC: Joint Chiefs of Staff, 2011.

Jones, Seth G. "The Rise of Afghanistan's Insurgency: State Failure and Jihad." *International Security* 32, no. 4 (Spring 2008): 7–40.

———. *In the Graveyard of Empires: America's War in Afghanistan.* New York: W. W. Norton & Company, 2010.

Joy, Charles Turner. *How Communists Negotiate.* New York: Macmillan, 1955.

———. *Negotiating While Fighting: The Diary of Admiral C. Turner Joy at the Korean Armistice Conference.* Stanford: Hoover Institution Press, 1978.

Bibliography

Kagan, Robert. *Of Paradise and Power: America and Europe in the New World Order.* New York: Vintage, 2004.

Kahneman, Daniel. *Thinking, Fast and Slow.* New York: Farrar, Straus and Giroux, 2011.

Kahneman, Daniel, Barbara L. Fredrickson, Charles A. Schreiber, and Donald A. Redelmeier. "When More Pain Is Preferred to Less: Adding a Better End." *Psychological Science* 4, no. 6 (November 1993): 401–5.

Kahneman, Daniel, and Jonathan Renshon. "Why Hawks Win." *Foreign Policy* 158 (January/February 2007): 34–38.

———. "Hawkish Biases." In *American Foreign Policy and the Politics of Fear: Threat Inflation Since 9/11,* edited by Trevor Thrall and Jane Cramer, 79–96. New York: Routledge, 2009.

Kaiser, David. *American Tragedy: Kennedy, Johnson, and the Origins of the Vietnam War.* Cambridge, MA: Harvard University Press, 2000.

———. "Strategy in War and Sports: A Comparison." In *Strategic Logic and Political Rationality,* edited by Bradford A. Lee and Karl F. Walling, 29–37. Portland, OR: Frank Cass, 2003.

Kalb, Marvin, and Deborah Kalb. *Haunting Legacy: Vietnam and the American Presidency from Ford to Obama.* Washington, DC: Brookings Institution Press, 2011.

Kalinovsky, Artemy M. *A Long Goodbye: The Soviet Withdrawal from Afghanistan.* Cambridge, MA: Harvard University Press, 2011.

Kalyvas, Stathis N. "The Changing Character of Civil Wars, 1800-2009." In *The Changing Character of War,* edited by Hew Strachan and Sibylle Scheipers, 202–19. New York: Oxford University Press, 2011.

Kaplan, Fred. *Daydream Believers: How a Few Grand Ideas Wrecked American Power.* Hoboken: Wiley, 2008.

———. *The Insurgents: David Petraeus and the Plot to Change the American Way of War.* New York: Simon & Schuster, 2013.

Kaplan, Mark S., Nathalie Huguet, Bentson H. McFarland, and Jason T. Newsom. "Suicide Among Male Veterans: A Prospective Population-Based Study." *Journal of Epidemiological Community Health* 61, no. 8 (August 2007): 619–24.

Kaplan, Robert D. "The Vietnam Solution." *The Atlantic* 309, no. 5 (June 2012): 54–62.

Kapstein, Ethan B. "Measuring Progress in Modern Warfare." *Survival* 54, no. 1 (February/March 2012): 137–58.

Keating, Susan Katz. *Prisoners of Hope: Exploiting the POW/MIA Myth in America.* New York: Random House, 1994.

Kennan, George F. *American Diplomacy.* Chicago: University of Chicago Press, 1984.

Kershaw, Ian. *Fateful Choices: Ten Decisions that Changed the World, 1940-1941.* New York: Penguin, 2007.

Khong, Yuen Foong. *Analogies at War: Korea, Munich, Dien Bien Phu, and the Vietnam Decisions of 1965.* Princeton, NJ: Princeton University Press, 1992.

Bibliography

Kilcullen, David. *The Accidental Guerrilla: Fighting Small Wars in the Midst of a Big One*. Oxford: Oxford University Press, 2009.

———. *Counterinsurgency*. New York: Oxford University Press, 2010.

Kimball, Jeffrey. *Nixon's Vietnam War*. Lawrence: University Press of Kansas, 1998.

———. "The Case of the 'Decent Interval': Do We Now Have a Smoking Gun?" *SHAFR Newsletter* 32, no. 3 (September 2001): 35–39.

Kissinger, Henry. *White House Years*. Boston: Little, Brown and Company, 1979.

———. *Diplomacy*. New York: Simon & Schuster, 1994.

———. *Ending the Vietnam War: A History of America's Involvement in and Extrication from the Vietnam War*. New York: Simon & Schuster, 2003.

Kocher, Matthew Adam, Thomas B. Pepinsky, and Stathis N. Kalyvas, "Aerial Bombing and Counterinsurgency in the Vietnam War," *American Journal of Political Science* 55, no. 2 (April 2011): 201–18.

Krebs, Ronald R. *Dueling Visions: U.S. Strategy Toward Eastern Europe Under Eisenhower*. College Station: Texas A&M University Press, 2001.

Krepinevich. Andrew F. *The Army and Vietnam*. Baltimore: Johns Hopkins University Press, 1986.

———. "How to Win in Iraq." *Foreign Affairs* 84, no. 5 (September/October 2005): 87–104.

Kupchan, Charles A. *How Enemies Become Friends: The Sources of Stable Peace*. Princeton, NJ: Princeton University Press, 2010.

Langguth, A. J. *Our Vietnam: The War 1954–1975*. New York: Touchstone, 2000.

Larson, Eric V. *Casualties and Consensus: The Historical Role of Casualties in Domestic Support for U.S. Military Operations*. Santa Monica: RAND, 1996.

Larson, Eric V., and Bogdan Savych. *American Public Support for U.S. Military Operations from Mogadishu to Baghdad*. Santa Monica: RAND, 2005.

Longworth, Richard, ed. *Churchill by Himself: The Definitive Collection of Quotations*. New York: PublicAffairs, 2011.

Lebovic, James H. *The Limits of U.S. Military Capability: Lessons from Vietnam and Iraq*. Baltimore: Johns Hopkins University Press, 2010.

Lebow, Richard Ned. *The Art of Bargaining*. Baltimore: Johns Hopkins University Press, 1996.

Lee, Bradford A. "Winning the War but Losing the Peace? The United States and the Strategic Issues of War Termination." In *Strategic Logic and Political Rationality,* edited by Bradford A. Lee and Karl F. Walling, 249–73. Portland, OR: Frank Cass, 2003.

Leffler, Melvyn P. *For the Soul of Mankind: The United States, the Soviet Union, and the Cold War*. New York: Hill & Wang, 2007.

Lind, Jennifer. "Apologies in International Politics." *Security Studies* 18, no. 3 (2009): 517–56.

Lindsay, Jon, and Roger Petersen. *CIWAG Case Study of Irregular Warfare and Armed Groups: Varieties of Insurgency and Counterinsurgency in Iraq, 2003–2009.*

Bibliography

Newport, RI: United States Naval War College, 2012. Available at: http://igcc.ucsd.edu/assets/001/503974.pdf.

Linn, Brian McAllister. *The Philippine War, 1899–1902.* Lawrence: University Press of Kansas, 2000.

Livingston, Ian S., and Michael O'Hanlon. "Afghanistan Index." *Brookings Institution* (May 16, 2012). Available at: http://www.brookings.edu/about/programs/foreign-policy/afghanistan-index.

Logevall, Fredrik. *Choosing War: The Lost Chance for Peace and the Escalation of War in Vietnam.* Berkeley: University of California Press, 1999.

———. *The Origins of the Vietnam War.* New York: Longman, 2001.

———. "What Really Happened in Vietnam: The North, the South, and the American Defeat." *Foreign Affairs* 91, no. 6 (November/December 2012): 129–36.

Lyall, Jason, and Isaiah Wilson III. "Rage Against the Machines: Explaining Outcomes in Counterinsurgency Wars." *International Organization* 63, no. 1 (January 2009): 67–106.

Lynch, Marc. "Explaining the Awakening: Engagement, Publicity, and the Transformation of Iraqi Sunni Political Attitudes." *Security Studies* 20, no. 1 (2011): 36–72.

McCann, David R., and Barry S. Strauss, eds. *War and Democracy: A Comparative Study of the Korean War and the Peloponnesian War.* Armonk, NY: M. E. Sharpe, 2001.

McChrystal, Stanley. *My Share of the Task: A Memoir.* New York: Penguin Books, 2013.

Macdonagh, Michael. "The Prime Minister." In *The Fortnightly Review,* Vol. 62, edited by W. L. Courtney, 176–98. New York: Leonard Scott, 1902.

Mack, Andrew. "Why Big Nations Lose Small Wars: The Politics of Asymmetric Conflict." *World Politics* 27, no. 2 (January 1975): 175–200.

McKee, Robert. *Story: Style, Structure, Substance, and the Principles of Screenwriting.* New York: HarperCollins, 2010.

MacLeod, Jenny, ed. *Defeat and Memory: Cultural Histories of Military Defeat in the Modern Era.* New York: Palgrave Macmillan, 2008.

McMahon, Robert J. "Credibility and World Power: Exploring the Psychological Dimension in Postwar Diplomacy," *Diplomatic History* 15, no. 4 (1991): 455–71.

———. "Contested Memory: The Vietnam War and American Society, 1975–2001." *Diplomatic History* 26, no. 2 (Spring 2002): 159–84.

———. "The Politics, and Geopolitics, of American Troop Withdrawals from Vietnam, 1968–1972." *Diplomatic History* 34, no. 3 (June 2010): 471–83.

McMahon, Patrice C., and Jon Western, eds. *The International Community and Statebuilding.* London: Routledge, 2012.

McMaster, H. R. *Dereliction of Duty: Lyndon Johnson, Robert McNamara, the Joint Chiefs of Staff, and the Lies that Led to Vietnam.* New York: HarperCollins, 1997.

McNamara, Robert S., James Blight, Robert Brigham, Thomas Biersteker, and Herbert Schandler. *Argument Without End: In Search of Answers to the Vietnam Tragedy.* New York: PublicAffairs, 1999.

Bibliography

McPherson, James M. *What They Fought For, 1861–1865*. Baton Rouge: Louisiana State University Press, 1994.

———. *Battle Cry of Freedom: The Civil War Era*. New York: Oxford University Press, 2003.

———. *Tried by War: Abraham Lincoln as Commander in Chief*. New York: Penguin Books, 2008.

Macrory, Patrick. *Retreat from Kabul: The Catastrophic British Defeat in Afghanistan, 1842*. Guilford, CT: Lyons Press, 2002.

Malkasian, Carter. *War Comes to Garmser: Thirty Years of Conflict on the Afghan Frontier*. New York: Oxford University Press, 2013.

Mangel, Marc, and Francisco J. Samaniego. "Abraham Wald's Work on Aircraft Survivability." *Journal of the American Statistical Association* 79, no. 386 (June 1984): 259–67.

Mao Tse-tung. *On Guerrilla Warfare*. Translated by Samuel B. Griffith. Champaign: University of Illinois Press, 2000.

Marshall, Frank J. *Marshall's Chess "Swindles."* New York: American Chess Bulletin, 1914.

Marston, Daniel, and Carter Malkasian, eds. *Counterinsurgency in Modern Warfare*. Oxford: Osprey, 2008.

Martel, William C. *Victory in War: Foundations of Modern Military Policy*. Cambridge: Cambridge University Press, 2007.

Mayo, James M. "The Manifestation of Politics in Architectural Practice." *Journal of Architectural Education* 50, no. 2 (November 1996): 76–88.

Mercer, Jonathan. *Reputation and International Politics*. Ithaca, NY: Cornell University Press, 1996.

Milburrn, Thomas W., and Daniel J. Christie. "Effort Justification as a Motive for Continuing War: The Vietnam Case." In *Psychological Dimensions of War*, edited by Betty Glad, 236–51. Newbury Park, CA: Sage, 1990.

Miller, Aaron David. *The Much Too Promised Land: America's Elusive Search for Arab-Israeli Peace*. New York: Bantam, 2008.

Miller, Linda B., and Michael Joseph Smith, eds. *Ideas & Ideals: Essays on Politics in Honor of Stanley Hoffmann*. Boulder: Westview Press, 1993.

Miller, Paul D. "The US and Afghanistan After 2014." *Survival* 55, no. 1 (February/March 2013): 67–86.

Millett, Allan R. *The War for Korea, 1950–1951: They Came from the North*. Lawrence: University Press of Kansas, 2010.

Mnookin, Robert. *Bargaining with the Devil: When to Negotiate, When to Fight*. New York: Simon & Schuster, 2010.

Montefiore, Simon Sebag. *Stalin: The Court of the Red Tsar*. New York: Vintage, 2005.

Morgan, Patrick M. "Saving Face for the Sake of Deterrence." In *Psychology and Deterrence*, edited by Robert Jervis, Richard Ned Lebow, and Janice Gross Stein, 125–52. Baltimore: Johns Hopkins University Press, 1985.

Morris, Edmund. *The Rise of Theodore Roosevelt*. New York: Random House, 2001.

Bibliography

Moten, Michael, ed. *Between War and Peace: How America Ends Its Wars*. New York: Free Press, 2011.

Moyar, Mark. *A Question of Command: Counterinsurgency from the Civil War to Iraq*. New Haven, CT: Yale University Press, 2009.

Mueller, John E. *War, Presidents and Public Opinion*. New York: John Wiley, 1973.

———. *The Remnants of War*. Ithaca, NY: Cornell University Press, 2004.

Nagl, John A. *Learning to Eat Soup with a Knife: Counterinsurgency Lessons from Malaya and Vietnam*. Chicago: University of Chicago Press, 2005.

———. "Let's Win the Wars We're In." *Joint Forces Quarterly* 52 (1st Quarter 2009): 20–26.

Nasr, Vali. *The Dispensable Nation: American Foreign Policy in Retreat*. New York: Doubleday, 2013.

Newtown, Jim. *Eisenhower: The White House Years*. New York: Anchor, 2012.

Nguyen, Lien-Hang T. *Hanoi's War: An International History of the War for Peace in Vietnam*. Chapel Hill: University of North Carolina Press, 2012.

Nietzsche, Friedrich. *Basic Writings of Nietzsche*. Translated and edited by Walter Kaufmann. New York: Modern Library, 2000.

Nye, Joseph S. *Soft Power: The Means to Success in World Politics*. New York: PublicAffairs, 2004.

O'Donnell, Patrick K. *Give Me Tomorrow: The Korean War's Greatest Untold Story — The Epic Stand of the Marines of George Company*. Cambridge: Da Capo Press, 2010.

O'Hanlon, Michael, and Bruce Riedel. "Plan A-Minus for Afghanistan." *Washington Quarterly* 34, no. 1 (2011): 123–32.

O'Neill, Bard E. *Insurgency & Terrorism: From Apocalypse to Revolution*. Dulles, VA: Potomac Books, 2005.

Overy, Richard J. *The Dictators: Hitler's Germany and Stalin's Russia*. New York: W. W. Norton & Company, 2004.

Packer, George. *The Assassin's Gate: America in Iraq*. New York: Farrar, Straus and Giroux, 2005.

Pape, Robert A. "Coercive Air Power in the Vietnam War." *International Security* 15, no. 2 (Autumn 1990): 103–46.

———. *Bombing to Win: Air Power and Coercion in War*. Ithaca, NY: Cornell University Press, 1996.

———. "When Duty Calls: A Pragmatic Standard of Humanitarian Intervention." *International Security* 37, no. 1 (Summer 2012): 41–80.

Parasiliti, Andrew. "Leaving Iraq." *Survival* 54, no. 1 (February/March 2012): 127–33.

Paris, Roland. *At War's End: Building Peace after Civil Conflict*. Cambridge: Cambridge University Press, 2004.

Paris, Roland, and Timothy D. Sisk, eds. *The Dilemmas of Statebuilding: Confronting the Contradictions of Postwar Peace Operations*. New York: Routledge, 2009.

Parker, Ned. "The Iraq We Left Behind." *Foreign Affairs* 91, no. 2 (March/April 2012): 94–110.

Bibliography

Paul, Christopher, Colin P. Clarke, Beth Grill, and Molly Dunigan. *Paths to Victory: Lessons from Modern Insurgencies.* Santa Monica: Rand, 2013.

Peeters, Guido, and Janusz Czapinski. "Positive-Negative Asymmetry in Evaluations: The Distinction between Affective and Informational Negativity Effects." *European Review of Social Psychology* 1, no. 1 (1990): 33–60.

Perry, Mark. *Talking to Terrorists: Why America Must Engage with Its Enemies.* New York: Basic Books, 2010.

Peters, Joel, and David Newman, eds. *The Routledge Handbook of the Israeli-Palestinian Conflict.* New York: Routledge, 2013.

Petraeus, David H. "How We Won in Iraq." *Foreign Policy* (October 29, 2013). Available at: http://www.foreignpolicy.com/articles/2013/10/29/david_petraeus _how_we_won_the_surge_in_iraq.

Pillar, Paul R. *Negotiating Peace: War Termination as a Bargaining Process.* Princeton, NJ: Princeton University Press, 1983.

———. "Ending Limited War: The Psychological Dynamics of the Termination Process." In *Psychological Dimensions of War,* edited by Betty Glad, 252–63. Newbury Park, CA: Sage, 1990.

Pinker, Steven. *The Better Angels of Our Nature: Why Violence Has Declined.* New York: Viking, 2011.

Polsky, Andrew J. *Elusive Victories: The American Presidency at War.* New York: Oxford University Press, 2012.

Powell, Colin L. "U.S. Forces: Challenges Ahead." *Foreign Affairs* 71, no. 5 (1992): 32–45.

———. *My American Journey.* New York: Random House, 1995.

Power, Samantha. *"A Problem from Hell": America and the Age of Genocide.* New York: Harper Perennial, 2003.

Powers, Kevin. *The Yellow Birds: A Novel.* New York: Little, Brown and Company, 2012.

Prados, John. "The Shape of the Table: Nguyen Van Thieu and Negotiations to End the Conflict." In *The Search for Peace in Vietnam,* edited by Lloyd C. Gardner and Ted Gittinger, 355–70. College Station: Texas A&M University Press Consortium, 2004.

Press, Daryl. *Calculating Credibility: How Leaders Assess Military Threats.* Ithaca, NY: Cornell University Press, 2005.

Preston, Diana. *The Dark Defile: Britain's Catastrophic Invasion of Afghanistan 1838–1842.* New York: Walker & Company, 2012.

Price, Bryan C. "Targeting Top Terrorists: How Leadership Decapitation Contributes to Counterterrorism." *International Security* 36, no. 4 (Spring 2012): 9–46.

Quester, George H. "The Psychological Effect of Bombing on Civilian Populations: Wars of the Past." In *Psychological Dimensions of War,* edited by Betty Glad, 201–14. Newbury Park, CA: Sage, 1990.

Bibliography

Rayburn, Joel. "The Last Exit from Iraq." *Foreign Affairs* 85, no. 2 (March/April 2006): 29–40.

———. *Descent into Chaos: The United States and the Failure of Nation Building in Pakistan, Afghanistan, and Central Asia*. New York: Viking, 2008.

———. "The Way Out of Afghanistan," *New York Review of Books*, January 13, 2011. Available at: http://www.nybooks.com/articles/archives/2011/jan/13/way-out-afghanistan/?pagination=false.

Record, Jeffrey. "Exit Strategy Delusions." *Parameters* 31, no. 4 (Winter 2001/2002): 21–27.

———. *Beating Goliath: Why Insurgencies Win*. Washington, DC: Potomac Books, 2007.

———. "Leaving Vietnam: Insights for Iraq?" *Diplomatic History* 34, no. 3 (June 2010): 567–76.

Ricks, Thomas E. *Fiasco: The American Military Adventure in Iraq*. New York: Penguin Press, 2006.

———. *The Gamble: General David Petraeus and the American Military Adventure in Iraq, 2006–2008*. New York: Penguin Press, 2009.

———. *The Generals: American Military Command from World War II to Today*. New York: Penguin Press, 2012.

———. "General Failure." *The Atlantic*, October 24, 2012. Available at: http://www.theatlantic.com/magazine/archive/2012/11/general-failure/309148/4/.

Ridgway, Matthew B. *The Korean War*. New York: Doubleday, 1967.

Robinson, Linda. *Tell Me How This Ends: General Petraeus and the Search for a Way Out of Iraq*. New York: PublicAffairs, 2009.

Rose, Gideon. "The Exit Strategy Delusion." *Foreign Affairs* 77, no. 1 (January/February 1998): 56–67.

———. *How Wars End: Why We Always Fight the Last Battle; A History of American Intervention from World War I to Afghanistan*. New York: Simon & Schuster, 2010.

Rose, Jonathan. *The Literary Churchill: Author, Reader, Actor*. New Haven, CT: Yale University Press, 2014.

Roselle, Laura. *Media and the Politics of Failure: Great Powers, Communication Strategies, and Military Defeats*. New York: Palgrave Macmillan, 2006.

Rosen, Stephen Peter. *War and Human Nature*. Princeton, NJ: Princeton University Press, 2005.

Rotmann, Philipp, David Tohn, and Jaron Wharton. "Learning Under Fire: Progress and Dissent in the US Military." *Survival* 51, no. 4 (August/September 2009): 31–48.

Rumsfeld, Donald. *Known and Unknown: A Memoir*. New York: Sentinel, 2011.

Russ, Martin. *Breakout: The Chosin Reservoir Campaign, Korea 1950*. New York: Penguin Books, 1999.

Salacuse, Jeswald W., and Jeffrey Z. Rubin. "Your Place or Mine? Site Location and Negotiation." *Negotiation Journal* 6, no. 1 (January 1990): 5–10.

Bibliography

Sandars, N. K., trans. *The Epic of Gilgamesh*. New York: Penguin Books, 1972.

Sandler, Stanley, ed. *The Korean War: An Encyclopedia*. New York: Taylor and Francis, 1995.

Sanger, David E. *Confront and Conceal: Obama's Secret Wars and Surprising Use of American Power*. New York: Crown, 2012.

Scales, Robert H. *Certain Victory: The U.S. Army in the Gulf War*. Dulles, VA: Brassey's, 1997.

———. "The Quality of Command: The Wrong Way and the Right Way to Make Better Generals." *Foreign Affairs* 91, no. 6 (November/December 2012): 137–43.

Schell, Jonathan. *The Time of Illusion*. New York: Vintage, 1976.

Schelling, Thomas C. *The Strategy of Conflict*. Cambridge, MA: Harvard University Press, 1980.

Schivelbusch, Wolfgang. *The Culture of Defeat: On National Trauma, Mourning, and Recovery*. New York: Picador, 2004.

Schoenbaum. Thomas J. *Waging Peace and War: Dean Rusk in the Truman, Kennedy, and Johnson Years*. New York: Simon & Schuster, 1988.

Schulzinger, Robert D. *A Time for Peace: The Legacy of the Vietnam War*. New York: Oxford University Press, 2006.

Schweikart, Larry. *America's Victories: Why the U.S. Wins Wars and Will Win the War on Terror*. New York: Sentinel, 2006.

Sebenius, James K., and Michael K. Singh. "Is a Nuclear Deal with Iran Possible? An Analytical Framework for the Iran Nuclear Negotiations." *International Security* 37, no. 3 (Winter 2012/2013): 52–91.

Seidel, Andrew D. "The Use of the Physical Environment in Peace Negotiations." *JAE* 32, no. 2 (November 1978): 19–23.

Semple, Michael, Theo Farrell, Anatol Lieven, and Rudra Chaudhuri. "Taliban Perspectives on Reconciliation." Royal United Services Institute Briefing Paper, September 2012. Available at: http://www.rusi.org/downloads/assets/Taliban_Perspectives_on_Reconciliation.pdf.

Sepp, Kalev I. "Best Practices in Counterinsurgency." *Military Review* (May/June 2005): 8–12. Available at: www.au.af.mil/au/awc/awcgate/milreview/sepp.pdf.

———. "From 'Shock and Awe' to 'Hearts and Minds': The Fall and Rise of U.S. Counterinsurgency Capability in Iraq." *Third World Quarterly* 28, no. 2 (2007): 217–30.

Seybolt, Taylor B. *Humanitarian Military Intervention: The Conditions for Success and Failure*. Oxford: Oxford University Press, 2007.

Shay, Jonathan. *Odysseus in America: Combat Trauma and the Trials of Homecoming*. New York: Scribner, 2002.

Sheehan, James J. *Where Have All the Soldiers Gone? The Transformation of Modern Europe*. New York: Houghton Mifflin Harcourt, 2008.

Sheehan, Neil. *A Bright Shining Lie: John Paul Vann and America in Vietnam*. London: Jonathan Cape, 1988.

Bibliography

Sherry, Michael S. *In the Shadow of War: The United States Since the 1930s*. New Haven, CT: Yale University Press, 1995.

Shinn, James, and James Dobbins. *Afghan Peace Talks: A Primer*. Santa Monica: RAND, 2011.

Shirer, William L. *The Rise and Fall of the Third Reich: A History of Nazi Germany*. New York: Simon & Schuster, 2011.

Simon, Steven. "The Price of the Surge." *Foreign Affairs* 87, no. 3 (May/June 2008), 57–76.

Simpson, Emile. *War from the Ground Up: Twenty-First-Century Combat as Politics*. New York: Oxford University Press, 2013.

Simpson, Erin M. "The Perils of Third-Party Counterinsurgency Campaigns." PhD diss., Harvard University, 2010.

Sky, Emma. "Iraq, From Surge to Sovereignty: Winding Down the War in Iraq." *Foreign Affairs* 90, no. 2 (March/April 2011): 117–27.

Sluglett, Peter. *Britain in Iraq: Contriving King and Country*. New York: I. B. Tauris, 2007.

Small, Melvin. *The Presidency of Richard Nixon*. Lawrence: University Press of Kansas, 1999.

Smith, James D. D. *Stopping Wars: Defining the Obstacles to Cease-Fire*. Boulder: Westview Press, 1995.

Smith, Niel A., and Nathan W. Toronto. "It's All the Rage: Why Mechanization Doesn't Explain COIN Outcomes." *Small Wars & Insurgencies* 21, no. 3 (September 2010): 519–28.

Smith, Rupert. *The Utility of Force: The Art of War in the Modern World*. New York: Penguin Books, 2006.

Solomon, Richard H., and Nigel Quinney. *American Negotiating Behavior: Wheelers-Dealers, Legal Eagles, Bullies and Preachers*. Washington, DC: United States Institute of Peace Press, 2010.

Soltis, Andy. *Frank Marshall, United States Chess Champion: A Biography with 220 Games*. Jefferson, NC: McFarland and Company, 1994.

Sparre, Kristen. "Megaphone Diplomacy in the Northern Irish Peace Process: Squaring the Circle by Talking to Terrorists through Journalists." *Harvard International Journal of Press/Politics* 6, no. 1 (Winter 2001): 88–104.

Special Inspector General for Iraq Reconstruction. *Hard Lessons: The Iraq Reconstruction Experience*. Washington, DC: Government Printing Office, 2009.

Spielvogel, Jackson J. *Western Civilization: Vol. I: To 1715*. 8th ed. Boston: Wadsworth, 2012.

Staniland, Paul. "States, Insurgents, and Wartime Political Orders." *Perspectives on Politics* 10, no. 2 (June 2012): 243–64.

Stanley, Elizabeth A. "Ending the Korean War: The Role of Domestic Coalition Shifts in Overcoming Obstacles to Peace." *International Security* 34, no. 1 (Summer 2009): 42–82.

———. *Paths to Peace: Domestic Coalition Shifts, War Termination and the Korean War*. Stanford: Stanford University Press, 2009.

Bibliography

Staw, Barry M., and Jerry Ross. "Understanding Behavior in Escalation Situations." *Science* 246, no. 4927 (October 1989): 216–20.

Steele, David. *Lord Salisbury: A Political Biography.* New York: Routledge, 2002.

Stewart, Rory, and Gerald Knaus. *Can Intervention Work?* New York: W. W. Norton & Company, 2011.

Strachan, Hew. *The First World War.* New York: Viking, 2004.

———. "The Lost Meaning of Strategy." *Survival* 47, no. 3 (Autumn 2005): 33–54.

Stueck, William. *The Korean War: An International History.* Princeton, NJ: Princeton University Press, 1995.

———. *Rethinking the Korean War: A New Diplomatic and Strategic History.* Princeton, NJ: Princeton University Press, 2002.

Stueck, William, ed. *The Korean War in World History.* Lexington: University Press of Kentucky, 2004.

Sweeney, Patrick J., Michael D. Matthews, and Paul B. Lester, eds. *Leadership in Dangerous Situations: A Handbook for the Armed Forces, Emergency Services, and First Responders.* Annapolis: Naval Institute Press, 2011.

Symonds, Craig L. *Lincoln and His Admirals.* New York: Oxford University Press, 2008.

Taleb, Nassim Nicholas. *The Black Swan: The Impact of the Highly Improbable.* 2nd ed. New York: Random House, 2010.

Taliaferro, Jeffrey W. *Balancing Risks: Great Power Intervention in the Periphery.* Ithaca: Cornell University Press, 2004.

Tanielian, Terri, and Lisa H. Jaycox, eds. *Invisible Wounds of War: Psychological and Cognitive Injuries, Their Consequences, and Services to Assist Recovery.* Santa Monica, CA: RAND, 2008.

Templer, Robert. *Shadows and Wind: A View of Modern Vietnam.* New York: Penguin Books, 1999.

Thomas-Symonds, Nicklaus. *Attlee: A Life in Politics.* New York: I. B. Tauris, 2010.

Thucydides. *History of the Peloponnesian War.* Translated by Rex Warner. New York: Penguin, 1972.

Tierney, Dominic. *How We Fight: Crusades, Quagmires, and the American Way of War.* New York: Little, Brown and Company, 2010.

———. "Mastering the Endgame of War." *Survival* 56, no. 5 (October/November 2014): 69–94.

———. "The Backlash Against Nation-Building." *Prism* (forthcoming).

Tocqueville, Alexis de. *Democracy in America.* Vol. 2. Translated by Henry Reeve. Stilwell, KS: Digireads, 2007.

Tomsen, Peter. *The Wars of Afghanistan: Messianic Terrorism, Tribal Conflicts, and the Failure of Great Powers.* New York: PublicAffairs, 2011.

Torricelli, Robert, and Andrew Carroll, eds. *In Our Own Words: Extraordinary Speeches of the American Century.* New York: Washington Square Press, 1999.

Tucker, Spencer C., ed. *The Encyclopedia of the Vietnam War: A Political, Social, and Military History.* 2nd ed. Santa Barbara: ABC-LIO, 2011.

Bibliography

————. *The Encyclopedia of the War of 1812: A Political, Social, and Military History.* Santa Barbara: ABC-CLIO, 2012.

Twain, Mark. *The Wit and Wisdom of Mark Twain.* Mineola, NY: Dover Publications, 2013.

Ucko, David H. *The New Counterinsurgency Era: Transforming the U.S. Military for Modern Wars.* Washington, DC: Georgetown University Press, 2009.

U.S. Army and Marine Corps. *The U.S. Army/Marine Corps Counterinsurgency Field Manual.* Chicago: University of Chicago Press, 2007.

Van Buren, Peter. *We Meant Well: How I Helped Lose the Battle for the Hearts and Minds of the Iraqi People.* New York: Metropolitan Books, 2011.

Van Creveld, Martin. *The Transformation of War: The Most Radical Reinterpretation of Armed Conflict Since Clausewitz.* New York: Free Press, 1991.

VanDeMark, Brian. *Into the Quagmire: Lyndon Johnson and the Escalation of the Vietnam War.* New York: Oxford University Press, 1995.

Vandiver, Frank E. *Shadows of Vietnam: Lyndon Johnson's Wars.* College Station: Texas A&M University Press, 1997.

Vasquez, John A., ed. *What Do We Know About War?* 2nd ed. Lanham, MD: Rowman & Littlefield Publishers, 2012.

Venkatesh, Sudhir Alladi. *American Project: The Rise and Fall of a Modern Ghetto.* Cambridge, MA: Harvard University Press, 2000.

Walder, Francis. *The Negotiators.* New York: McDowell, Obolensky, 1959.

Wall, Irwin M. *France, the United States, and the Algerian War.* Berkeley: University of California Press, 2001.

Wallis, W. Allen. "The Statistical Research Group, 1942-1945." *Journal of the American Statistical Association* 75, no. 370 (June 1980): 320–30.

Walt, Stephen M. *Taming American Power: The Global Response to U.S. Primacy.* New York: W. W. Norton & Company, 2005.

————. "Cutting Losses in Wars of Choice: Obstacles and Strategies." In *The Prudent Use of Power in American National Security Strategy,* edited by Stephen Van Evera and Sidharth Shah, 131–55. Boston: The Tobin Project, 2010.

Walter, Barbara F. *Committing to Peace: The Successful Settlement of Civil Wars.* Princeton, NJ: Princeton University Press, 2002.

Watkins, Michael, and Susan Rosegrant. *Breakthrough International Negotiation: How Great Negotiators Transformed the World's Toughest Post-Cold War Conflicts.* San Francisco: Jossey-Bass, 2001.

Weigley, Russell F. *The American Way of War: A History of United States Military Strategy and Policy.* New York: Macmillan, 1973.

Weiss, Thomas G. *Military-Civilian Interactions: Humanitarian Crises and the Responsibility to Protect.* 2nd ed. New York: Rowman & Littlefield, 2005.

Welch, David A. *Painful Choices: A Theory of Foreign Policy Change.* Princeton, NJ: Princeton University Press, 2005.

West, Bing. *The Wrong War: Grit, Strategy and the Way Out of Afghanistan.* New York: Random House, 2011.

Bibliography

Westad, Odd Arne. *The Global Cold War: Third World Intervention and the Making of Our Times*. New York: Cambridge University Press, 2005.

Westen, Drew. *The Political Brain: The Role of Emotion in Deciding the Fate of the Nation*. New York: PublicAffairs, 2007.

Woodward, Bob. *Bush at War*. New York: Simon & Schuster, 2002.

———. *Plan of Attack*. New York: Simon & Schuster, 2004.

———. *Obama's Wars*. New York: Simon & Schuster, 2010.

Yafeng Xia. *Negotiating with the Enemy: U.S.-China Talks During the Cold War, 1949–1972*. Bloomington: Indiana University Press, 2006.

Young, Marilyn B. *The Vietnam Wars, 1945–1990*. New York: Harper Perennial, 1991.

Zakaria, Fareed. *The Post-American World*. New York: W. W. Norton & Company, 2009.

Zenko, Micah, and Michael A. Cohen. "Clear and Present Safety: The United States Is More Secure than Washington Thinks." *Foreign Affairs* 91, no. 2 (March/April 2012): 79–93.

Index

Note: Italic page numbers refer to illustrations.

Index

Index

Chandrasekaran, Rajiv, 175–76
chess, 32, 68–70, *69*, 72–73, 92, 308
China: Afghanistan war narrative and, 228; aid to mujahideen, 261; Communist guerrilla tactics in, 27, 28; Korean War and, 10, 44, 46–48, 99, 103, 111, 158, 251–52; U.S. competition with, 299; U.S. partisan politics and, 85; Vietnam and, 28, 49, 52, 56, 83, 84, 158, 217–18, 265, 266–67
Chosin Reservoir battle, 44, 46
Churchill, Winston, 10, 40, 101, 111, 188, 198, 240
Civil War: Britain and, 224–25, *225*; casualties from, 9; Confederate morale, 31, 158; Lincoln's relationships with generals, 181–82; as threat to national survival, 29, 318n13; war narrative and, 7, 140, 224, 284; war's aftermath and, 10, 279, 284, *285*
civil wars: in Bosnia, 190, 249, 302; COIN tactics and, 162, 167–68; foreign aid and, 28, 343n26; foreign financing and, 28, 274; international peacekeeping forces and, 249, 301; Iraq War as, 62; legality of, 303–05; negotiated peace and, 194, 197; power as disadvantage in, 16–17, 23, 24–25, 27, 29, 163; as prevailing contemporary mode of conflict, 30, 291, 296–300; replacing interstate conflicts, 21–22, 28, 286, 319–20n48; training of local troops and, 246; ugly stability scenario and, 119; veterans' recovery and, 277. *See also* counterinsurgency campaigns; insurgencies
Clausewitz, Carl von, 31, 112–13, 167, 306, 308
Clay, Henry, 98, 99, 127
Clinton, Bill, 89, 184, 222, 257, 267
Clinton, Hillary, 33, 192, 268
COIN (population-centric counterinsurgency), 155, 161–68, 170, 175–78, 305, 333n14, 17, 333–34n19

cold war, 19, 21, 25, 121–22, 229
concessions, 225–26
Continuation War, 124–26
counterinsurgency campaigns: assessing progress in, 41, 107–10; beacon of freedom scenario and, 241–42, 311; COIN tactics, 161–68, 333–34n19; compared to interstate wars, 25, 88, 276, 286, 298–300, 318n13; foreign financing and, 28, 274; international peacekeepers and, 301–02; legality of, 303–05; objectives and, 113, 117; phobic reactions to war and, 283; security and, 166–67, 169; Spanish-American War and, 264; training for, 246, 281, 296–300, 345n8; troop surges and, 159; U.S. attitudes toward, 87–89, 91, 186, 281, 298; U.S. failure to adapt to, 286–87; veterans' recovery and, 277. *See also* civil wars; insurgencies
Crocker, Ryan C., 35, 104, 184, 195, 208, 269–70, *269*
Cronkite, Walter, 14, 319n37
crusader mentality, 309–12
cut and run scenarios, 117, 131, 160, 257

dangerous myths, 280, 284–86
deadlines, 240–43, 271
deal and no-deal scenarios, 207–09, 212, 259, 290, 338n37
de Gaulle, Charles, 36, 103, 134–37, 227
Dekel, Udi, 235–36
democracy, 18–19, 21, 309–10
democratization, 167–68
Desert Fox operation, 71
divide and woo strategy, 265–68, 287
domino effect, 49, 128, 300
Dost Mohammad Khan, 38, 40
dovish pressures, 77, 87–89, 91, 115

economic aid, 221, 269–70, 272–73, 343n26
economic choices, 109–10

Index

veterans' recovery, 264, 265, 275–79, 287

victory culture, 33–34, 35, 41–42, 73–76, 113–14, 310

Vietcong: assessment of progress against, 107–09; negotiations to end war and, 54, 56, 204–05, *204, 205*; recuperative abilities of, 24, 320n55; Rolling Thunder campaign and, 210; Tet Offensive and, 185; unification of Vietnam and, 49; U.S. inability to defeat, *51,* 52, 281

Vietnam, 265, 266–68

Vietnamization, 53–54, 244, 245

Vietnam War: antiwar movement, 150, 226–27; assessing battlefield information and, 107–09; bombing encourages insurgent support, 25; China and, 28, 49, 52, 56, 83, 84, 158, 217–18, 265, 266–67; Communist guerrilla tactics in, 27; decision to use force and, 301, 302; as fiasco, 43, 49, 51–52, 53, 55, 56, 300; final casualties of, 4, 5, 295; as guerrilla war, 88; as interstate war, 297, 327n64; Joint Chiefs of Staff and, 180; as military defeat, 11, 12, 14, 23, 35, 268, 284; military withdrawal and, 4, 91, 148, 257, 268; nationalism and, 28, 183; negotiations to end, 53–56, 128, 148, 192, 194, 197, 198, 201, 204–05, *204, 205,* 209–13, 217–18, 226–27, 230, 245, 253; 1954 Geneva Accords and, 48–49; numbers of casualties, 11, 53, 54, 56, 108, 148, 312; objectives of, 112, 128; POW/MIAs and, 253, *254,* 255, 267; as pre-cold war, 19; public support for, 327n64; recalibration of Afghanistan War objectives and, 130; Rolling Thunder campaign, 49, 209–11, *210,* 338n43; security of local population and, 166; Soviet Union and, 49, 52, 83, 158, 183, 217–18;

sunk costs and, 81; Tet Offensive, 53, 185–86; troop surges and, 158, 160–61, 287, 290; unconventional war preparation after, 26; U.S. amnesia about, 281, 345n8; U.S. exit strategy and, 3–4, 6, 11, 31–32, 35, 36, 43, 52–57, 65, 80, 82–85, 90–91, 128–29, 131, 147–51, 188, 201, 217, 227, 230, 253, 284, 290, 291, 326n44; U.S. fear of reputational loss, 82, 87, 227, 326n46; U.S. phobia about, 283; U.S. reconciliation with Vietnam and, 267–69; Vietcong's recuperative abilities, 24, 320n55; Vietnamization campaign, 53–54, 244, 245; war narrative and, 139, 143, 147–51, 257, *258,* 344n54

waiting for success, 227, 229

Wald, Abraham, 105–06, 109, 110

Wallace, William, 76, *164*

war games, 72, 74, 76

war narrative: Afghanistan War and, 139–40, 142–44, 151–53, 172, 206, 228, 270; Civil War and, 7, 140, 224, 284; for foreign audiences, 152–53, 186; foreign nationalism and, 183–84; French war in Algeria and, 134–37; Gilgamesh epic as, 137, *138,* 139, 147, 312; Korean War and, 139, 251; military withdrawal and, 239, 255–59, 290, 291; negotiations and, 198, 202, 224; presidential communication and, 141–43, 145–47, 150–52, 288; reconciliation of former enemies and, 267; shaping historical memory, 280–86; Soviet Union in Afghanistan and, 262, *262;* troop surges and, 160, 186; understanding war and, 140–42, 145; veterans' recovery and, 275; Vietnam War and, 139, 143, 147–51, 257, *258,* 344n54; World War II and, 139, 145, 147

Index

About the Author

DOMINIC TIERNEY is an associate professor of political science at Swarthmore College and holds a PhD in international relations from Oxford University. He is a senior fellow at the Foreign Policy Research Institute, a former visiting associate professor at Princeton University, and a former research fellow at Harvard University. He is the author of three other books: *FDR and the Spanish Civil War, How We Fight,* and *Failing to Win,* which won the International Studies Association Best Book of the Year Award and was nominated for its Best Book of the Decade Award.